RADIANT

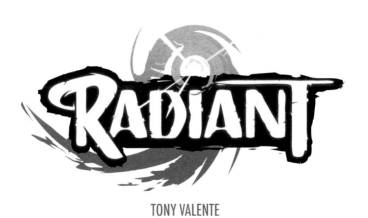

TONY VALENTE

CONTENTS

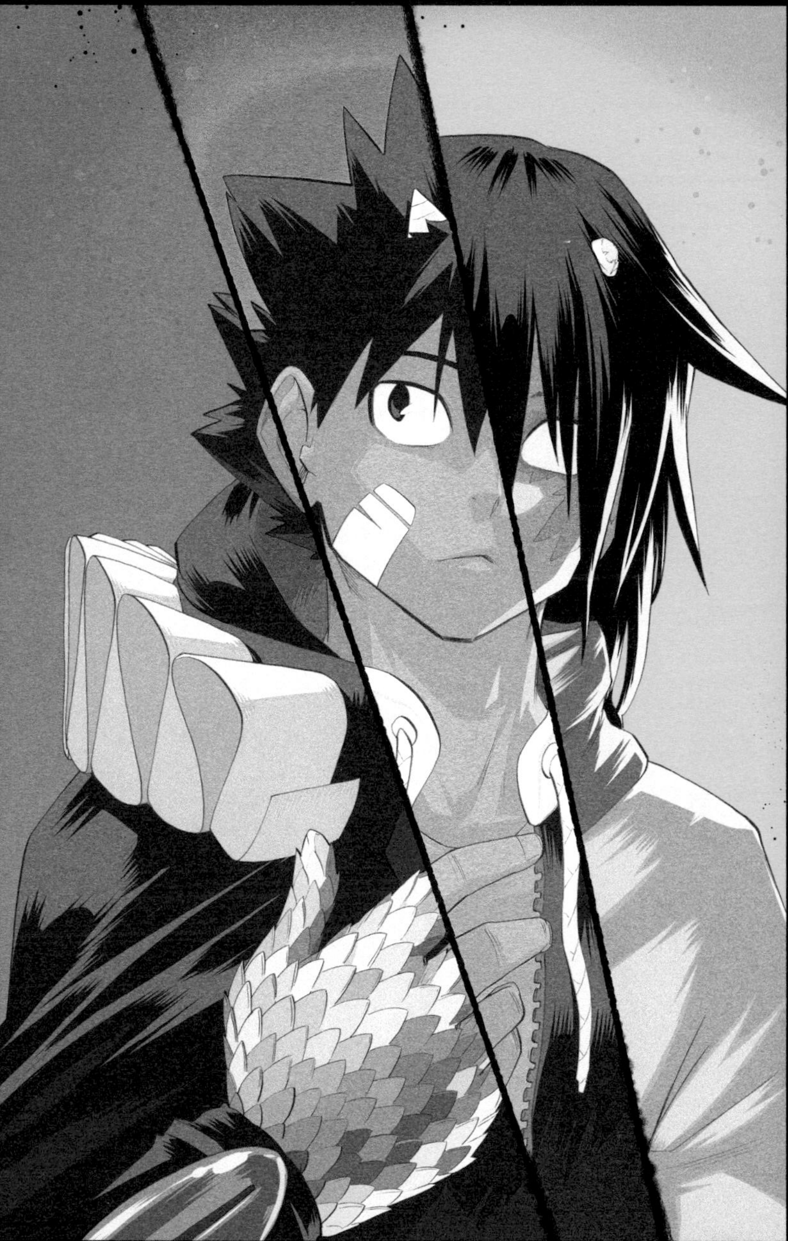

Summary of the previous volume:

To celebrate the promotion of Ullmina Bagliore to the rank of Colonel, a grand parade is organized and used to exhibit the armed forces of the Inquisition, as well as the Infected and the Nemesis they had recently captured. Mélie and Ocoho decide to go to the parade, as they're still looking for Seth and Doc, who have been missing since they all arrived in Bôme. Unfortunately for Doc, he's been brought along by Vérone to join the parade. Meanwhile, Seth attempts to help Lupa get her Nemesis back. And just as everything seemed to line up perfectly for our friends to find each other again during the event, Adhès and his group of Domitors decide to attack the Inquisition and take the people hostage.

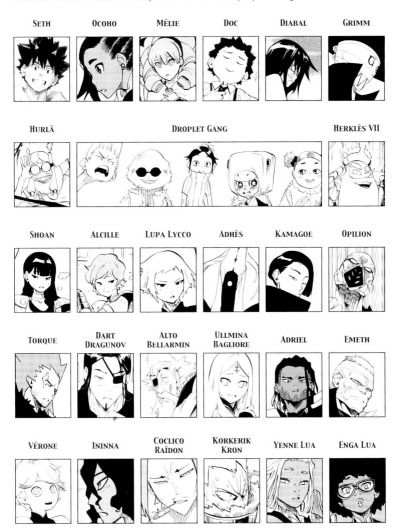

Seth
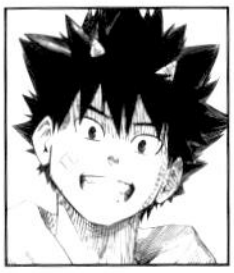

Ocoho
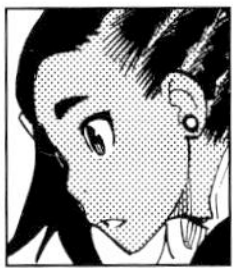

Mélie
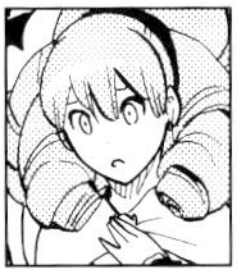

Doc
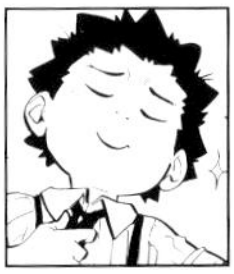

Diabal
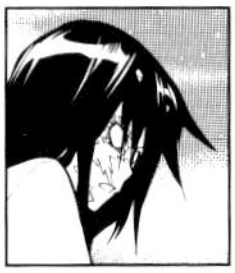

Grimm
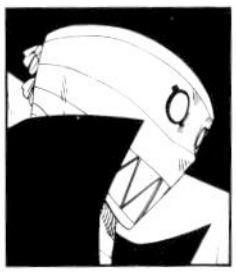

Hurlä
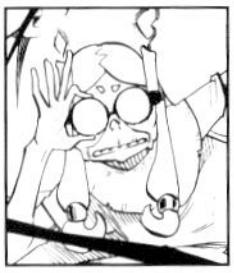

Droplet Gang
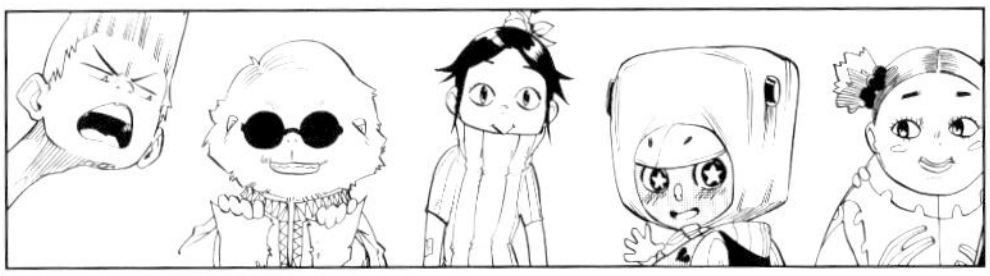

Herklès VII
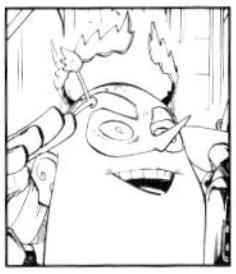

Shoan
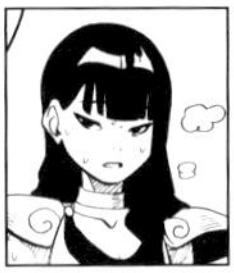

Alcille
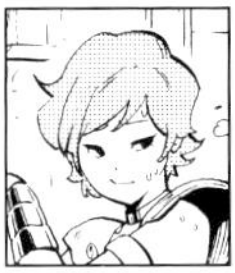

Lupa Lycco
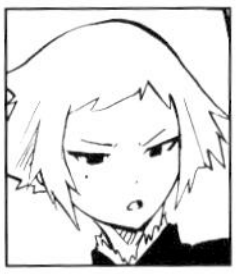

Adhès
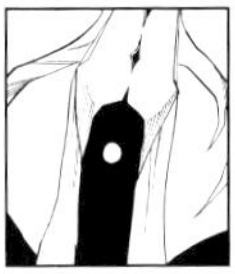

Kamagoe
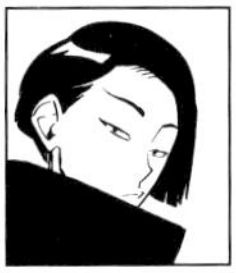

Opilion
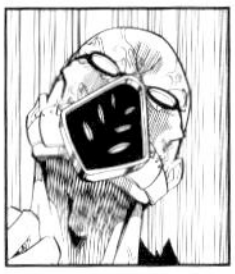

Torque
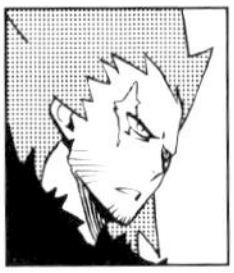

Dart Dragunov
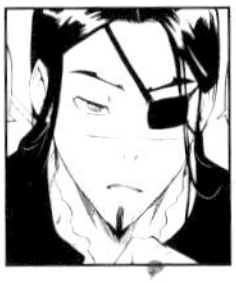

Alto Bellarmin
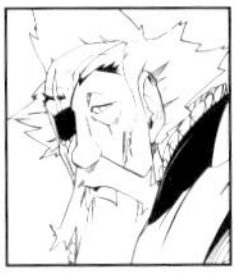

Ullmina Bagliore
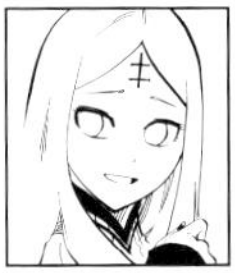

Adriel
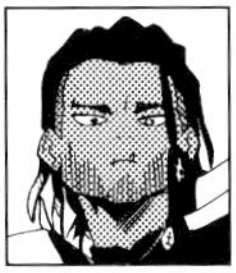

Emeth
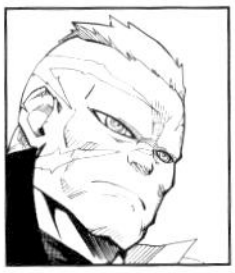

Vérone
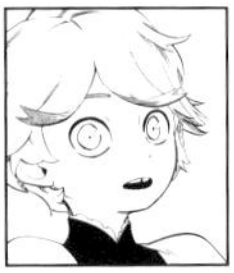

Ininna
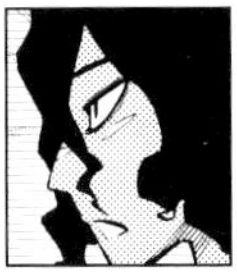

Coclico Raïdon
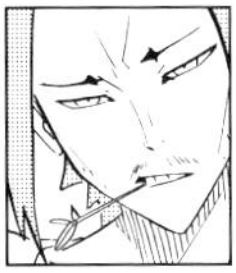

Korkerik Kron
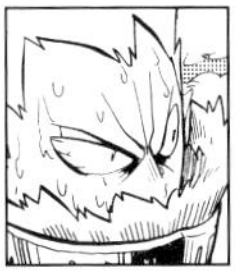

Yenne Lua
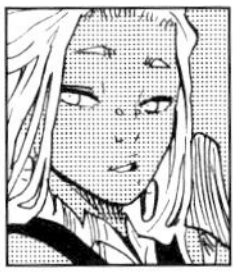

Enga Lua
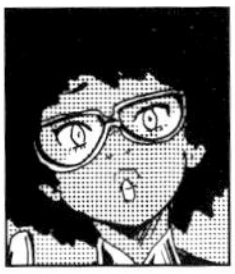

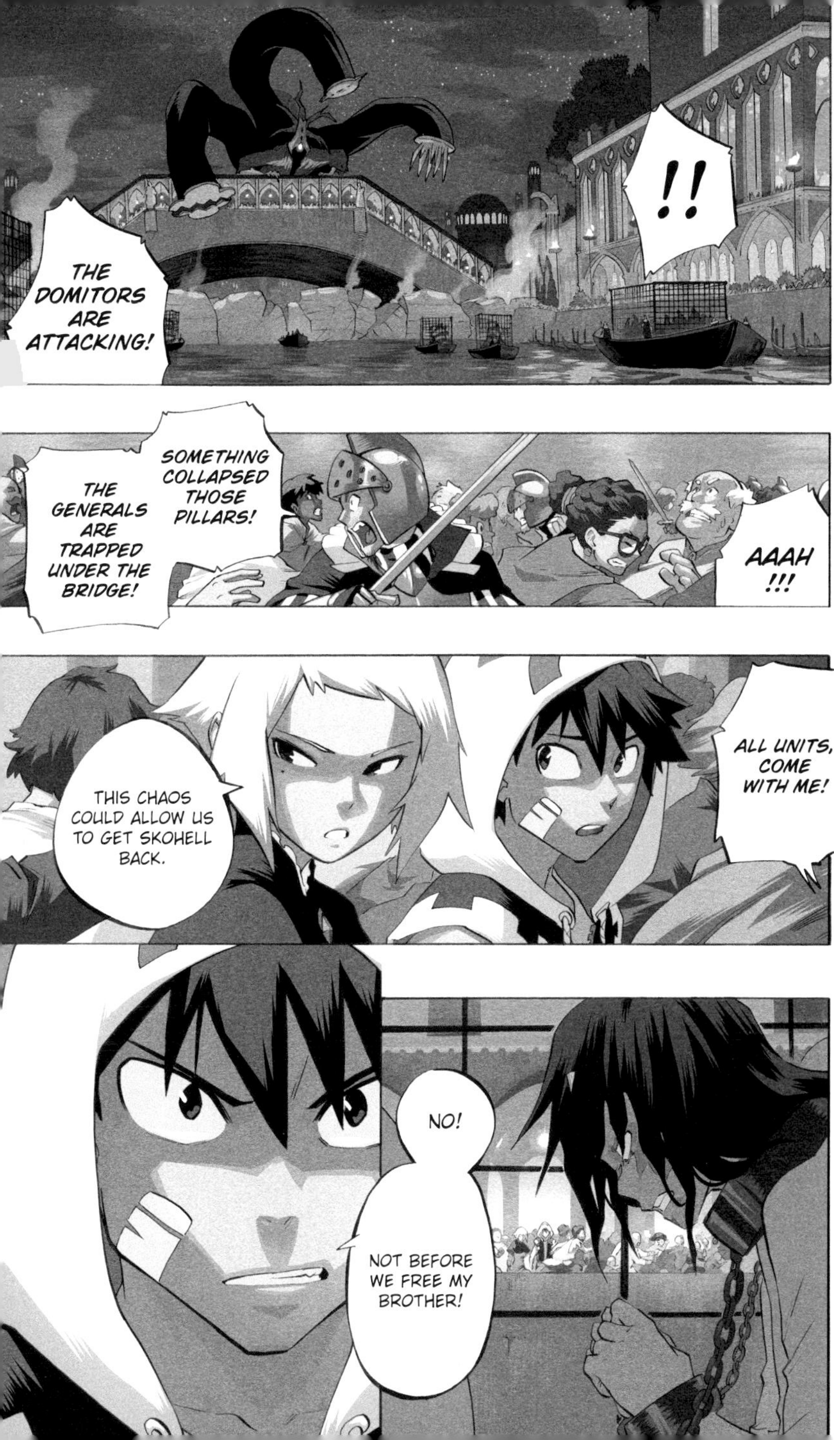
!!
THE DOMITORS ARE ATTACKING!
AAAH!!!
SOMETHING COLLAPSED THOSE PILLARS!
THE GENERALS ARE TRAPPED UNDER THE BRIDGE!
ALL UNITS, COME WITH ME!
THIS CHAOS COULD ALLOW US TO GET SKOHELL BACK.
NO!
NOT BEFORE WE FREE MY BROTHER!

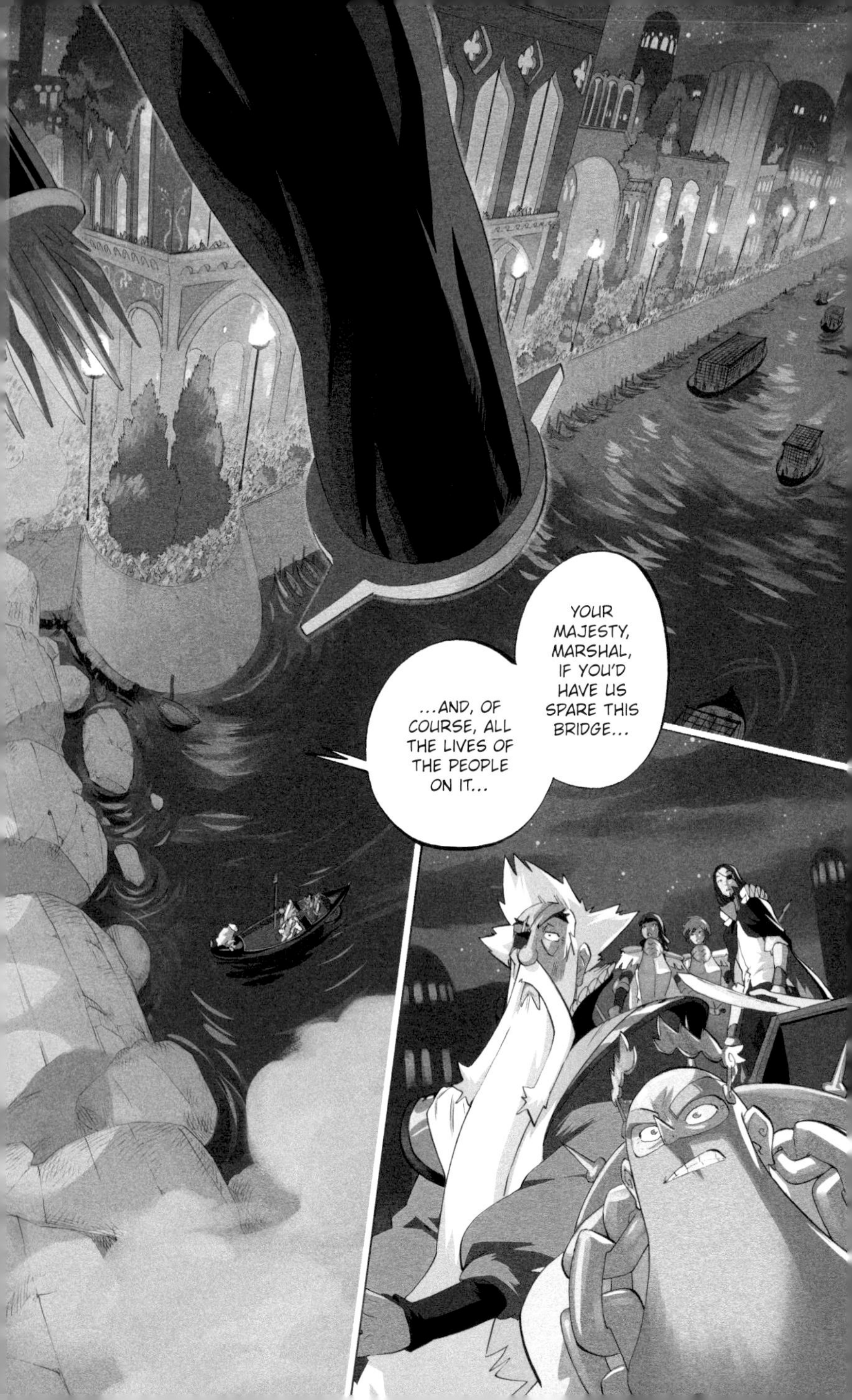
YOUR MAJESTY, MARSHAL, IF YOU'D HAVE US SPARE THIS BRIDGE...
...AND, OF COURSE, ALL THE LIVES OF THE PEOPLE ON IT...

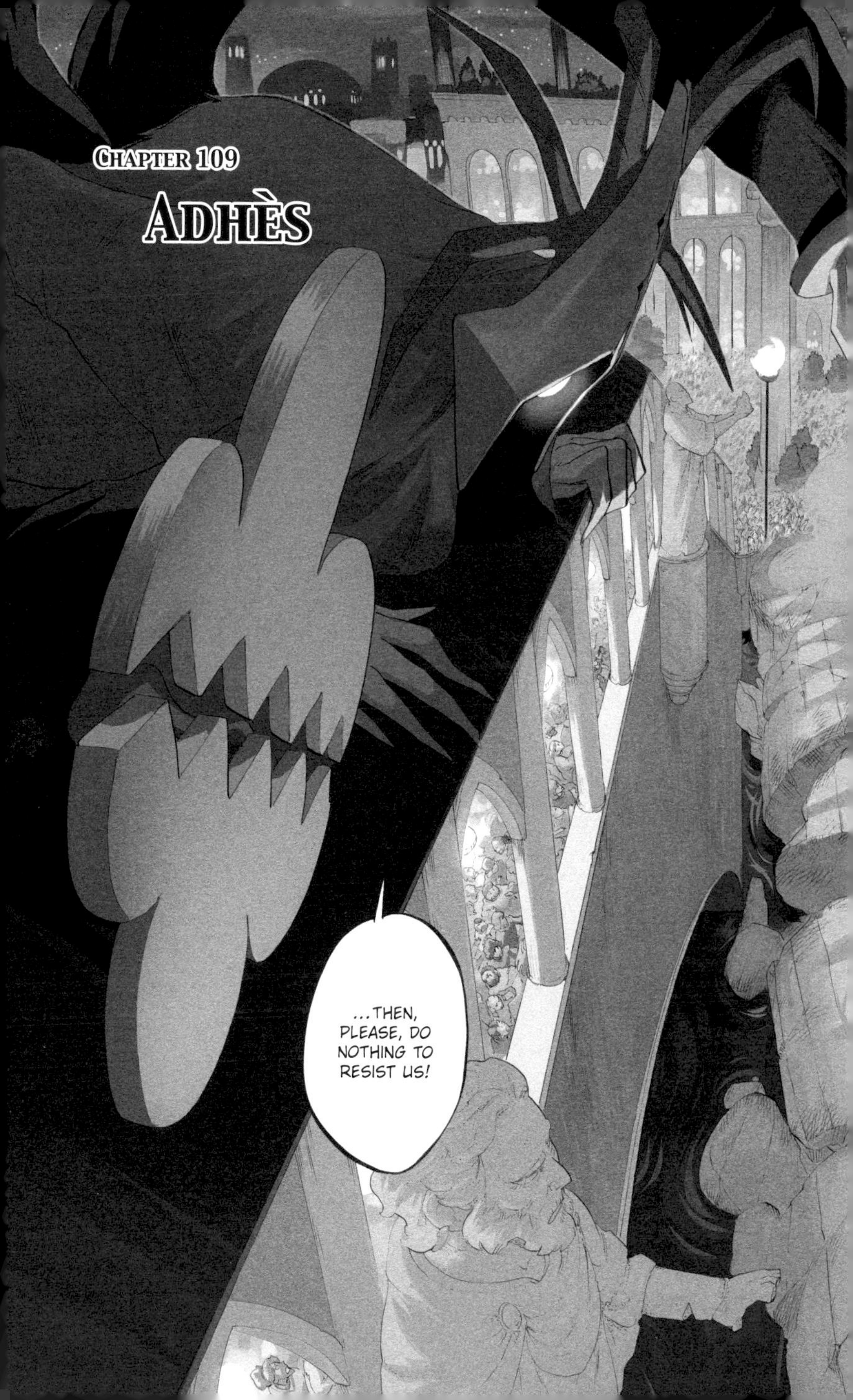
Chapter 109
Adhès
...Then, please, do nothing to resist us!

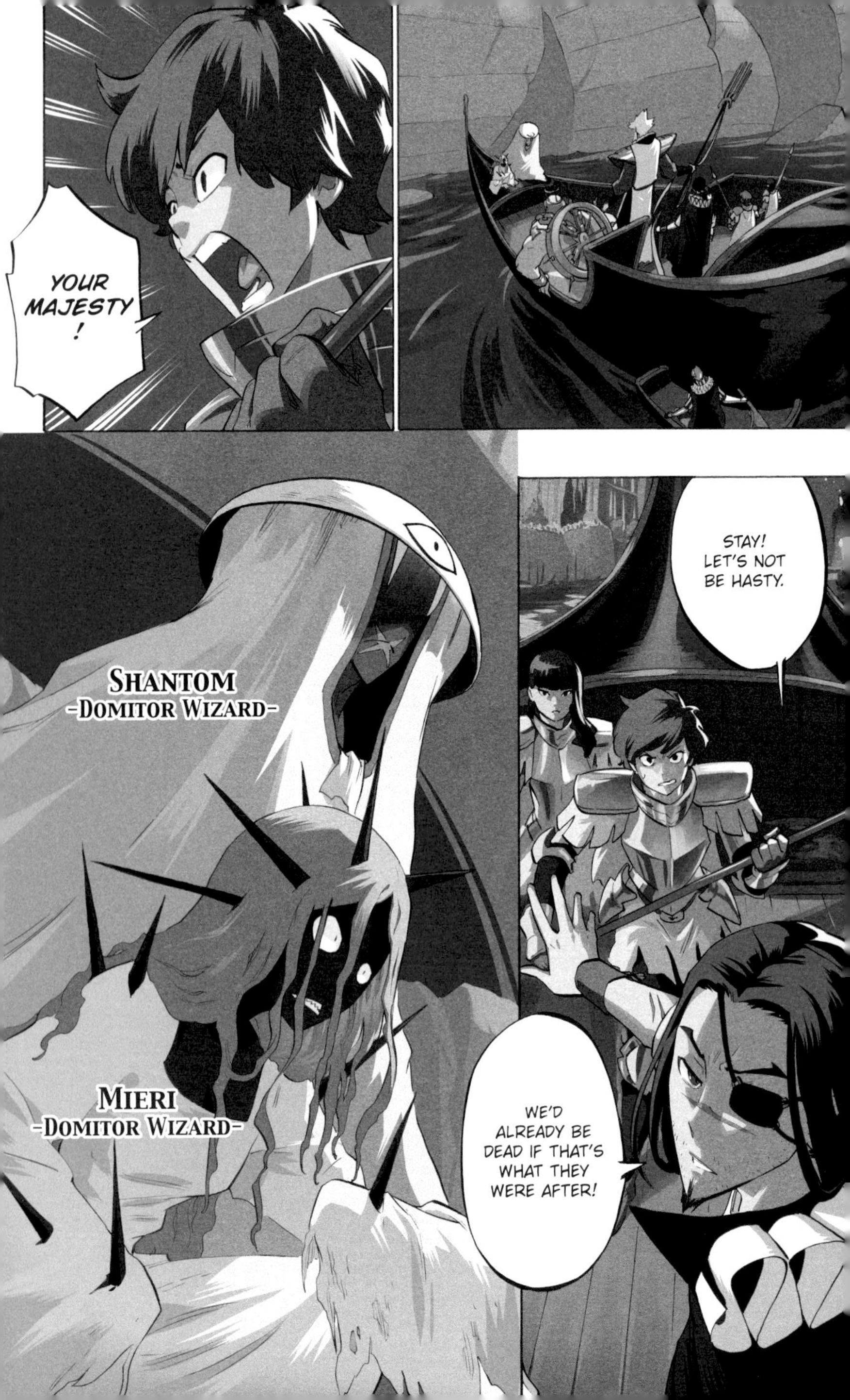
YOUR MAJESTY!
STAY! LET'S NOT BE HASTY.
WE'D ALREADY BE DEAD IF THAT'S WHAT THEY WERE AFTER!
Shantom
-Domitor Wizard-
Mieri
-Domitor Wizard-

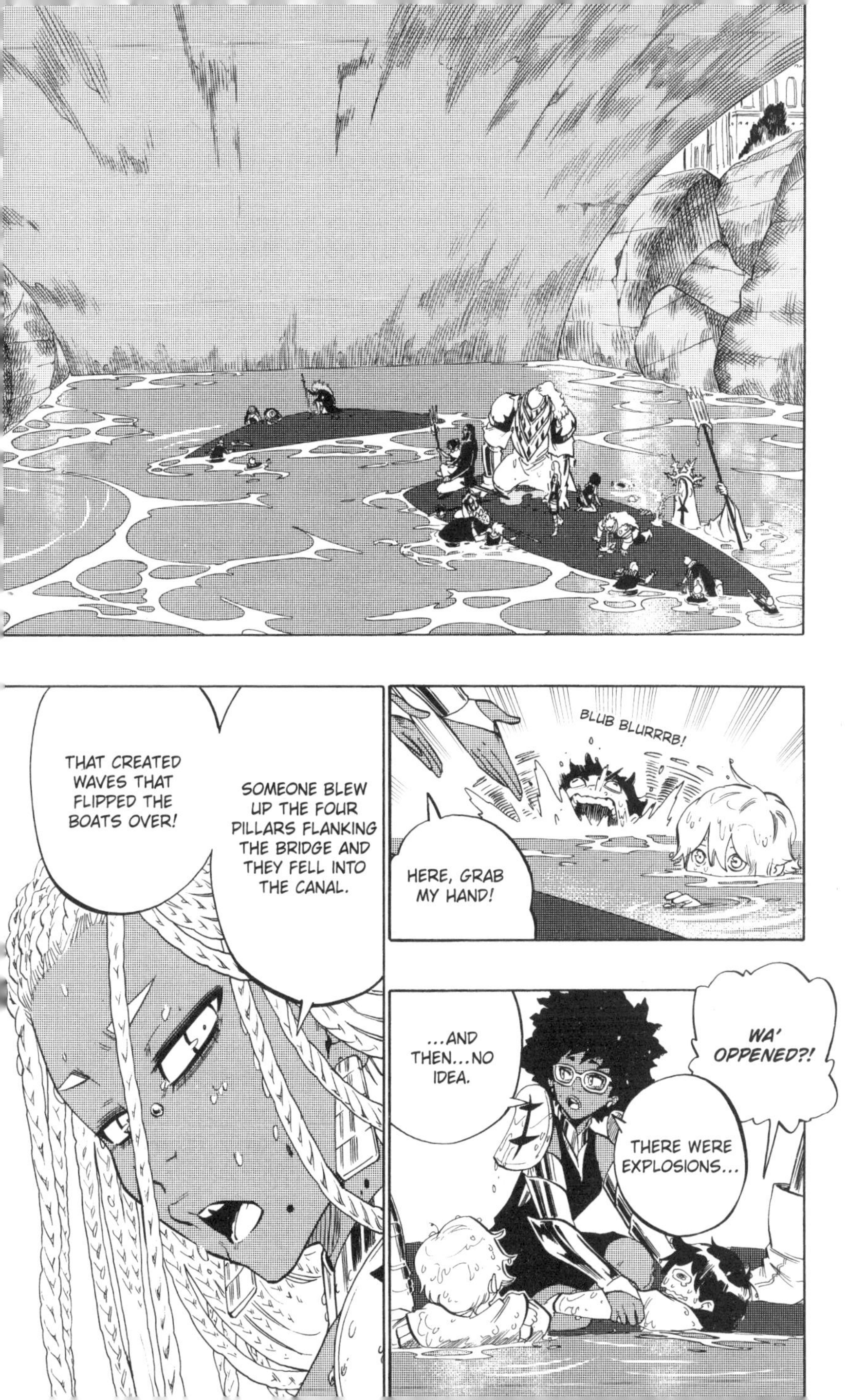
BLUB BLURRRB!
HERE, GRAB MY HAND!
WA' OPPENED?!
THERE WERE EXPLOSIONS...
...AND THEN...NO IDEA.
SOMEONE BLEW UP THE FOUR PILLARS FLANKING THE BRIDGE AND THEY FELL INTO THE CANAL.
THAT CREATED WAVES THAT FLIPPED THE BOATS OVER!

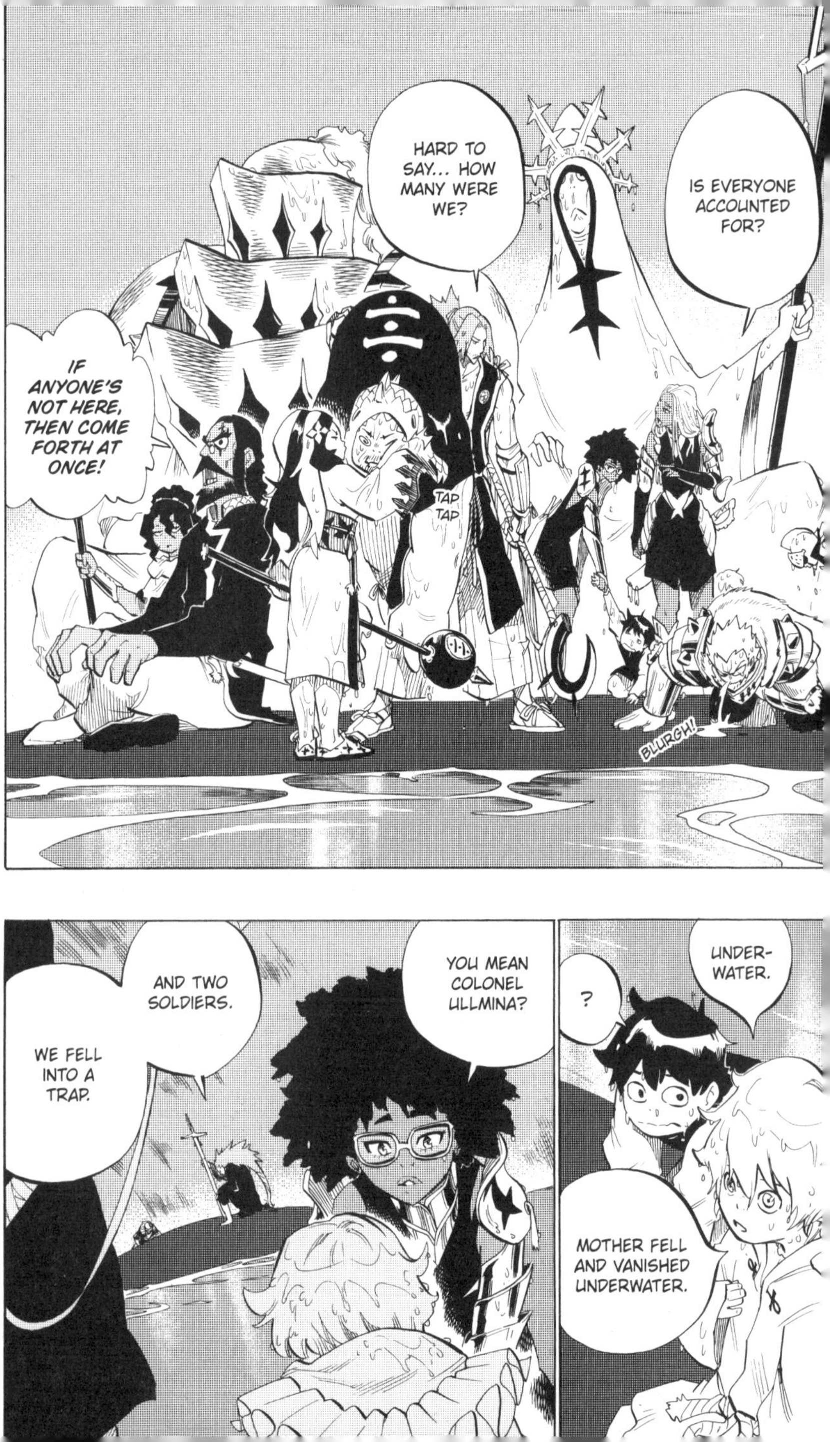
IS EVERYONE ACCOUNTED FOR?
HARD TO SAY... HOW MANY WERE WE?
IF ANYONE'S NOT HERE, THEN COME FORTH AT ONCE!
TAP TAP
BLURGH!
UNDER-WATER.
?
MOTHER FELL AND VANISHED UNDERWATER.
YOU MEAN COLONEL ULLMINA?
AND TWO SOLDIERS.
WE FELL INTO A TRAP.

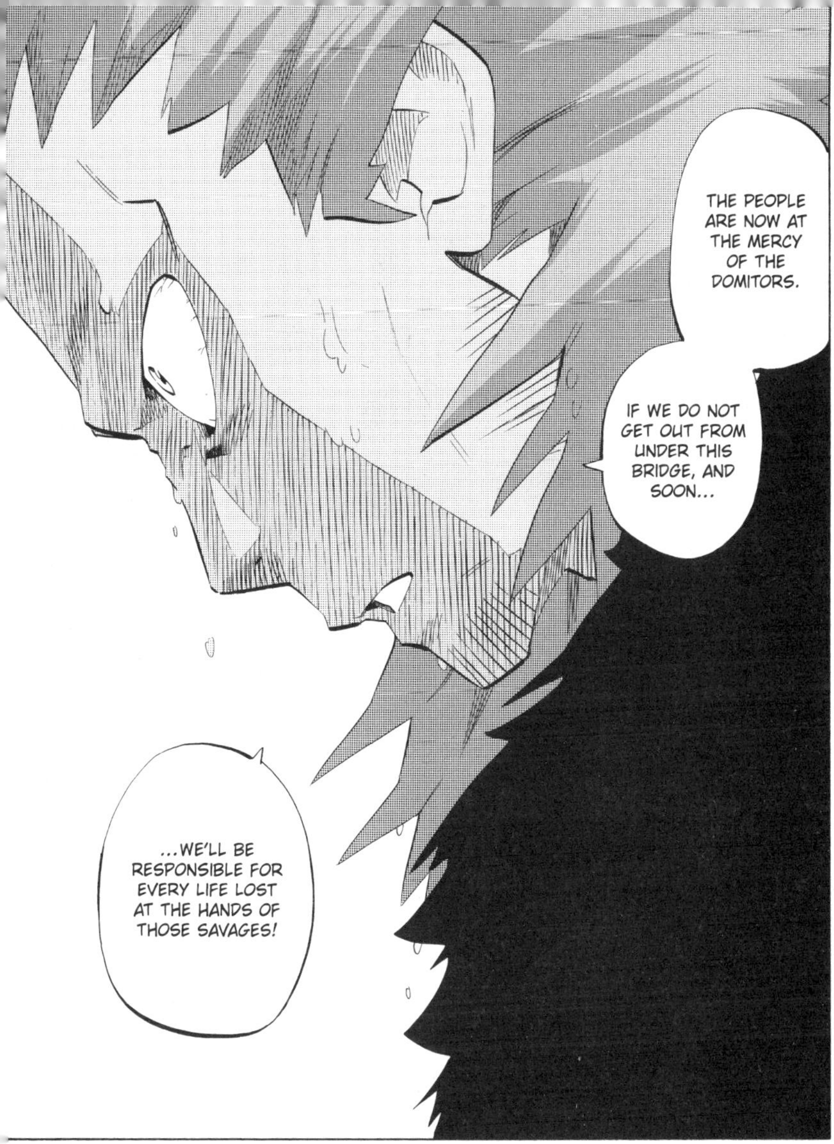
THE PEOPLE ARE NOW AT THE MERCY OF THE DOMITORS.
IF WE DO NOT GET OUT FROM UNDER THIS BRIDGE, AND SOON...
...WE'LL BE RESPONSIBLE FOR EVERY LIFE LOST AT THE HANDS OF THOSE SAVAGES!

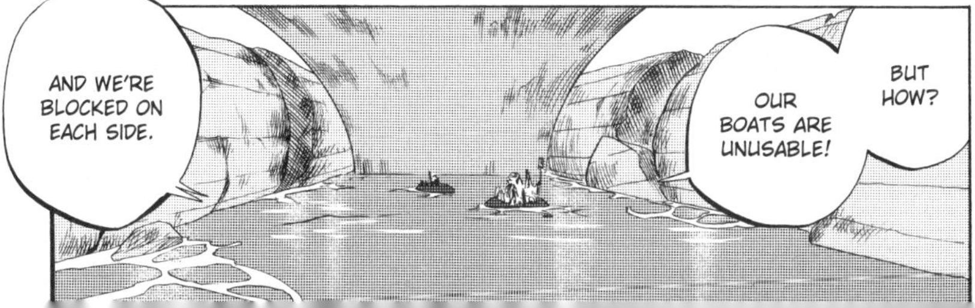
BUT HOW?
OUR BOATS ARE UNUSABLE!
AND WE'RE BLOCKED ON EACH SIDE.

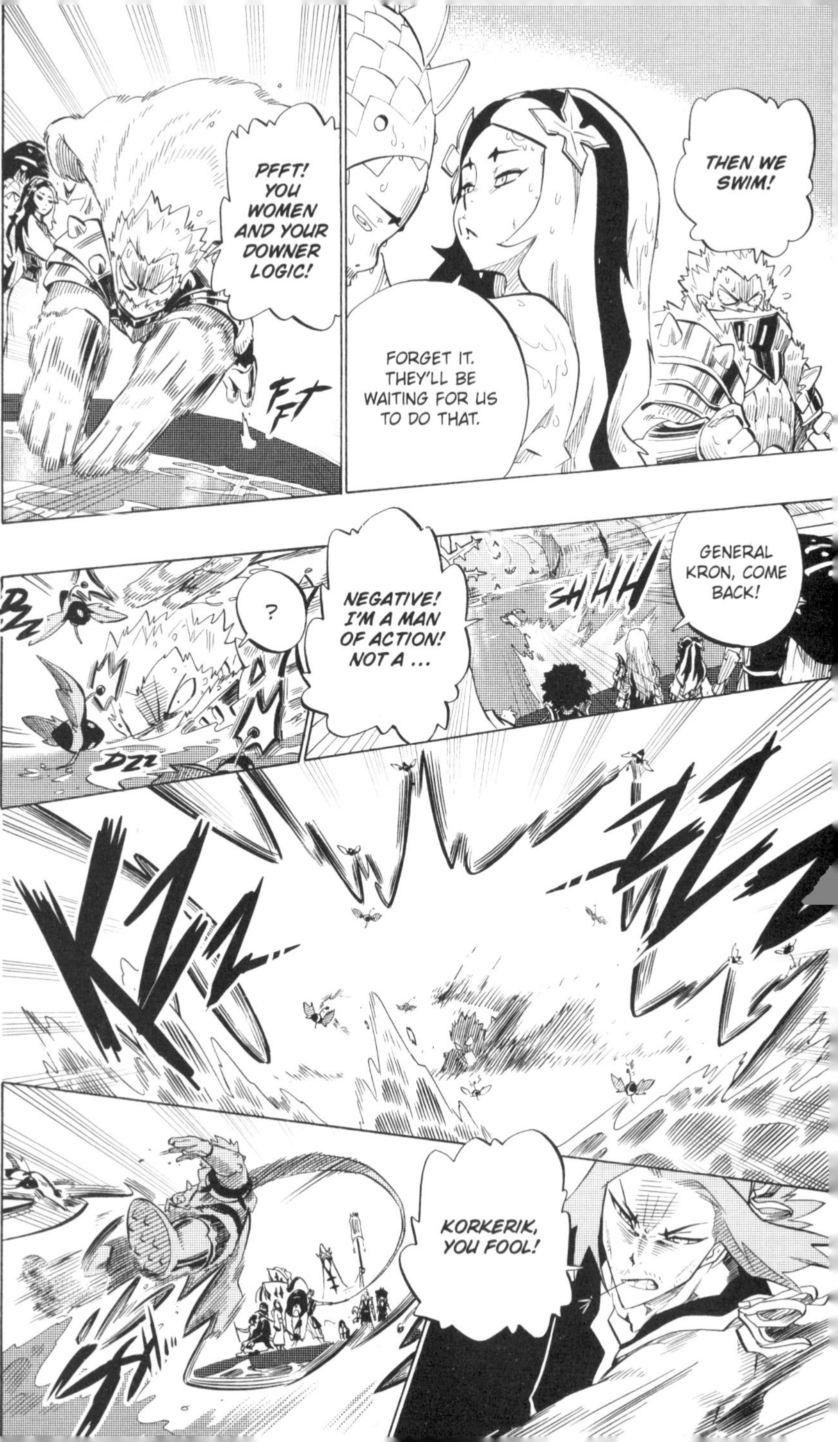
THEN WE SWIM!
FORGET IT. THEY'LL BE WAITING FOR US TO DO THAT.
PFFT! YOU WOMEN AND YOUR DOWNER LOGIC!
FFT
GENERAL KRON, COME BACK!
SHHH
NEGATIVE! I'M A MAN OF ACTION! NOT A ...
?
DZZ
DZZ
KORKERIK, YOU FOOL!

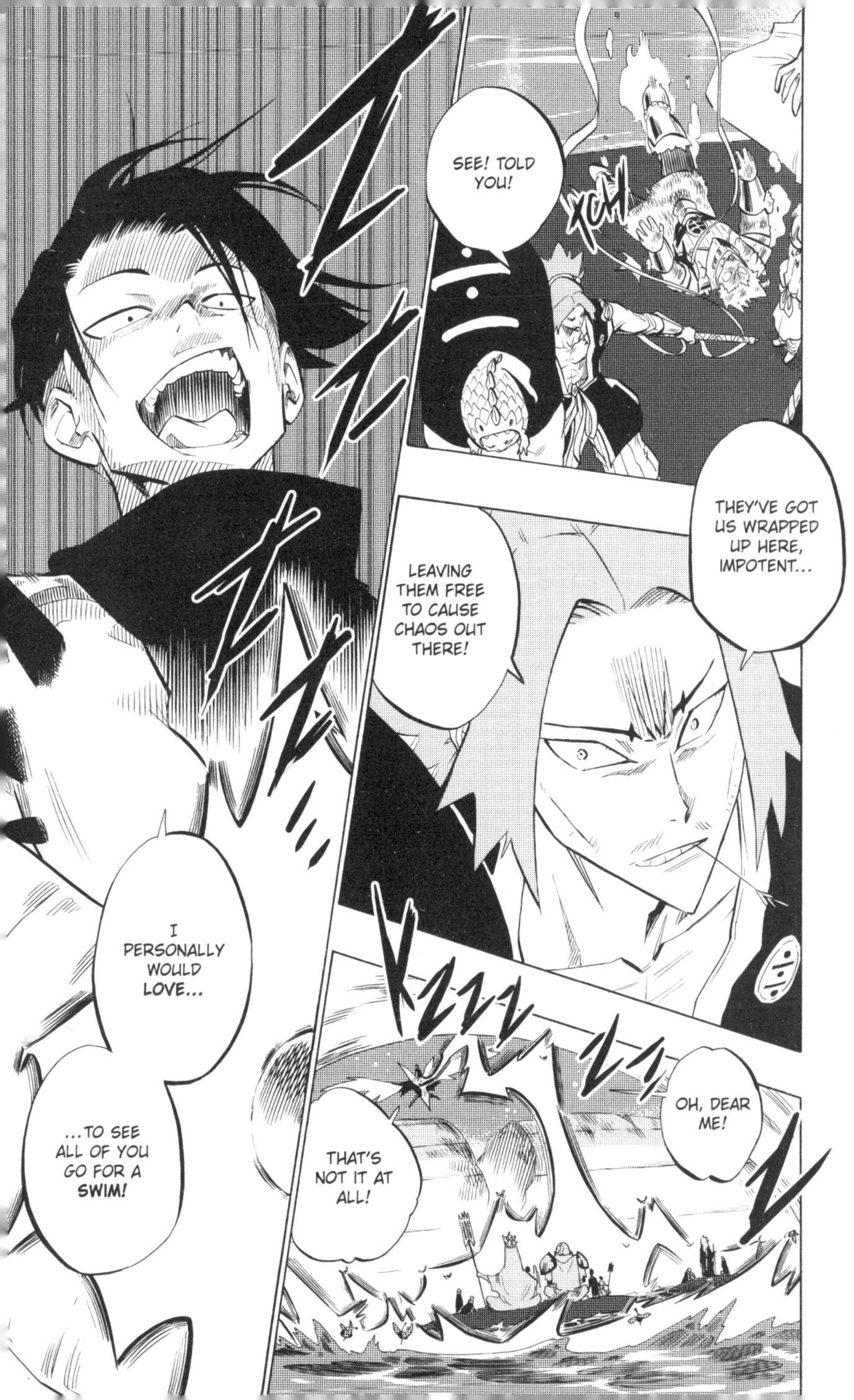
SEE! TOLD YOU!
XCH
THEY'VE GOT US WRAPPED UP HERE, IMPOTENT...
LEAVING THEM FREE TO CAUSE CHAOS OUT THERE!
OH, DEAR ME!
THAT'S NOT IT AT ALL!
I PERSONALLY WOULD LOVE...
...TO SEE ALL OF YOU GO FOR A SWIM!

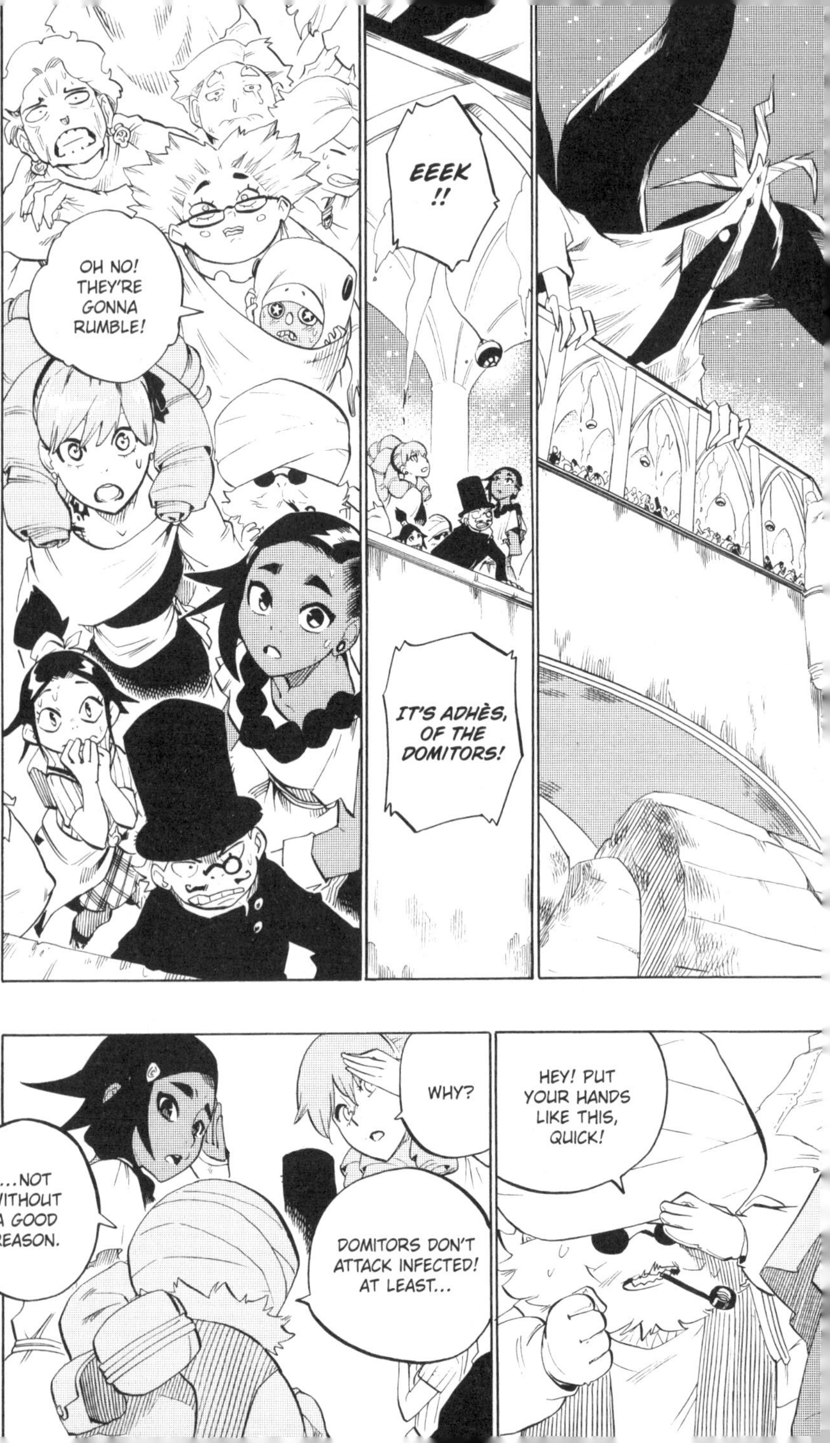
EEEK !!
IT'S ADHÈS, OF THE DOMITORS!
OH NO! THEY'RE GONNA RUMBLE!
HEY! PUT YOUR HANDS LIKE THIS, QUICK!
WHY?
DOMITORS DON'T ATTACK INFECTED! AT LEAST...
...NOT WITHOUT A GOOD REASON.

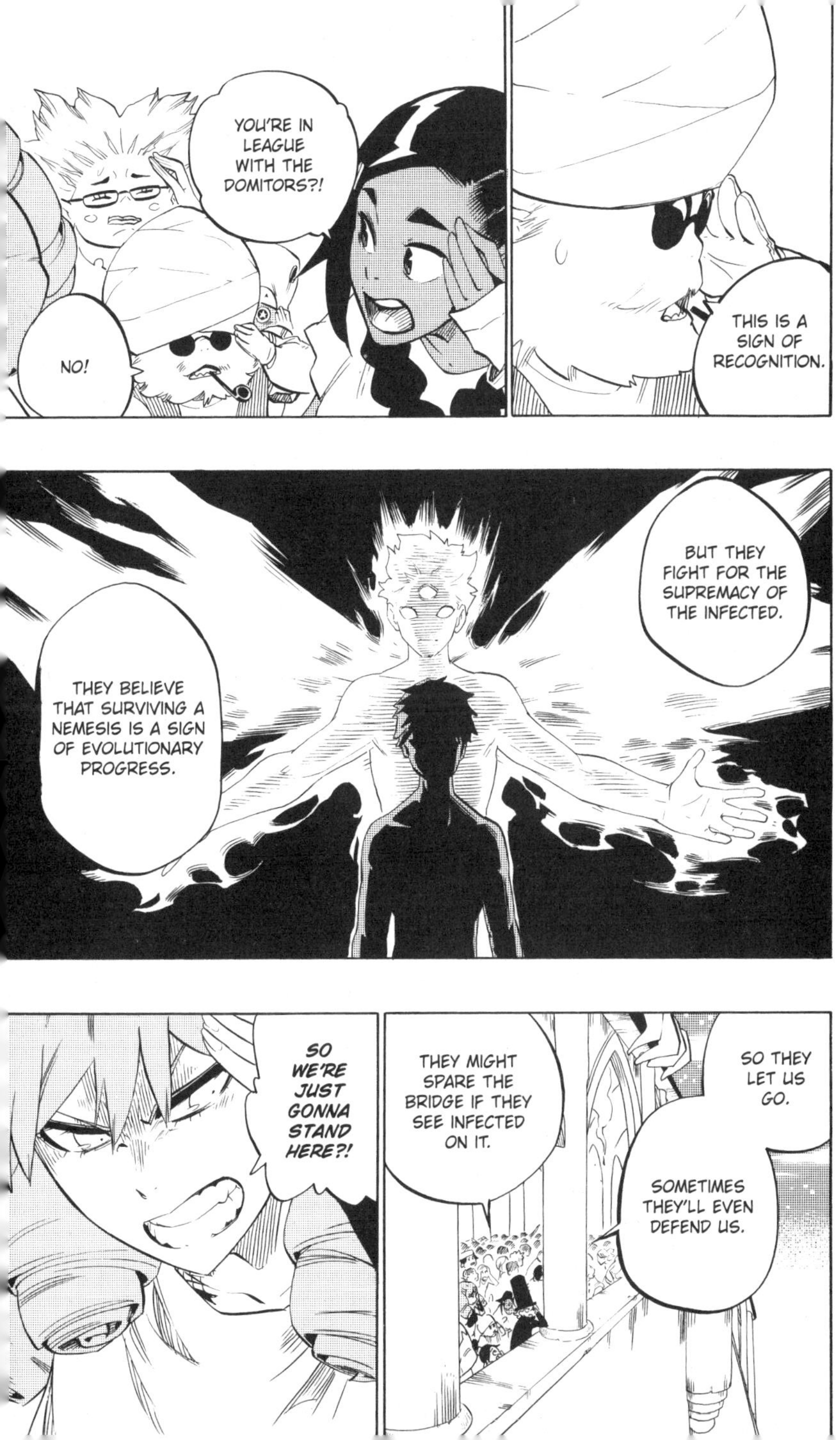
THIS IS A SIGN OF RECOGNITION.
YOU'RE IN LEAGUE WITH THE DOMITORS?!
NO!
BUT THEY FIGHT FOR THE SUPREMACY OF THE INFECTED.
THEY BELIEVE THAT SURVIVING A NEMESIS IS A SIGN OF EVOLUTIONARY PROGRESS.
SO THEY LET US GO.
SOMETIMES THEY'LL EVEN DEFEND US.
THEY MIGHT SPARE THE BRIDGE IF THEY SEE INFECTED ON IT.
SO WE'RE JUST GONNA STAND HERE?!

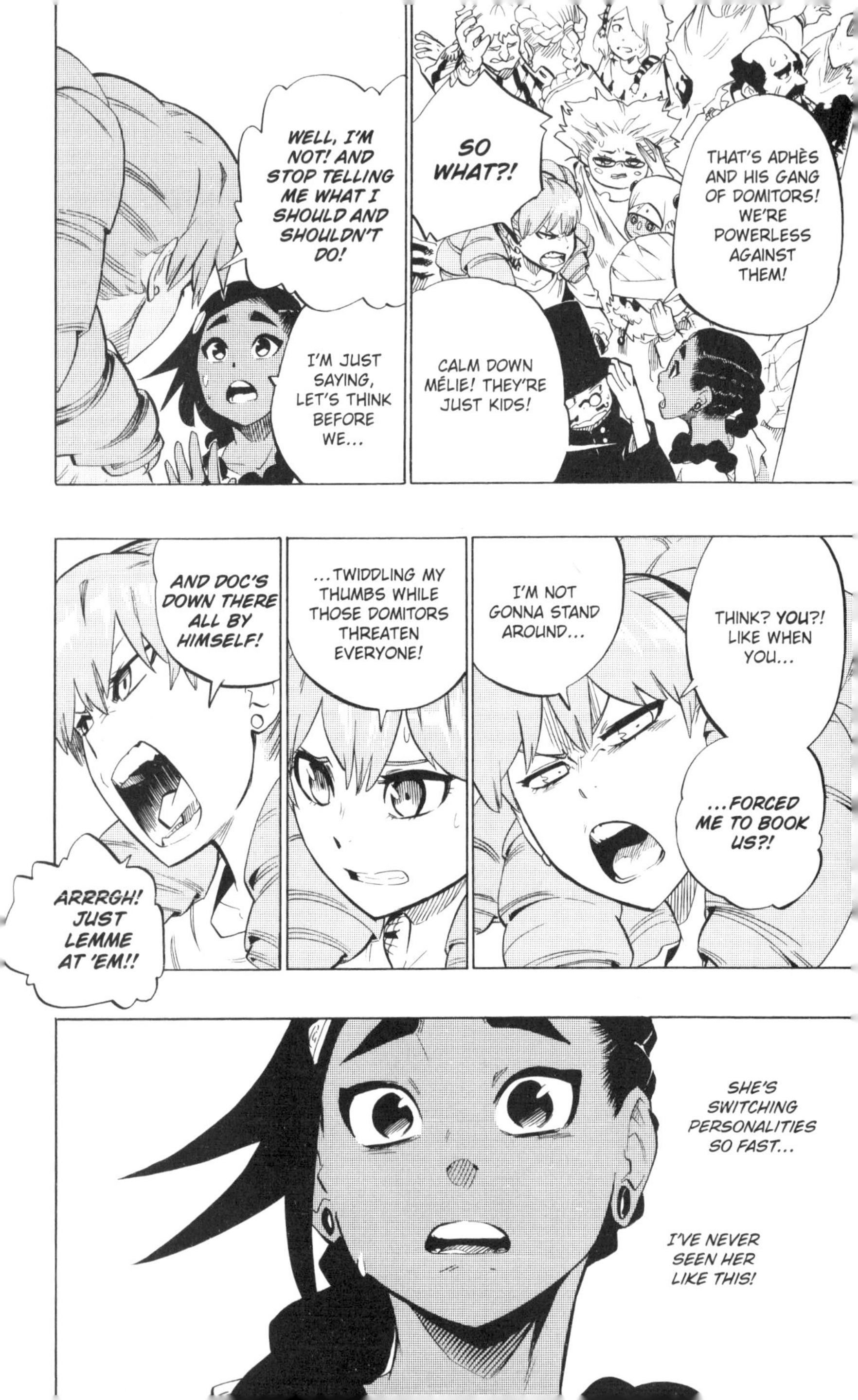
THAT'S ADHÈS AND HIS GANG OF DOMITORS! WE'RE POWERLESS AGAINST THEM!
SO WHAT?!
CALM DOWN MÉLIE! THEY'RE JUST KIDS!
WELL, I'M NOT! AND STOP TELLING ME WHAT I SHOULD AND SHOULDN'T DO!
I'M JUST SAYING, LET'S THINK BEFORE WE...
THINK? YOU?! LIKE WHEN YOU...
...FORCED ME TO BOOK US?!
I'M NOT GONNA STAND AROUND...
...TWIDDLING MY THUMBS WHILE THOSE DOMITORS THREATEN EVERYONE!
AND DOC'S DOWN THERE ALL BY HIMSELF!
ARRRGH! JUST LEMME AT 'EM!!
SHE'S SWITCHING PERSONALITIES SO FAST...
I'VE NEVER SEEN HER LIKE THIS!

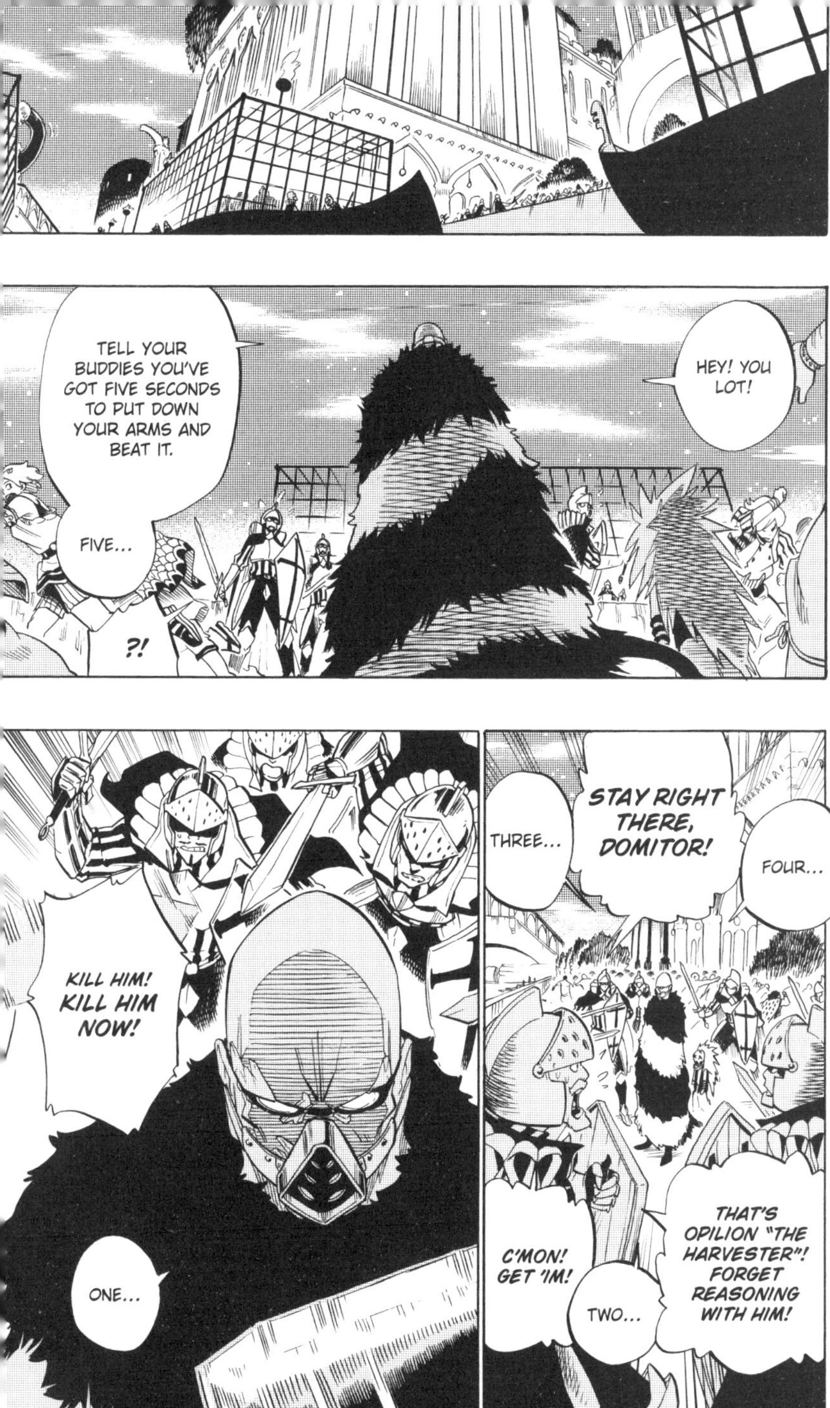
HEY! YOU LOT!
TELL YOUR BUDDIES YOU'VE GOT FIVE SECONDS TO PUT DOWN YOUR ARMS AND BEAT IT.
FIVE...
?!
FOUR...
STAY RIGHT THERE, DOMITOR!
THREE...
THAT'S OPILION "THE HARVESTER"! FORGET REASONING WITH HIM!
TWO...
C'MON! GET 'IM!
KILL HIM! KILL HIM NOW!
ONE...

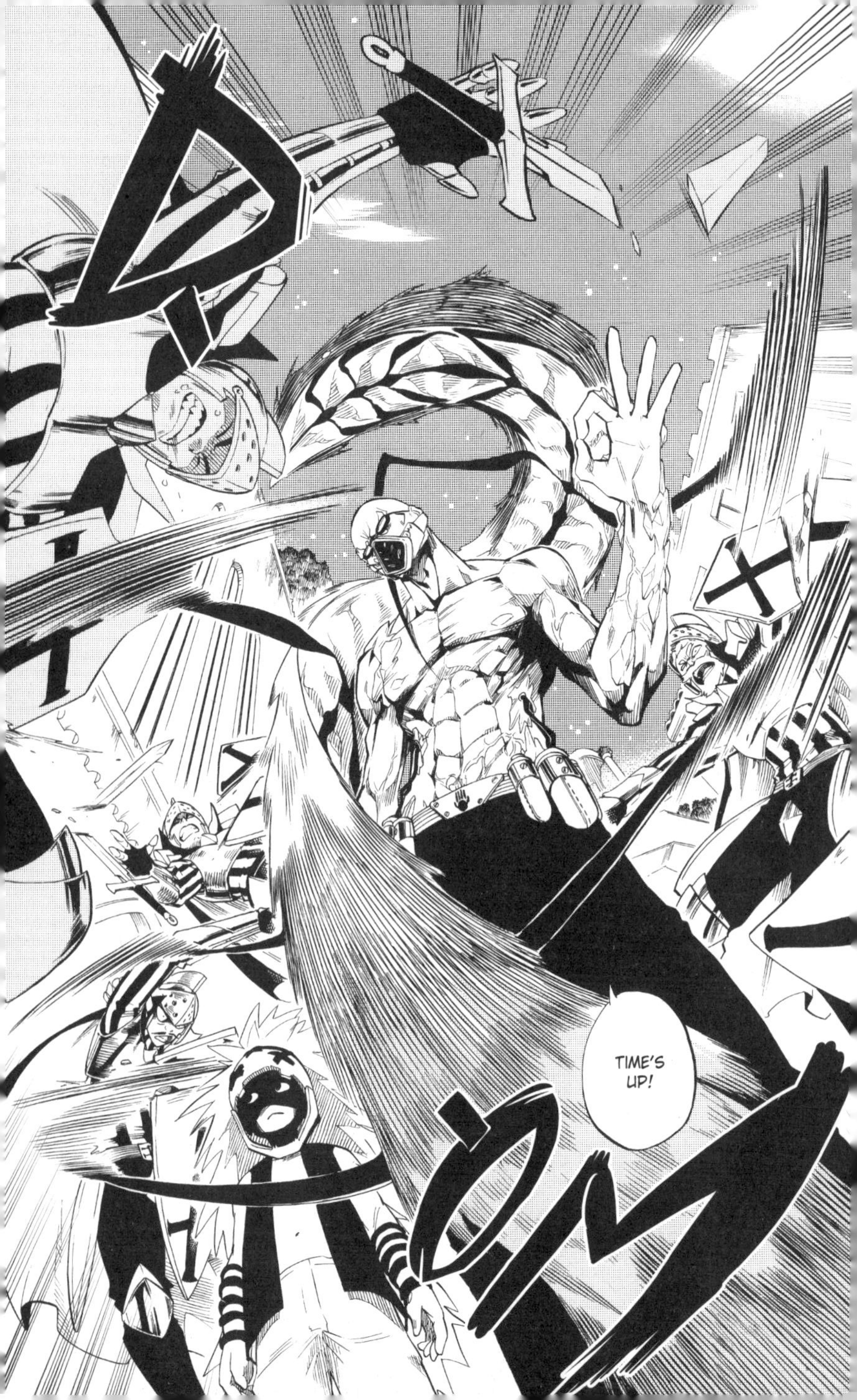
TIME'S UP!

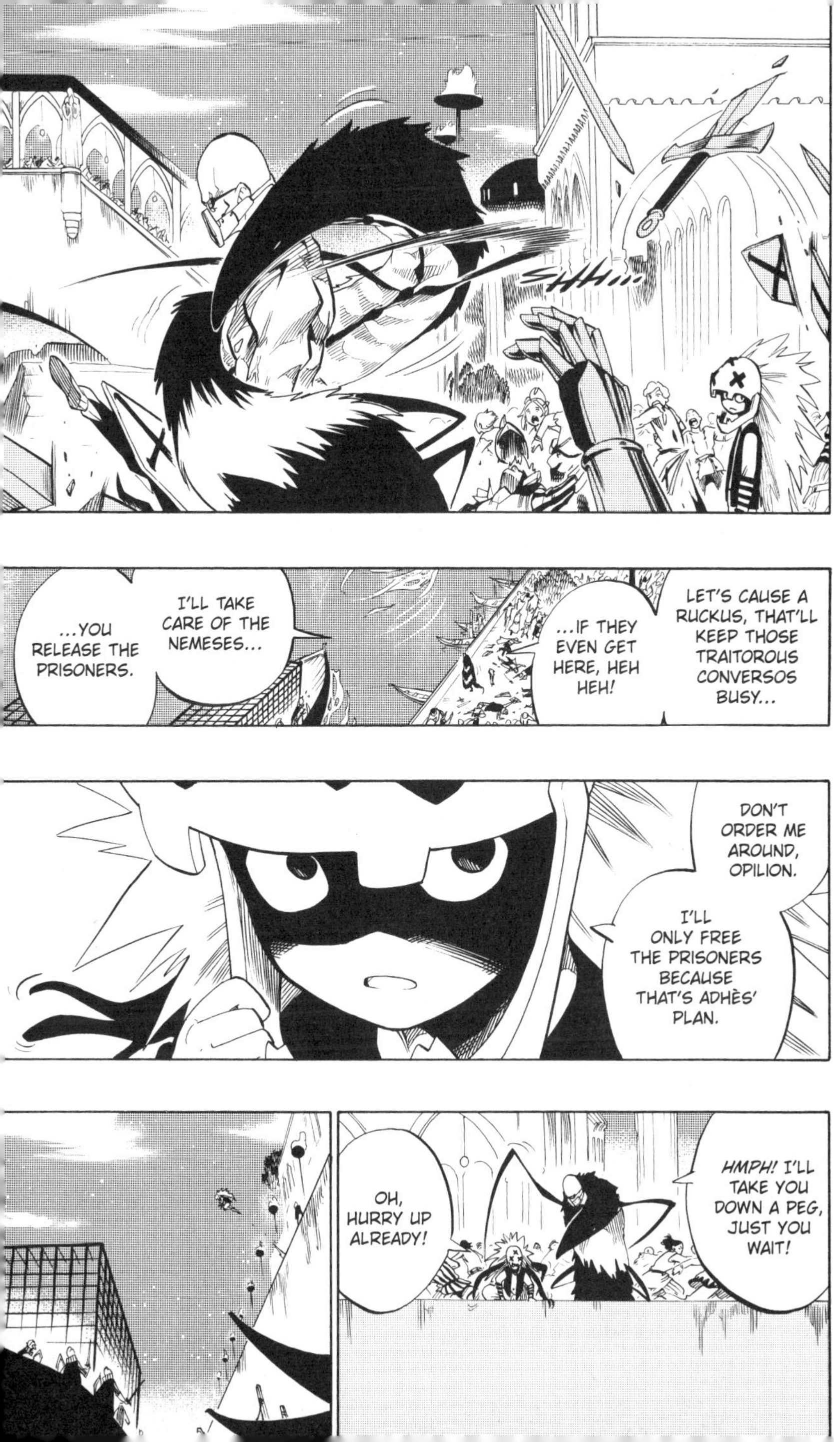
SHHH...
LET'S CAUSE A RUCKUS, THAT'LL KEEP THOSE TRAITOROUS CONVERSOS BUSY...
...IF THEY EVEN GET HERE, HEH HEH!
I'LL TAKE CARE OF THE NEMESES...
...YOU RELEASE THE PRISONERS.
DON'T ORDER ME AROUND, OPILION.
I'LL ONLY FREE THE PRISONERS BECAUSE THAT'S ADHÈS' PLAN.
HMPH! I'LL TAKE YOU DOWN A PEG, JUST YOU WAIT!
OH, HURRY UP ALREADY!

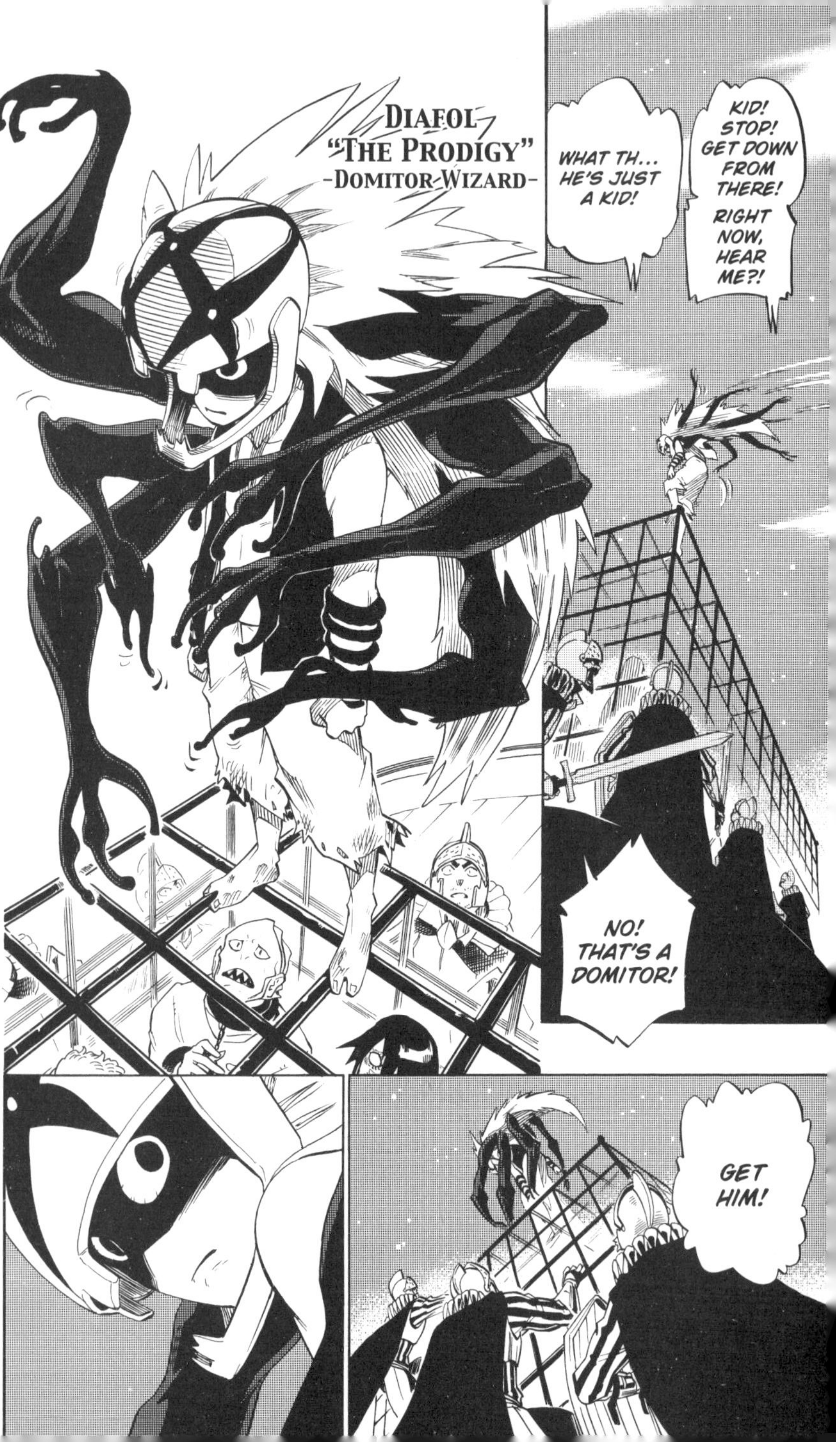
KID! STOP! GET DOWN FROM THERE! RIGHT NOW, HEAR ME?!
WHAT TH... HE'S JUST A KID!
NO! THAT'S A DOMITOR!
DIAFOL "THE PRODIGY"
-DOMITOR-WIZARD-
GET HIM!

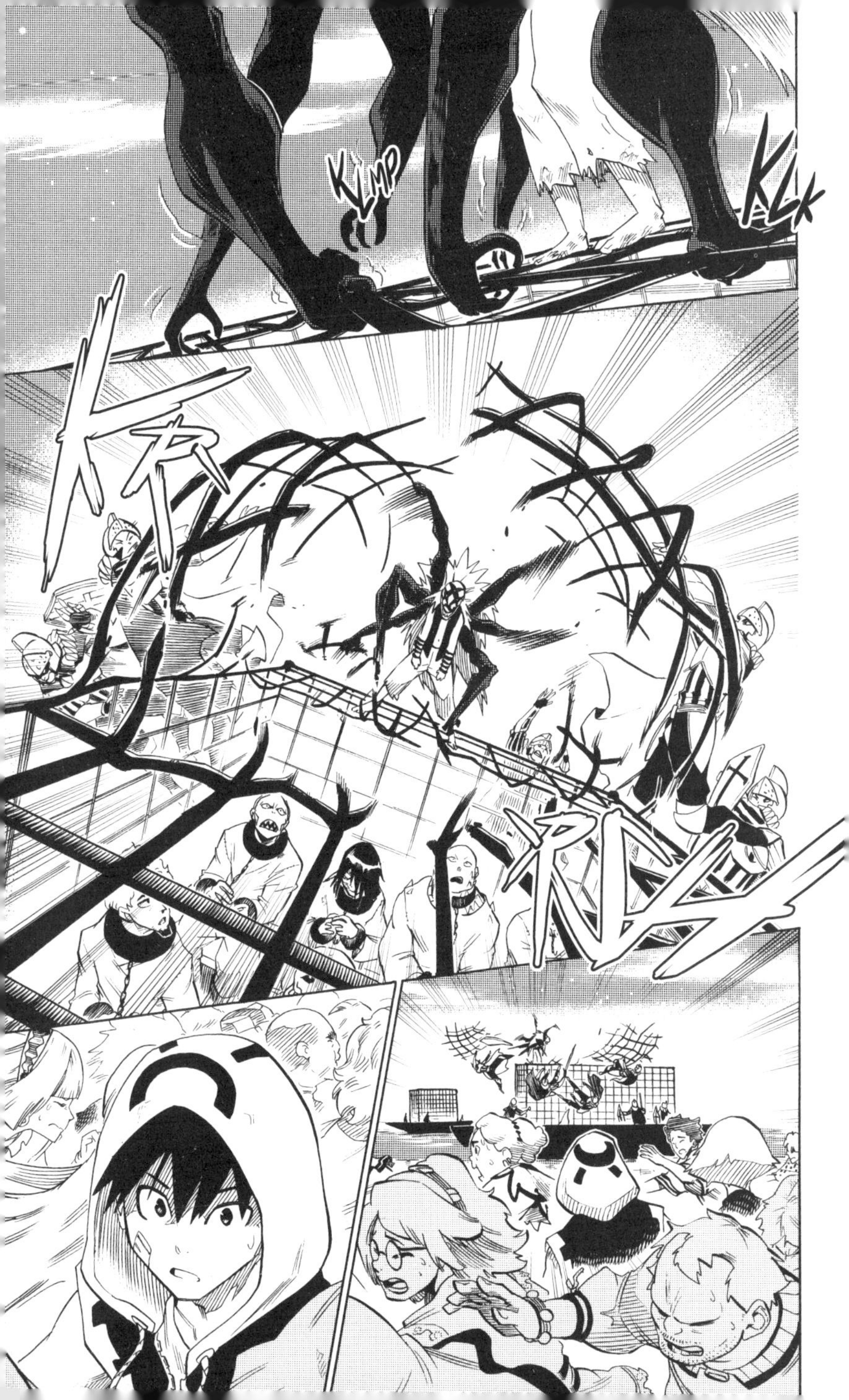
KLK
KLMP
KR
RNK

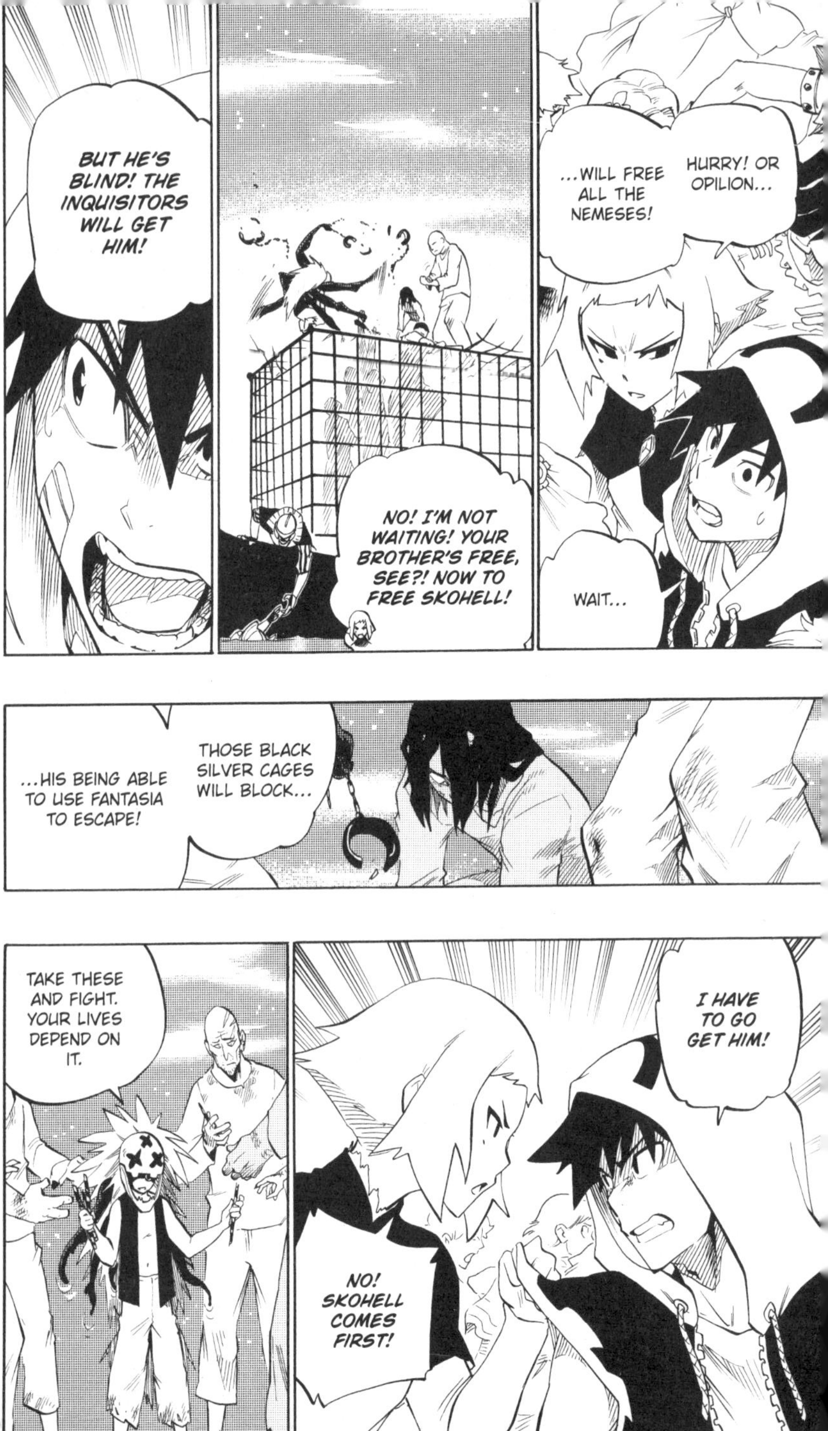
HURRY! OR OPILION...
...WILL FREE ALL THE NEMESES!
WAIT...
NO! I'M NOT WAITING! YOUR BROTHER'S FREE, SEE?! NOW TO FREE SKOHELL!
BUT HE'S BLIND! THE INQUISITORS WILL GET HIM!
THOSE BLACK SILVER CAGES WILL BLOCK...
...HIS BEING ABLE TO USE FANTASIA TO ESCAPE!
I HAVE TO GO GET HIM!
NO! SKOHELL COMES FIRST!
TAKE THESE AND FIGHT. YOUR LIVES DEPEND ON IT.

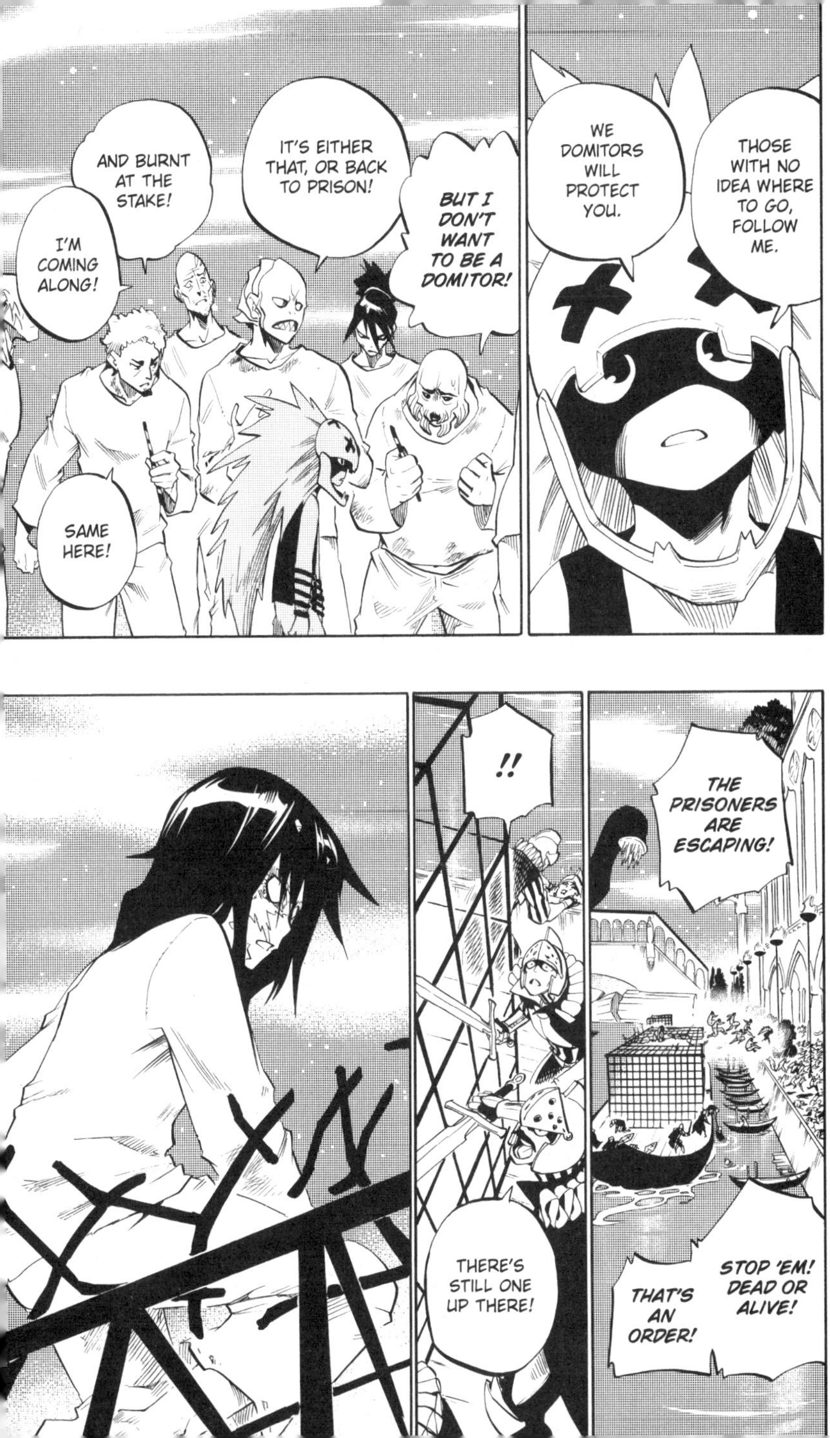
THOSE WITH NO IDEA WHERE TO GO, FOLLOW ME.
WE DOMITORS WILL PROTECT YOU.
BUT I DON'T WANT TO BE A DOMITOR!
IT'S EITHER THAT, OR BACK TO PRISON!
AND BURNT AT THE STAKE!
I'M COMING ALONG!
SAME HERE!
THE PRISONERS ARE ESCAPING!
STOP 'EM! DEAD OR ALIVE!
THAT'S AN ORDER!
!!
THERE'S STILL ONE UP THERE!

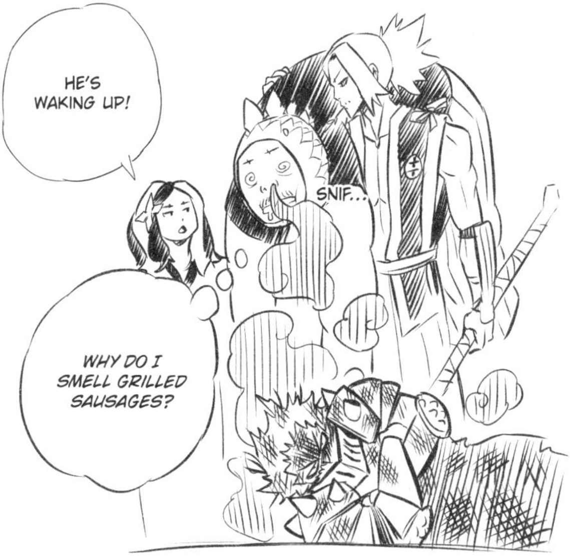
SNIF...
HE'S WAKING UP!
WHY DO I SMELL GRILLED SAUSAGES?

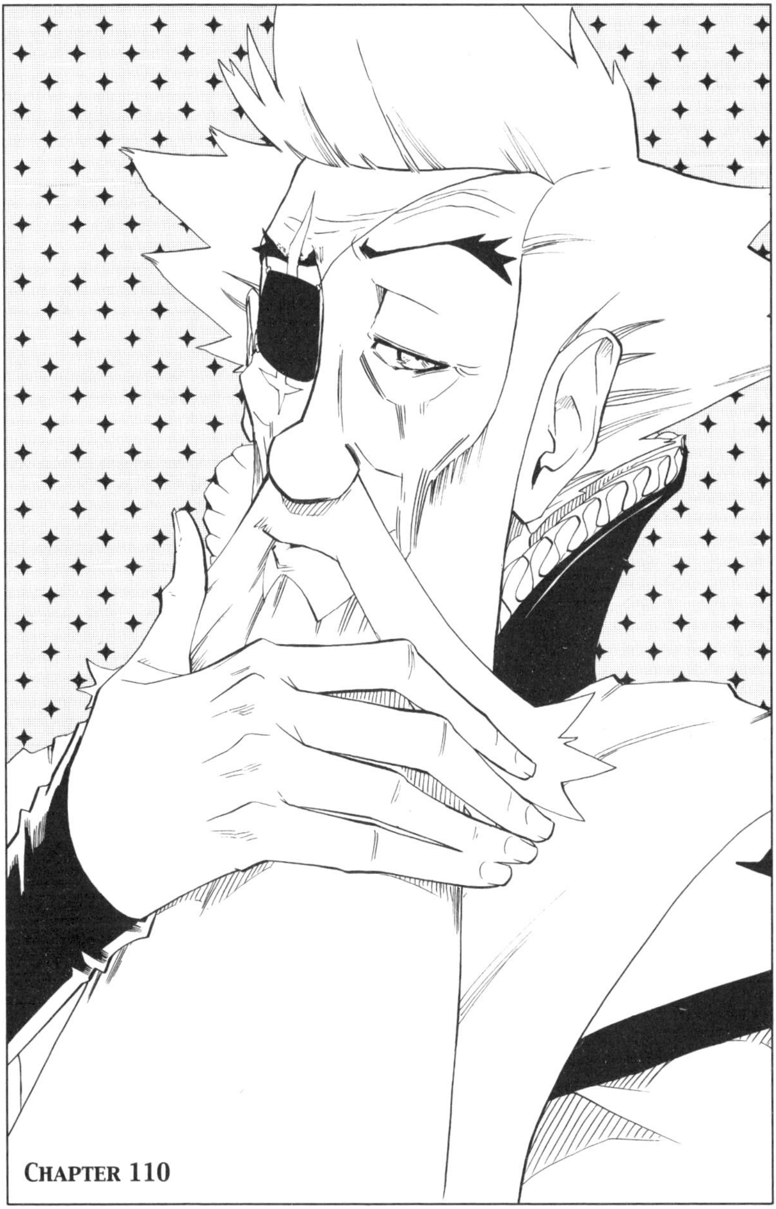

Chapter 110

With My Respect and Thanks

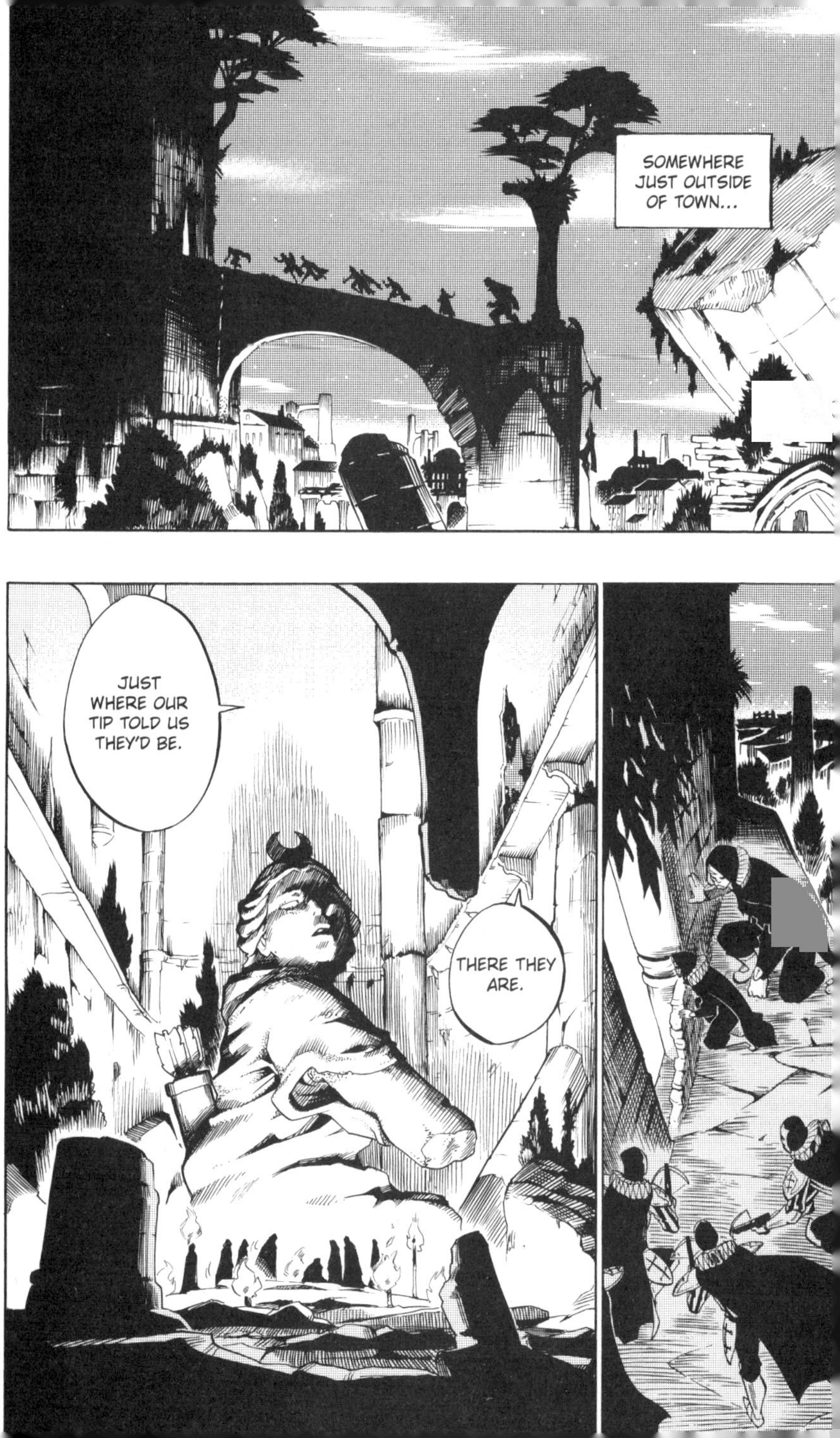
SOMEWHERE JUST OUTSIDE OF TOWN...
JUST WHERE OUR TIP TOLD US THEY'D BE.
THERE THEY ARE.

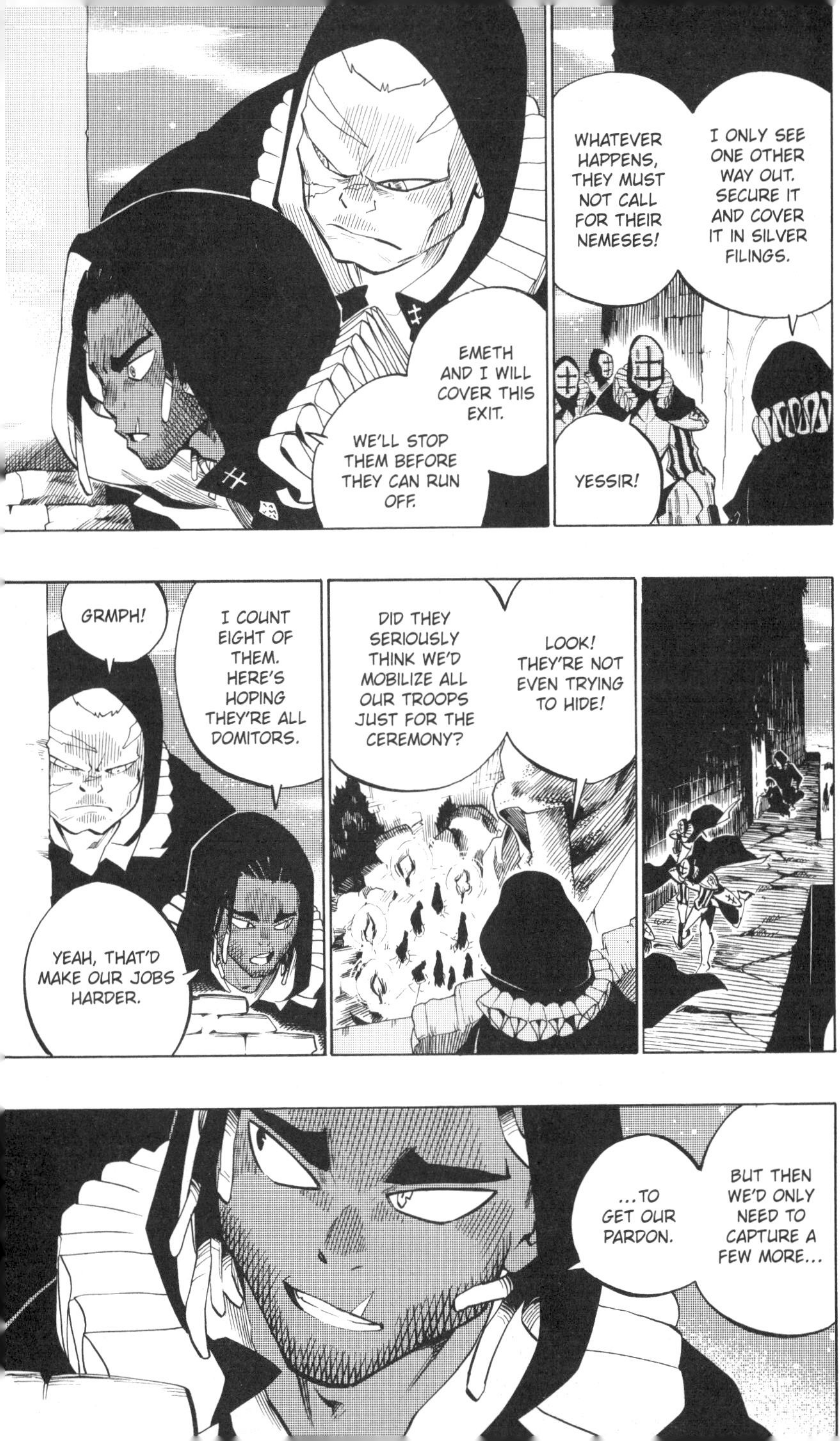
I ONLY SEE ONE OTHER WAY OUT. SECURE IT AND COVER IT IN SILVER FILINGS.
WHATEVER HAPPENS, THEY MUST NOT CALL FOR THEIR NEMESES!
YESSIR!
EMETH AND I WILL COVER THIS EXIT.
WE'LL STOP THEM BEFORE THEY CAN RUN OFF.
LOOK! THEY'RE NOT EVEN TRYING TO HIDE!
DID THEY SERIOUSLY THINK WE'D MOBILIZE ALL OUR TROOPS JUST FOR THE CEREMONY?
I COUNT EIGHT OF THEM. HERE'S HOPING THEY'RE ALL DOMITORS.
GRMPH!
YEAH, THAT'D MAKE OUR JOBS HARDER.
BUT THEN WE'D ONLY NEED TO CAPTURE A FEW MORE...
...TO GET OUR PARDON.

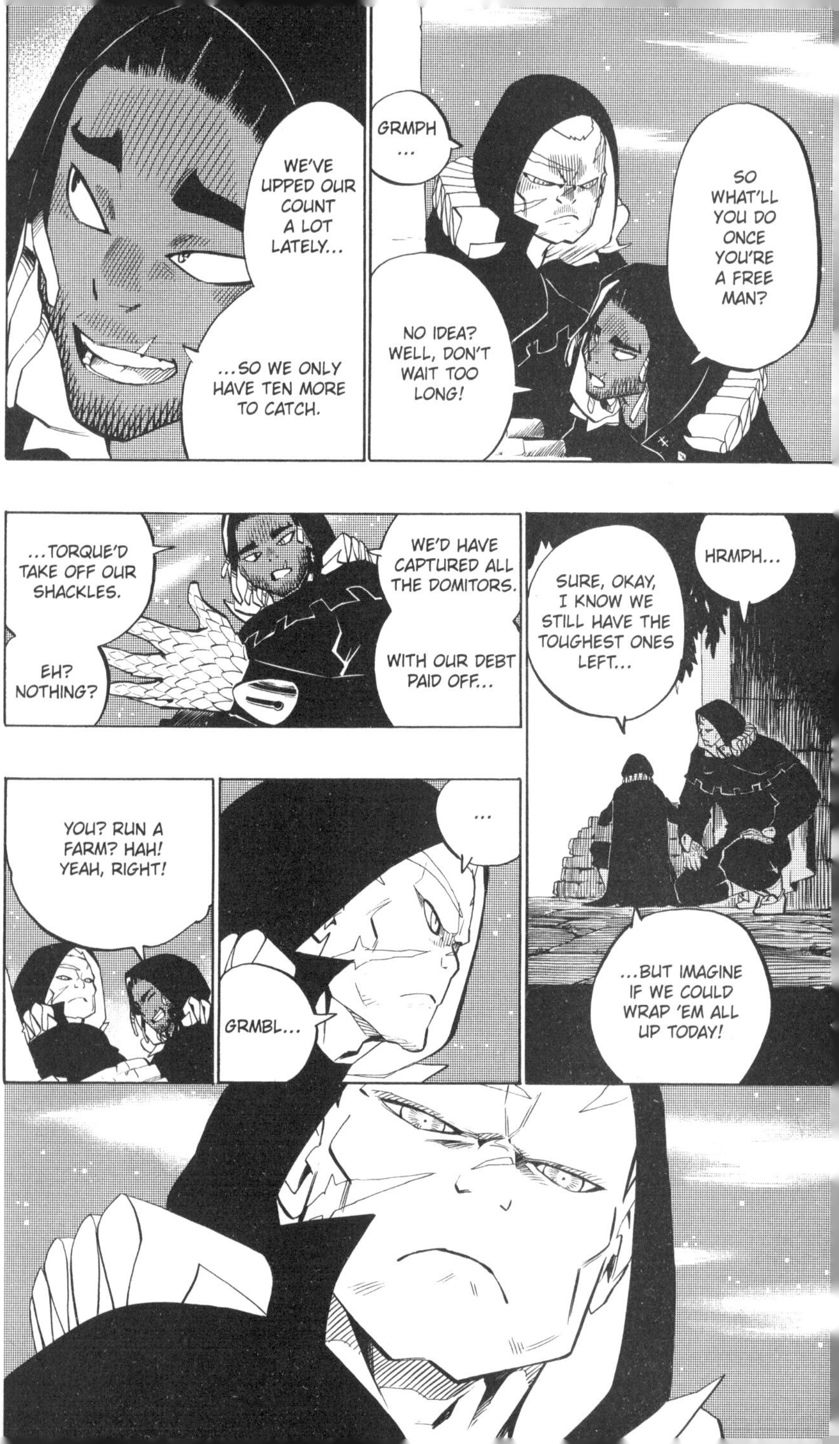
SO WHAT'LL YOU DO ONCE YOU'RE A FREE MAN?
GRMPH...
NO IDEA? WELL, DON'T WAIT TOO LONG!
WE'VE UPPED OUR COUNT A LOT LATELY...
...SO WE ONLY HAVE TEN MORE TO CATCH.
HRMPH...
SURE, OKAY, I KNOW WE STILL HAVE THE TOUGHEST ONES LEFT...
...BUT IMAGINE IF WE COULD WRAP 'EM ALL UP TODAY!
WE'D HAVE CAPTURED ALL THE DOMITORS.
WITH OUR DEBT PAID OFF...
...TORQUE'D TAKE OFF OUR SHACKLES.
EH? NOTHING?
...
GRMBL...
YOU? RUN A FARM? HAH! YEAH, RIGHT!

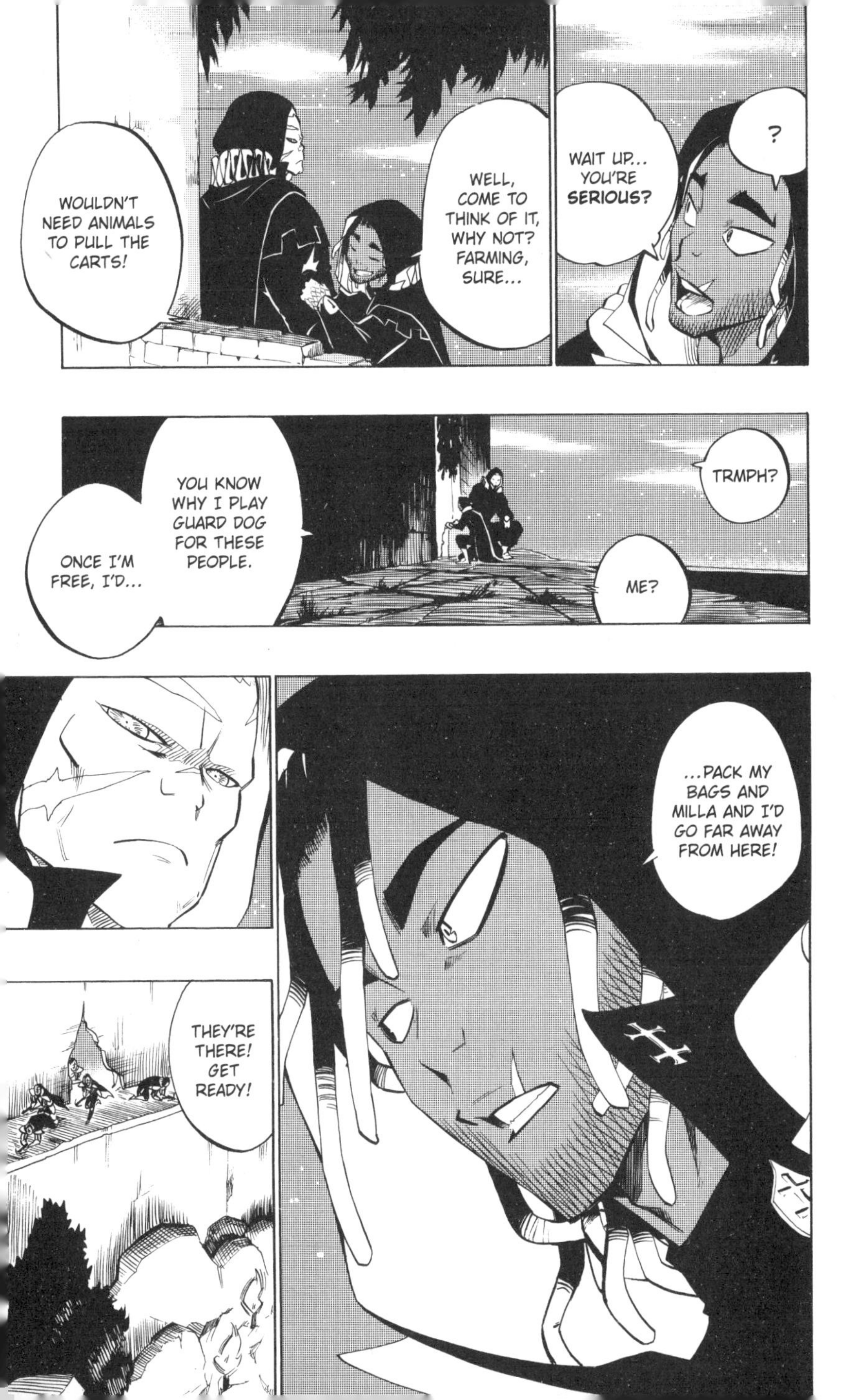
?
WAIT UP... YOU'RE **SERIOUS?**
WELL, COME TO THINK OF IT, WHY NOT? FARMING, SURE...
WOULDN'T NEED ANIMALS TO PULL THE CARTS!
TRMPH?
ME?
YOU KNOW WHY I PLAY GUARD DOG FOR THESE PEOPLE.
ONCE I'M FREE, I'D...
...PACK MY BAGS AND MILLA AND I'D GO FAR AWAY FROM HERE!
THEY'RE THERE! GET READY!

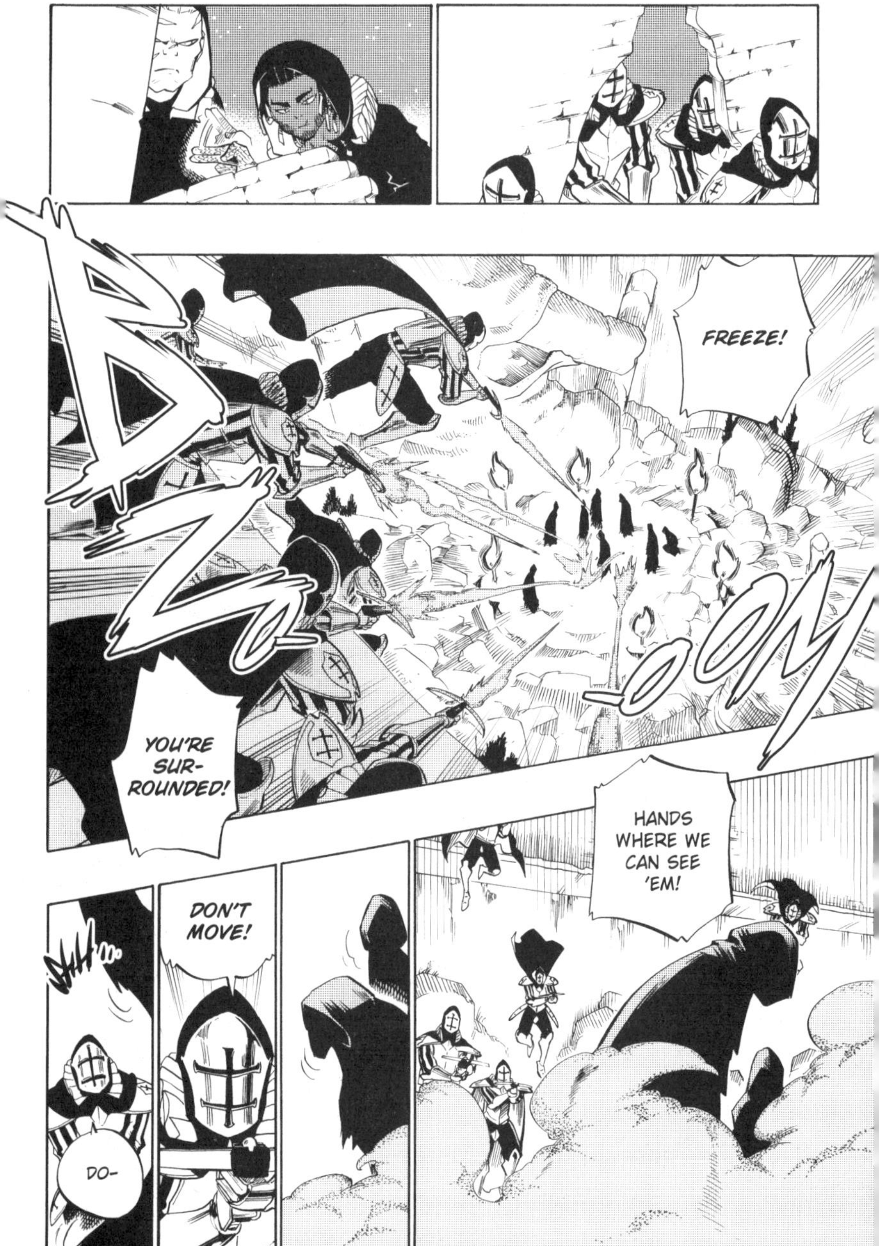
FREEZE!
YOU'RE SUR-ROUNDED!
HANDS WHERE WE CAN SEE 'EM!
DON'T MOVE!
DO-

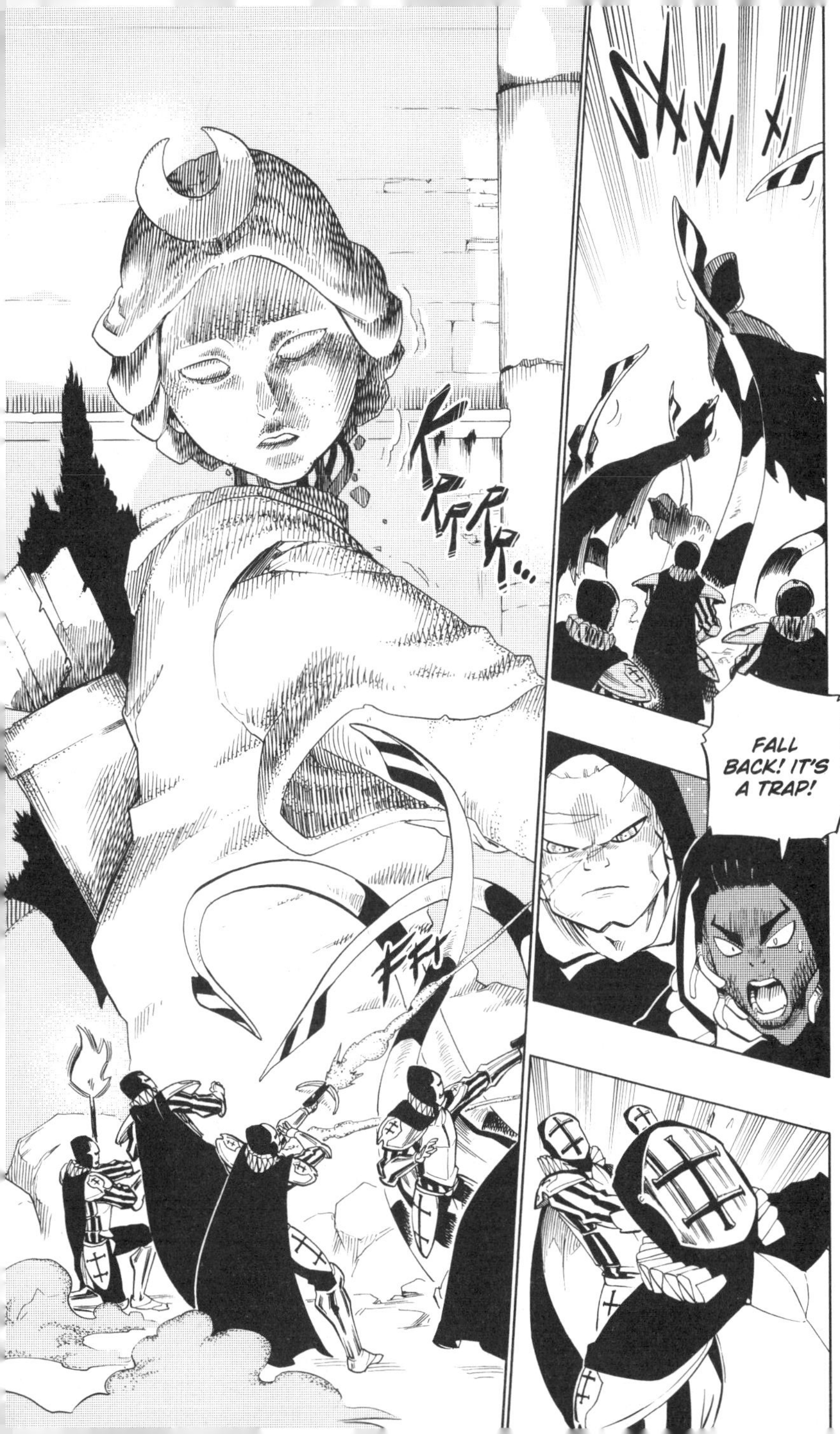
FALL BACK! IT'S A TRAP!
KRRRRR...

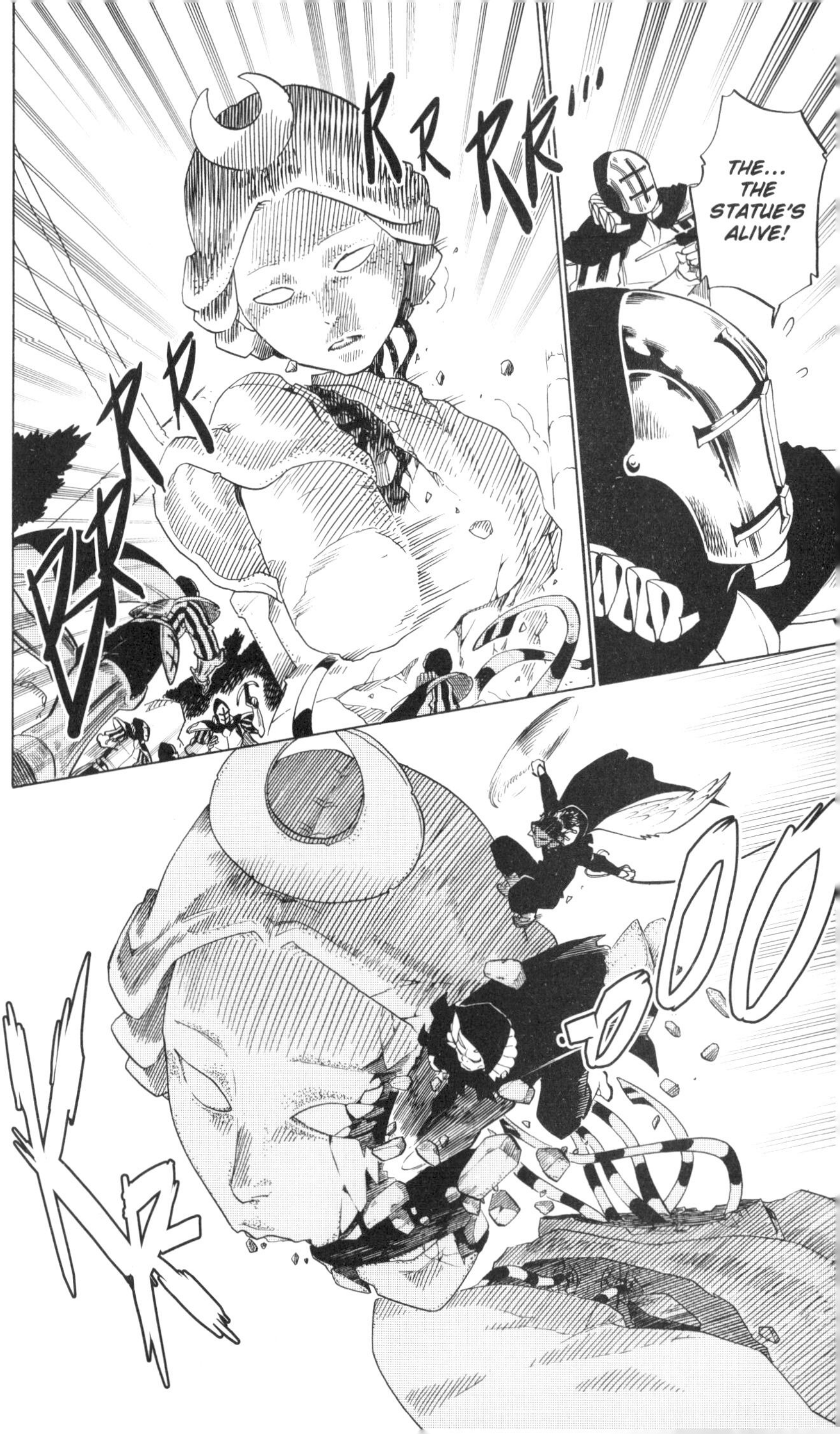
THE... THE STATUE'S ALIVE!
RRRRR...
BRRR
KRR

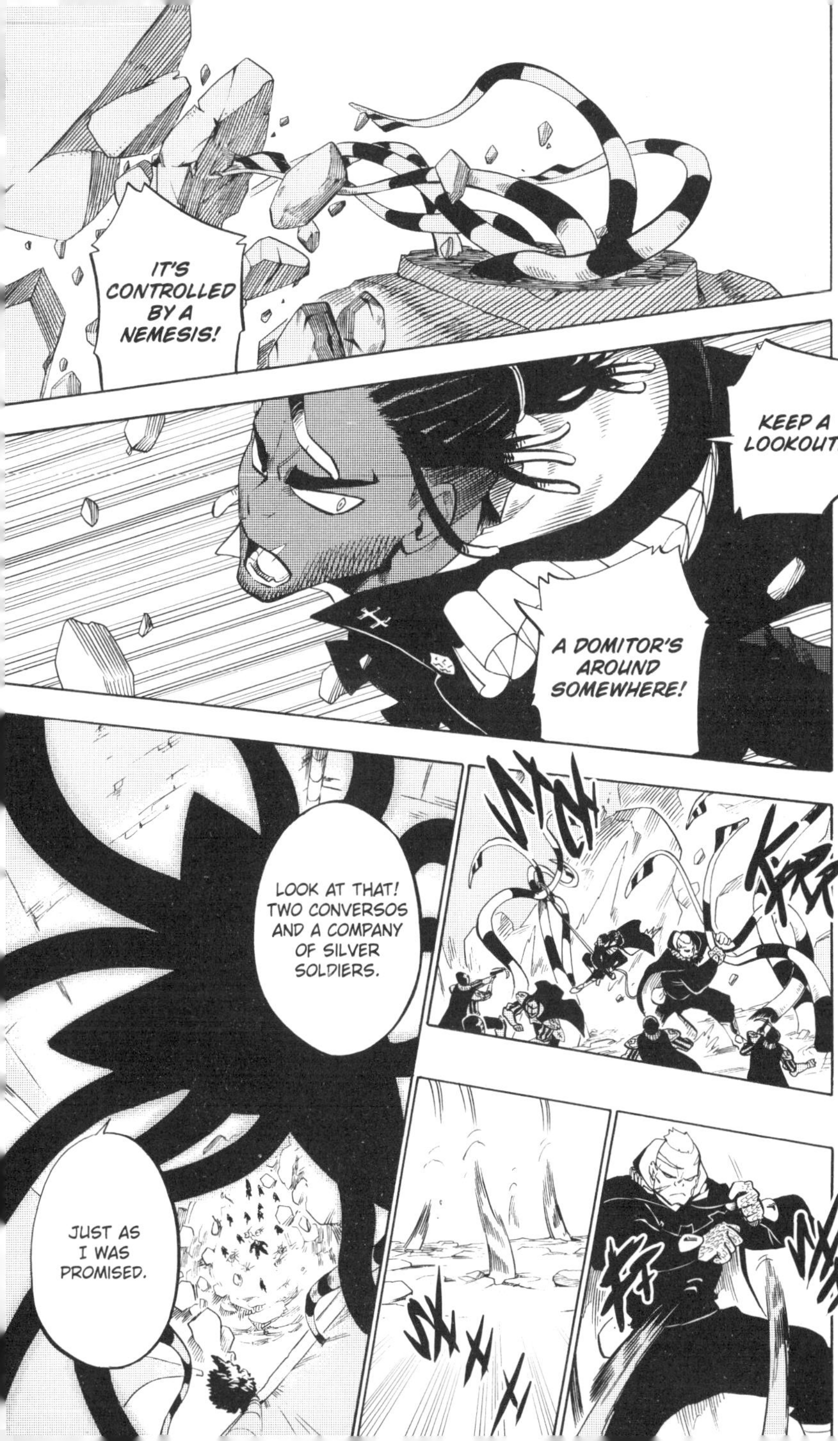

IT'S CONTROLLED BY A NEMESIS!
KEEP A LOOKOUT!
A DOMITOR'S AROUND SOMEWHERE!
LOOK AT THAT! TWO CONVERSOS AND A COMPANY OF SILVER SOLDIERS.
JUST AS I WAS PROMISED.

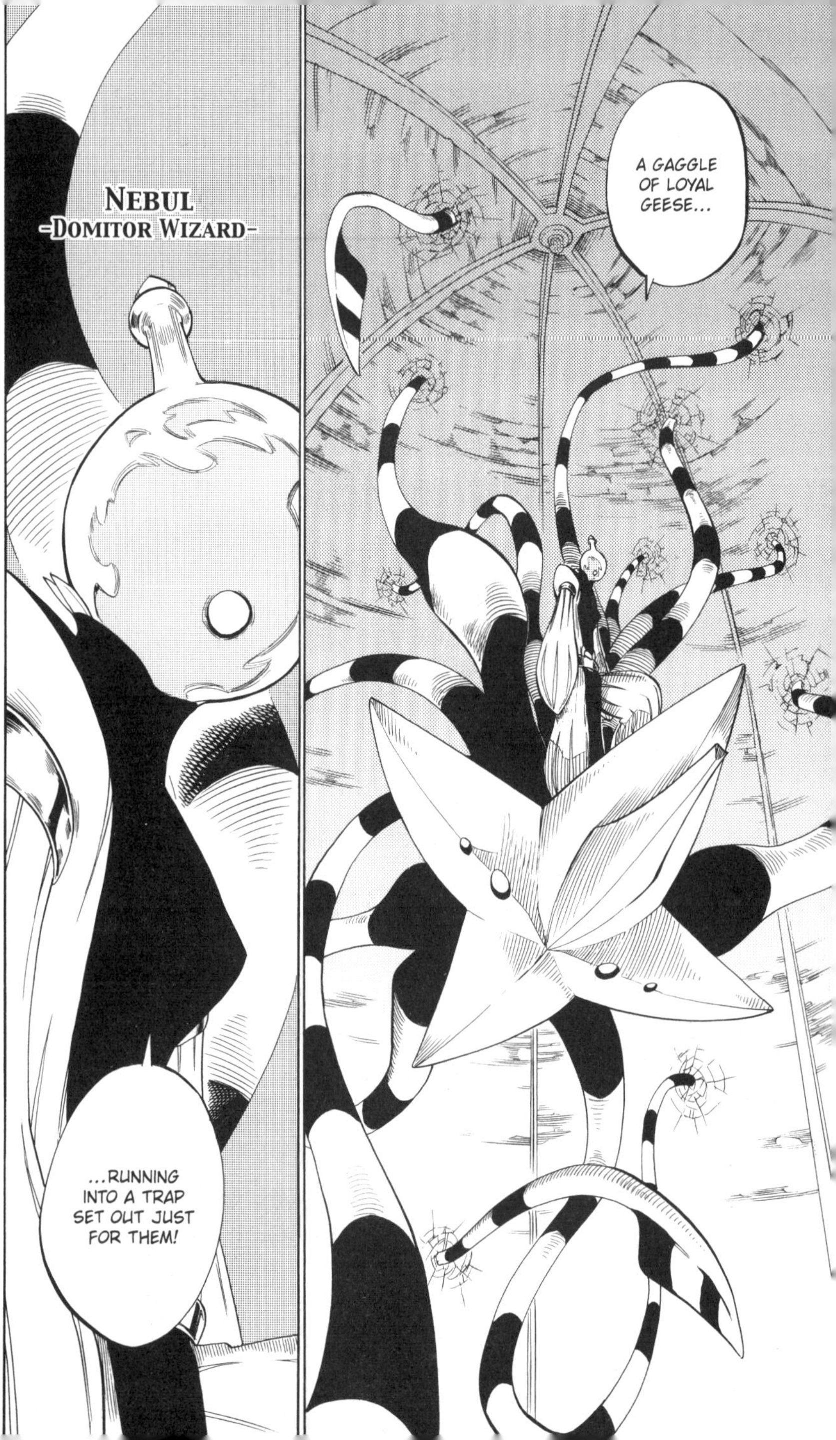
A GAGGLE OF LOYAL GEESE...
NEBUL
-DOMITOR WIZARD-
...RUNNING INTO A TRAP SET OUT JUST FOR THEM!

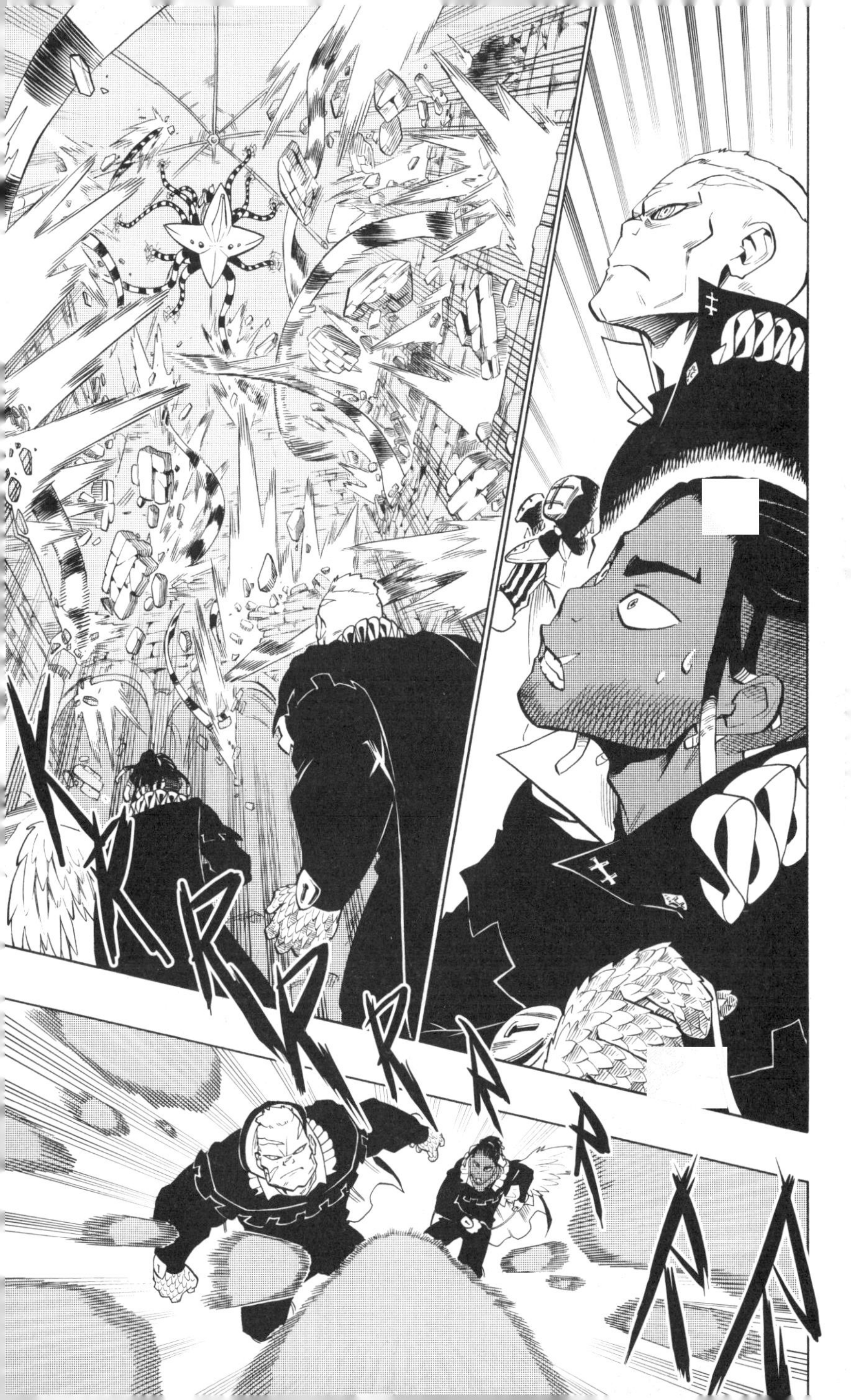
KRRRRRRRRR

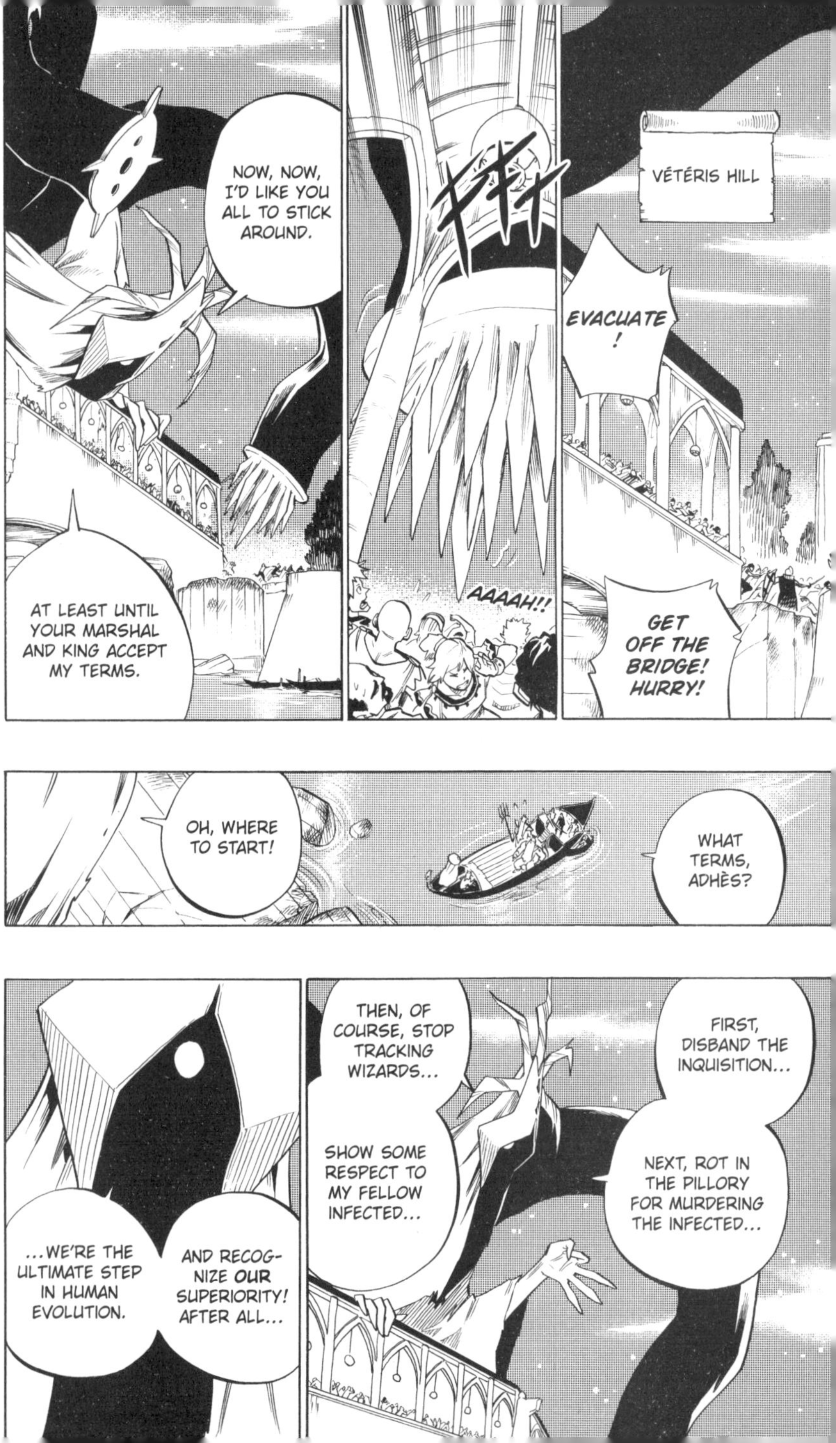
VÉTÉRIS HILL
EVACUATE!
GET OFF THE BRIDGE! HURRY!
AAAAH!!
NOW, NOW, I'D LIKE YOU ALL TO STICK AROUND.
AT LEAST UNTIL YOUR MARSHAL AND KING ACCEPT MY TERMS.
WHAT TERMS, ADHÈS?
OH, WHERE TO START!
FIRST, DISBAND THE INQUISITION...
THEN, OF COURSE, STOP TRACKING WIZARDS...
NEXT, ROT IN THE PILLORY FOR MURDERING THE INFECTED...
SHOW SOME RESPECT TO MY FELLOW INFECTED...
AND RECOG-NIZE **OUR** SUPERIORITY! AFTER ALL...
...WE'RE THE ULTIMATE STEP IN HUMAN EVOLUTION.

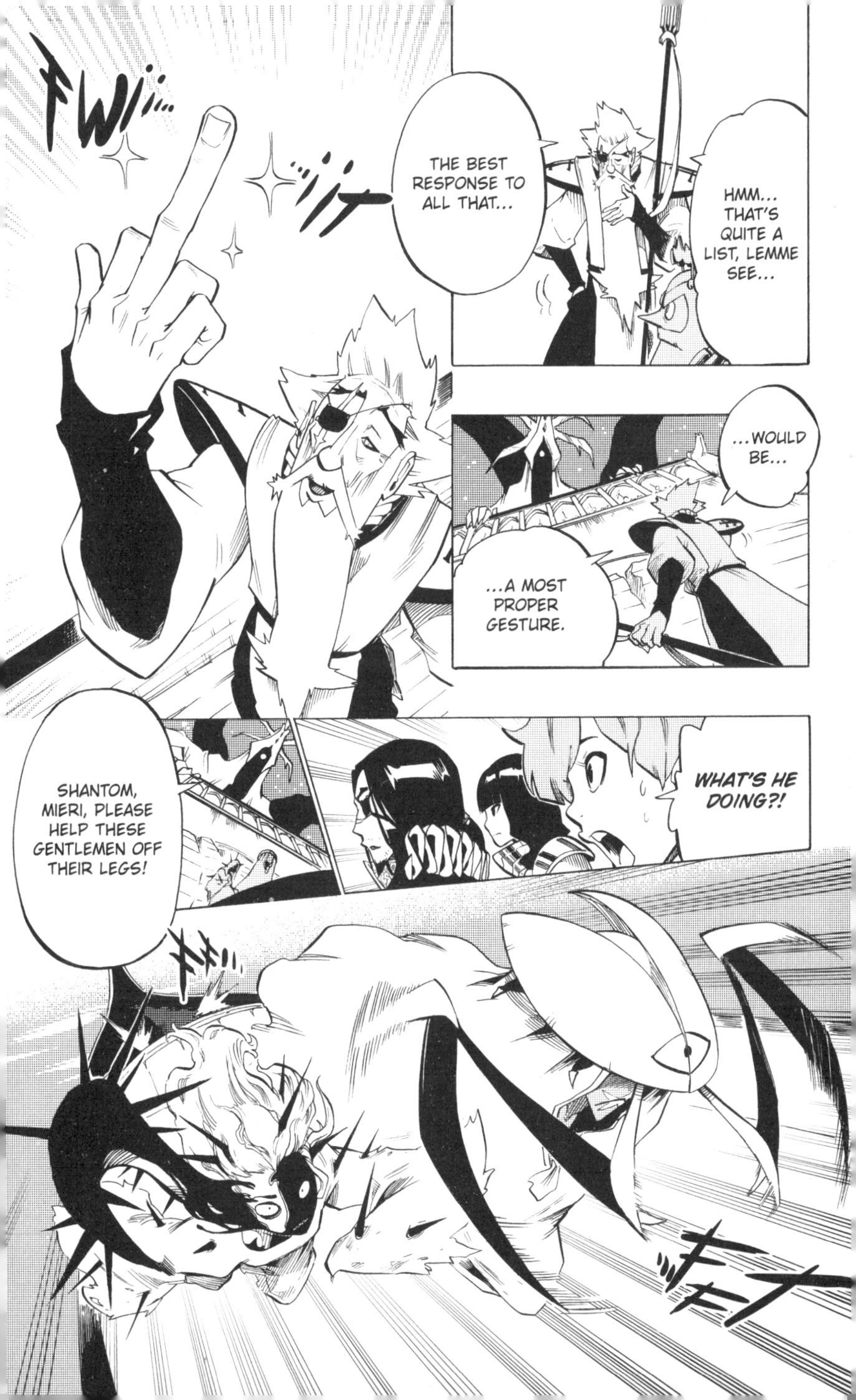
HMM... THAT'S QUITE A LIST, LEMME SEE...
THE BEST RESPONSE TO ALL THAT...
...WOULD BE...
...A MOST PROPER GESTURE.
WHAT'S HE DOING?!
SHANTOM, MIERI, PLEASE HELP THESE GENTLEMEN OFF THEIR LEGS!

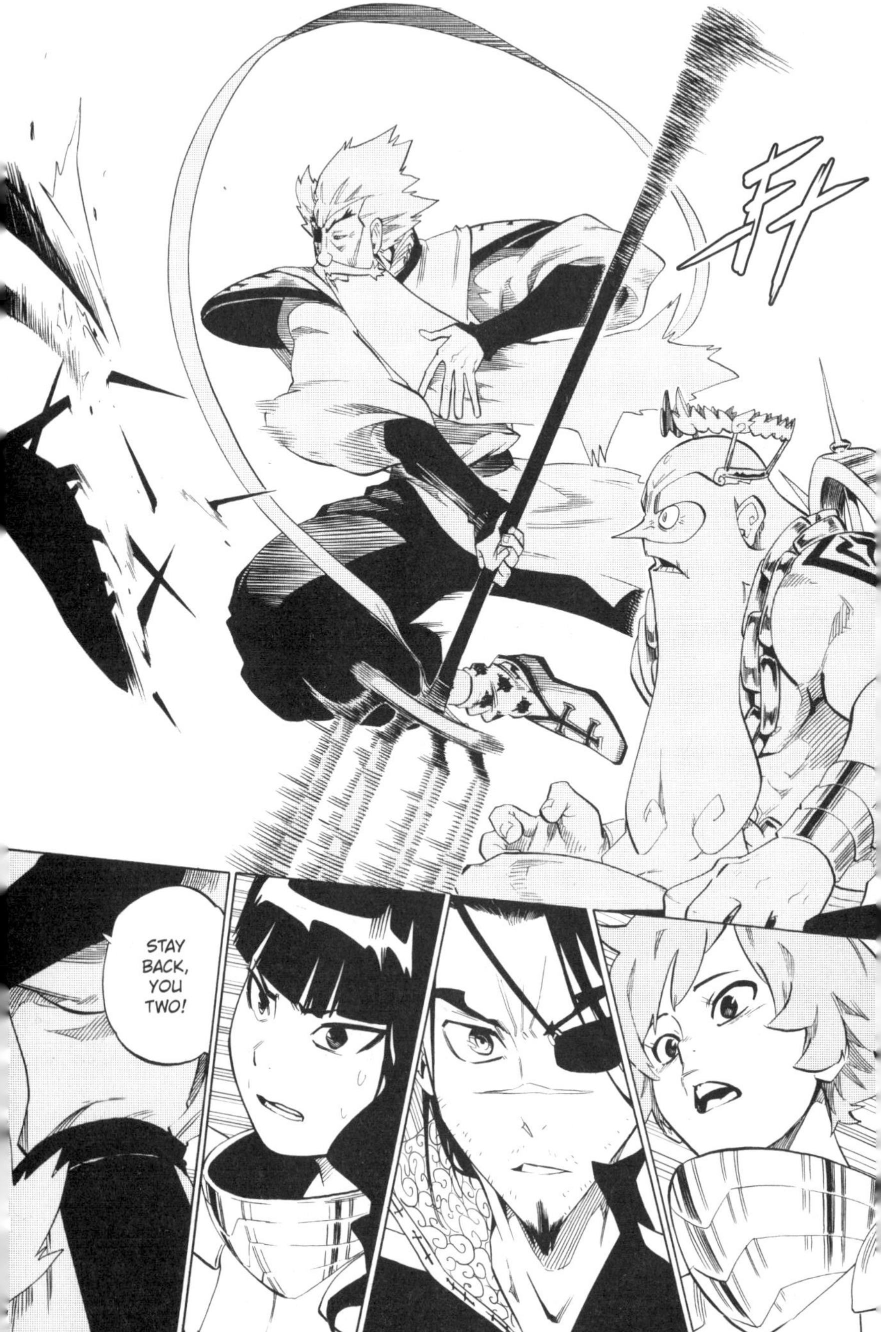
STAY BACK, YOU TWO!

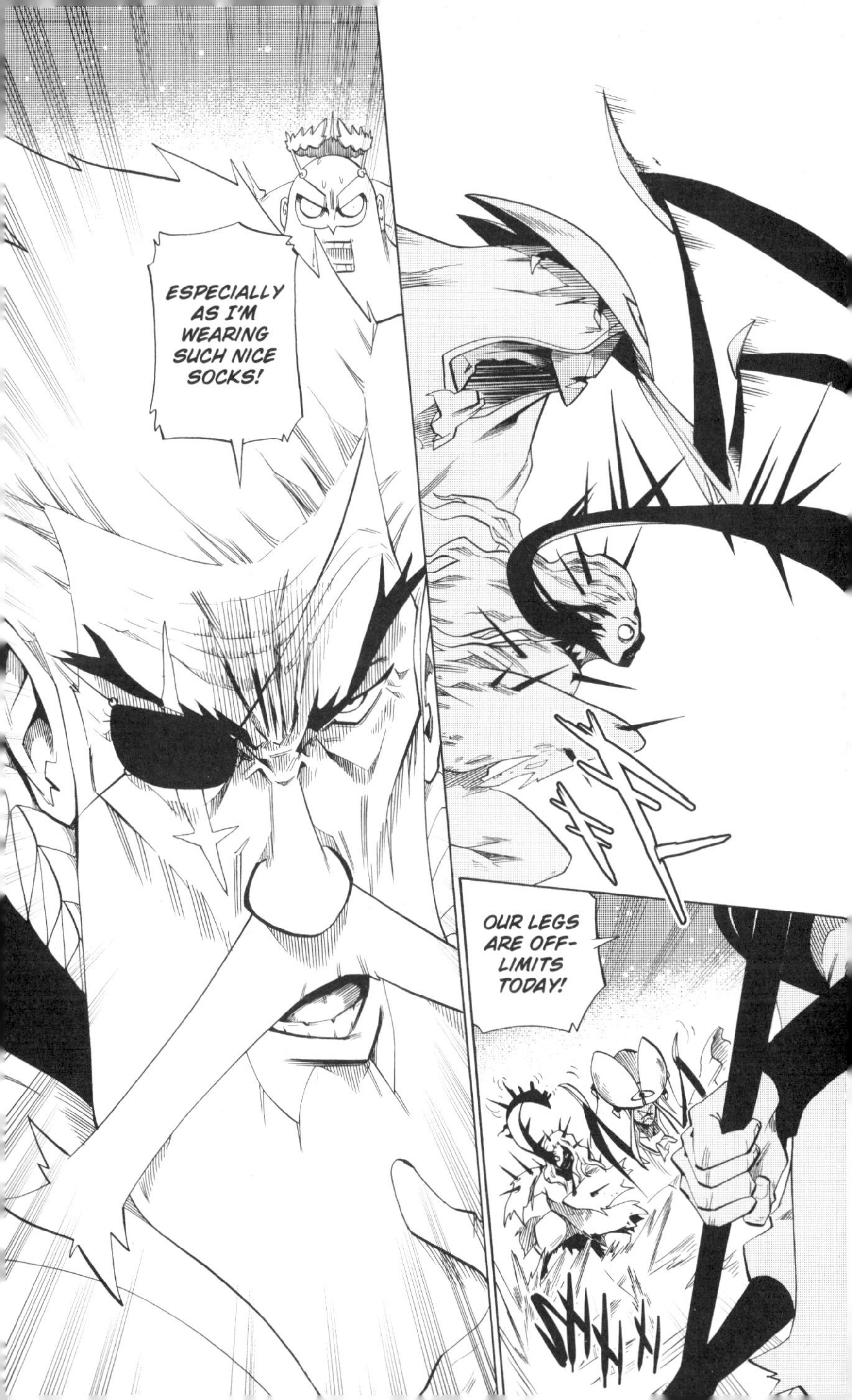
OUR LEGS ARE OFF-LIMITS TODAY!
ESPECIALLY AS I'M WEARING SUCH NICE SOCKS!

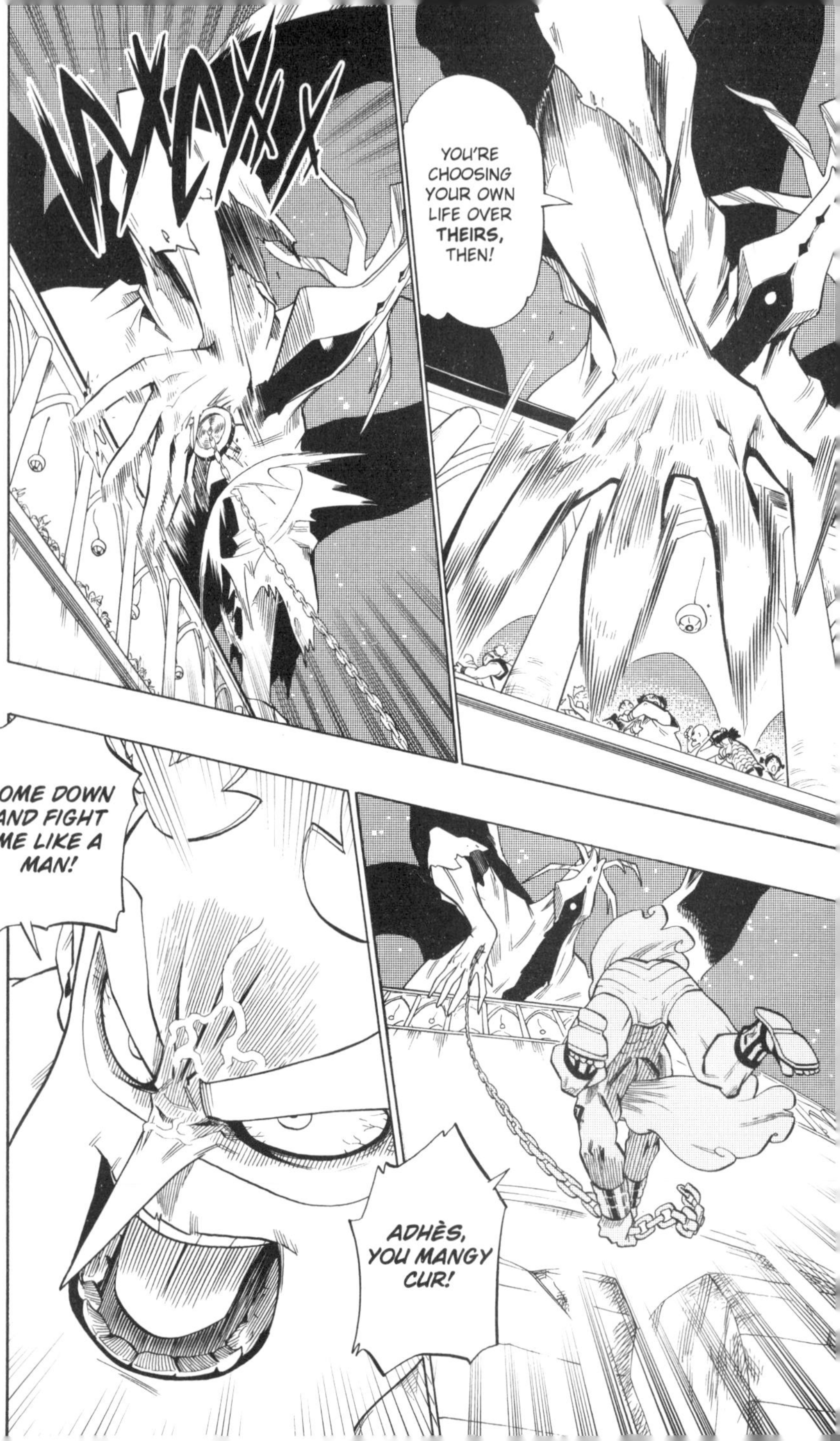
YOU'RE CHOOSING YOUR OWN LIFE OVER **THEIRS,** THEN!
ADHÈS, YOU MANGY CUR!
COME DOWN AND FIGHT ME LIKE A MAN!

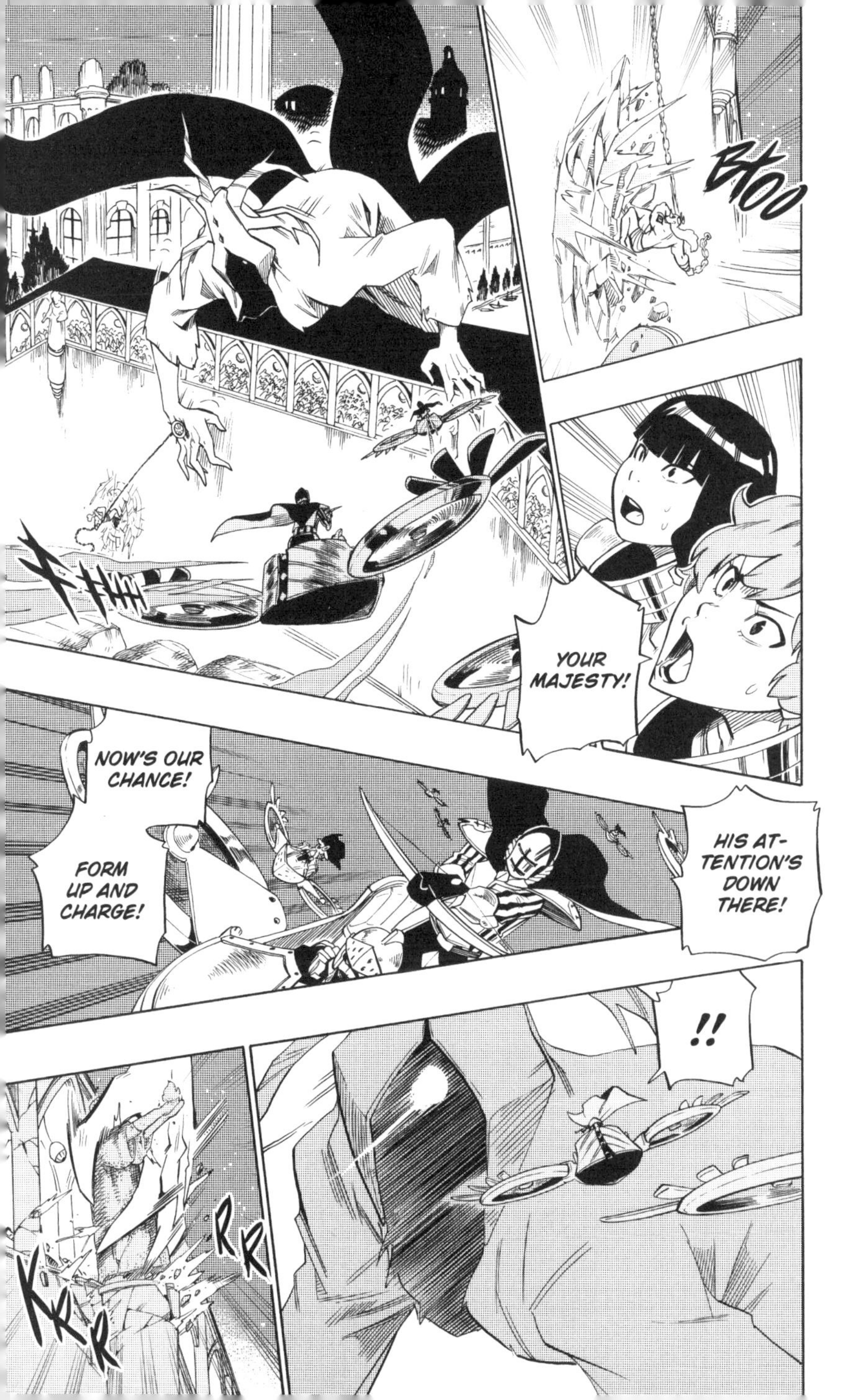
BTOO
YOUR MAJESTY!
HIS AT-TENTION'S DOWN THERE!
NOW'S OUR CHANCE!
FORM UP AND CHARGE!
!!
KRRRR

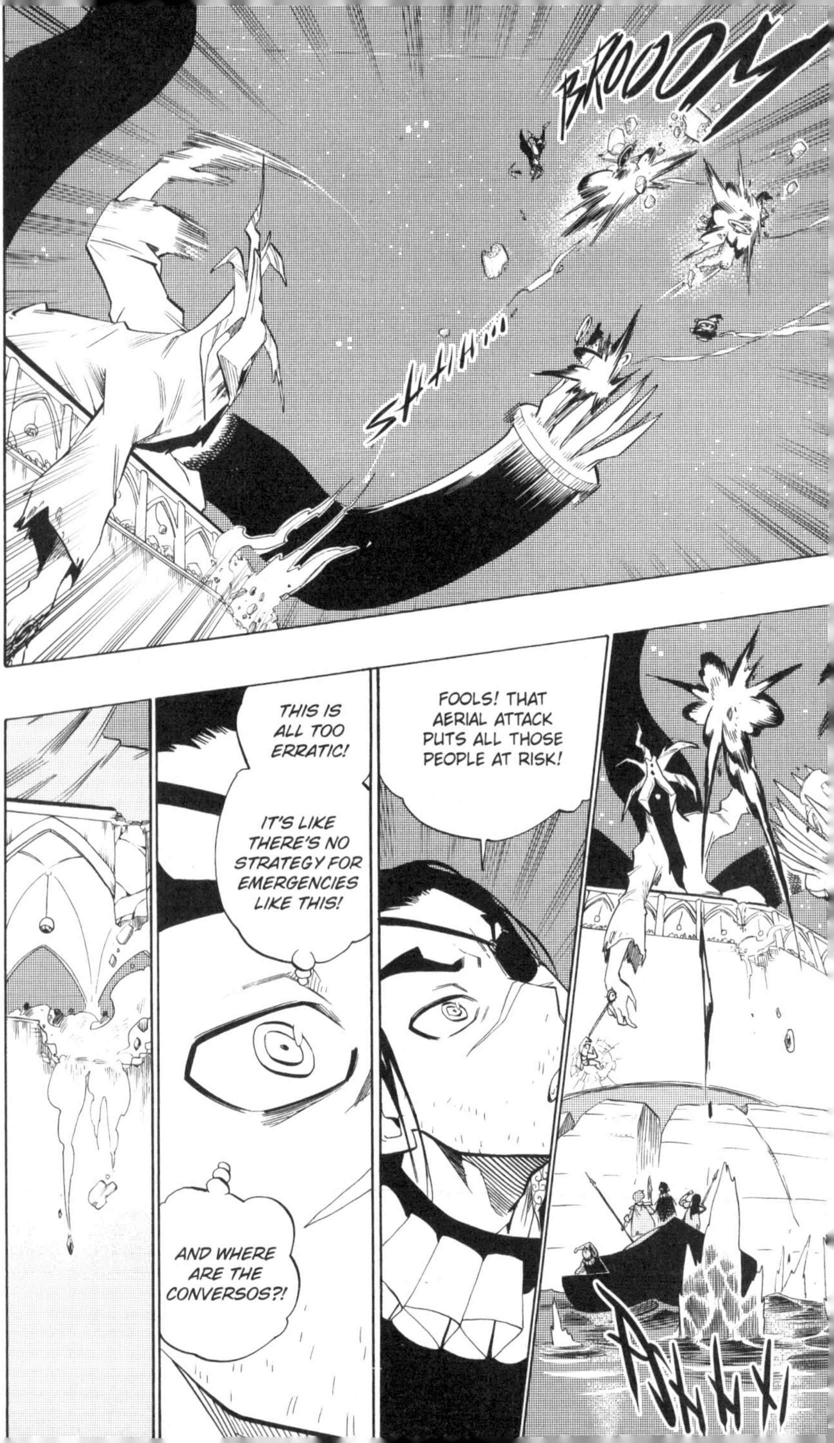
BROOOM
SHHH...
FOOLS! THAT AERIAL ATTACK PUTS ALL THOSE PEOPLE AT RISK!
FSHHH
THIS IS ALL TOO ERRATIC!
IT'S LIKE THERE'S NO STRATEGY FOR EMERGENCIES LIKE THIS!
AND WHERE ARE THE CONVERSOS?!

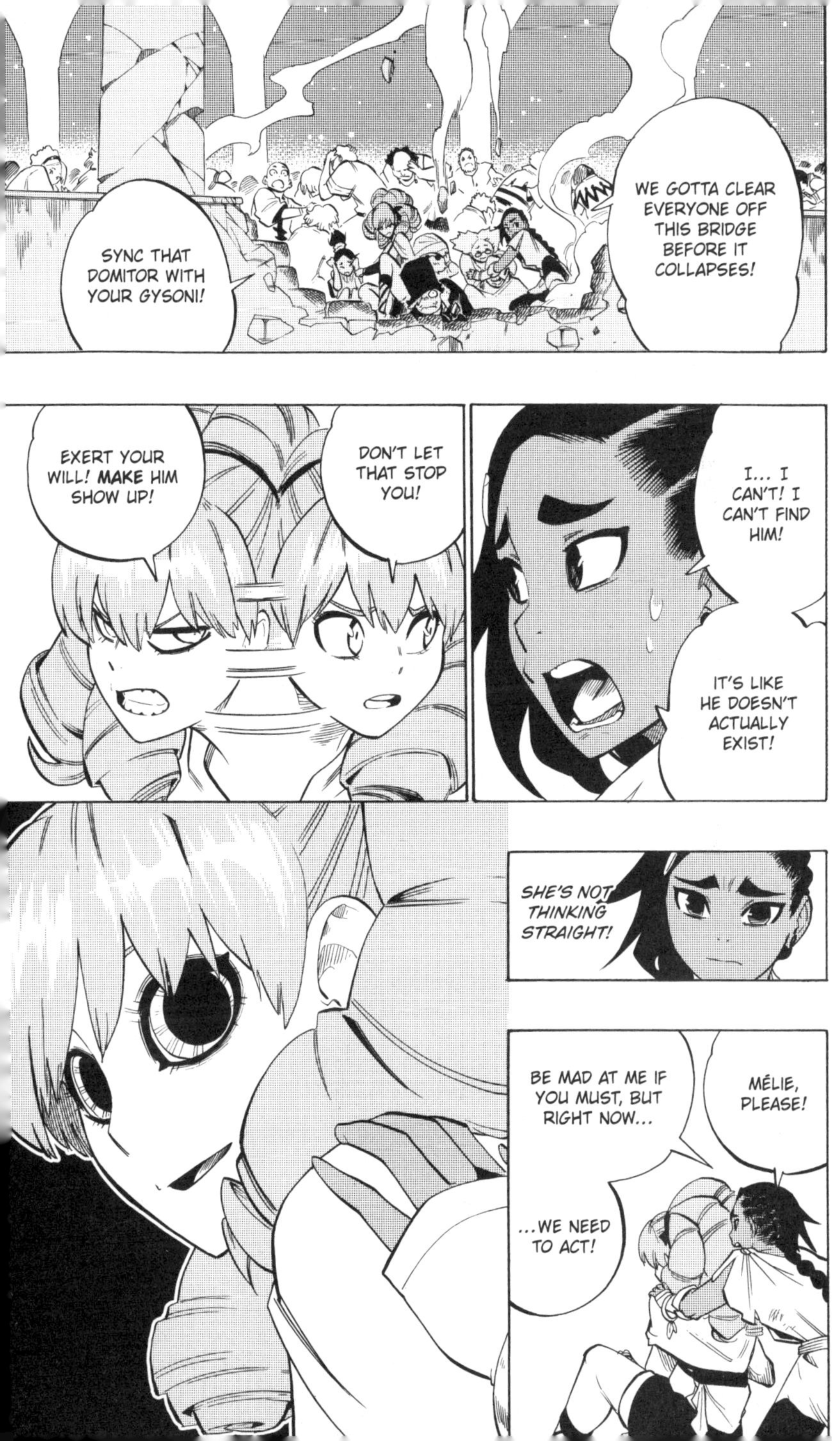
WE GOTTA CLEAR EVERYONE OFF THIS BRIDGE BEFORE IT COLLAPSES!
SYNC THAT DOMITOR WITH YOUR GYSONI!
I... I CAN'T! I CAN'T FIND HIM!
IT'S LIKE HE DOESN'T ACTUALLY EXIST!
DON'T LET THAT STOP YOU!
EXERT YOUR WILL! **MAKE** HIM SHOW UP!
SHE'S NOT THINKING STRAIGHT!
MÉLIE, PLEASE!
BE MAD AT ME IF YOU MUST, BUT RIGHT NOW...
...WE NEED TO ACT!

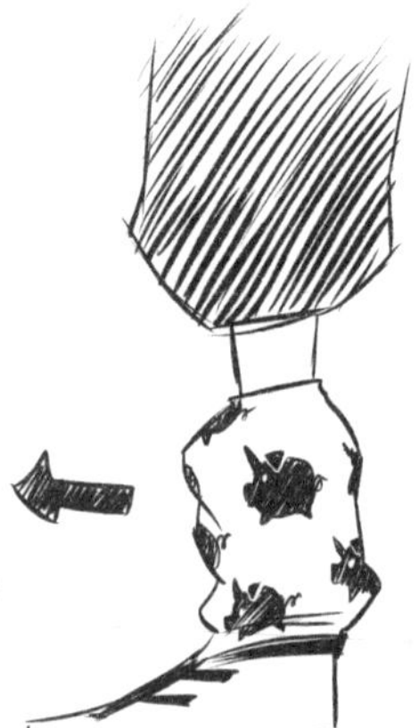

THE BEAUTIFUL SOCKS OF
MARSHAL BELLARMIN...

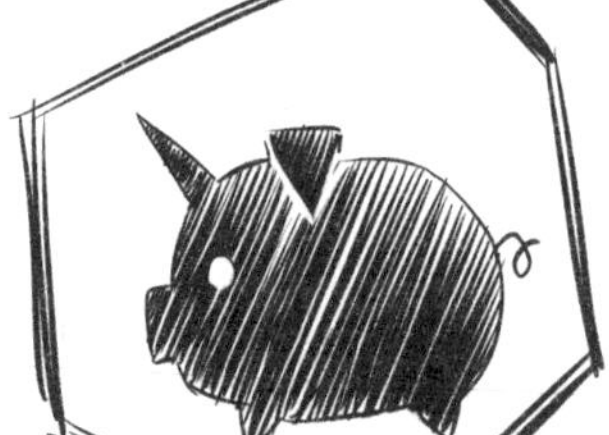

WITH A UNIPIG MOTIF!

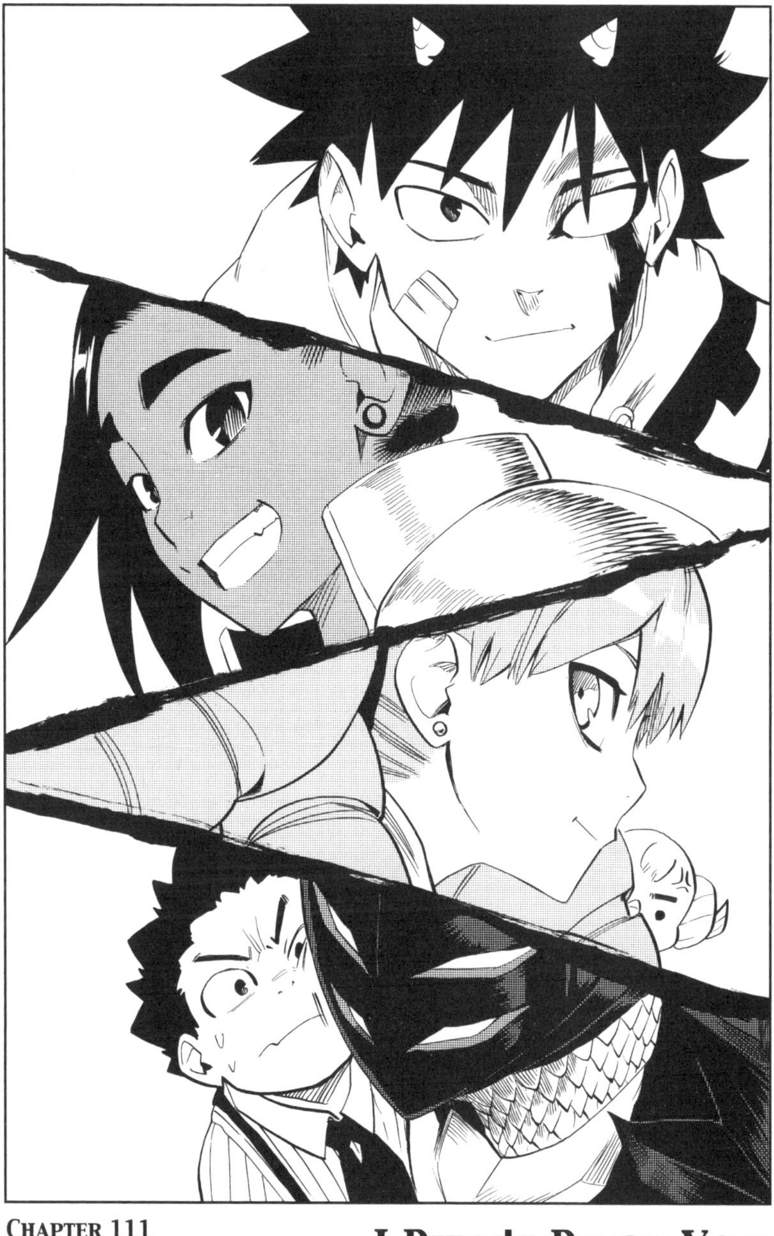

Chapter 111

I Didn't Ditch You

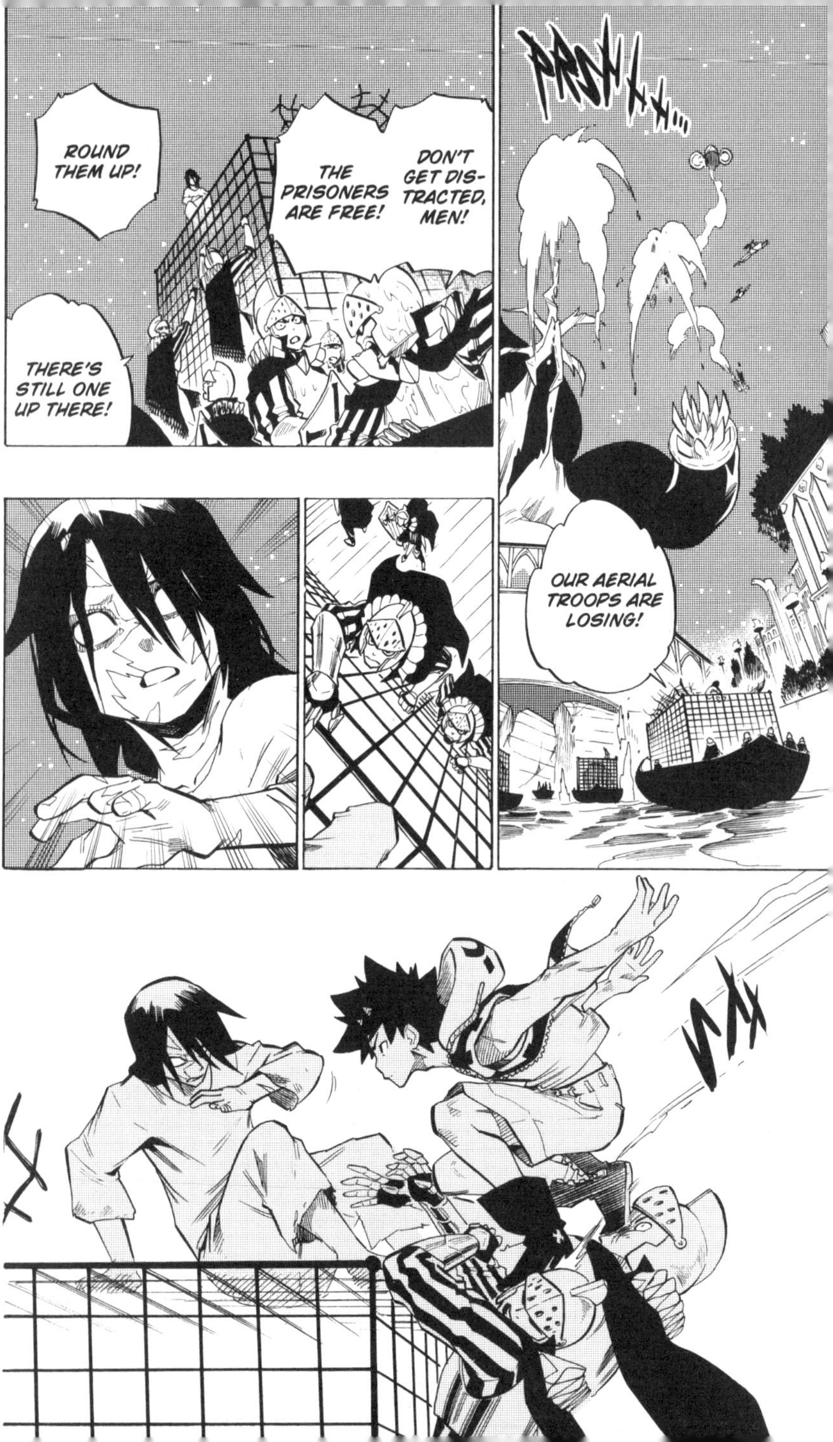
OUR AERIAL TROOPS ARE LOSING!
DON'T GET DIS-TRACTED, MEN!
THE PRISONERS ARE FREE!
ROUND THEM UP!
THERE'S STILL ONE UP THERE!

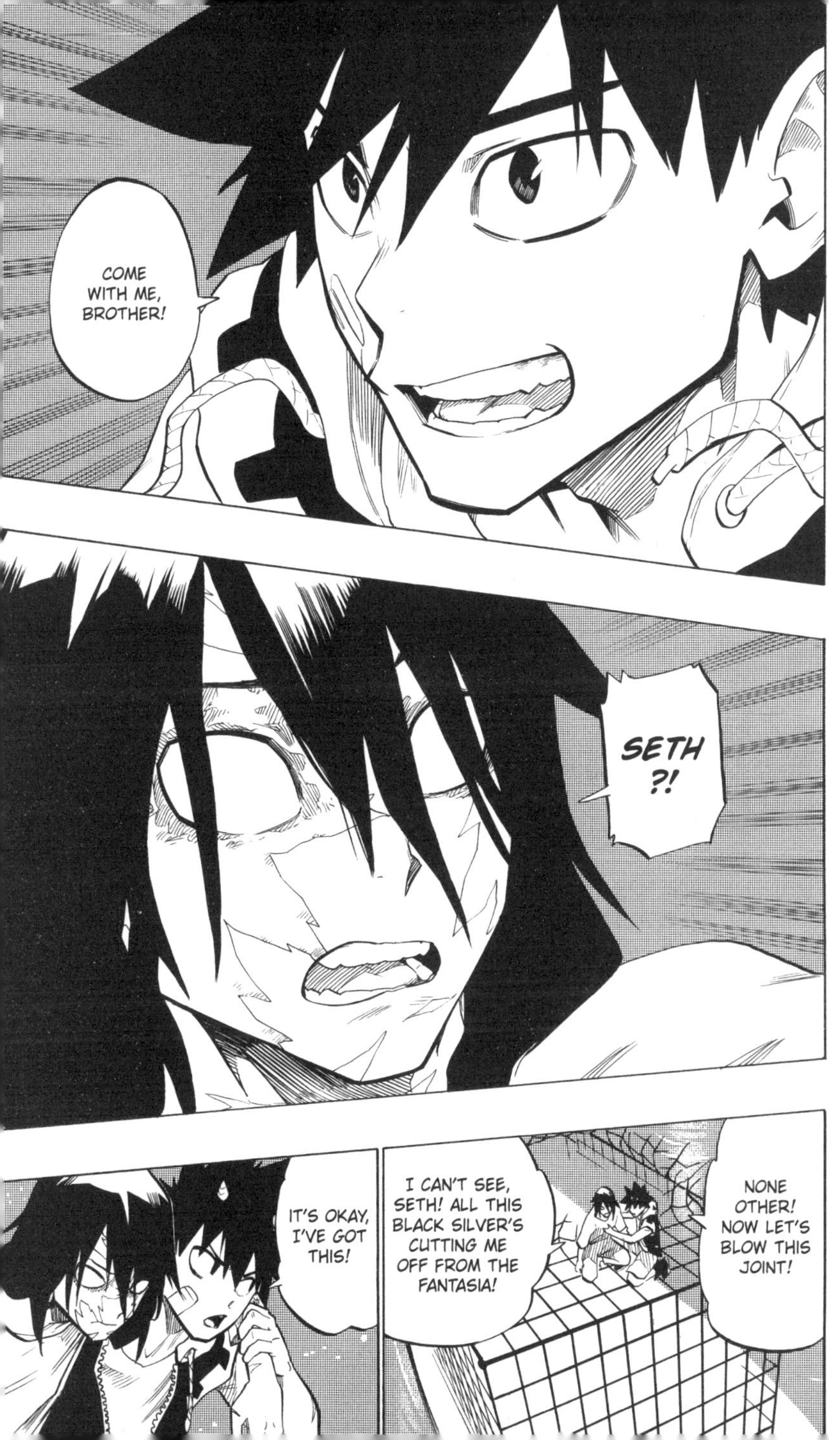
COME WITH ME, BROTHER!
SETH ?!
NONE OTHER! NOW LET'S BLOW THIS JOINT!
I CAN'T SEE, SETH! ALL THIS BLACK SILVER'S CUTTING ME OFF FROM THE FANTASIA!
IT'S OKAY, I'VE GOT THIS!

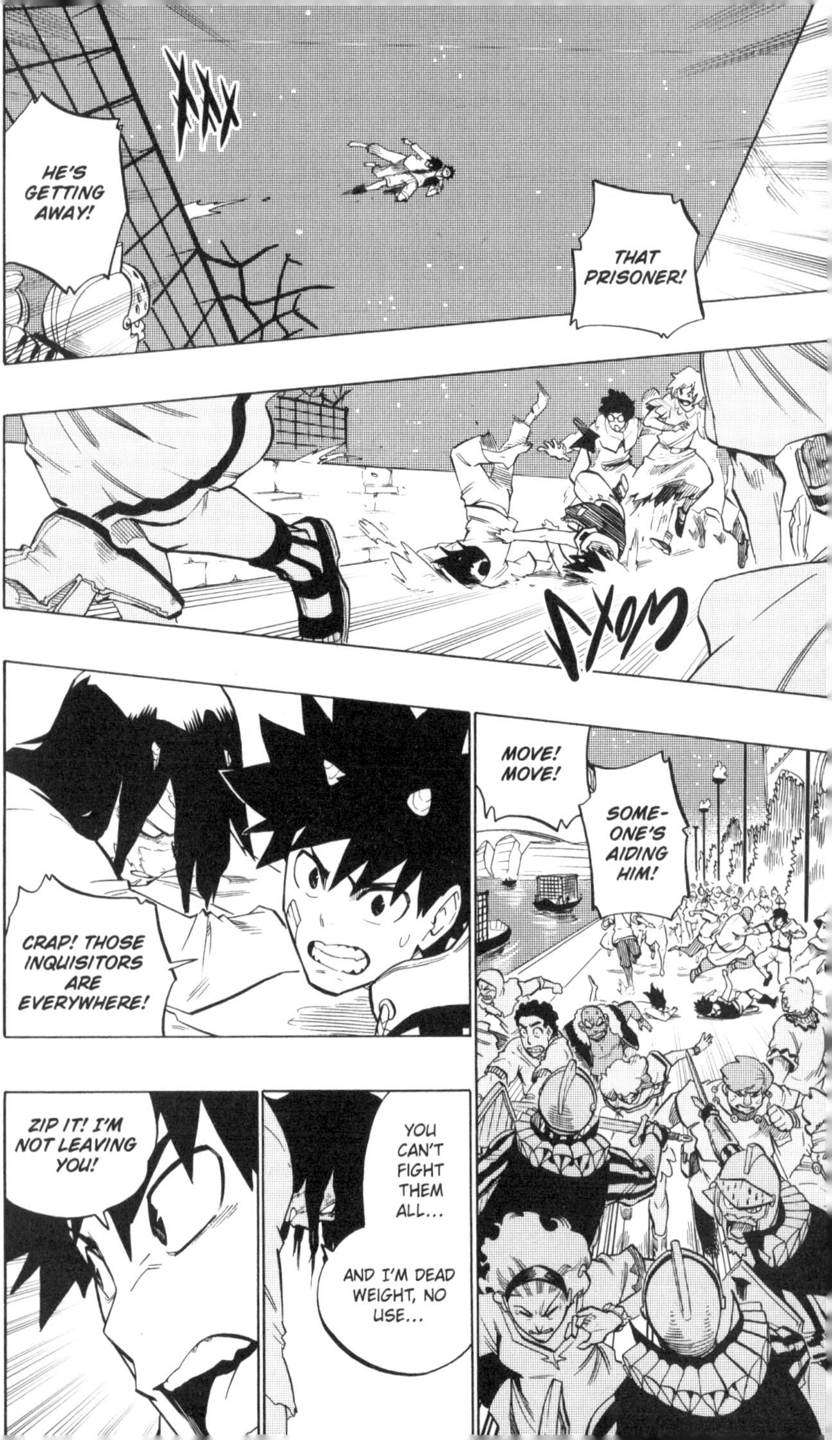
THAT PRISONER!
HE'S GETTING AWAY!
SOME-ONE'S AIDING HIM!
MOVE! MOVE!
CRAP! THOSE INQUISITORS ARE EVERYWHERE!
YOU CAN'T FIGHT THEM ALL...
AND I'M DEAD WEIGHT, NO USE...
ZIP IT! I'M NOT LEAVING YOU!

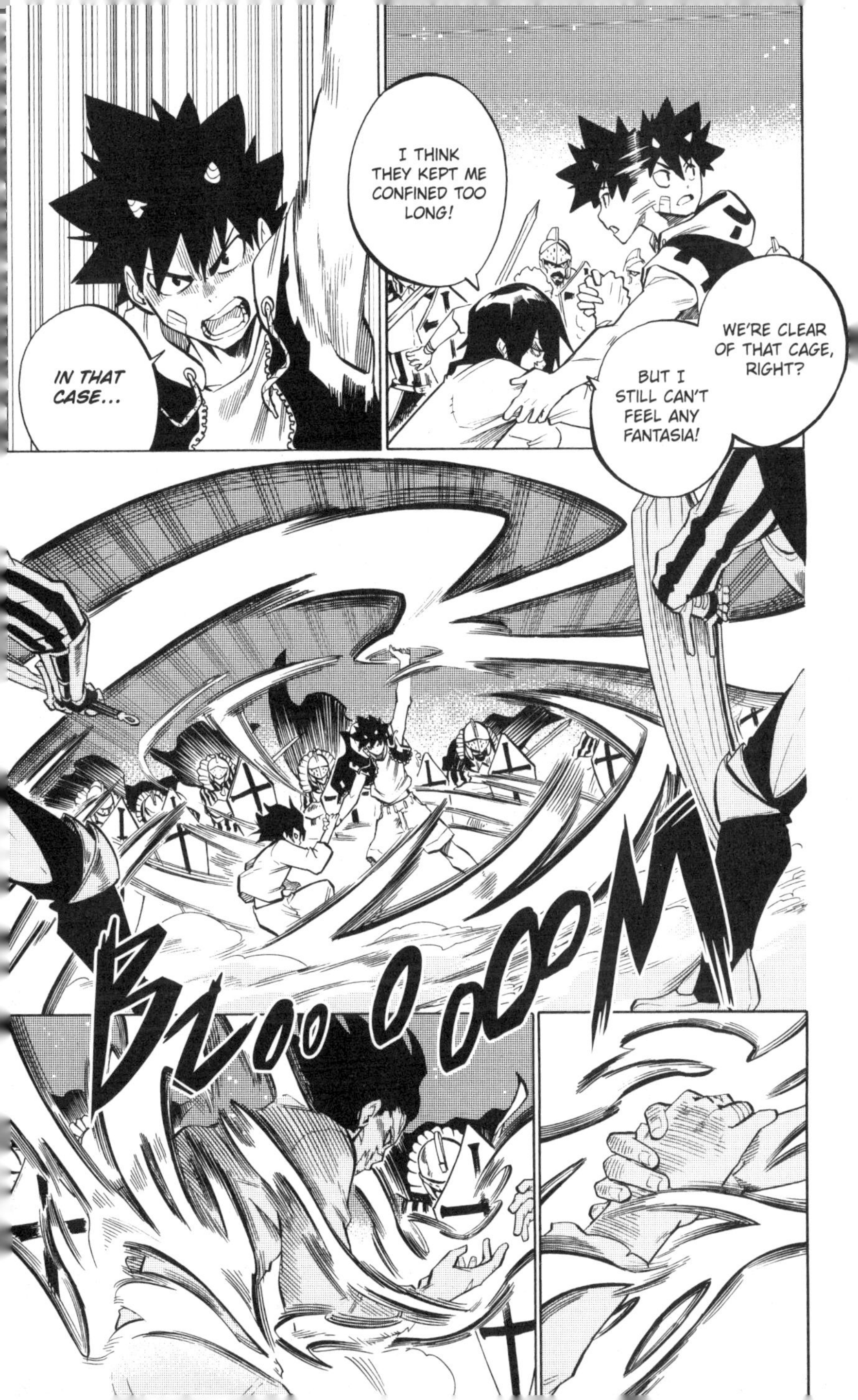
WE'RE CLEAR OF THAT CAGE, RIGHT?
BUT I STILL CAN'T FEEL ANY FANTASIA!
I THINK THEY KEPT ME CONFINED TOO LONG!
IN THAT CASE...
BLOOOOOOM

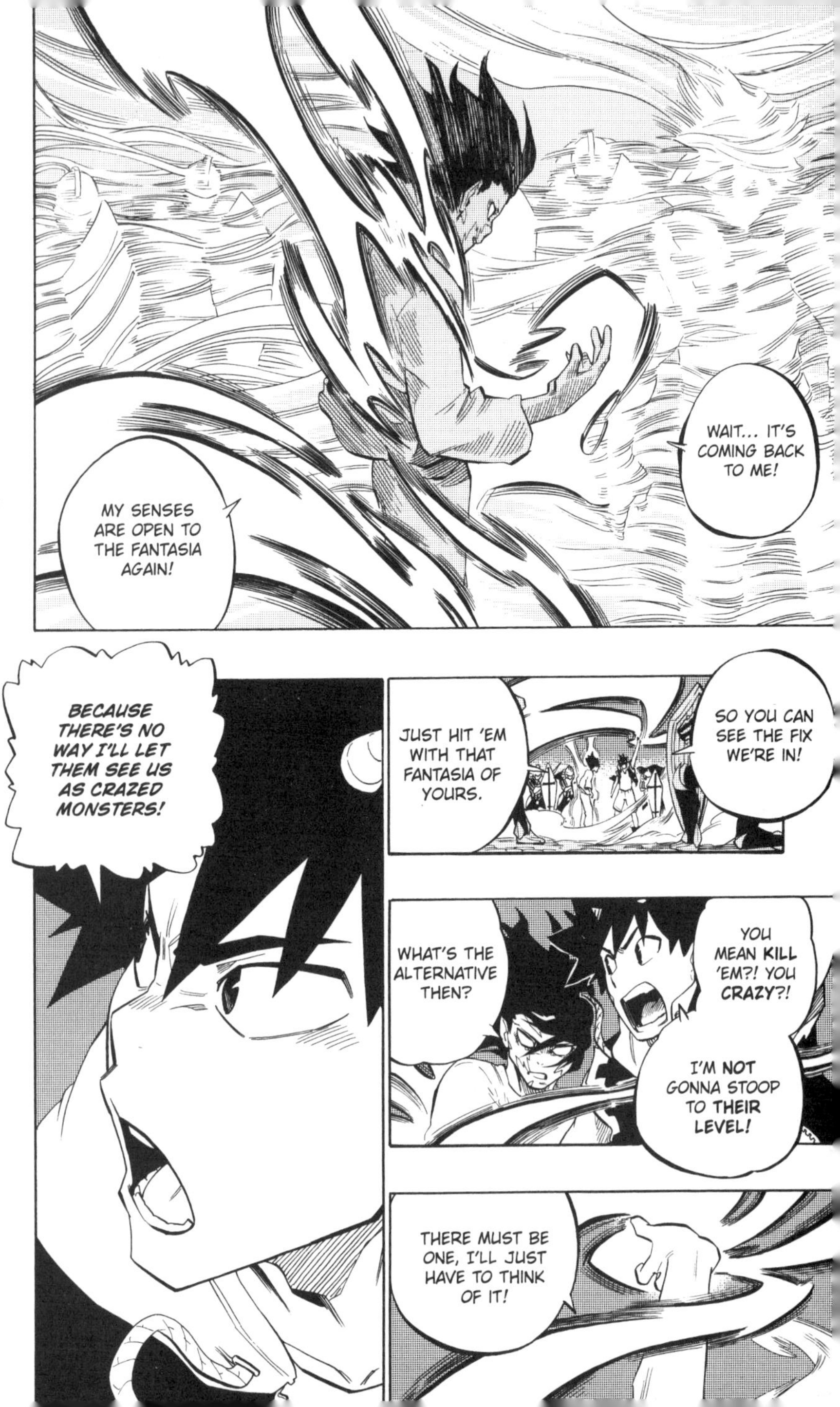
WAIT... IT'S COMING BACK TO ME!
MY SENSES ARE OPEN TO THE FANTASIA AGAIN!
SO YOU CAN SEE THE FIX WE'RE IN!
JUST HIT 'EM WITH THAT FANTASIA OF YOURS.
YOU MEAN **KILL** 'EM?! YOU **CRAZY?!**
WHAT'S THE ALTERNATIVE THEN?
I'M **NOT** GONNA STOOP TO **THEIR LEVEL!**
THERE MUST BE ONE, I'LL JUST HAVE TO THINK OF IT!
BECAUSE THERE'S NO WAY I'LL LET THEM SEE US AS CRAZED MONSTERS!

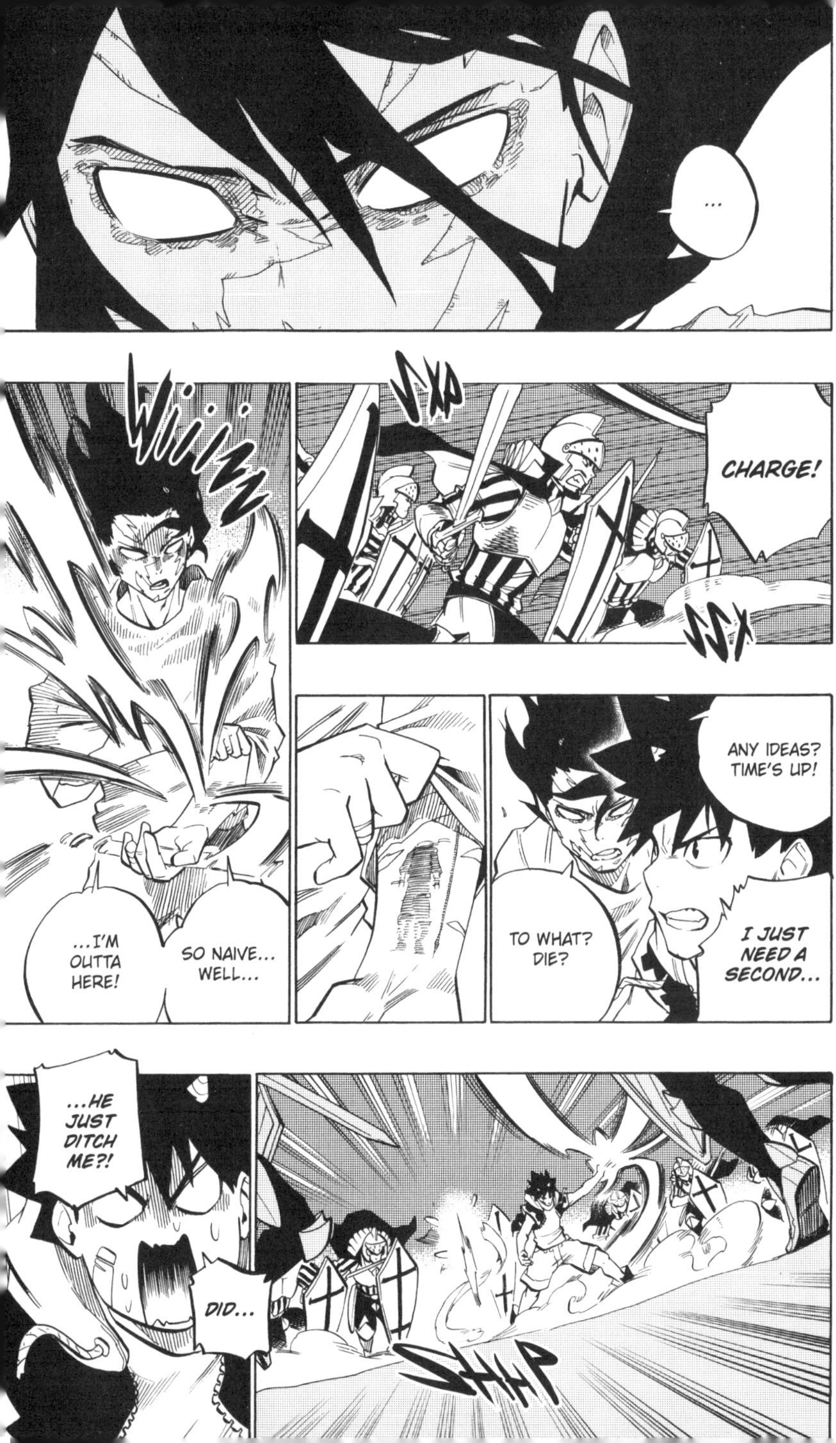
...
CHARGE!
SKP
ANY IDEAS? TIME'S UP!
I JUST NEED A SECOND...
TO WHAT? DIE?
WIIIZZ
SO NAIVE... WELL...
...I'M OUTTA HERE!
SHHP
DID...
...HE JUST DITCH ME?!

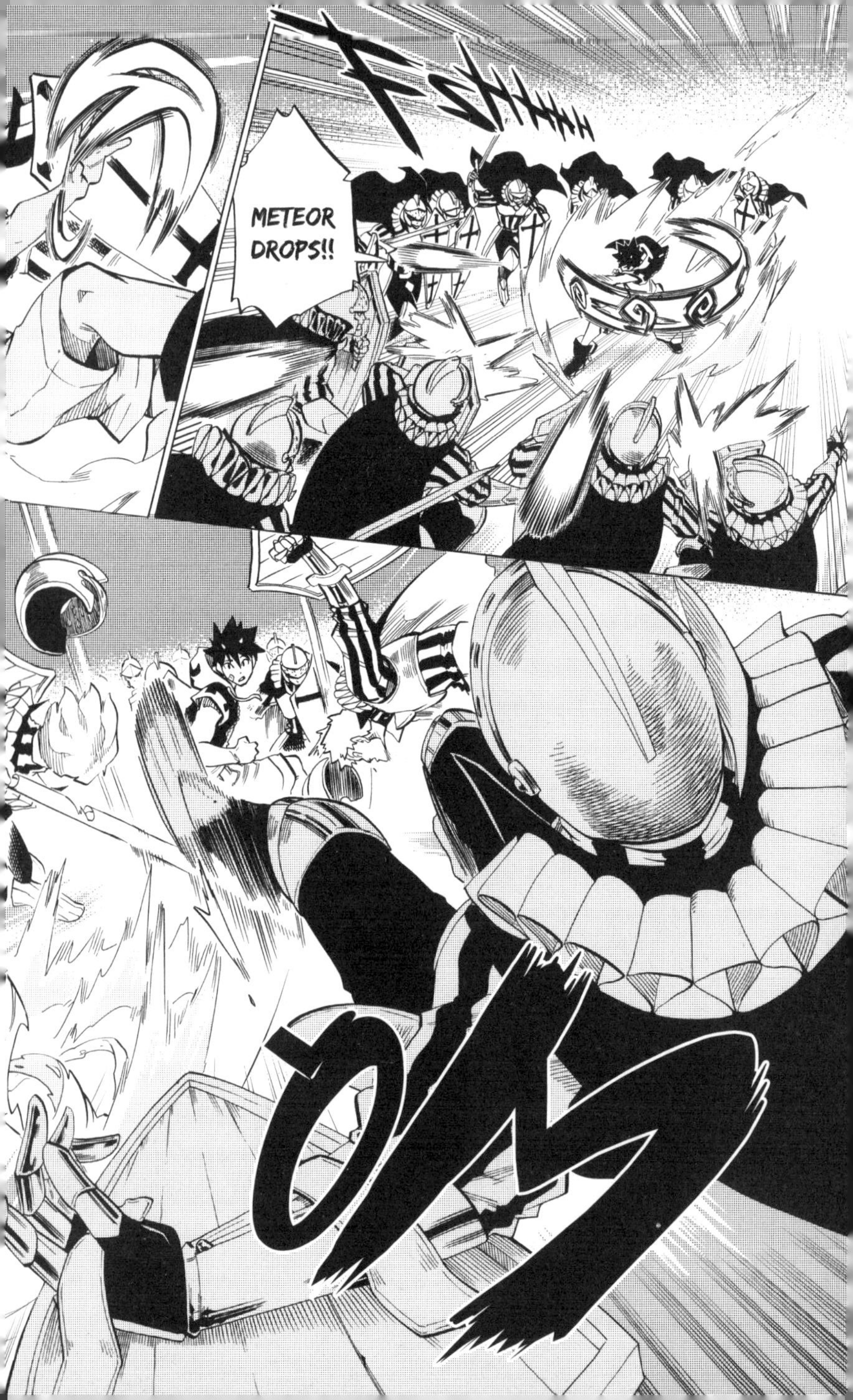
METEOR DROPS!!

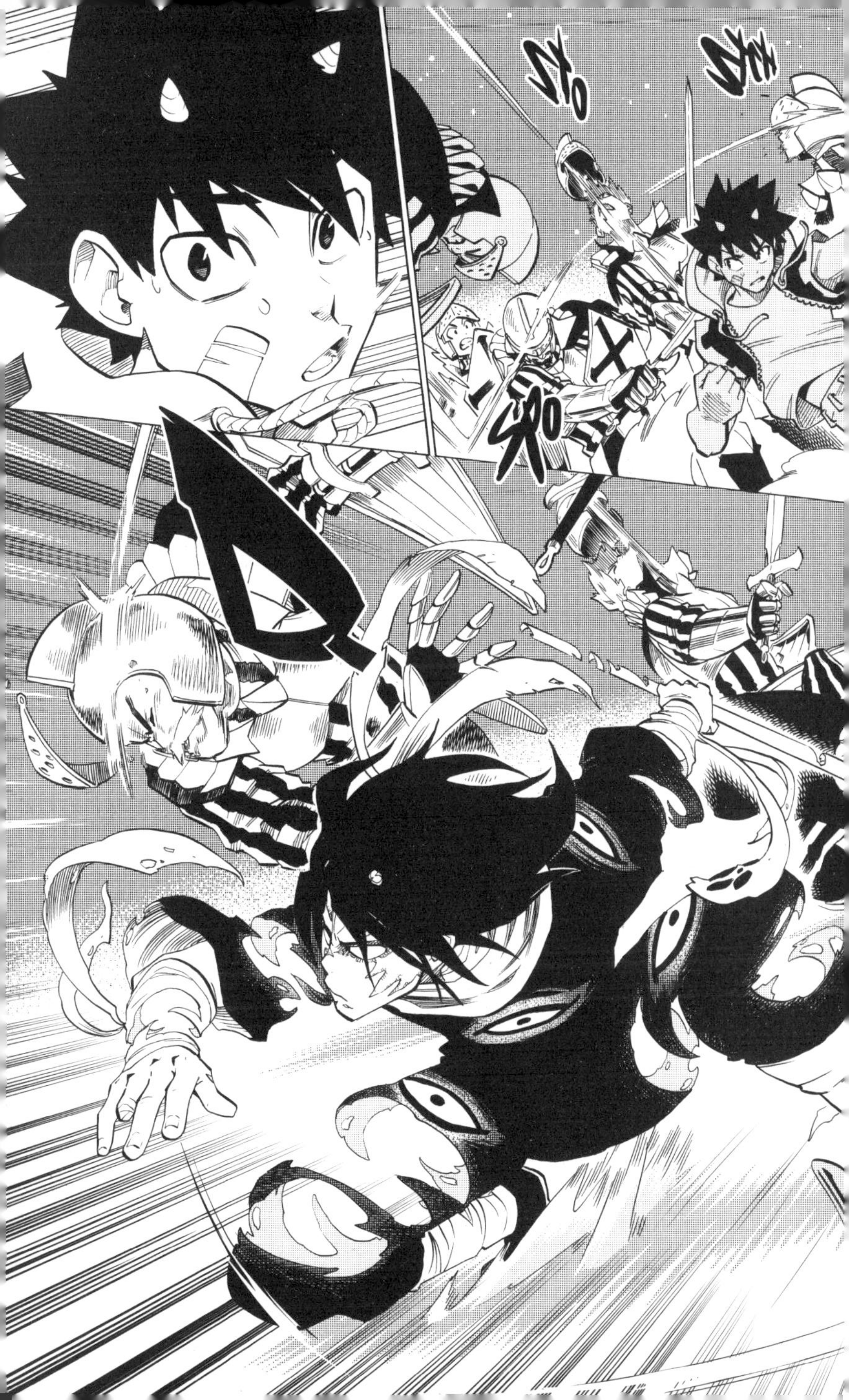

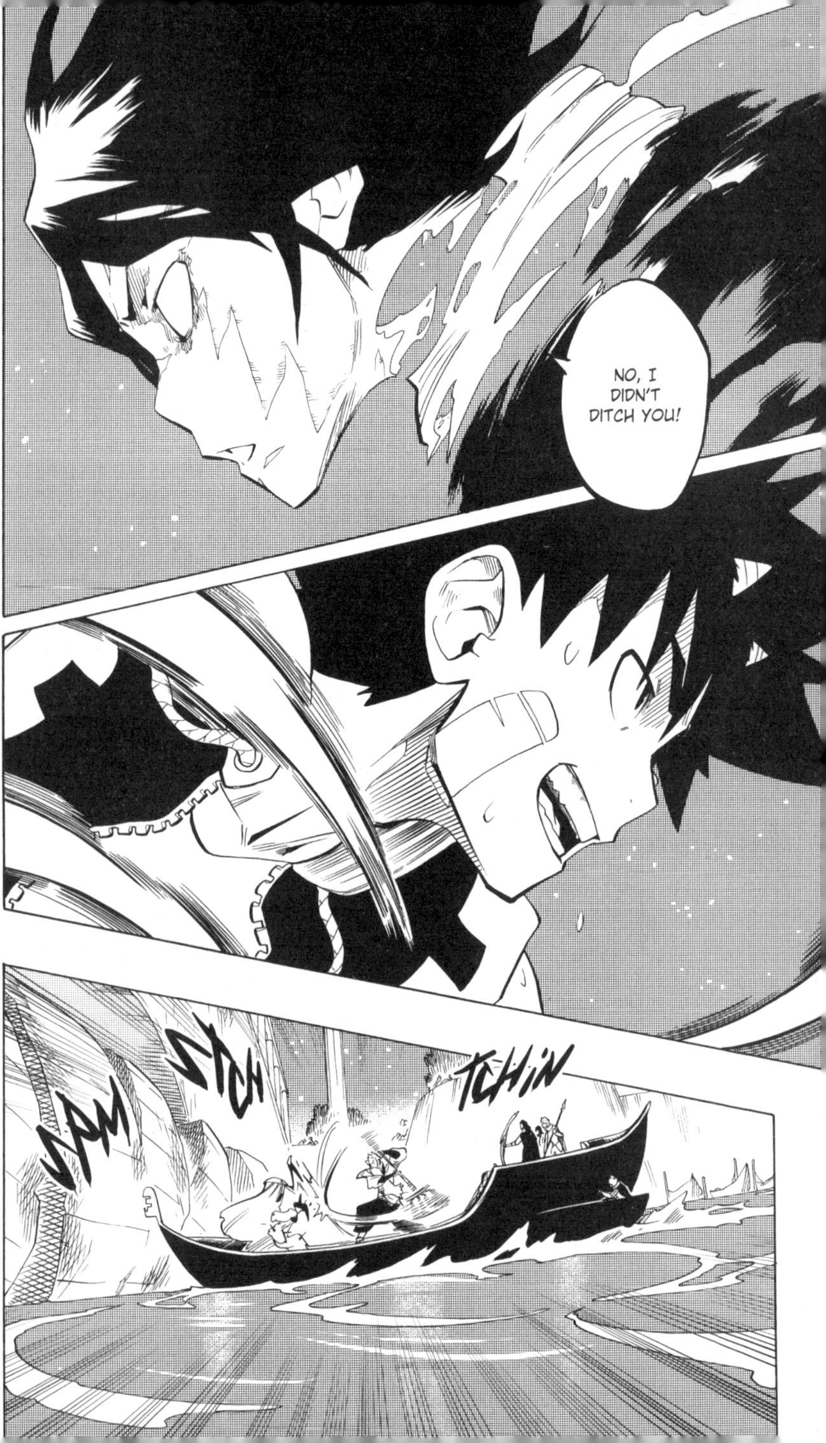
NO, I DIDN'T DITCH YOU!
TCHIN
STCH
SPM

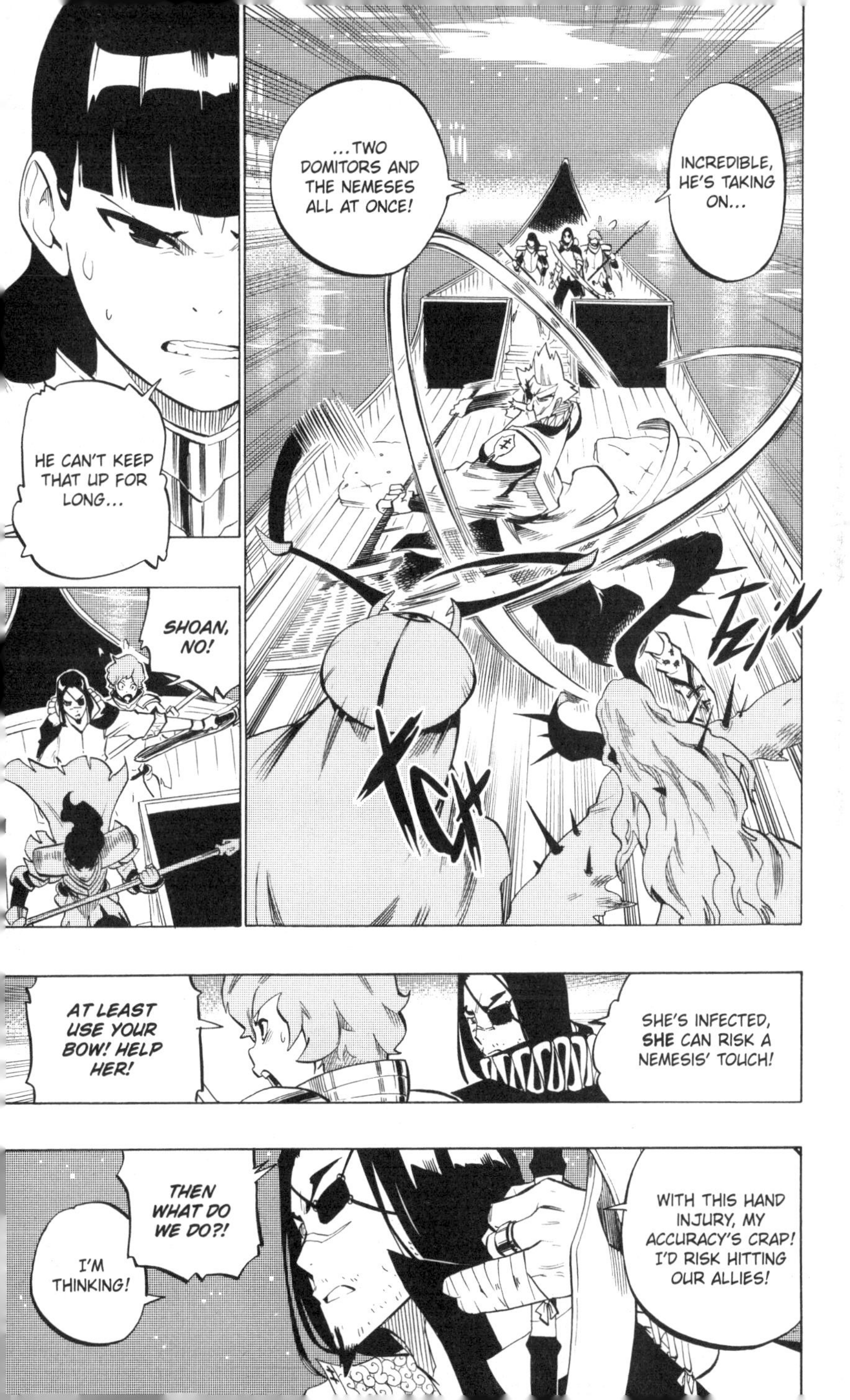
INCREDIBLE, HE'S TAKING ON...
...TWO DOMITORS AND THE NEMESES ALL AT ONCE!
KZIN
KCH
HE CAN'T KEEP THAT UP FOR LONG...
SHOAN, NO!
SHE'S INFECTED, SHE CAN RISK A NEMESIS' TOUCH!
AT LEAST USE YOUR BOW! HELP HER!
WITH THIS HAND INJURY, MY ACCURACY'S CRAP! I'D RISK HITTING OUR ALLIES!
THEN WHAT DO WE DO?!
I'M THINKING!

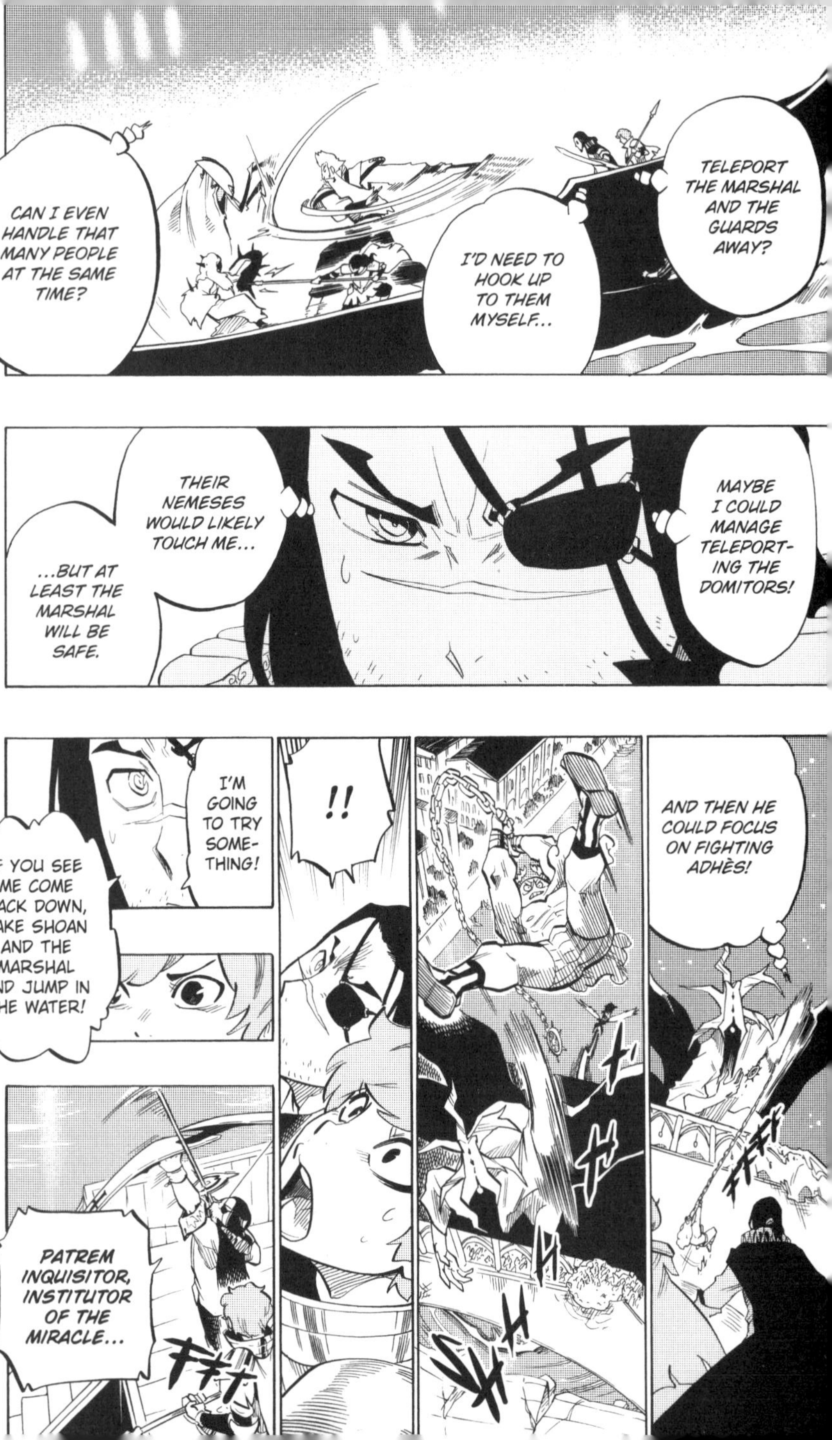
TELEPORT THE MARSHAL AND THE GUARDS AWAY?
I'D NEED TO HOOK UP TO THEM MYSELF...
CAN I EVEN HANDLE THAT MANY PEOPLE AT THE SAME TIME?
MAYBE I COULD MANAGE TELEPORT-ING THE DOMITORS!
THEIR NEMESES WOULD LIKELY TOUCH ME...
...BUT AT LEAST THE MARSHAL WILL BE SAFE.
AND THEN HE COULD FOCUS ON FIGHTING ADHÈS!
!!
I'M GOING TO TRY SOME-THING!
IF YOU SEE ME COME BACK DOWN, TAKE SHOAN AND THE MARSHAL AND JUMP IN THE WATER!
PATREM INQUISITOR, INSTITUTOR OF THE MIRACLE...

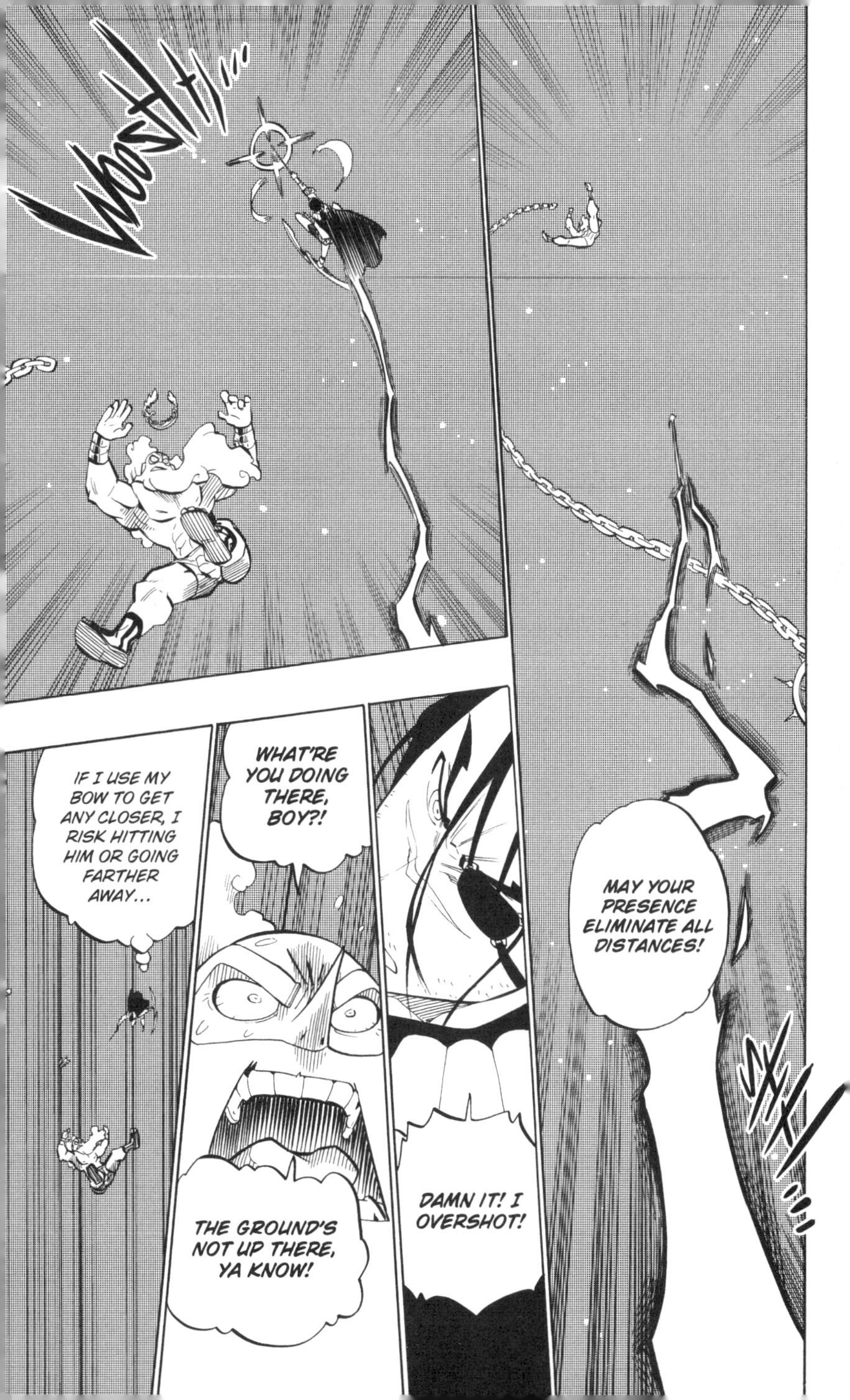
MAY YOUR PRESENCE ELIMINATE ALL DISTANCES!
WHOOSH!!...
DAMN IT! I OVERSHOT!
WHAT'RE YOU DOING THERE, BOY?!
THE GROUND'S NOT UP THERE, YA KNOW!
IF I USE MY BOW TO GET ANY CLOSER, I RISK HITTING HIM OR GOING FARTHER AWAY...

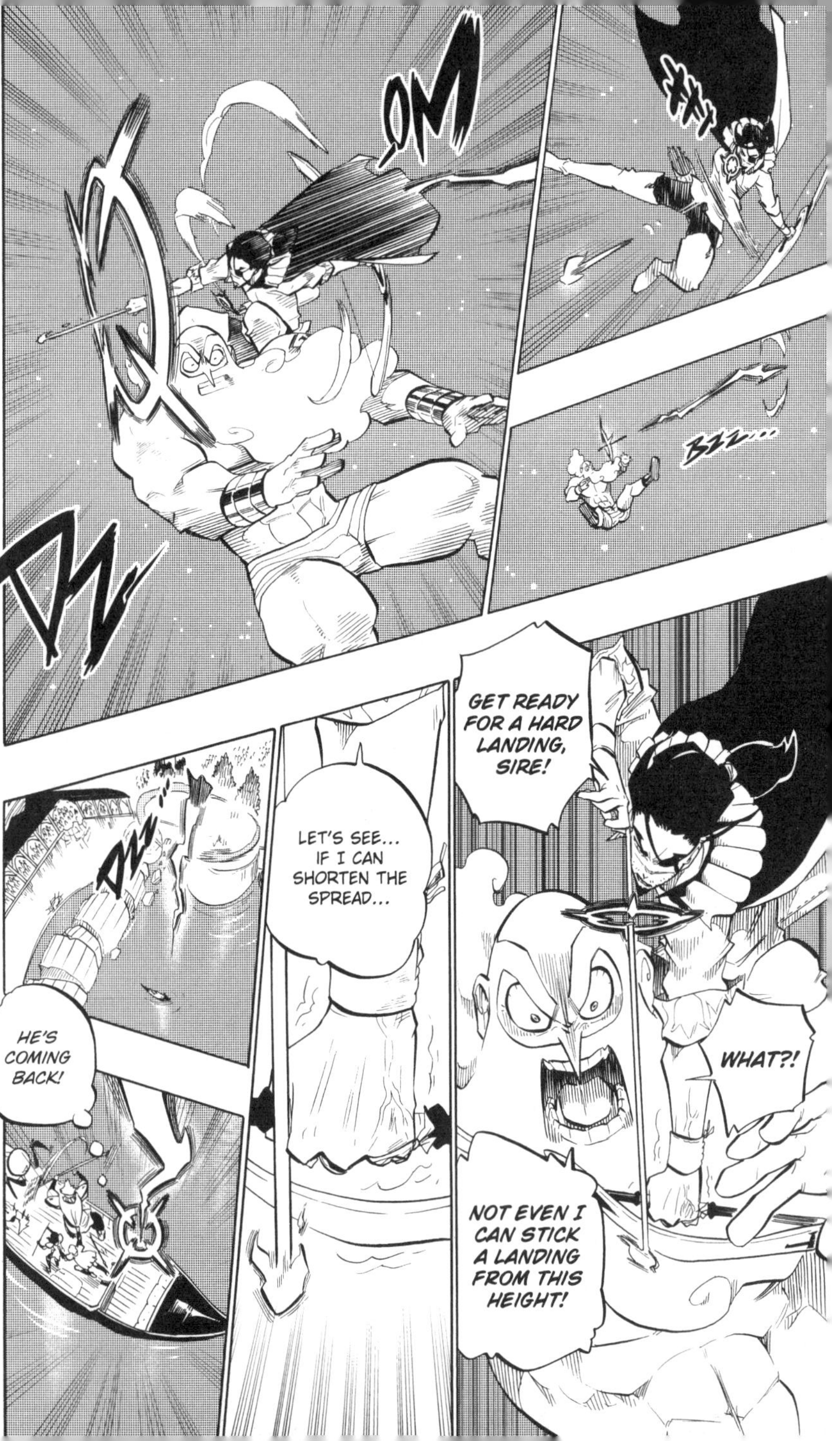
BZZ...
GET READY FOR A HARD LANDING, SIRE!
WHAT?!
NOT EVEN I CAN STICK A LANDING FROM THIS HEIGHT!
LET'S SEE... IF I CAN SHORTEN THE SPREAD...
HE'S COMING BACK!

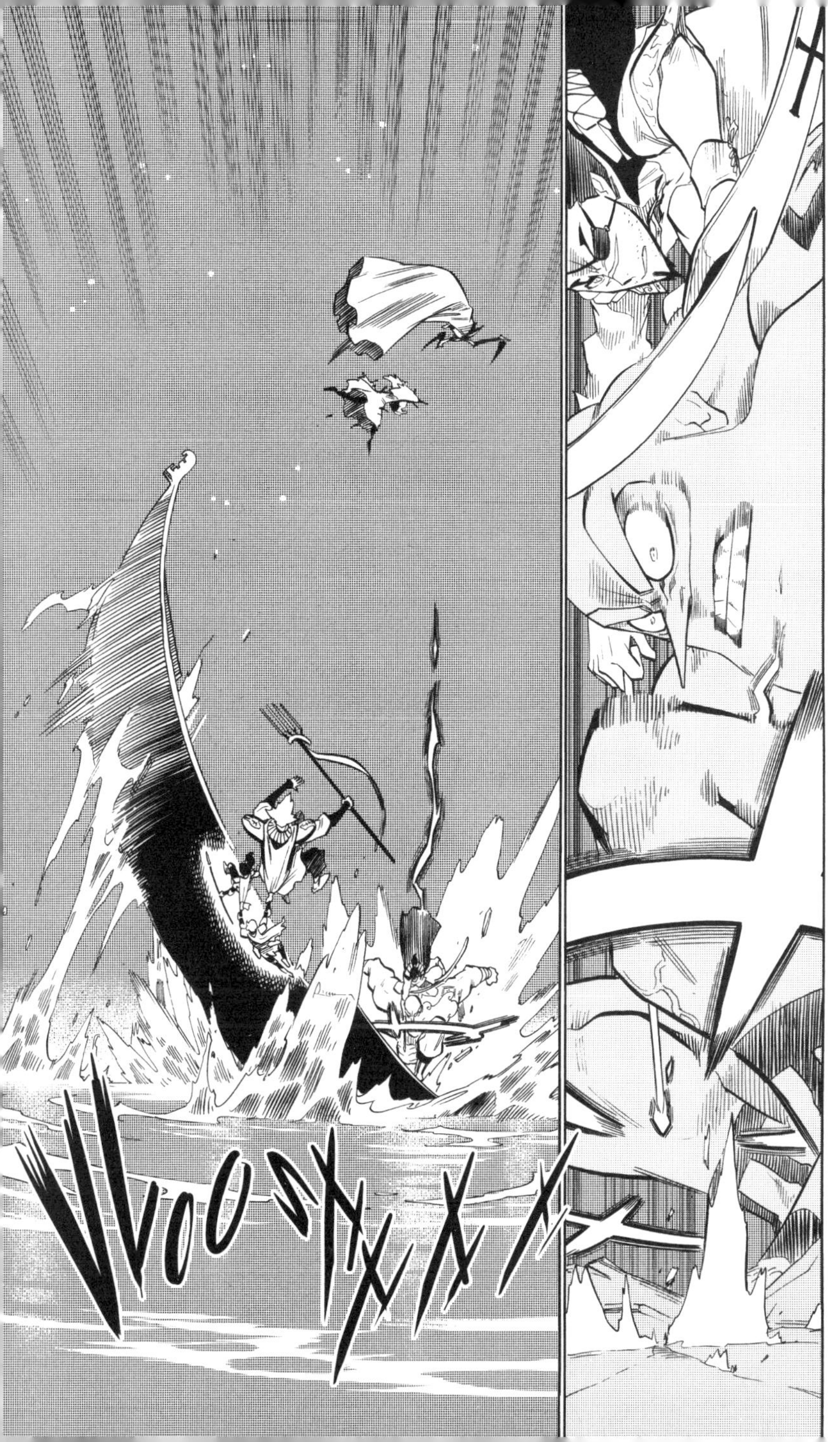
WOOSHHH

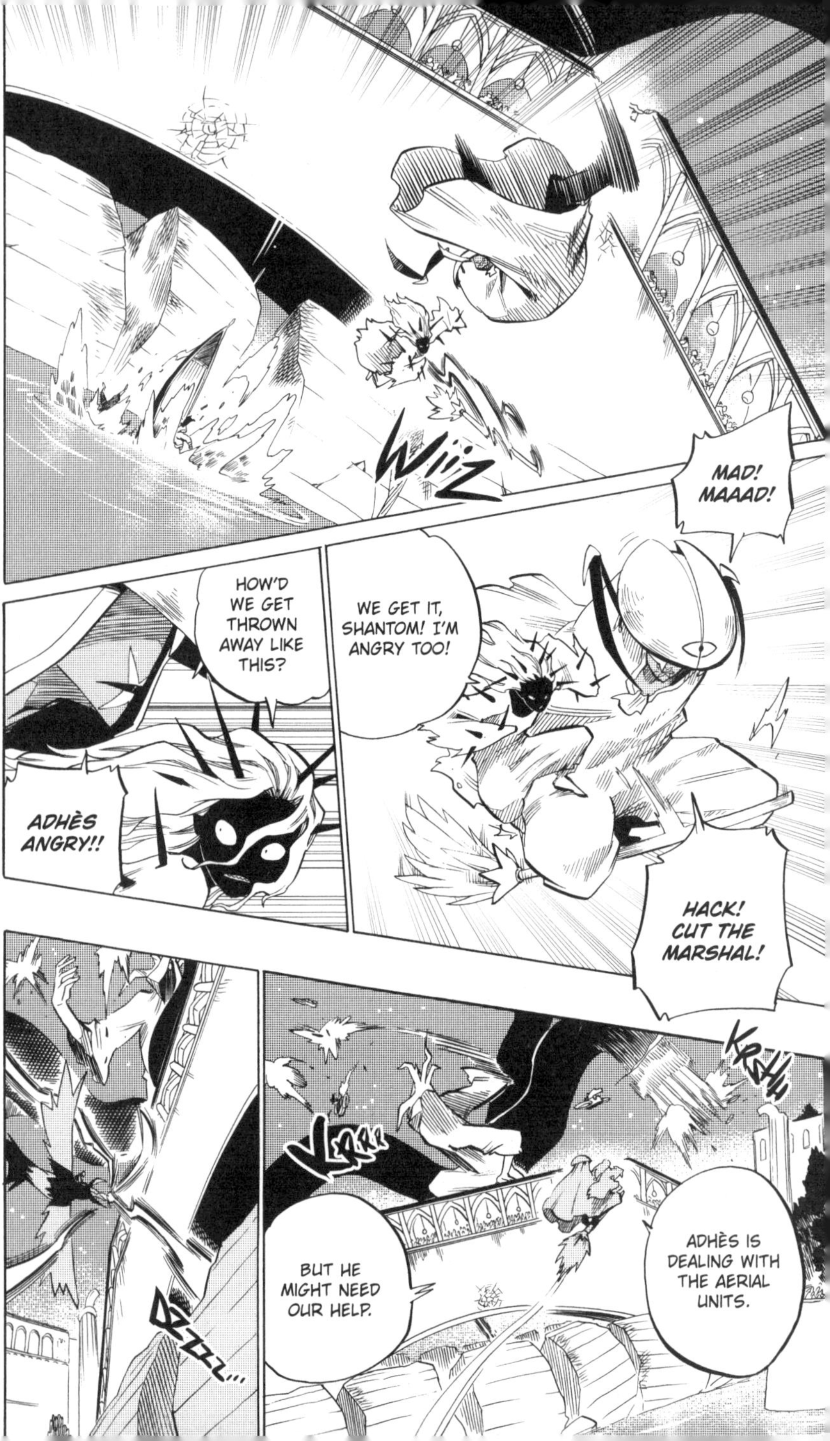

WIIZ
MAD! MAAAD!
WE GET IT, SHANTOM! I'M ANGRY TOO!
HACK! CUT THE MARSHAL!
HOW'D WE GET THROWN AWAY LIKE THIS?
ADHÈS ANGRY!!
KRSHH
VRRR
ADHÈS IS DEALING WITH THE AERIAL UNITS.
BUT HE MIGHT NEED OUR HELP.
DZZZZ...

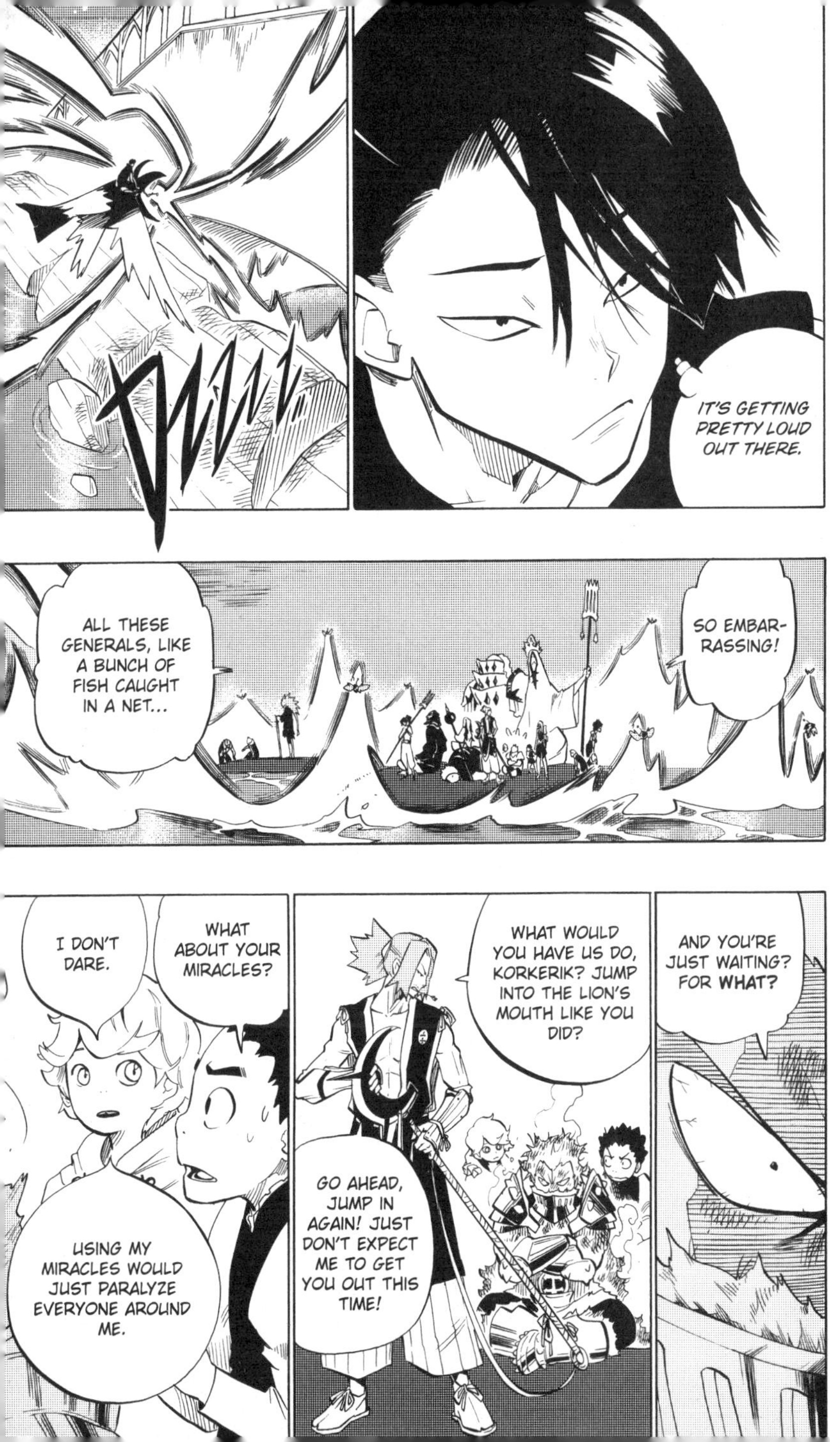
IT'S GETTING PRETTY LOUD OUT THERE.
SO EMBAR-RASSING!
ALL THESE GENERALS, LIKE A BUNCH OF FISH CAUGHT IN A NET...
AND YOU'RE JUST WAITING? FOR **WHAT**?
WHAT WOULD YOU HAVE US DO, KORKERIK? JUMP INTO THE LION'S MOUTH LIKE YOU DID?
GO AHEAD, JUMP IN AGAIN! JUST DON'T EXPECT ME TO GET YOU OUT THIS TIME!
WHAT ABOUT YOUR MIRACLES?
I DON'T DARE.
USING MY MIRACLES WOULD JUST PARALYZE EVERYONE AROUND ME.

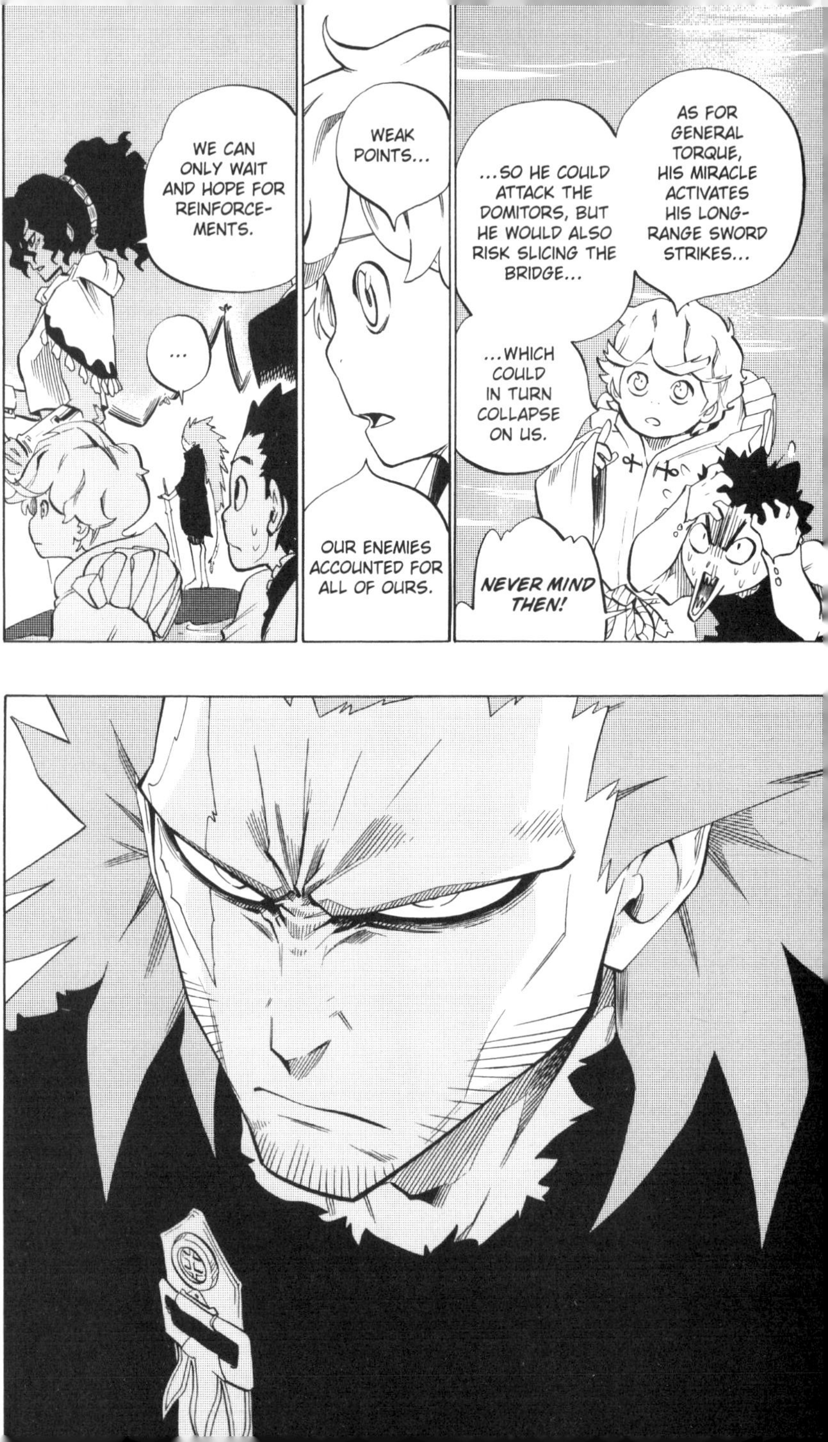
AS FOR GENERAL TORQUE, HIS MIRACLE ACTIVATES HIS LONG-RANGE SWORD STRIKES...
...SO HE COULD ATTACK THE DOMITORS, BUT HE WOULD ALSO RISK SLICING THE BRIDGE...
...WHICH COULD IN TURN COLLAPSE ON US.
NEVER MIND THEN!
WEAK POINTS...
OUR ENEMIES ACCOUNTED FOR ALL OF OURS.
WE CAN ONLY WAIT AND HOPE FOR REINFORCE-MENTS.
...

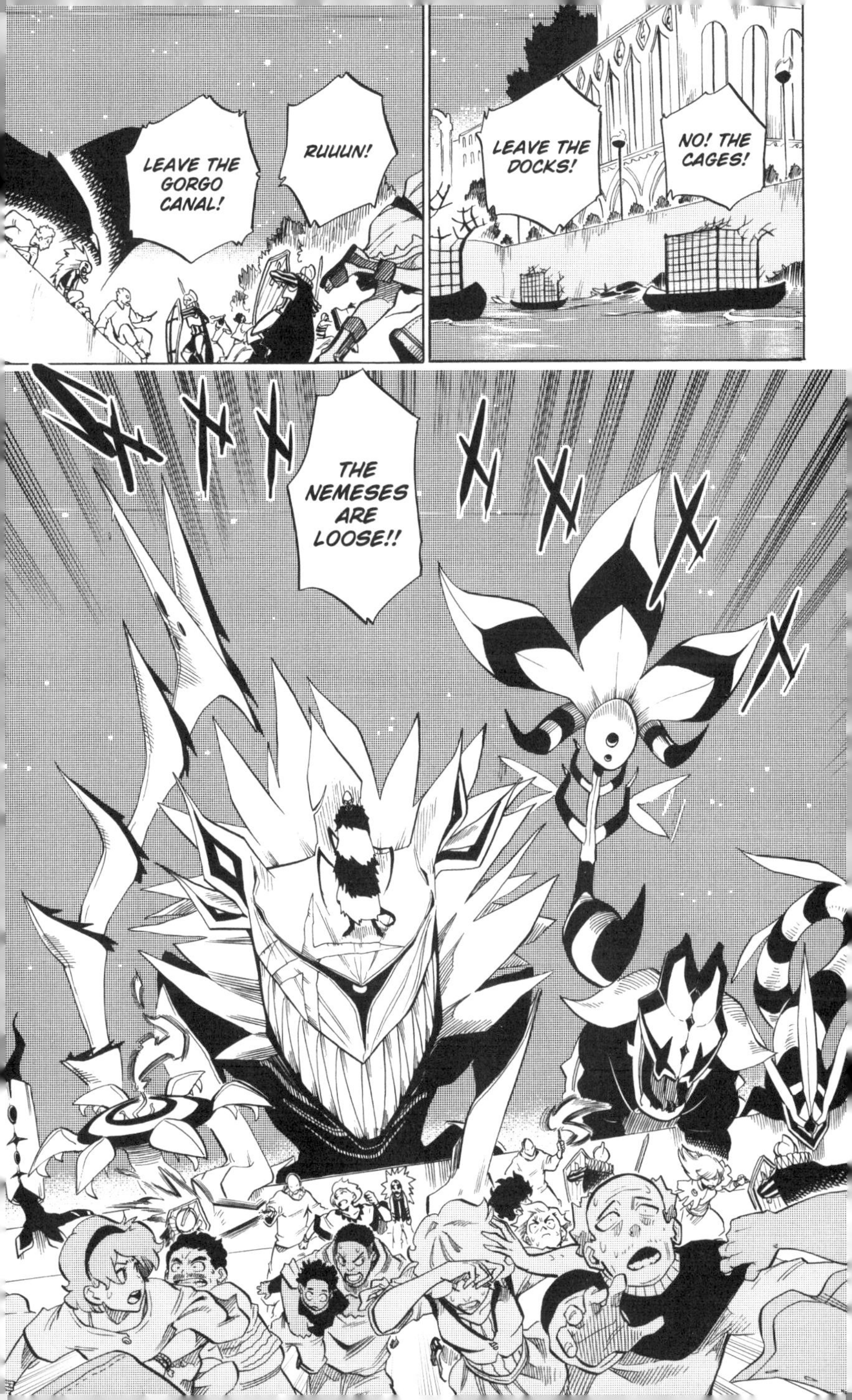
NO! THE CAGES!
LEAVE THE DOCKS!
RUUUN!
LEAVE THE GORGO CANAL!
THE NEMESES ARE LOOSE!!

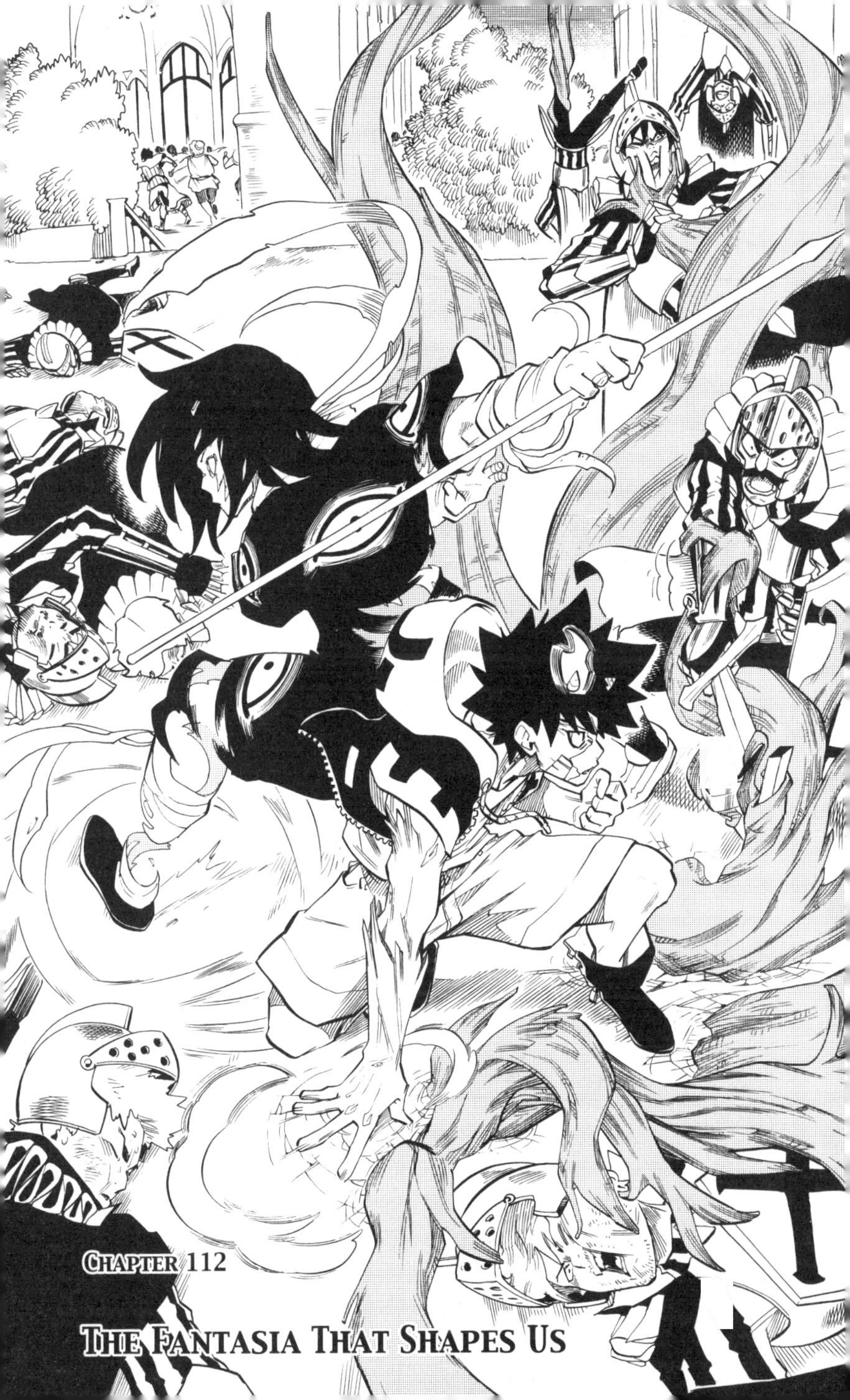

Chapter 112

The Fantasia That Shapes Us

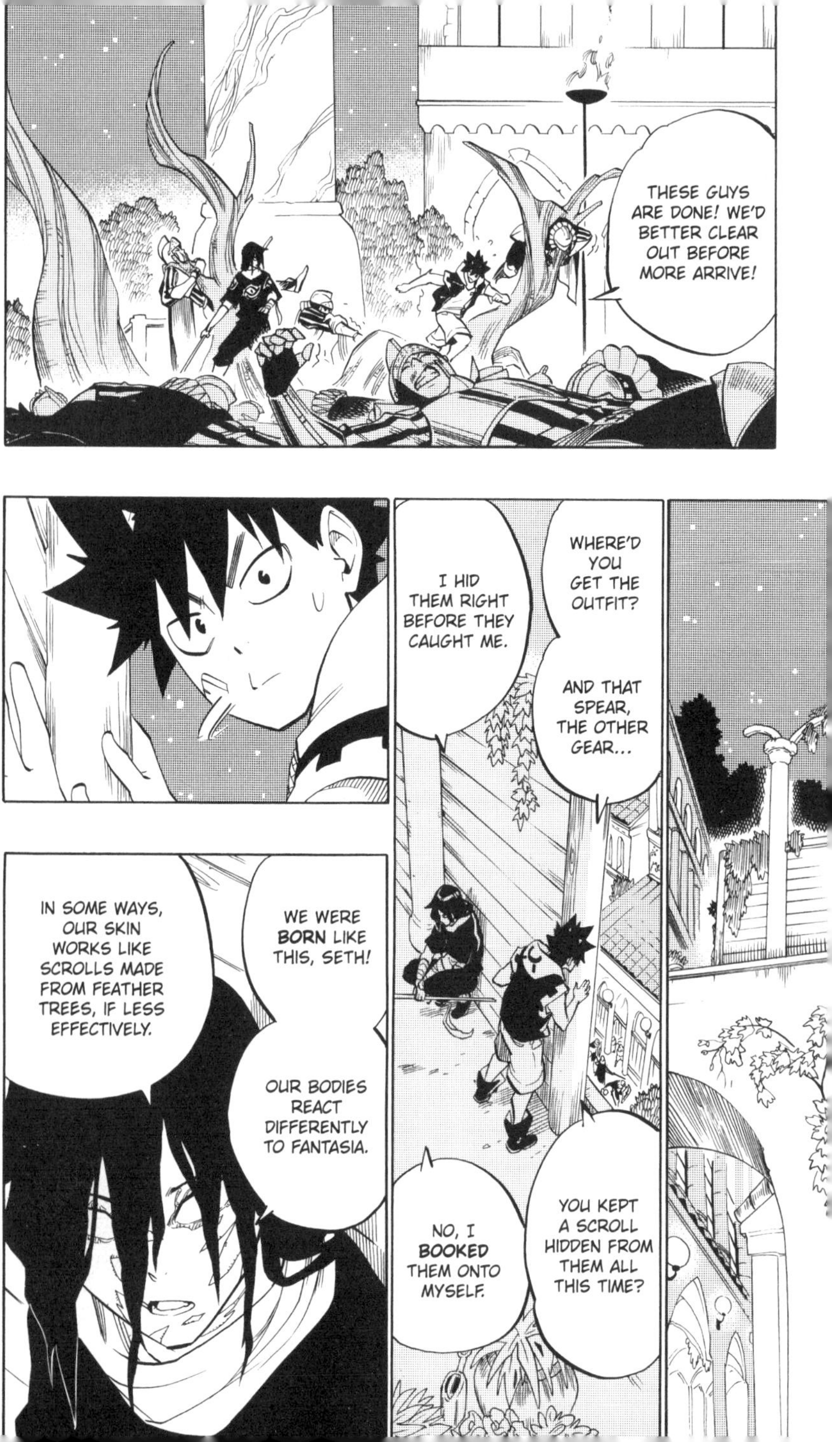
THESE GUYS ARE DONE! WE'D BETTER CLEAR OUT BEFORE MORE ARRIVE!
WHERE'D YOU GET THE OUTFIT?
AND THAT SPEAR, THE OTHER GEAR...
I HID THEM RIGHT BEFORE THEY CAUGHT ME.
YOU KEPT A SCROLL HIDDEN FROM THEM ALL THIS TIME?
NO, I **BOOKED** THEM ONTO MYSELF.
WE WERE **BORN** LIKE THIS, SETH!
IN SOME WAYS, OUR SKIN WORKS LIKE SCROLLS MADE FROM FEATHER TREES, IF LESS EFFECTIVELY.
OUR BODIES REACT DIFFERENTLY TO FANTASIA.

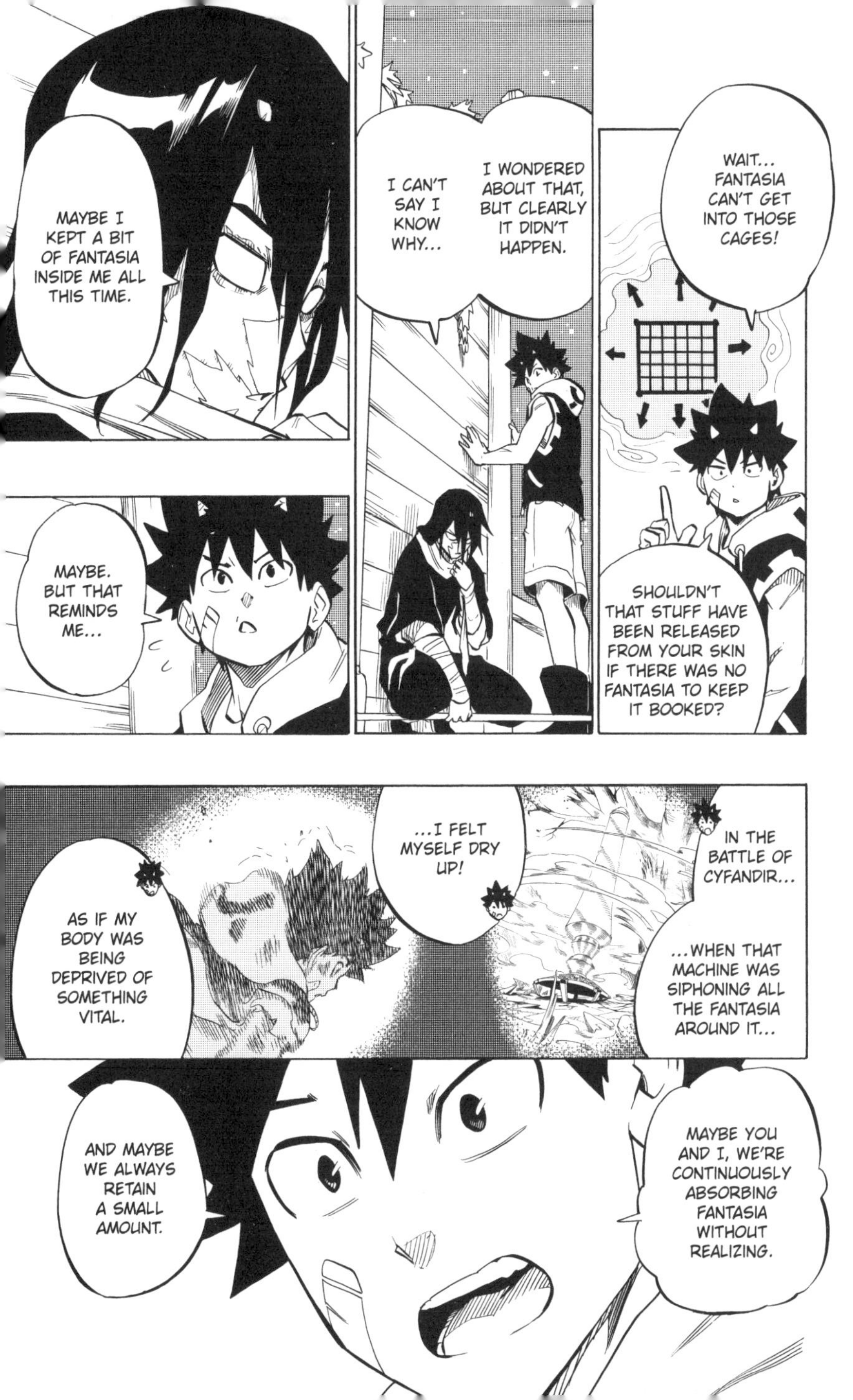
WAIT... FANTASIA CAN'T GET INTO THOSE CAGES!
SHOULDN'T THAT STUFF HAVE BEEN RELEASED FROM YOUR SKIN IF THERE WAS NO FANTASIA TO KEEP IT BOOKED?
I WONDERED ABOUT THAT, BUT CLEARLY IT DIDN'T HAPPEN.
I CAN'T SAY I KNOW WHY...
MAYBE I KEPT A BIT OF FANTASIA INSIDE ME ALL THIS TIME.
MAYBE. BUT THAT REMINDS ME...
IN THE BATTLE OF CYFANDIR...
...WHEN THAT MACHINE WAS SIPHONING ALL THE FANTASIA AROUND IT...
...I FELT MYSELF DRY UP!
AS IF MY BODY WAS BEING DEPRIVED OF SOMETHING VITAL.
MAYBE YOU AND I, WE'RE CONTINUOUSLY ABSORBING FANTASIA WITHOUT REALIZING.
AND MAYBE WE ALWAYS RETAIN A SMALL AMOUNT.

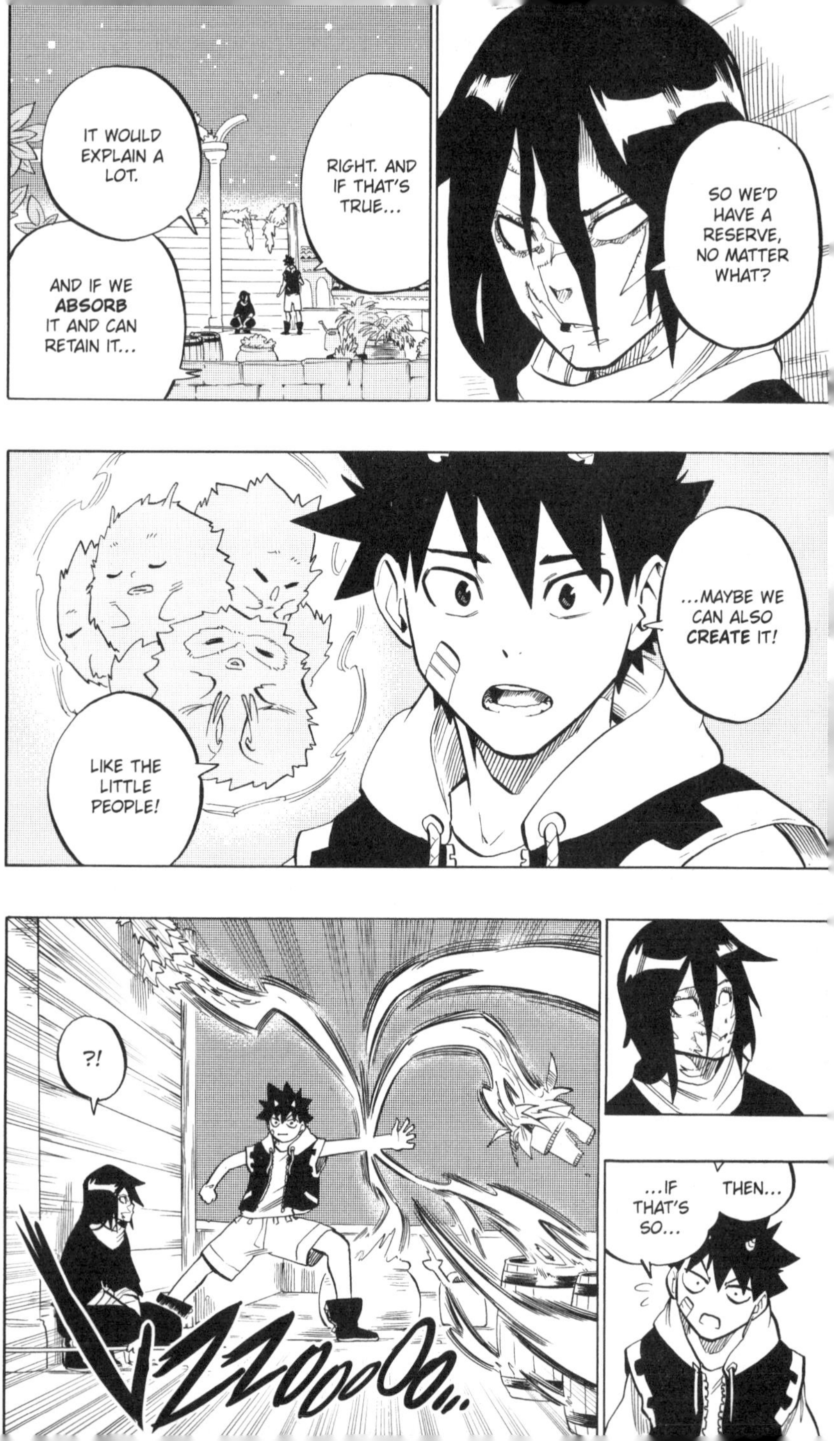
SO WE'D HAVE A RESERVE, NO MATTER WHAT?
RIGHT. AND IF THAT'S TRUE...
IT WOULD EXPLAIN A LOT.
AND IF WE **ABSORB** IT AND CAN RETAIN IT...
...MAYBE WE CAN ALSO **CREATE** IT!
LIKE THE LITTLE PEOPLE!
THEN...
...IF THAT'S SO...
?!
VZZOoooo...

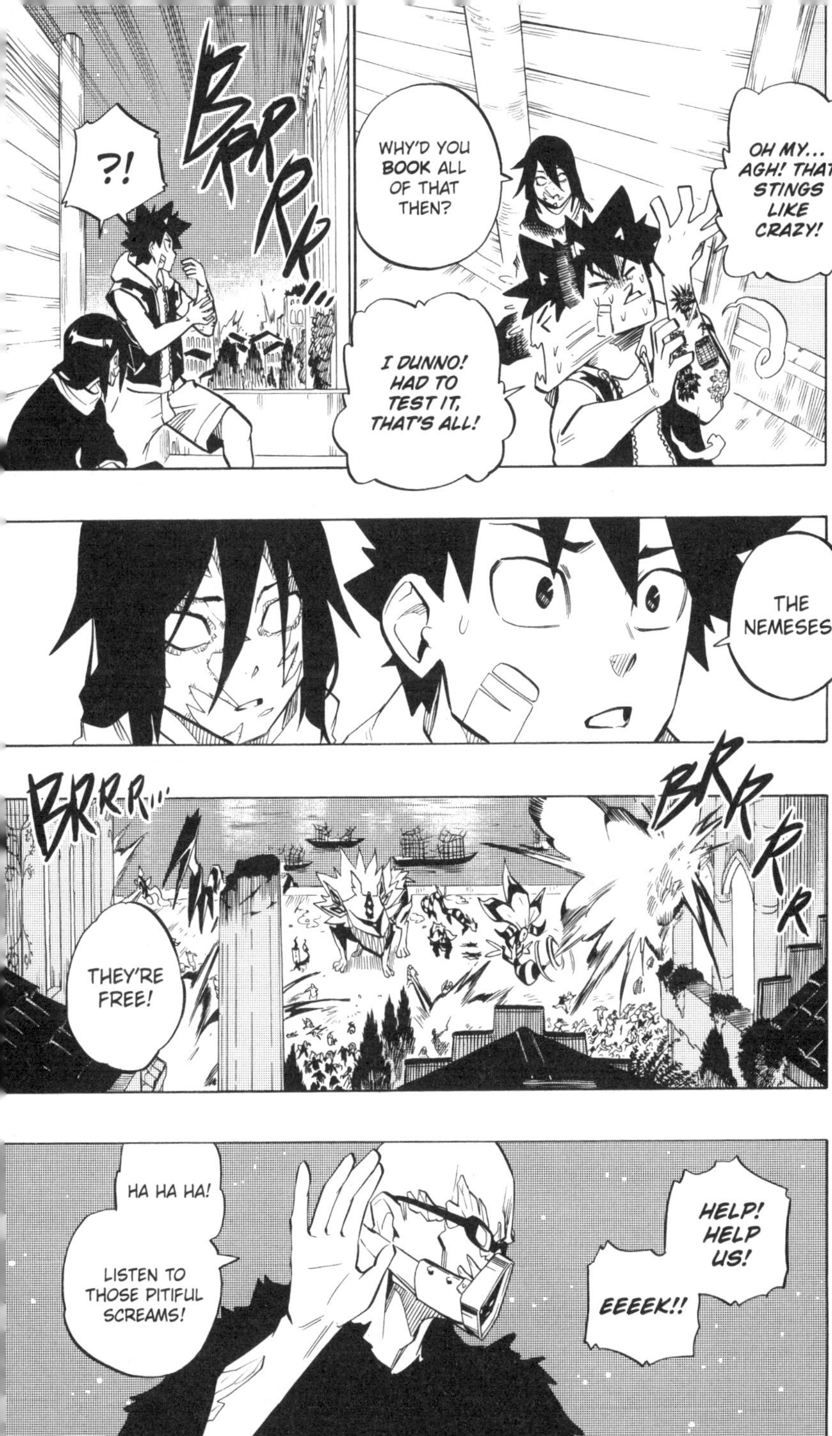
OH MY... AGH! THAT STINGS LIKE CRAZY!
WHY'D YOU BOOK ALL OF THAT THEN?
I DUNNO! HAD TO TEST IT, THAT'S ALL!
BRRRK...
?!
THE NEMESES!
BRRRR
BRRR...
THEY'RE FREE!
HELP! HELP US!
EEEEK!!
HA HA HA!
LISTEN TO THOSE PITIFUL SCREAMS!

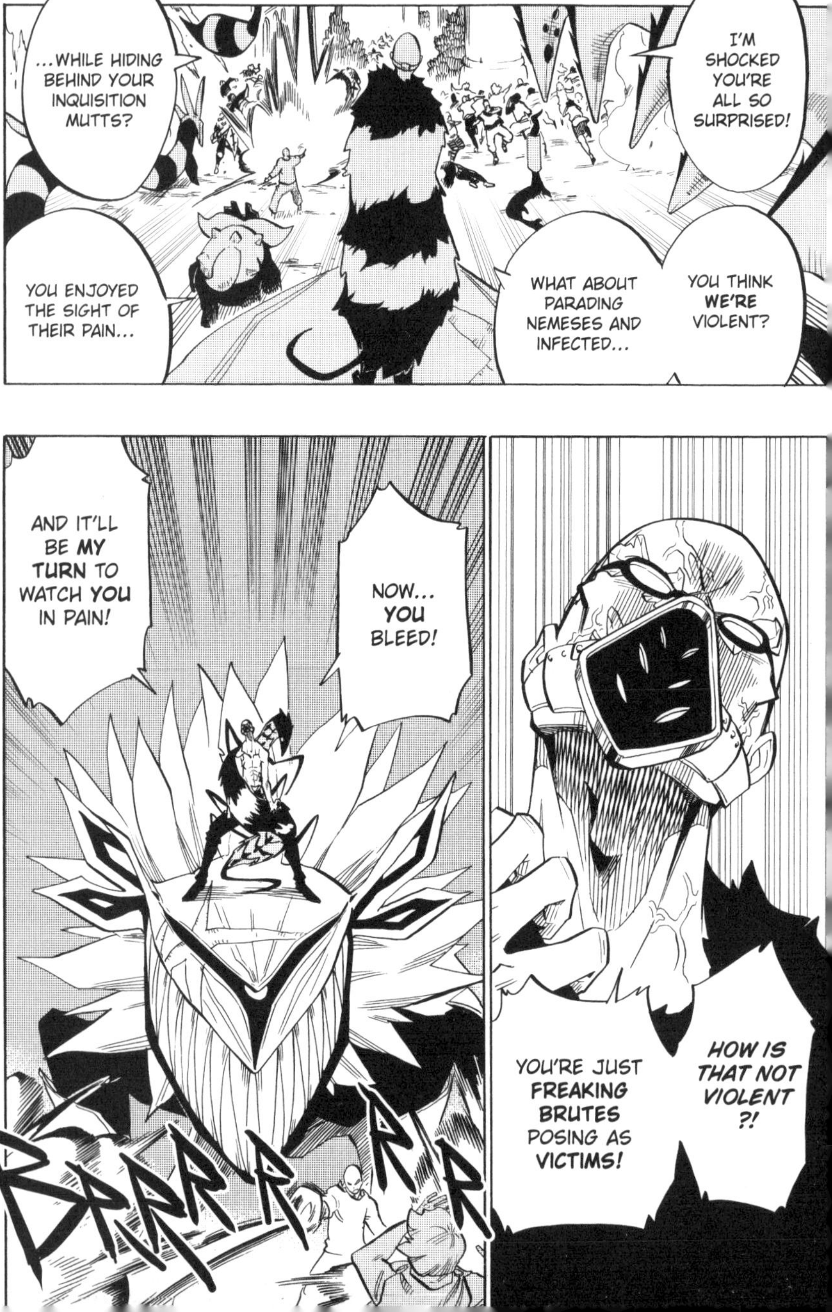
I'M SHOCKED YOU'RE ALL SO SURPRISED!
YOU THINK WE'RE VIOLENT?
WHAT ABOUT PARADING NEMESES AND INFECTED...
...WHILE HIDING BEHIND YOUR INQUISITION MUTTS?
YOU ENJOYED THE SIGHT OF THEIR PAIN...
HOW IS THAT NOT VIOLENT?!
YOU'RE JUST FREAKING BRUTES POSING AS VICTIMS!
NOW... YOU BLEED!
AND IT'LL BE MY TURN TO WATCH YOU IN PAIN!
BRRRRR

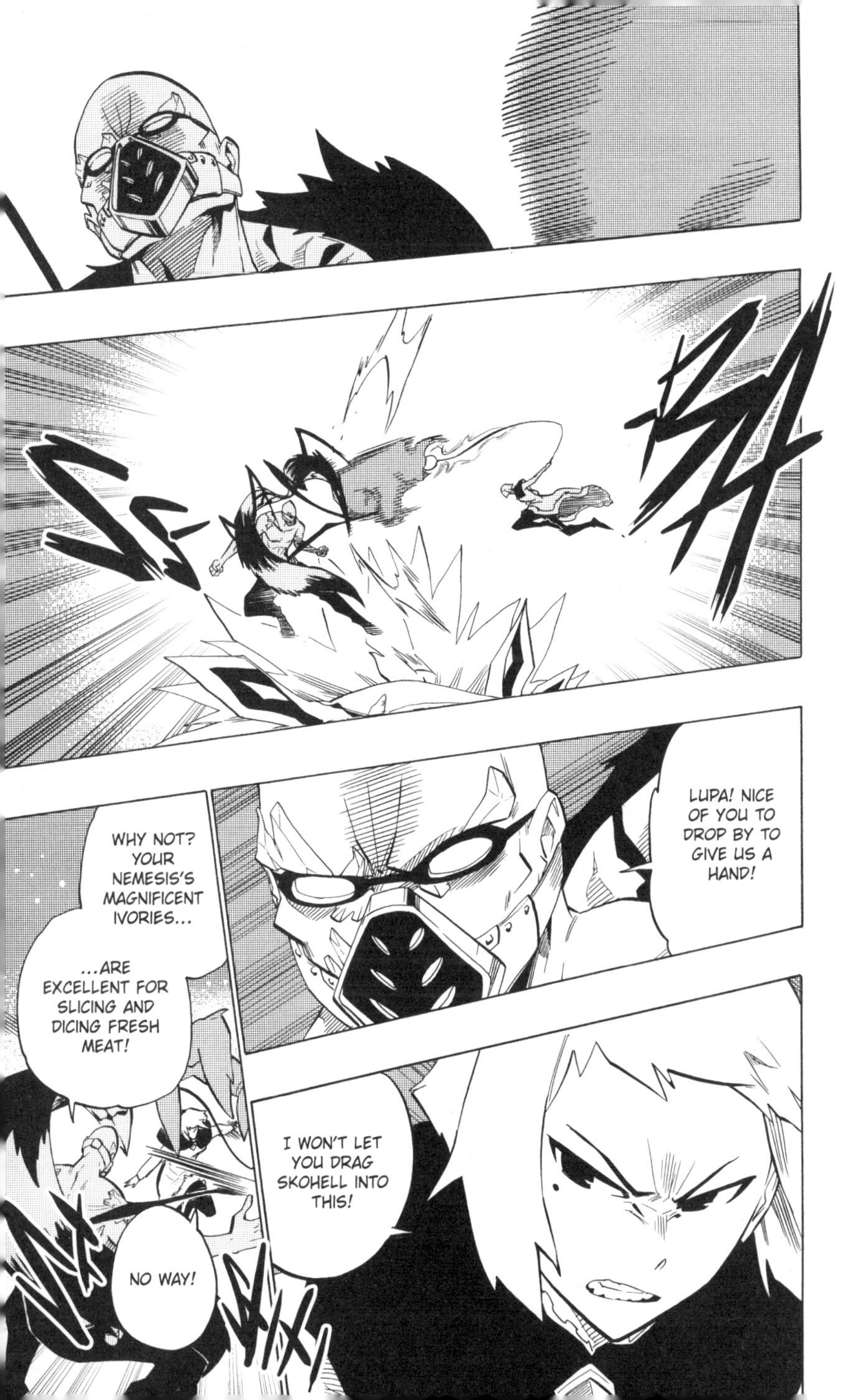
LUPA! NICE OF YOU TO DROP BY TO GIVE US A HAND!
WHY NOT? YOUR NEMESIS'S MAGNIFICENT IVORIES...
...ARE EXCELLENT FOR SLICING AND DICING FRESH MEAT!
I WON'T LET YOU DRAG SKOHELL INTO THIS!
NO WAY!

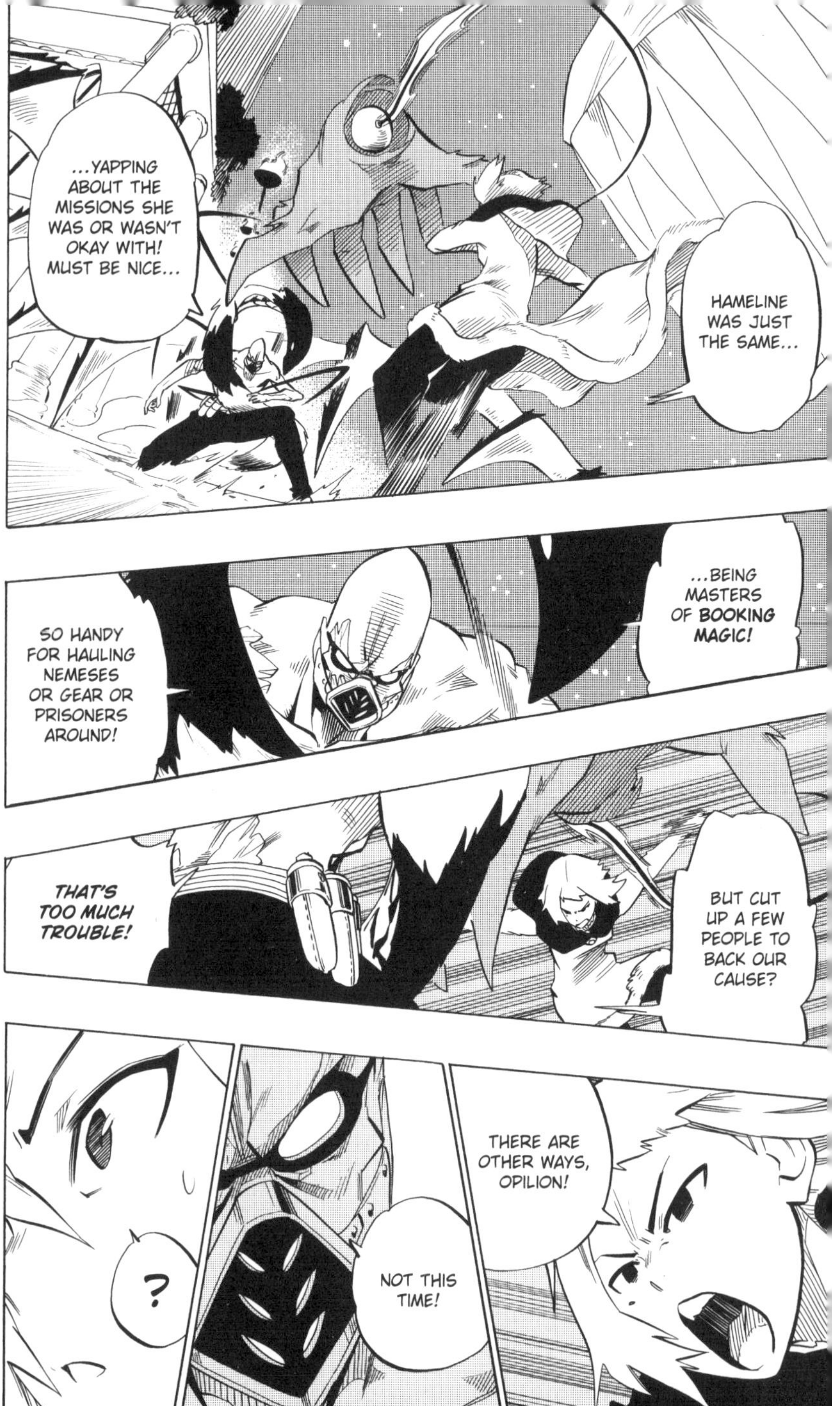
HAMELINE WAS JUST THE SAME...
...YAPPING ABOUT THE MISSIONS SHE WAS OR WASN'T OKAY WITH! MUST BE NICE...
...BEING MASTERS OF **BOOKING MAGIC!**
SO HANDY FOR HAULING NEMESES OR GEAR OR PRISONERS AROUND!
BUT CUT UP A FEW PEOPLE TO BACK OUR CAUSE?
THAT'S TOO MUCH TROUBLE!
THERE ARE OTHER WAYS, OPILION!
NOT THIS TIME!
?

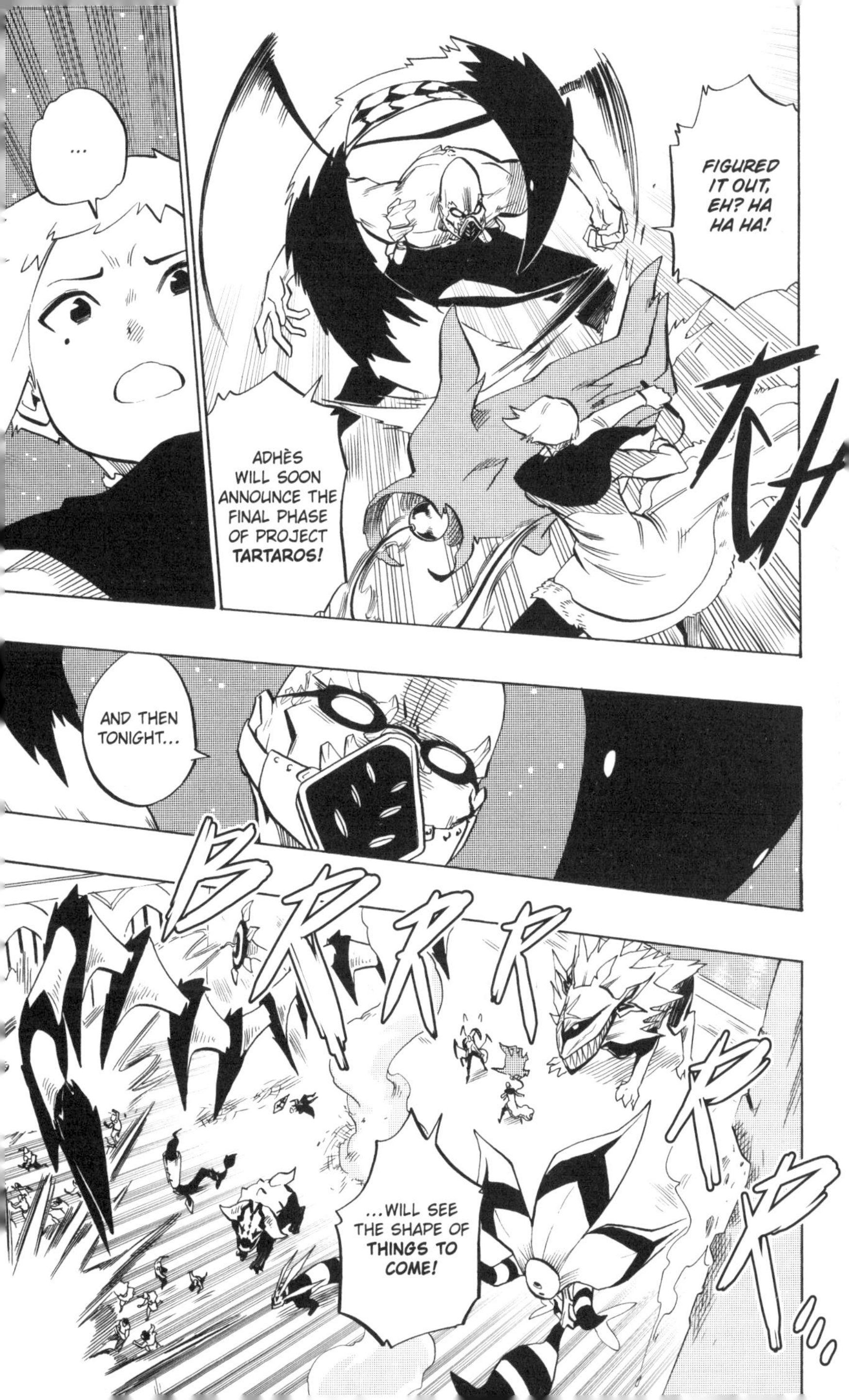
FIGURED IT OUT, EH? HA HA HA!
ADHÈS WILL SOON ANNOUNCE THE FINAL PHASE OF PROJECT TARTAROS!
...
AND THEN TONIGHT...
...WILL SEE THE SHAPE OF THINGS TO COME!

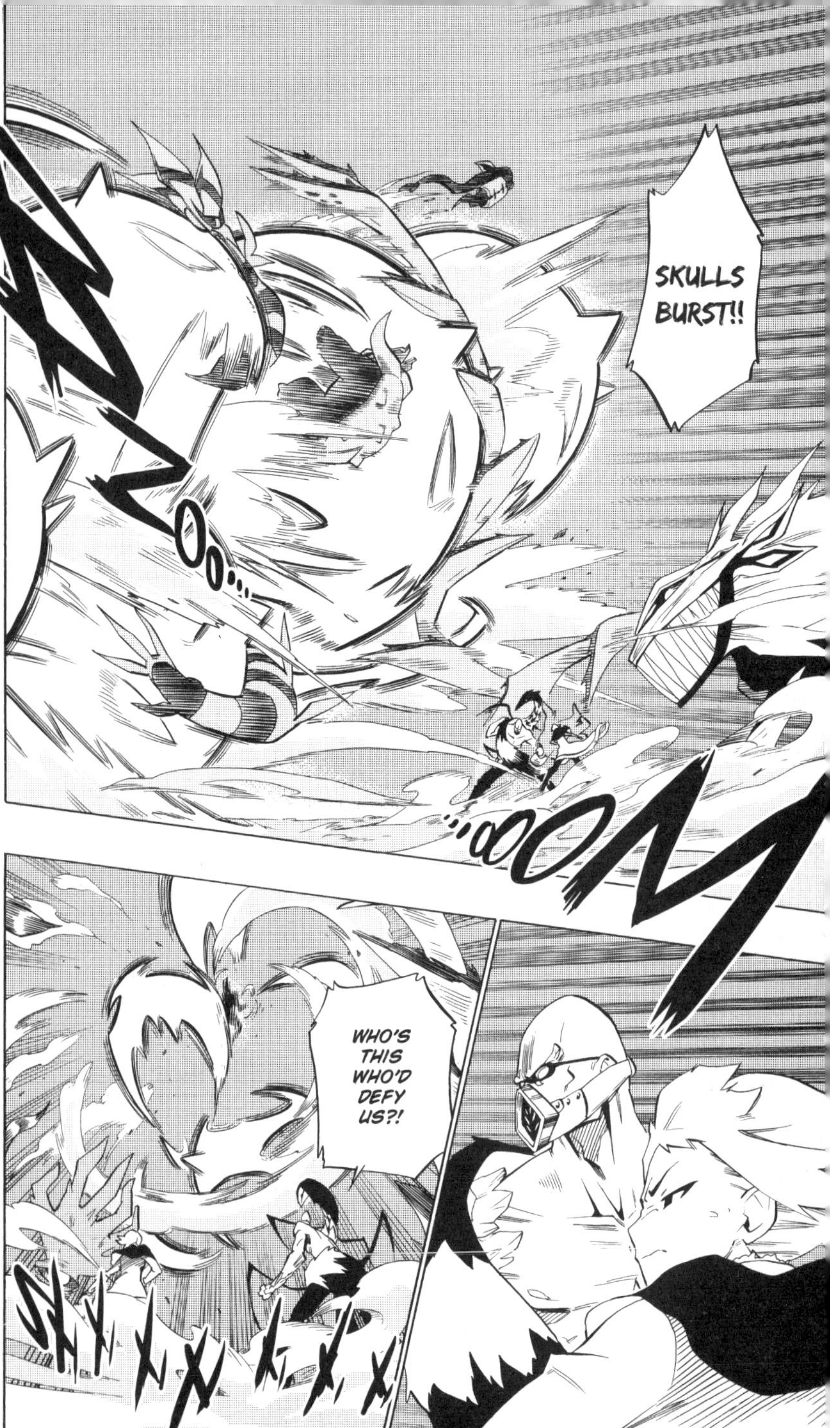
SKULLS BURST!!
ZWOO...
...OOM
WHO'S THIS WHO'D DEFY US?!
SHXXXXX

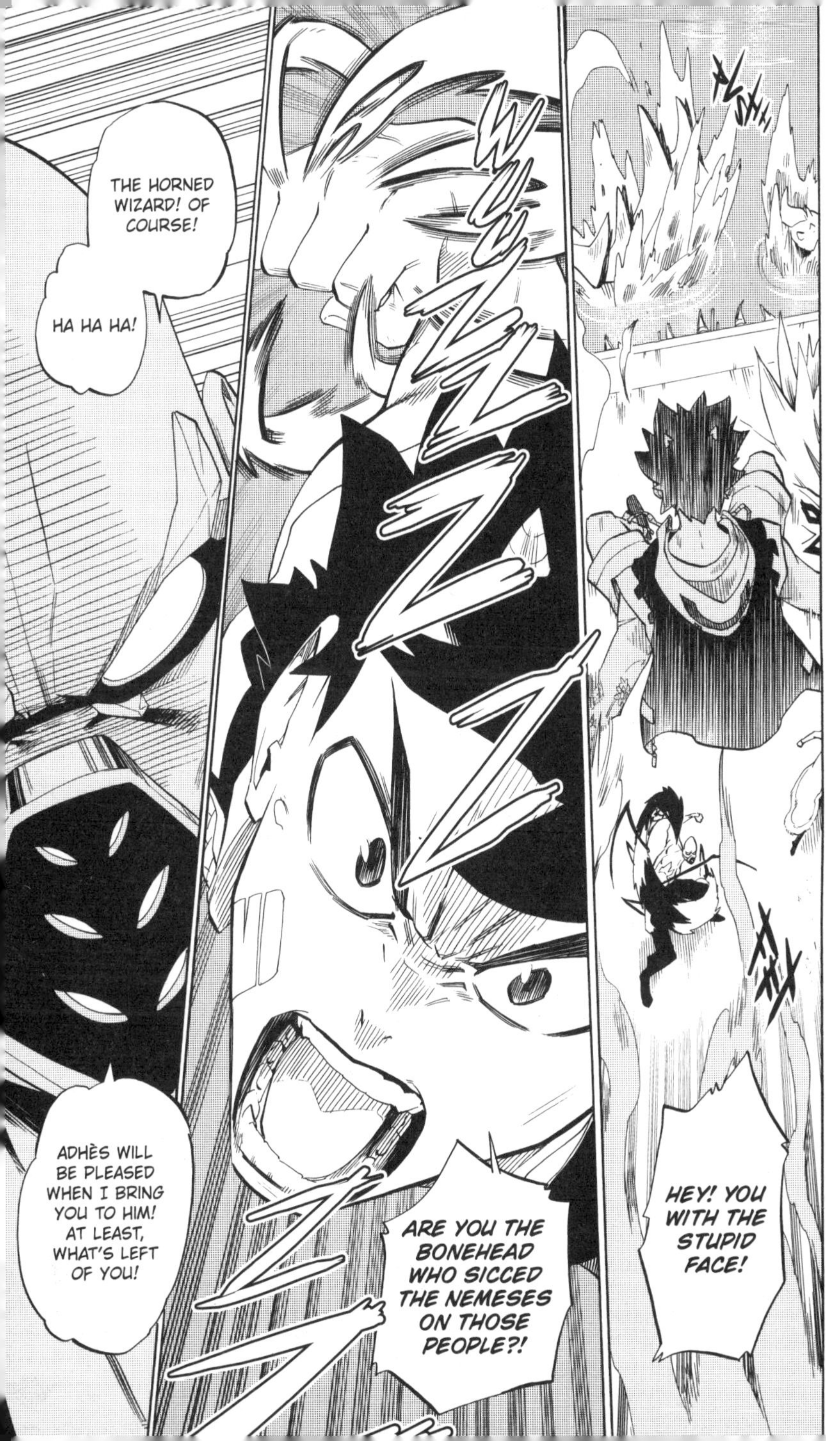

HEY! YOU WITH THE STUPID FACE!
ARE YOU THE BONEHEAD WHO SICCED THE NEMESES ON THOSE PEOPLE?!
THE HORNED WIZARD! OF COURSE!
HA HA HA!
ADHÈS WILL BE PLEASED WHEN I BRING YOU TO HIM! AT LEAST, WHAT'S LEFT OF YOU!

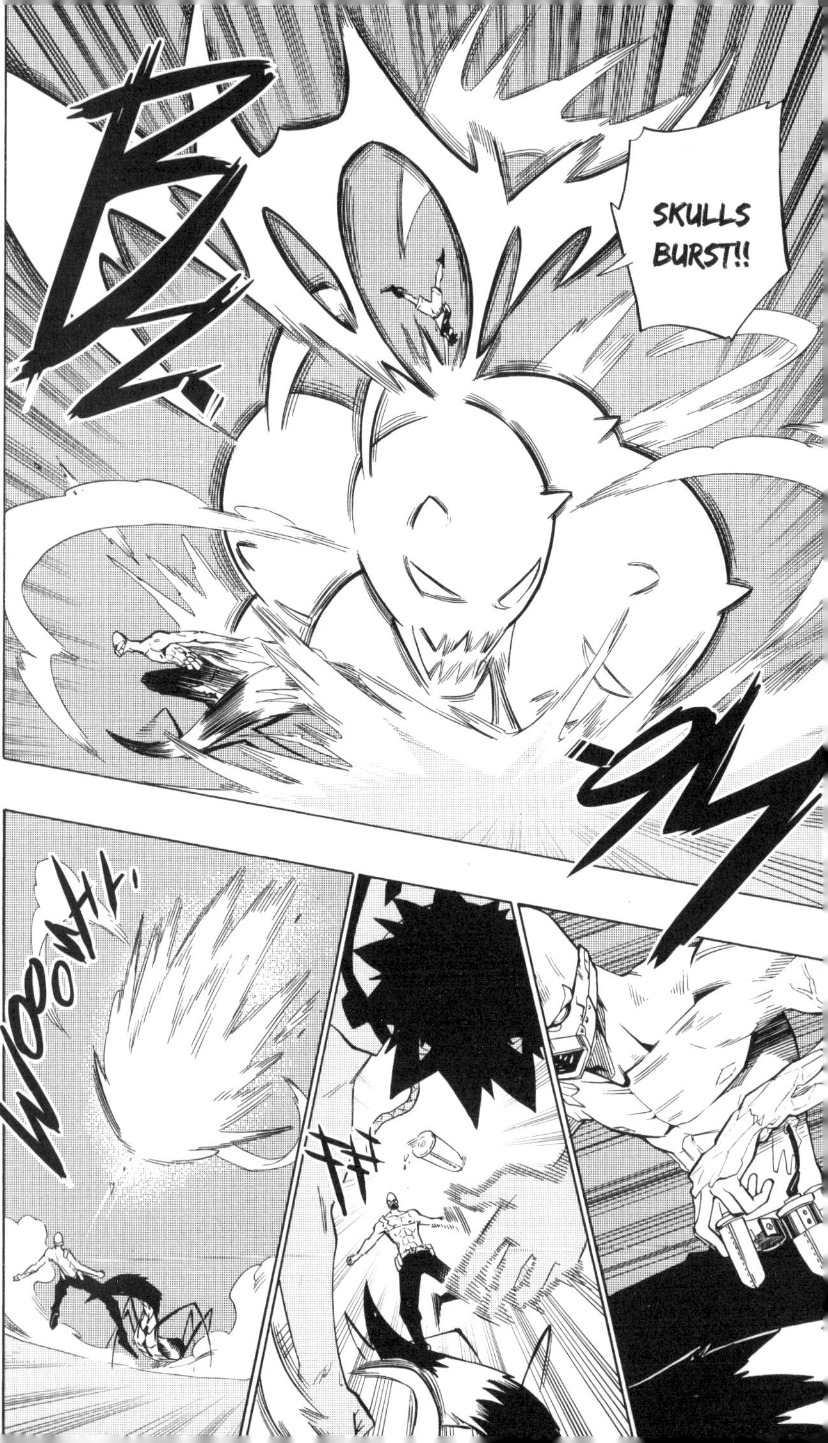
SKULLS BURST!!
WOOOSH!!

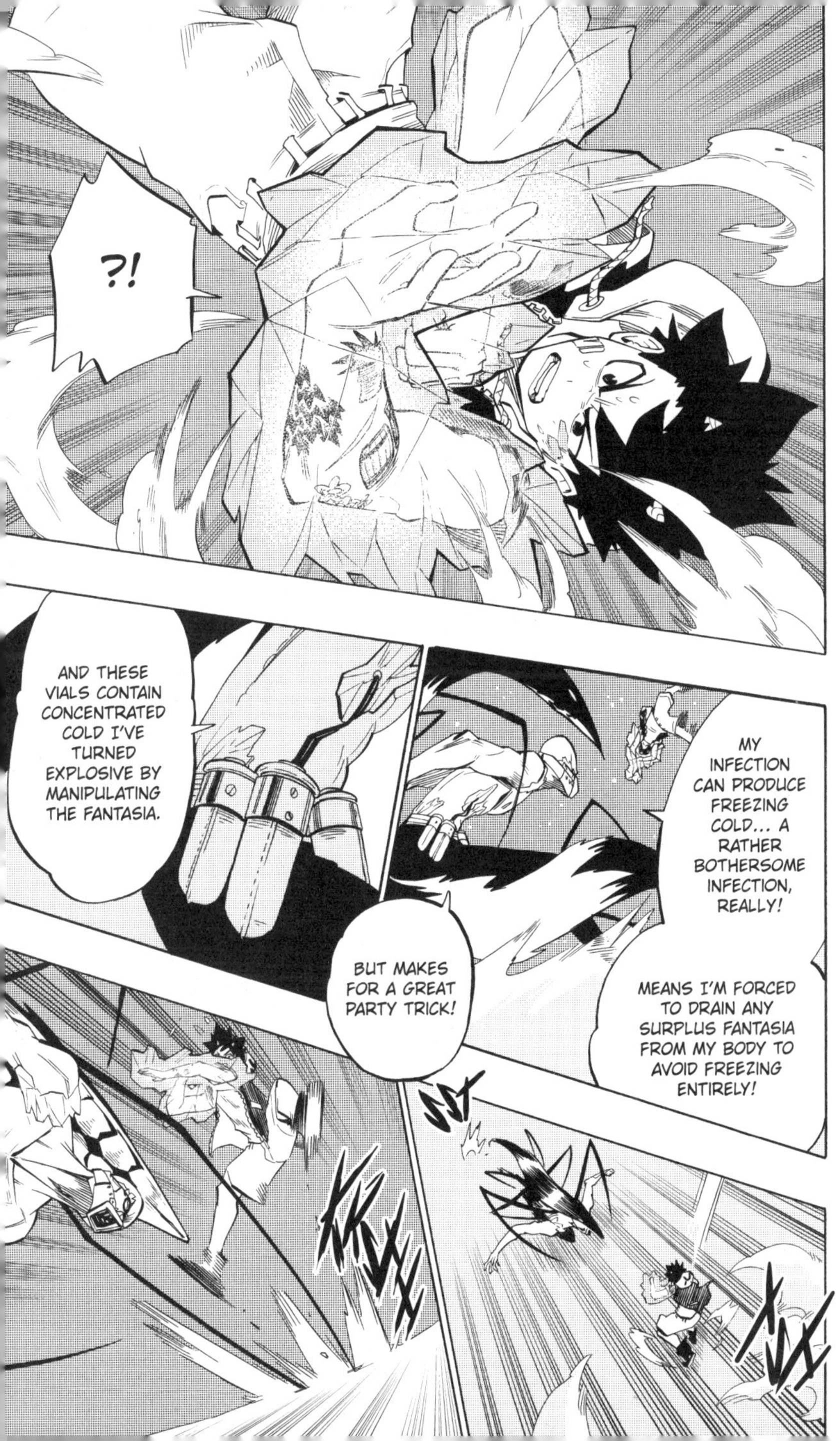
?!
MY INFECTION CAN PRODUCE FREEZING COLD... A RATHER BOTHERSOME INFECTION, REALLY!
MEANS I'M FORCED TO DRAIN ANY SURPLUS FANTASIA FROM MY BODY TO AVOID FREEZING ENTIRELY!
BUT MAKES FOR A GREAT PARTY TRICK!
AND THESE VIALS CONTAIN CONCENTRATED COLD I'VE TURNED EXPLOSIVE BY MANIPULATING THE FANTASIA.
SST

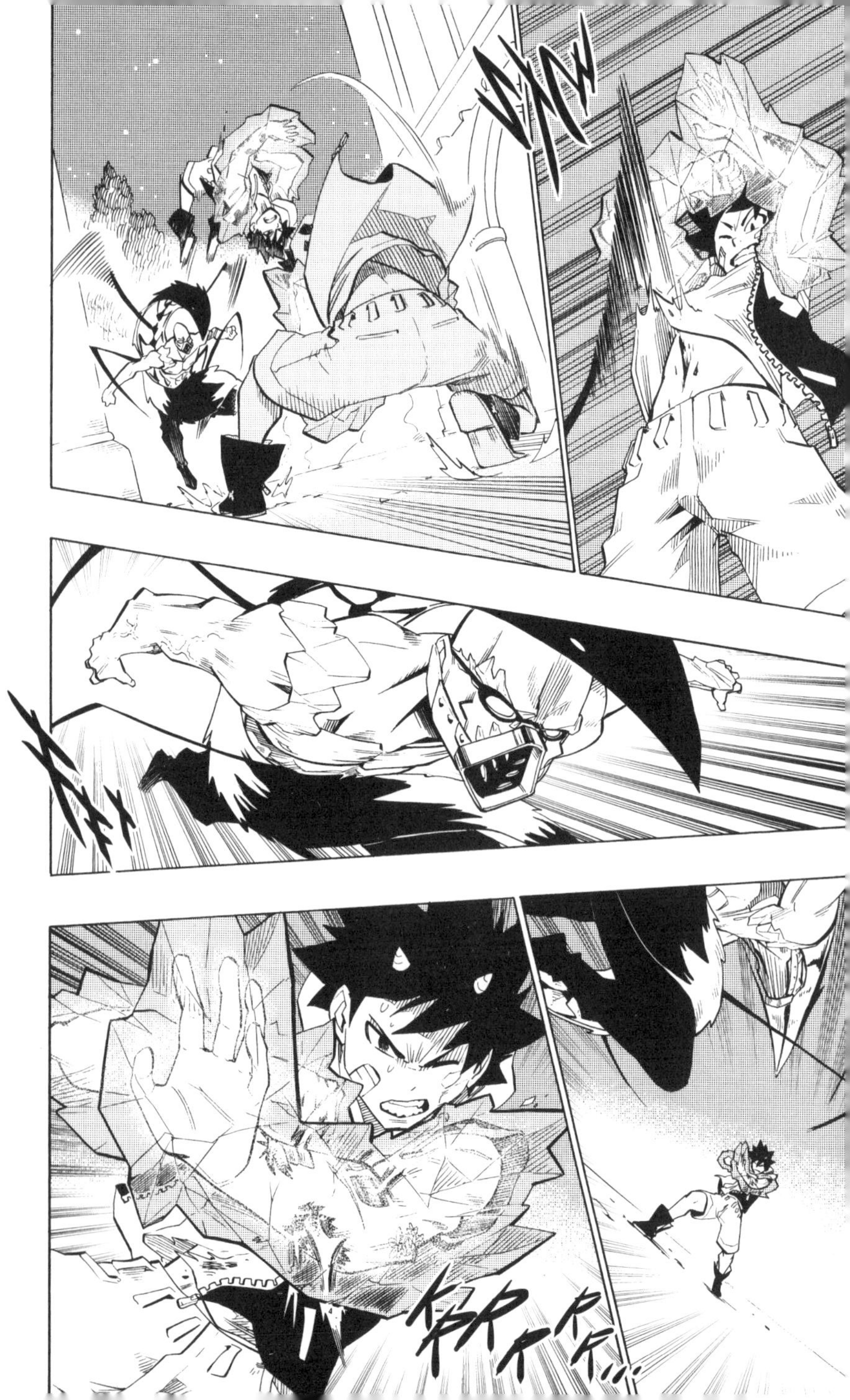
KRRRRR...

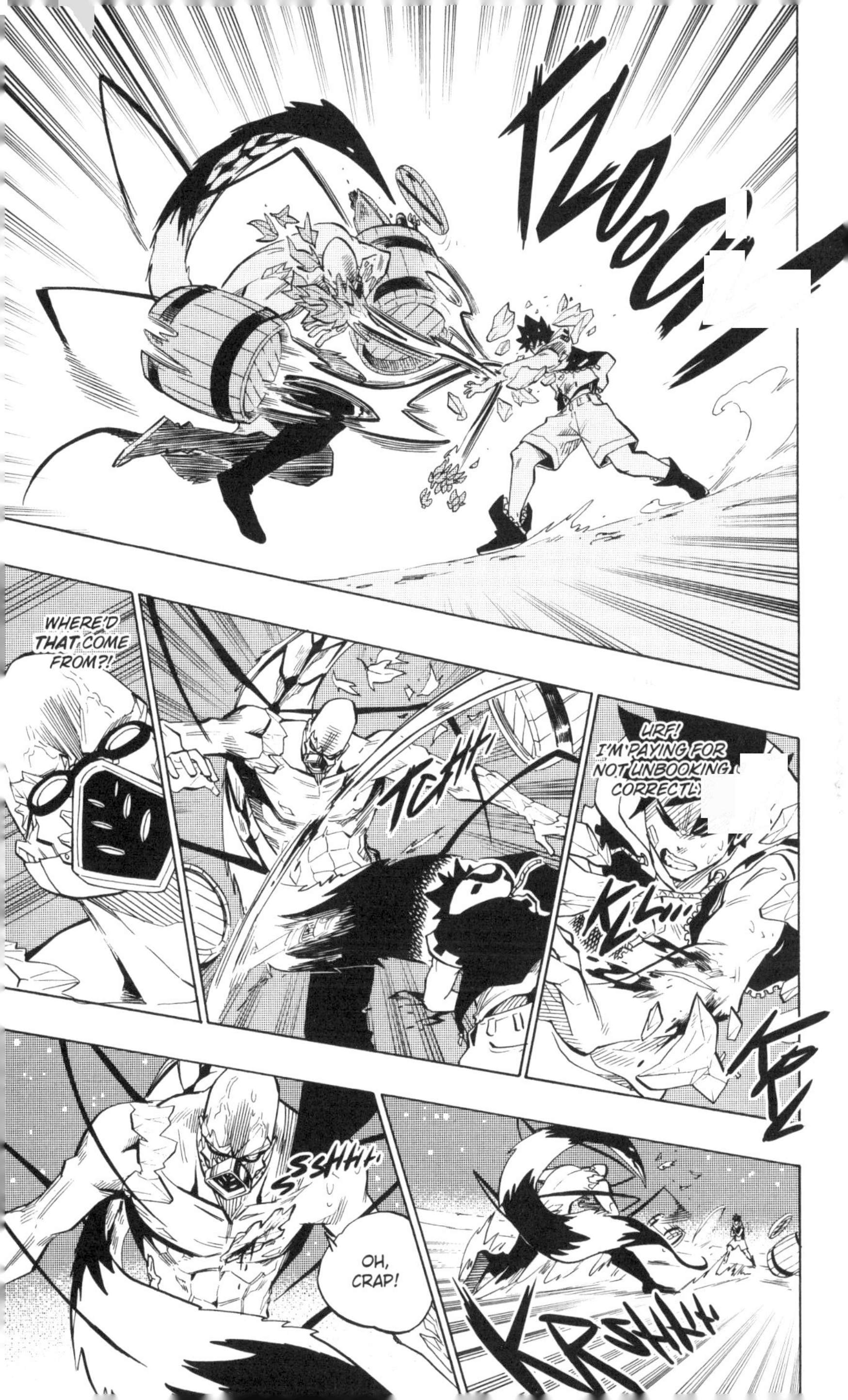
URF! I'M PAYING FOR NOT UNBOOKING CORRECTLY
KRSHH
SSHHH
OH, CRAP!
TCHH
WHERE'D THAT COME FROM?!

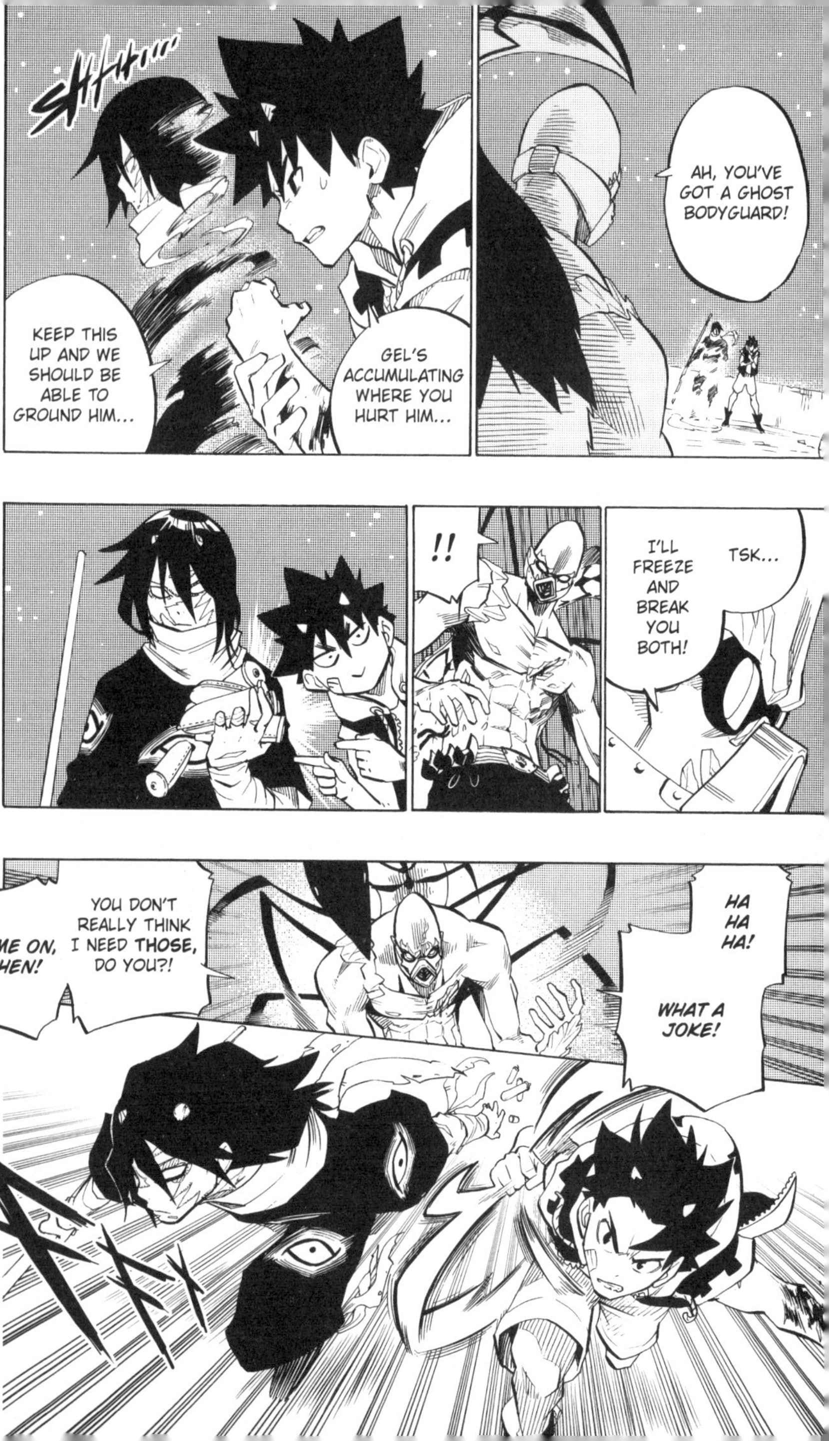
AH, YOU'VE GOT A GHOST BODYGUARD!
GEL'S ACCUMULATING WHERE YOU HURT HIM...
KEEP THIS UP AND WE SHOULD BE ABLE TO GROUND HIM...
TSK...
I'LL FREEZE AND BREAK YOU BOTH!
!!
HA HA HA!
WHAT A JOKE!
YOU DON'T REALLY THINK I NEED THOSE, DO YOU?!
COME ON, THEN!

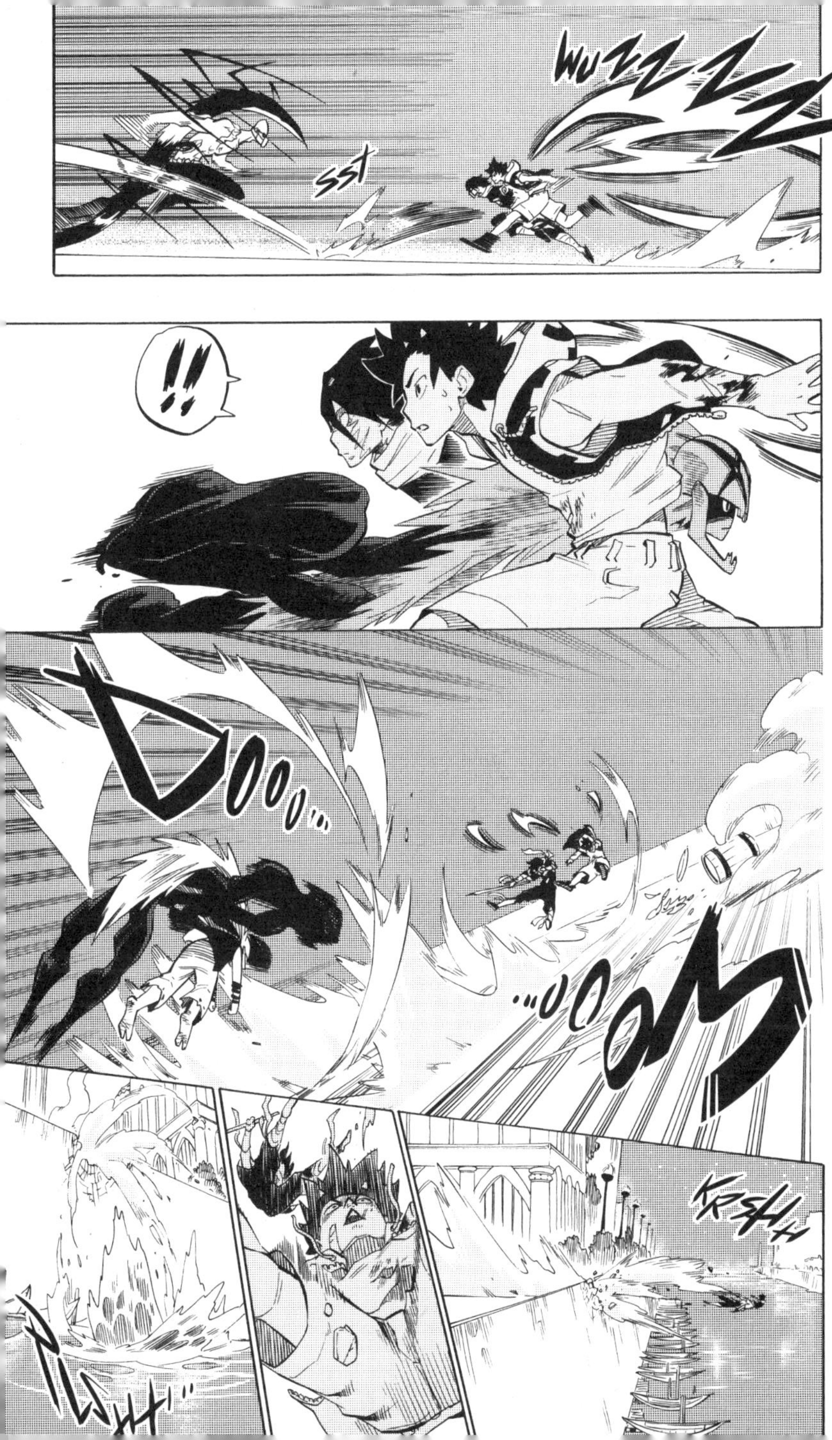
WUZZZZZ
SST
!!
DOOO...
...OOOM
KRSHH
PLSHH

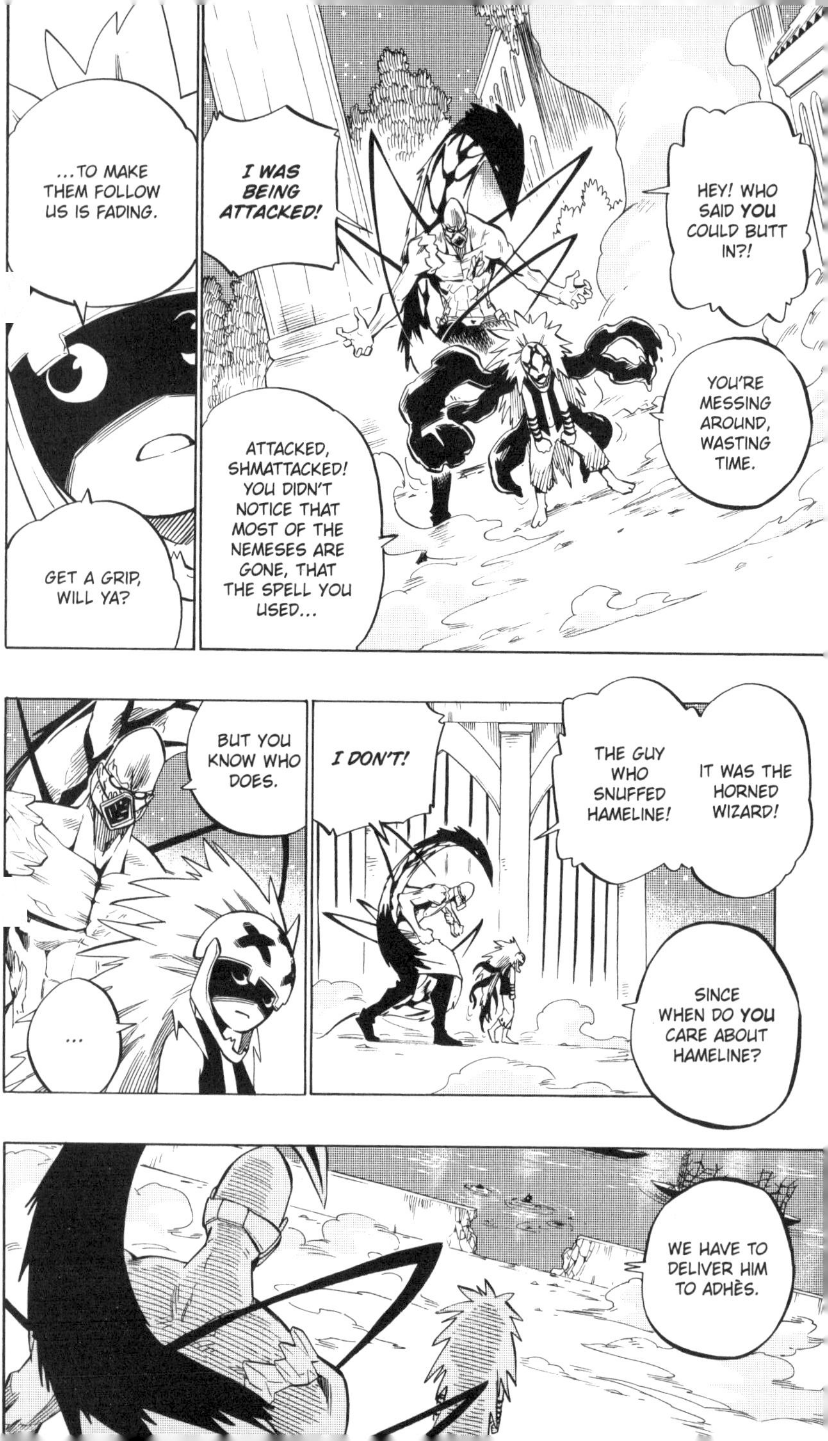
HEY! WHO SAID YOU COULD BUTT IN?!
YOU'RE MESSING AROUND, WASTING TIME.
I WAS BEING ATTACKED!
ATTACKED, SHMATTACKED! YOU DIDN'T NOTICE THAT MOST OF THE NEMESES ARE GONE, THAT THE SPELL YOU USED...
...TO MAKE THEM FOLLOW US IS FADING.
GET A GRIP, WILL YA?
IT WAS THE HORNED WIZARD!
THE GUY WHO SNUFFED HAMELINE!
SINCE WHEN DO YOU CARE ABOUT HAMELINE?
I DON'T!
BUT YOU KNOW WHO DOES.
...
WE HAVE TO DELIVER HIM TO ADHÈS.

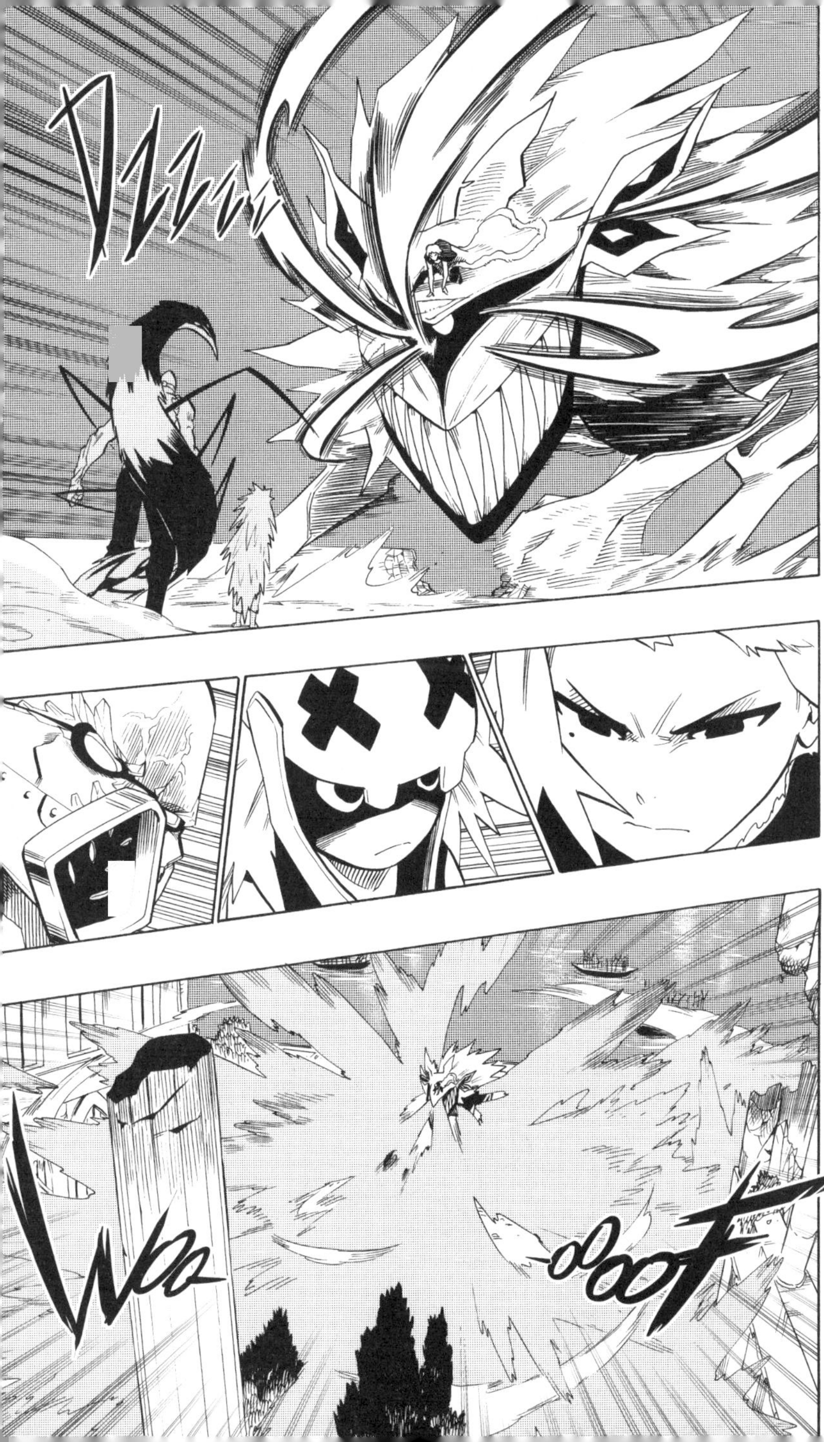
Dzzzz
Waa
-oooof

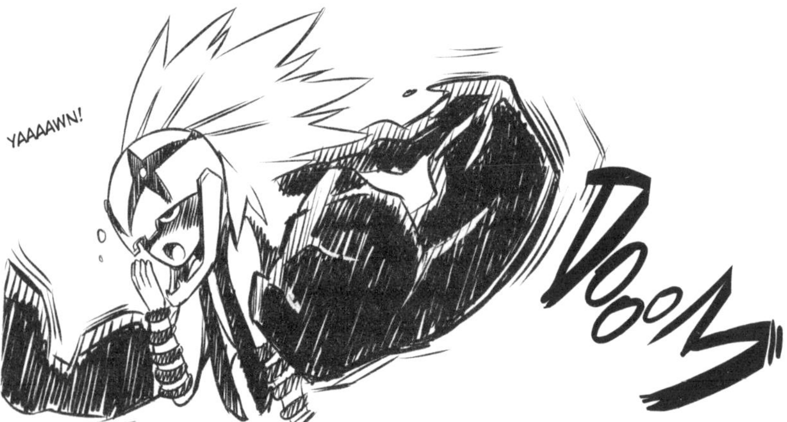
YAAAAWN!
DOOOM

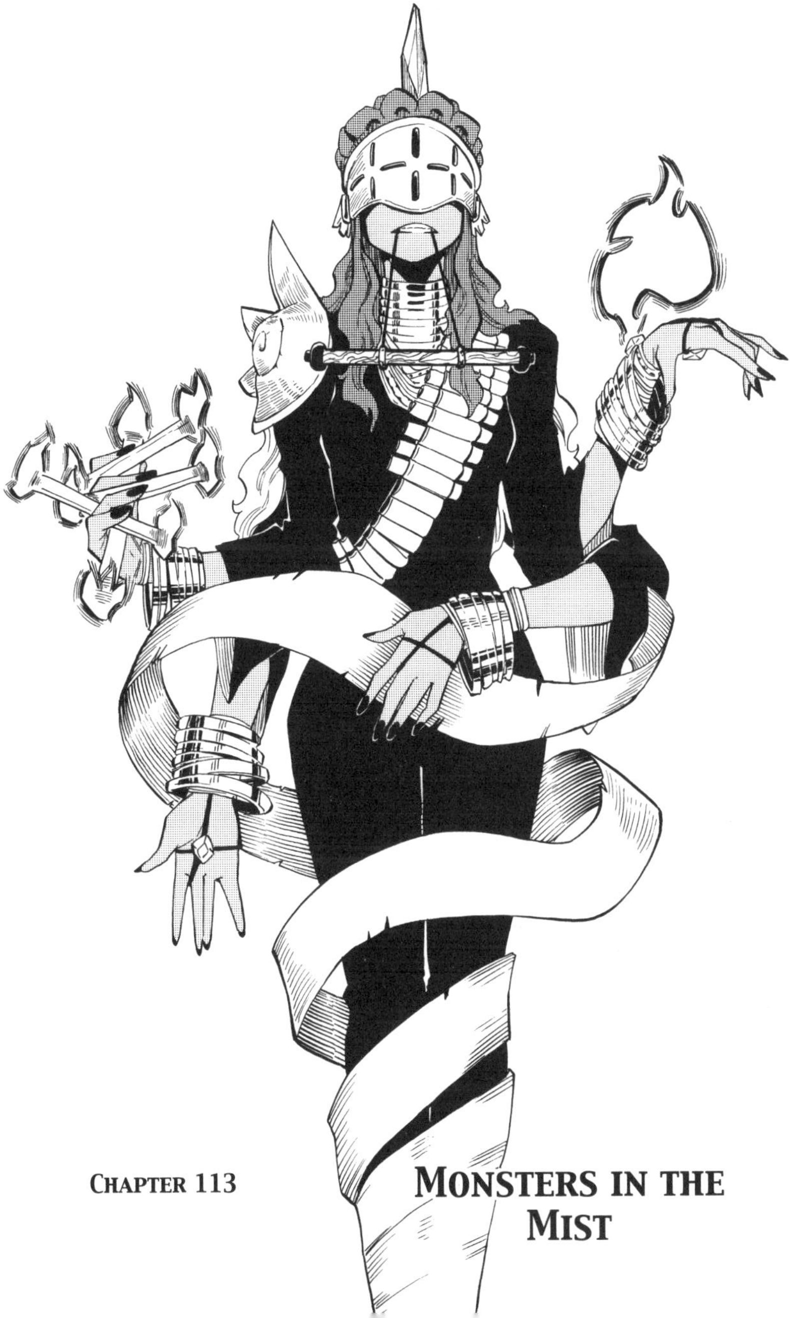

Chapter 113

Monsters in the Mist

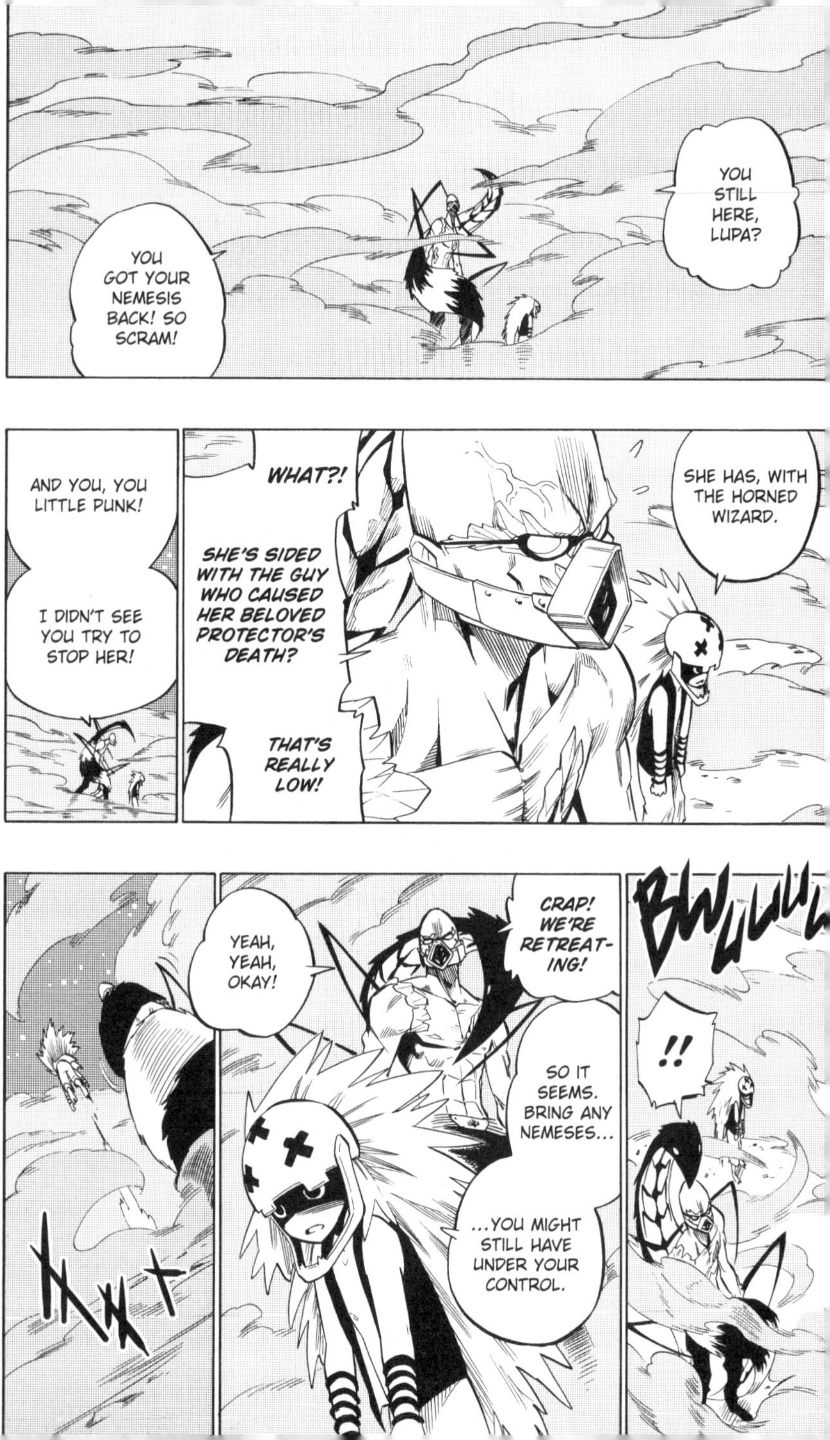

YOU STILL HERE, LUPA?
YOU GOT YOUR NEMESIS BACK! SO SCRAM!
SHE HAS, WITH THE HORNED WIZARD.
WHAT?!
SHE'S SIDED WITH THE GUY WHO CAUSED HER BELOVED PROTECTOR'S DEATH?
THAT'S REALLY LOW!
AND YOU, YOU LITTLE PUNK!
I DIDN'T SEE YOU TRY TO STOP HER!
BWUUUU
!!
CRAP! WE'RE RETREAT-ING!
YEAH, YEAH, OKAY!
SO IT SEEMS. BRING ANY NEMESES...
...YOU MIGHT STILL HAVE UNDER YOUR CONTROL.

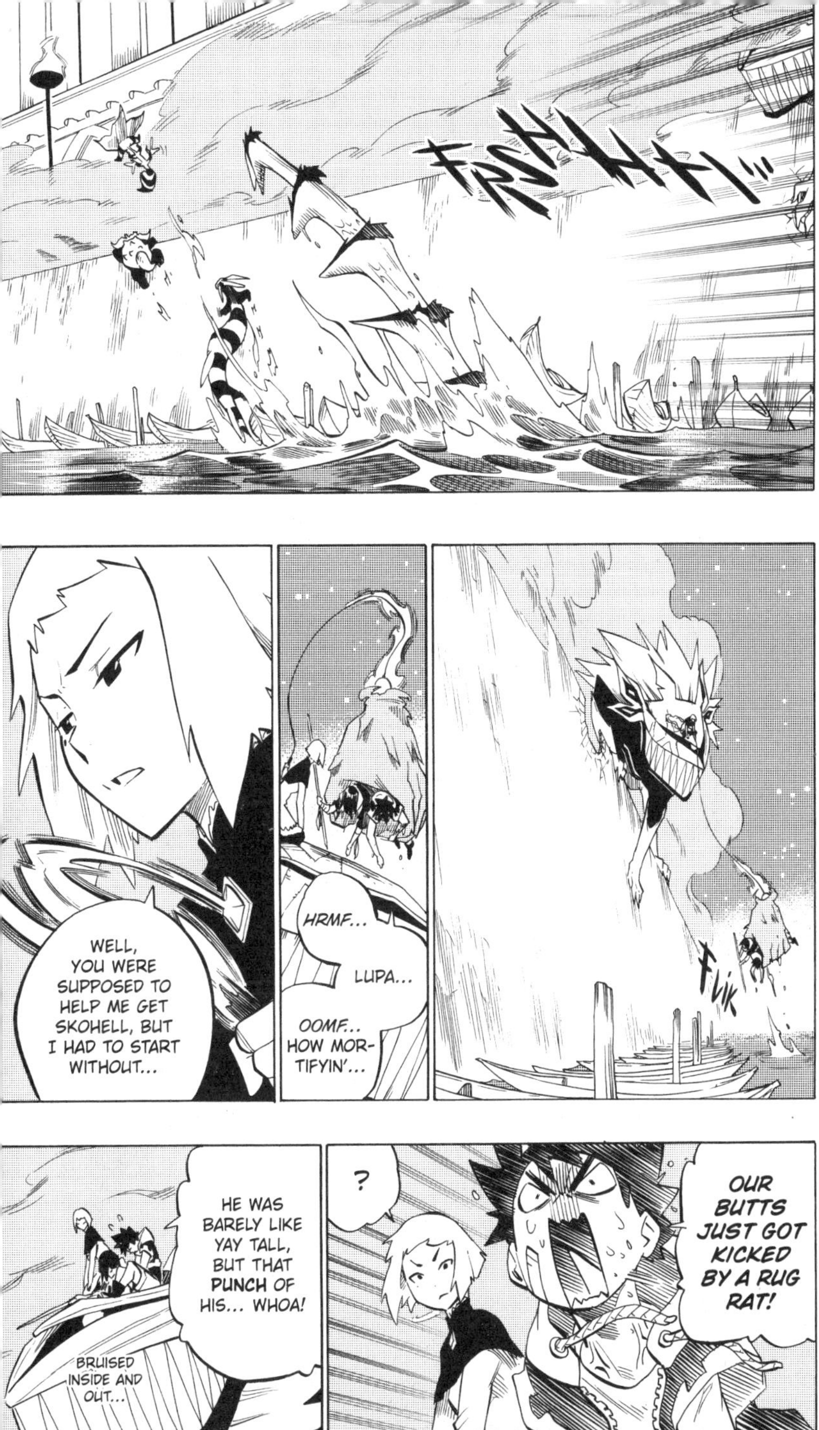
FRSHHHT
FLIK
HRMF...
LUPA...
OOMF... HOW MORTIFYIN'...
WELL, YOU WERE SUPPOSED TO HELP ME GET SKOHELL, BUT I HAD TO START WITHOUT...
OUR BUTTS JUST GOT KICKED BY A RUG RAT!
?
HE WAS BARELY LIKE YAY TALL, BUT THAT **PUNCH** OF HIS... WHOA!
BRUISED INSIDE AND OUT...

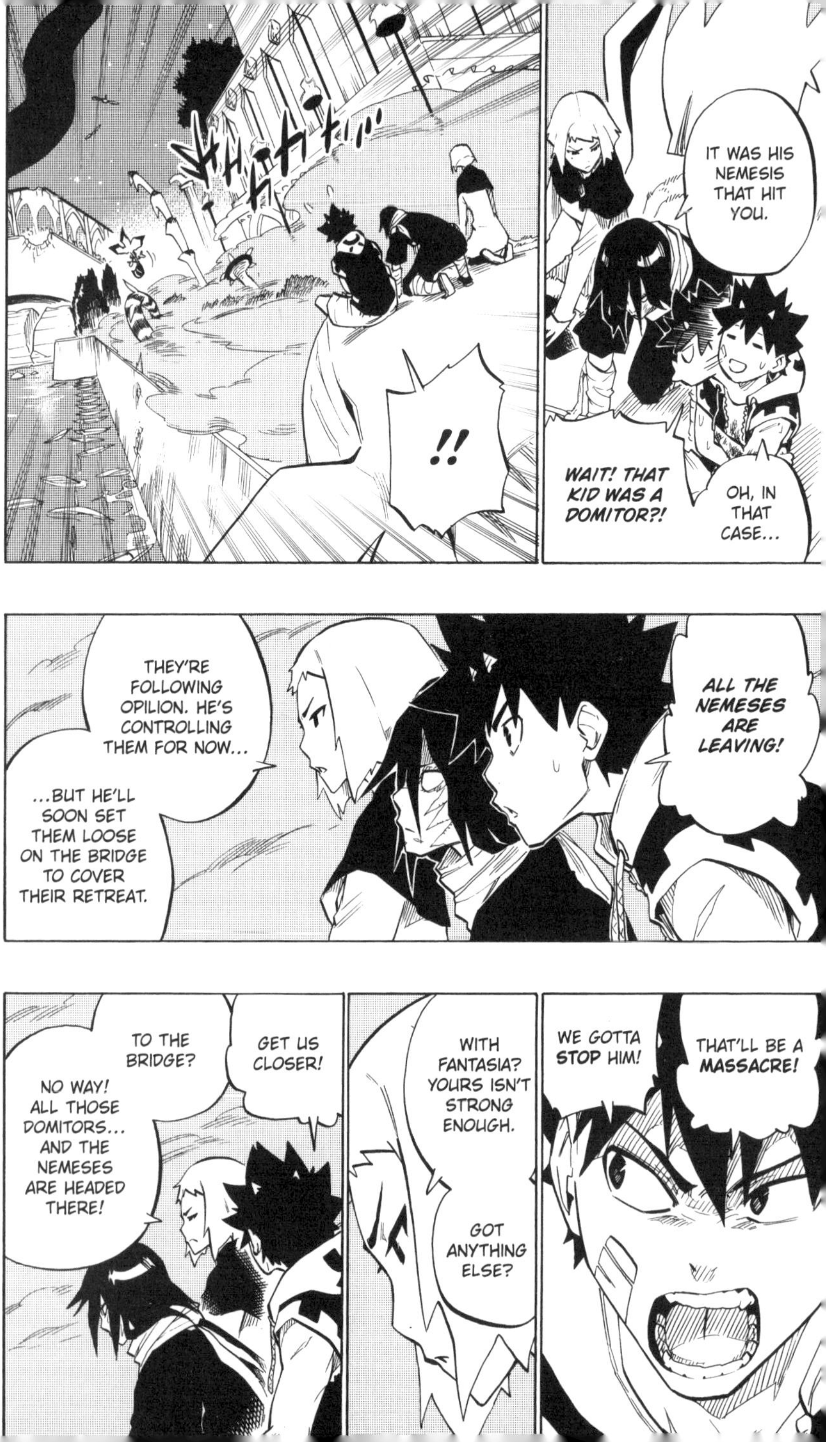
IT WAS HIS NEMESIS THAT HIT YOU.
OH, IN THAT CASE...
WAIT! THAT KID WAS A DOMITOR?!
!!
ALL THE NEMESES ARE LEAVING!
THEY'RE FOLLOWING OPILION. HE'S CONTROLLING THEM FOR NOW...
...BUT HE'LL SOON SET THEM LOOSE ON THE BRIDGE TO COVER THEIR RETREAT.
THAT'LL BE A MASSACRE!
WE GOTTA STOP HIM!
WITH FANTASIA? YOURS ISN'T STRONG ENOUGH.
GOT ANYTHING ELSE?
GET US CLOSER!
TO THE BRIDGE?
NO WAY! ALL THOSE DOMITORS... AND THE NEMESES ARE HEADED THERE!

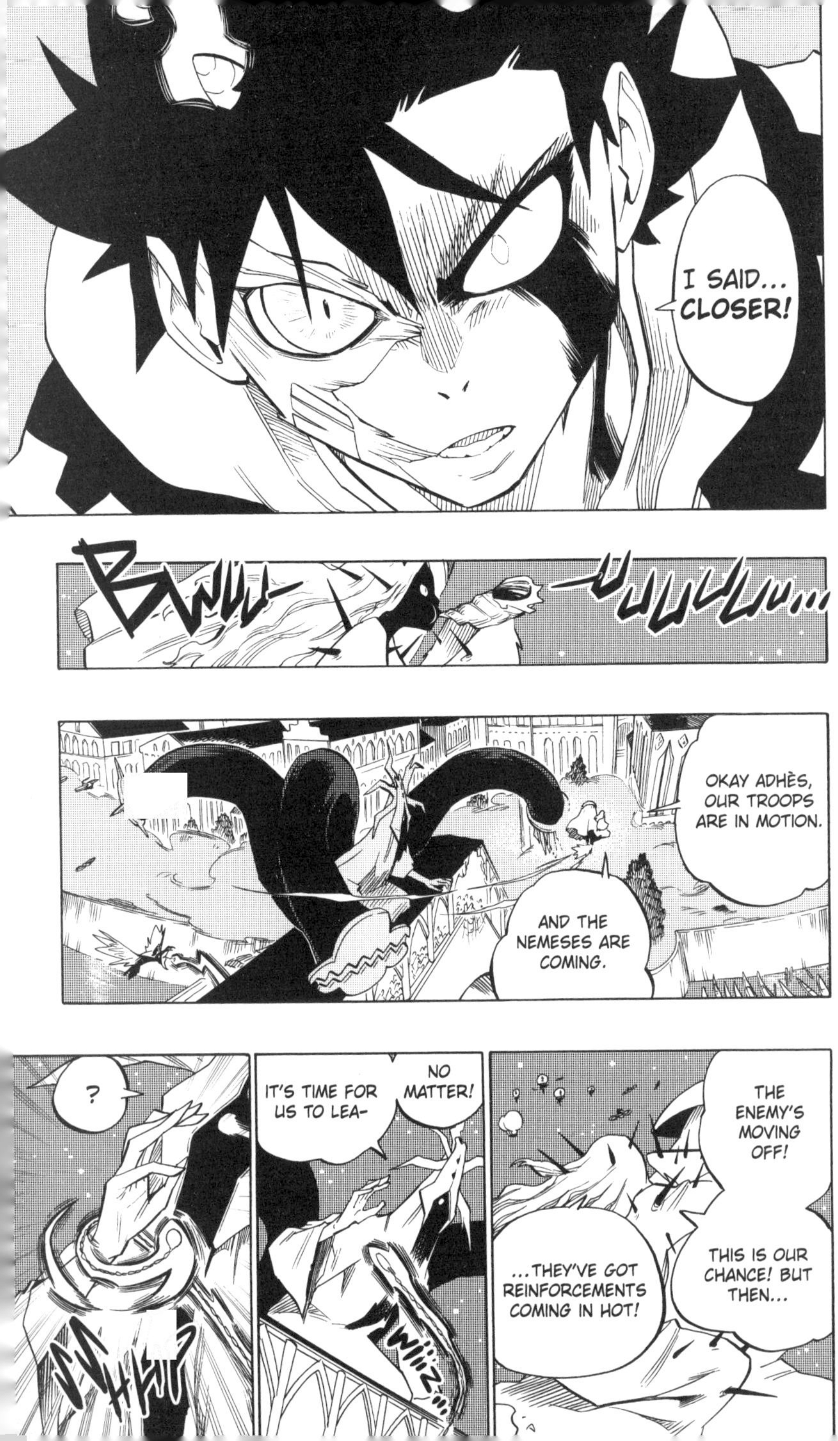
I SAID... CLOSER!
BWUU-
UUUUUU...
OKAY ADHÈS, OUR TROOPS ARE IN MOTION.
AND THE NEMESES ARE COMING.
THE ENEMY'S MOVING OFF!
THIS IS OUR CHANCE! BUT THEN...
...THEY'VE GOT REINFORCEMENTS COMING IN HOT!
NO MATTER!
IT'S TIME FOR US TO LEA-
?

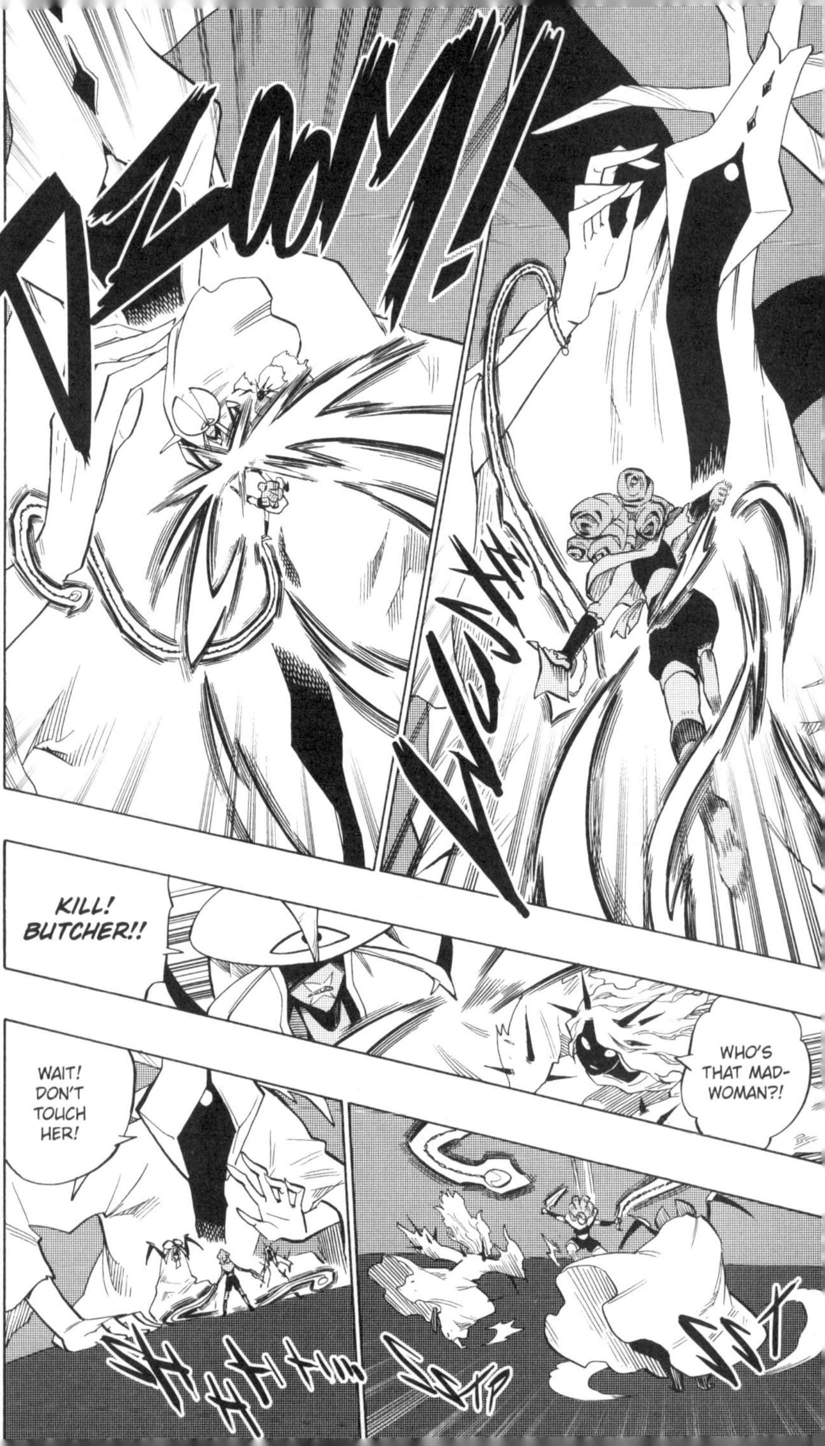
DZOOM!!
KILL! BUTCHER!!
WHO'S THAT MAD-WOMAN?!
WAIT! DON'T TOUCH HER!

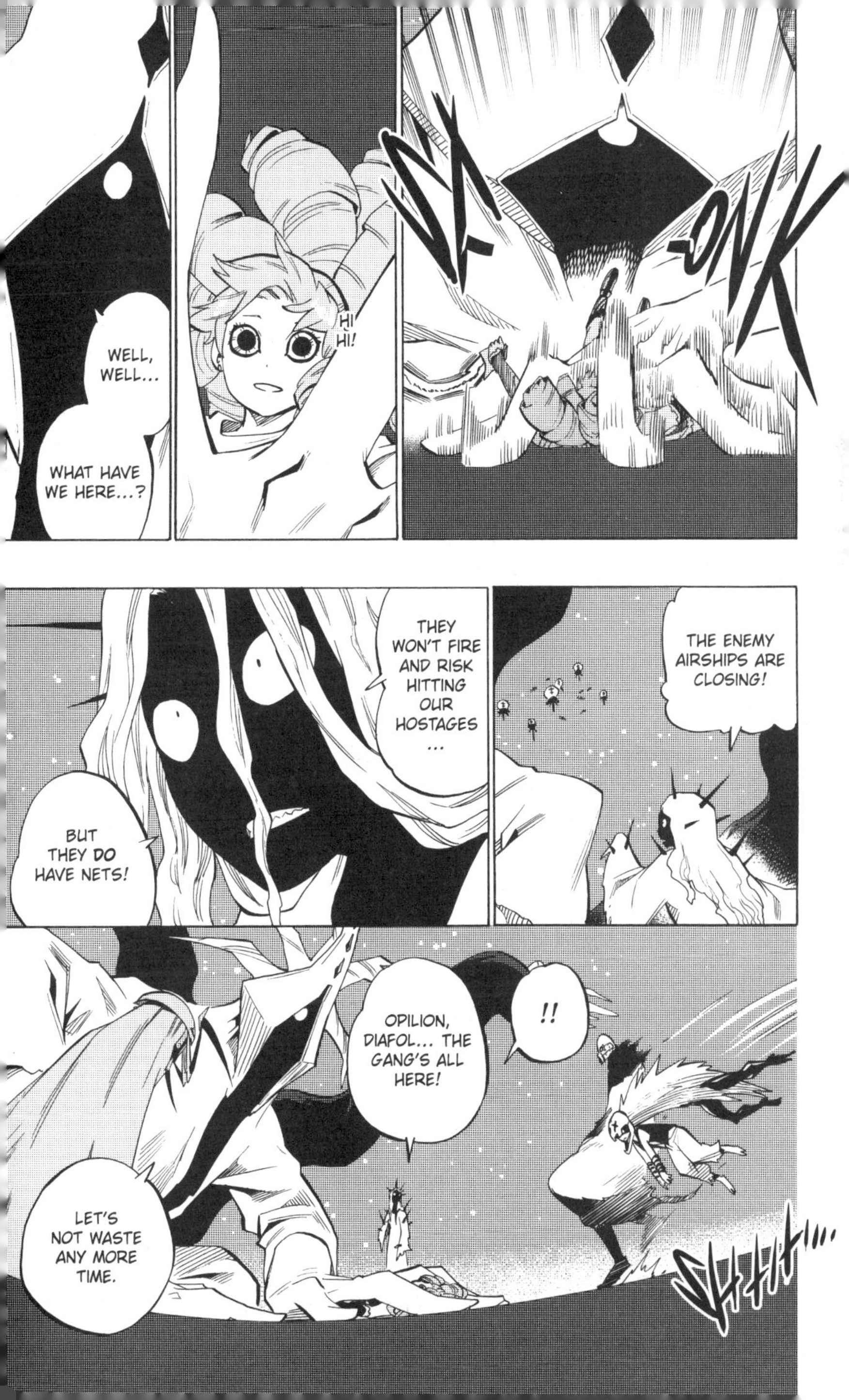
DA
-ONK
HI HI!
WELL, WELL...
WHAT HAVE WE HERE...?
THE ENEMY AIRSHIPS ARE CLOSING!
THEY WON'T FIRE AND RISK HITTING OUR HOSTAGES ...
BUT THEY DO HAVE NETS!
!!
OPILION, DIAFOL... THE GANG'S ALL HERE!
LET'S NOT WASTE ANY MORE TIME.

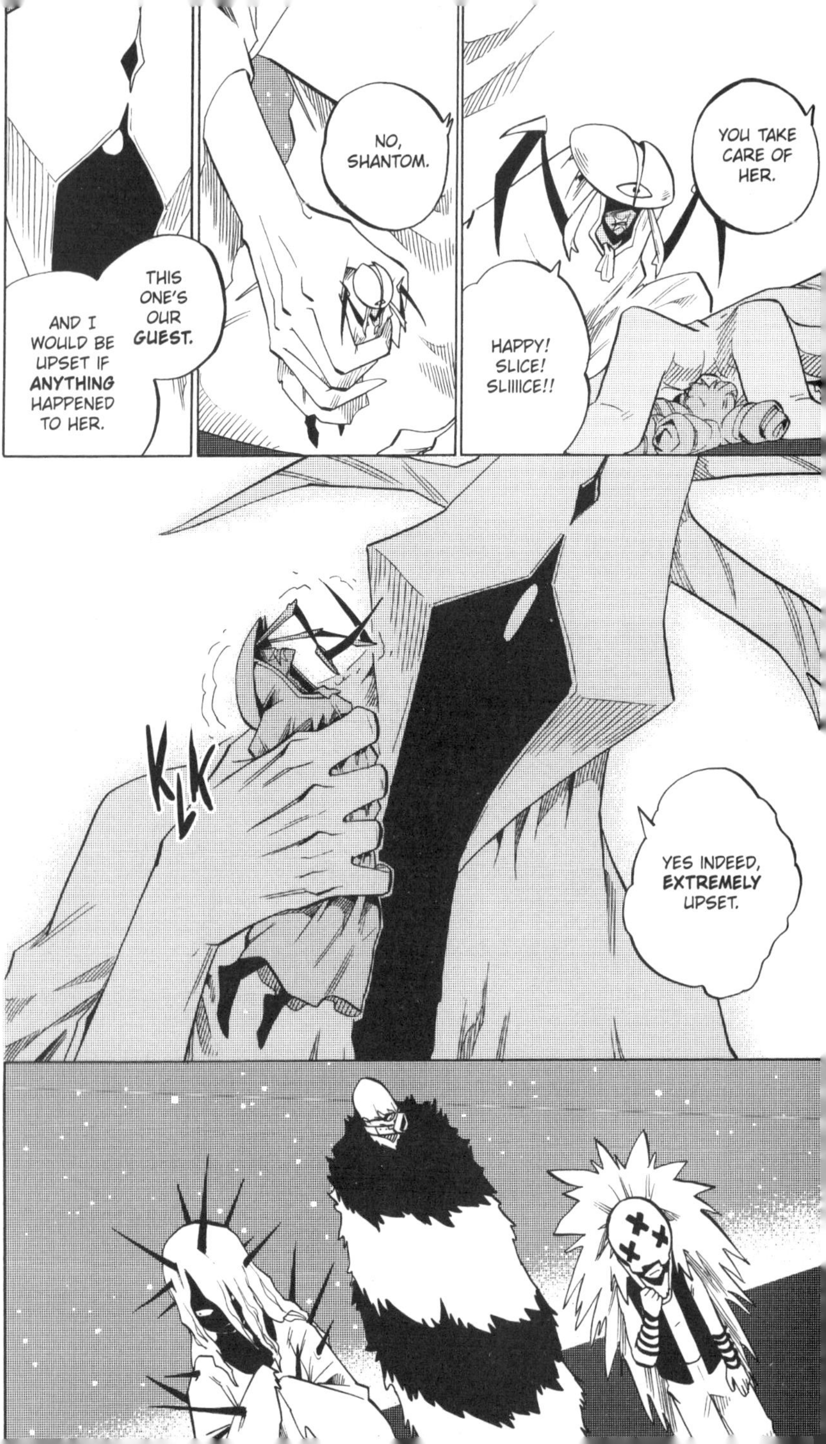
YOU TAKE CARE OF HER.
HAPPY! SLICE! SLIIIICE!!
NO, SHANTOM.
THIS ONE'S OUR GUEST.
AND I WOULD BE UPSET IF ANYTHING HAPPENED TO HER.
KLK
YES INDEED, EXTREMELY UPSET.

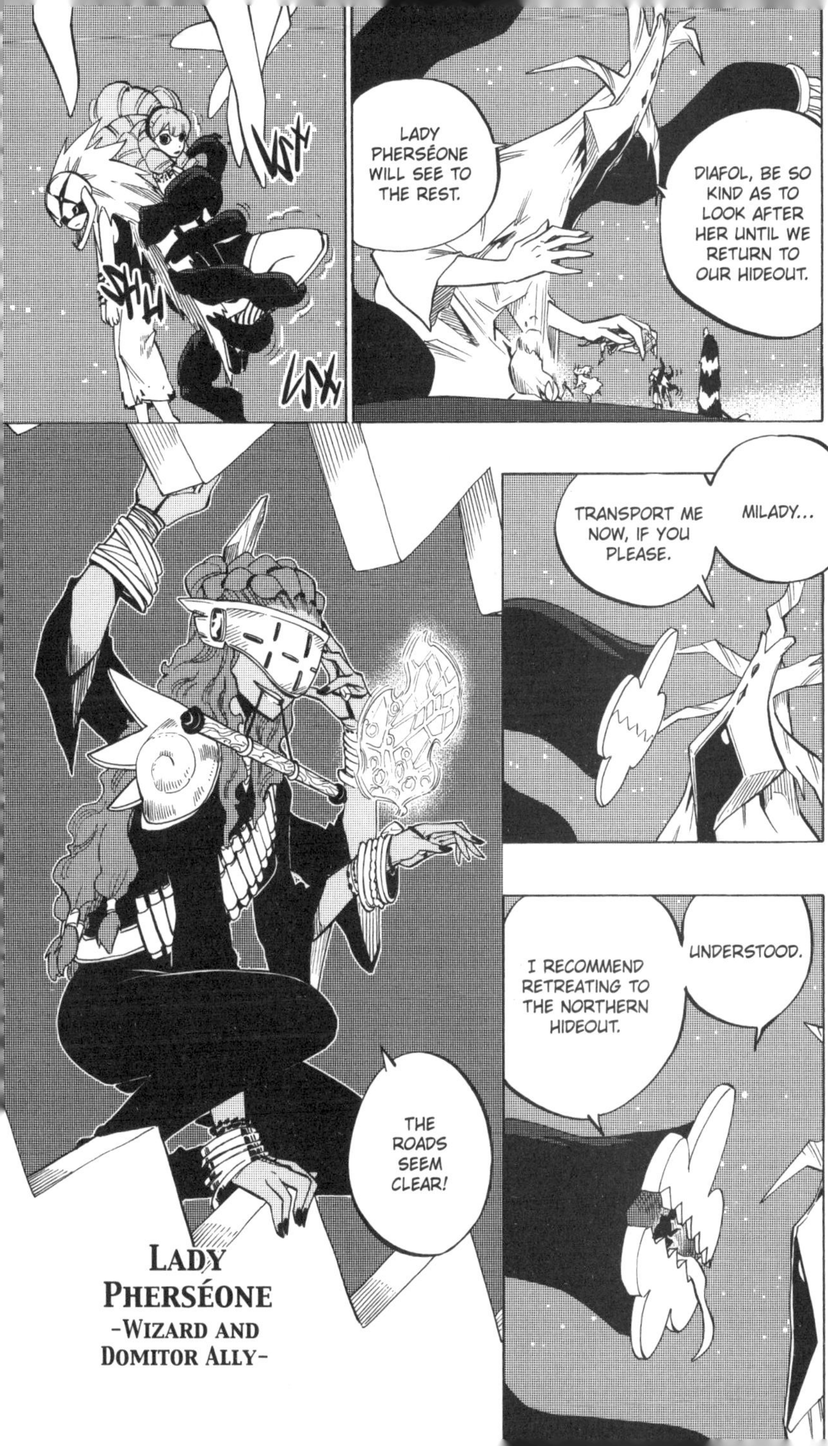
DIAFOL, BE SO KIND AS TO LOOK AFTER HER UNTIL WE RETURN TO OUR HIDEOUT.
LADY PHERSÉONE WILL SEE TO THE REST.
MILADY...
TRANSPORT ME NOW, IF YOU PLEASE.
UNDERSTOOD.
I RECOMMEND RETREATING TO THE NORTHERN HIDEOUT.
THE ROADS SEEM CLEAR!
LADY PHERSÉONE
-WIZARD AND DOMITOR ALLY-

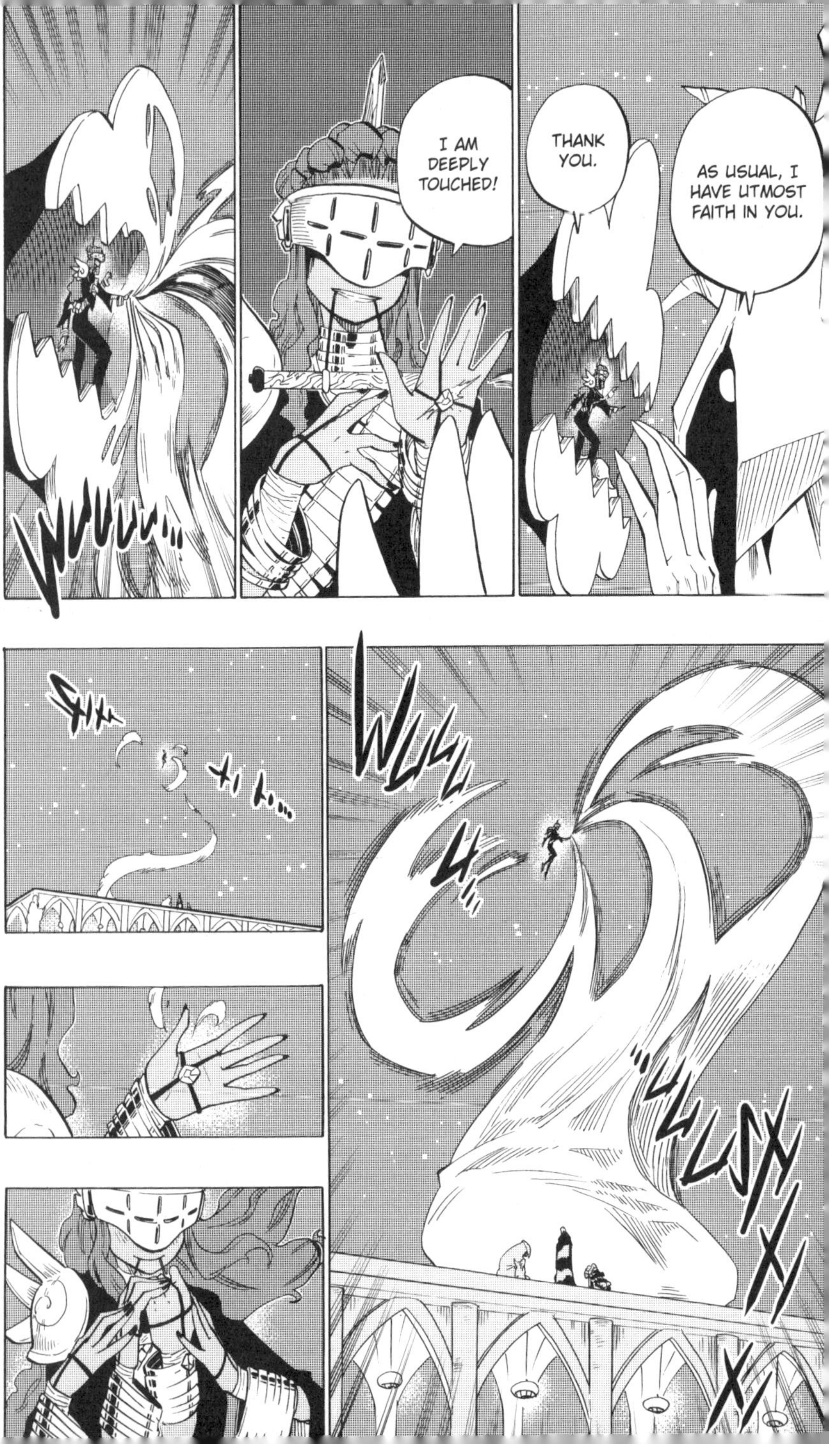
AS USUAL, I HAVE UTMOST FAITH IN YOU.
THANK YOU.
I AM DEEPLY TOUCHED!

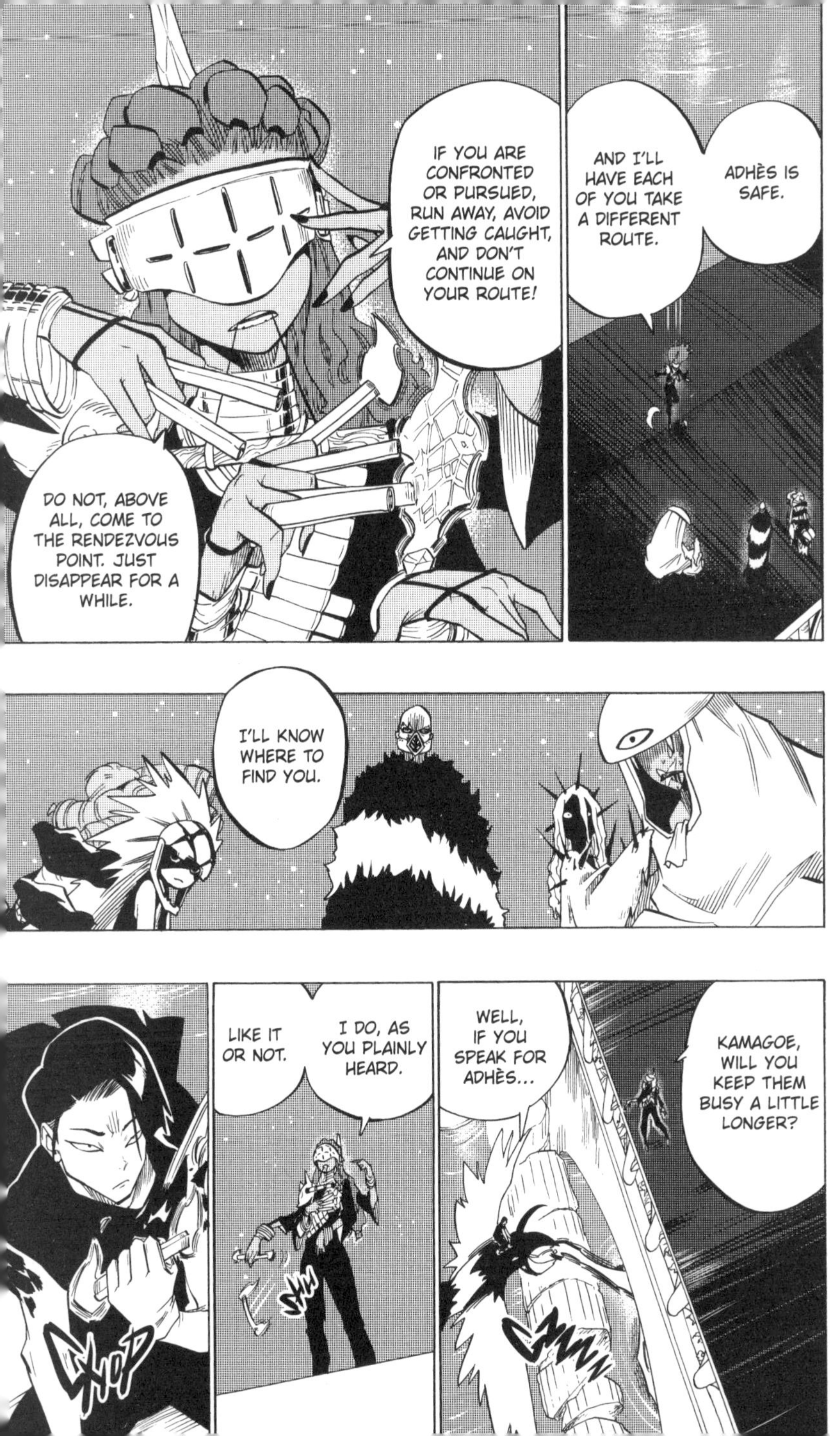
ADHÈS IS SAFE.
AND I'LL HAVE EACH OF YOU TAKE A DIFFERENT ROUTE.
IF YOU ARE CONFRONTED OR PURSUED, RUN AWAY, AVOID GETTING CAUGHT, AND DON'T CONTINUE ON YOUR ROUTE!
DO NOT, ABOVE ALL, COME TO THE RENDEZVOUS POINT. JUST DISAPPEAR FOR A WHILE.
I'LL KNOW WHERE TO FIND YOU.
KAMAGOE, WILL YOU KEEP THEM BUSY A LITTLE LONGER?
WELL, IF YOU SPEAK FOR ADHÈS...
I DO, AS YOU PLAINLY HEARD.
LIKE IT OR NOT.

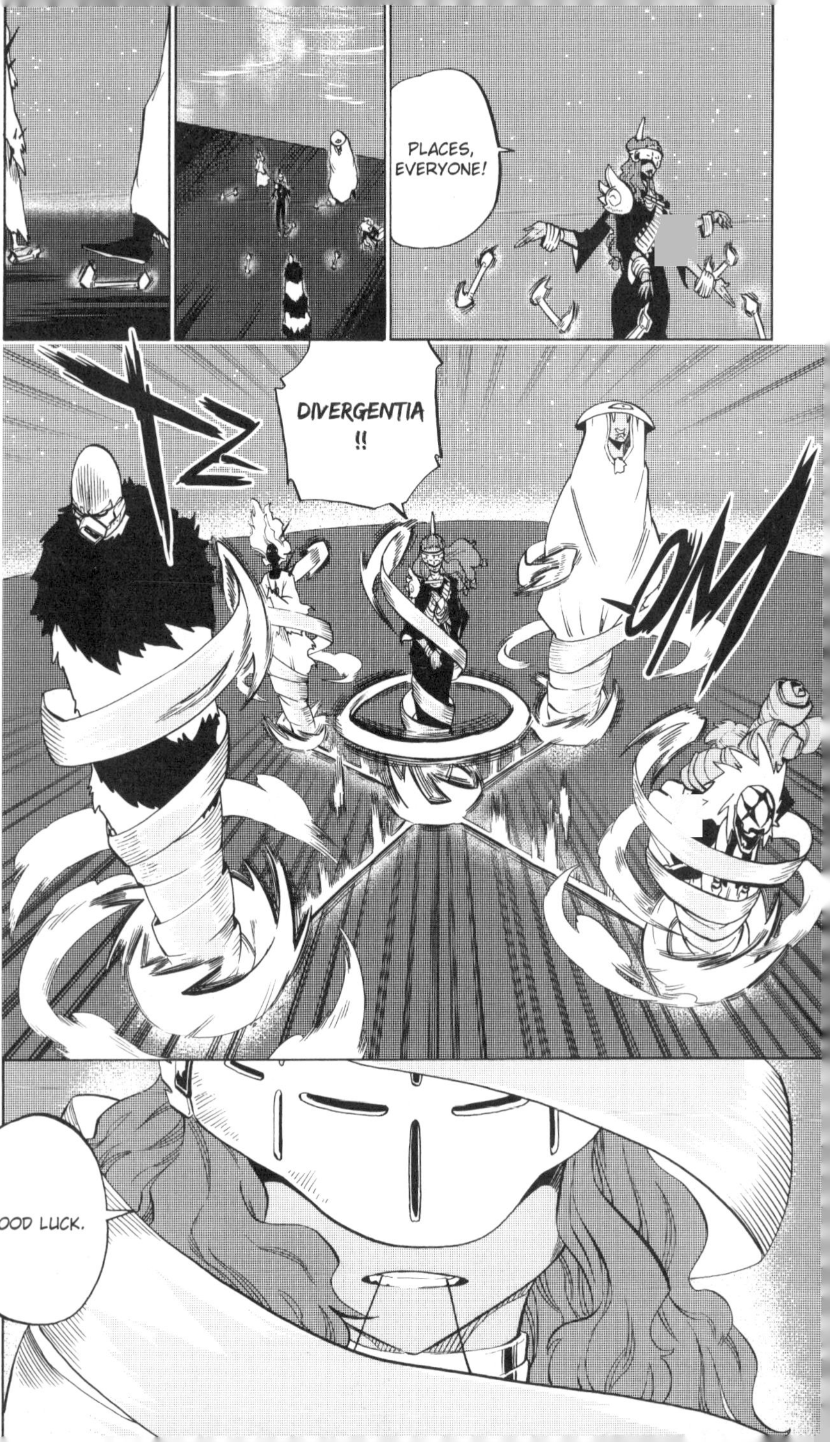
PLACES, EVERYONE!
DIVERGENTIA !!
GOOD LUCK.

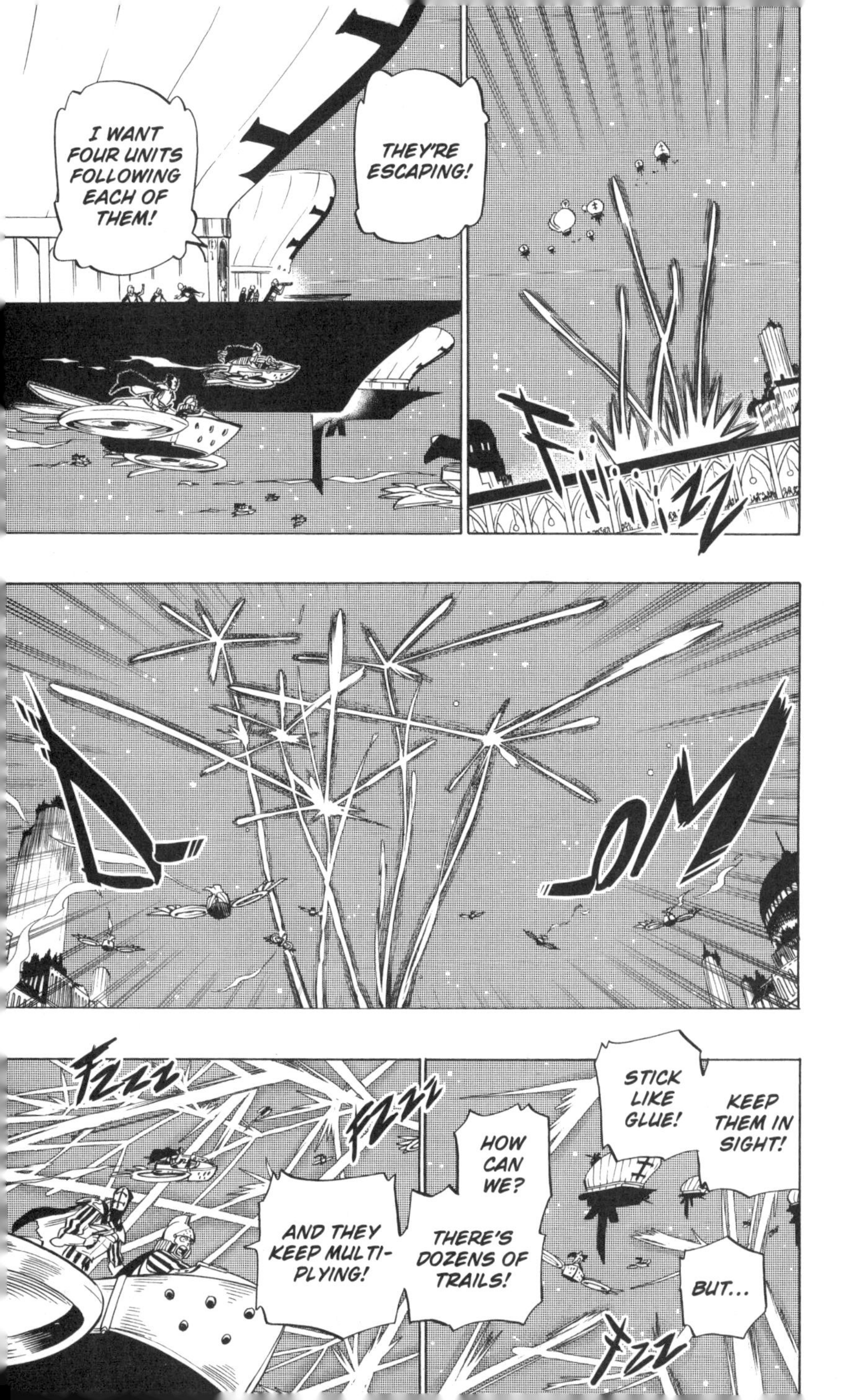
FIIIIZZ
THEY'RE ESCAPING!
I WANT FOUR UNITS FOLLOWING EACH OF THEM!
DOOM
KEEP THEM IN SIGHT!
STICK LIKE GLUE!
BUT...
FZZ
HOW CAN WE?
THERE'S DOZENS OF TRAILS!
AND THEY KEEP MULTI-PLYING!
FZZZ
FZZZ

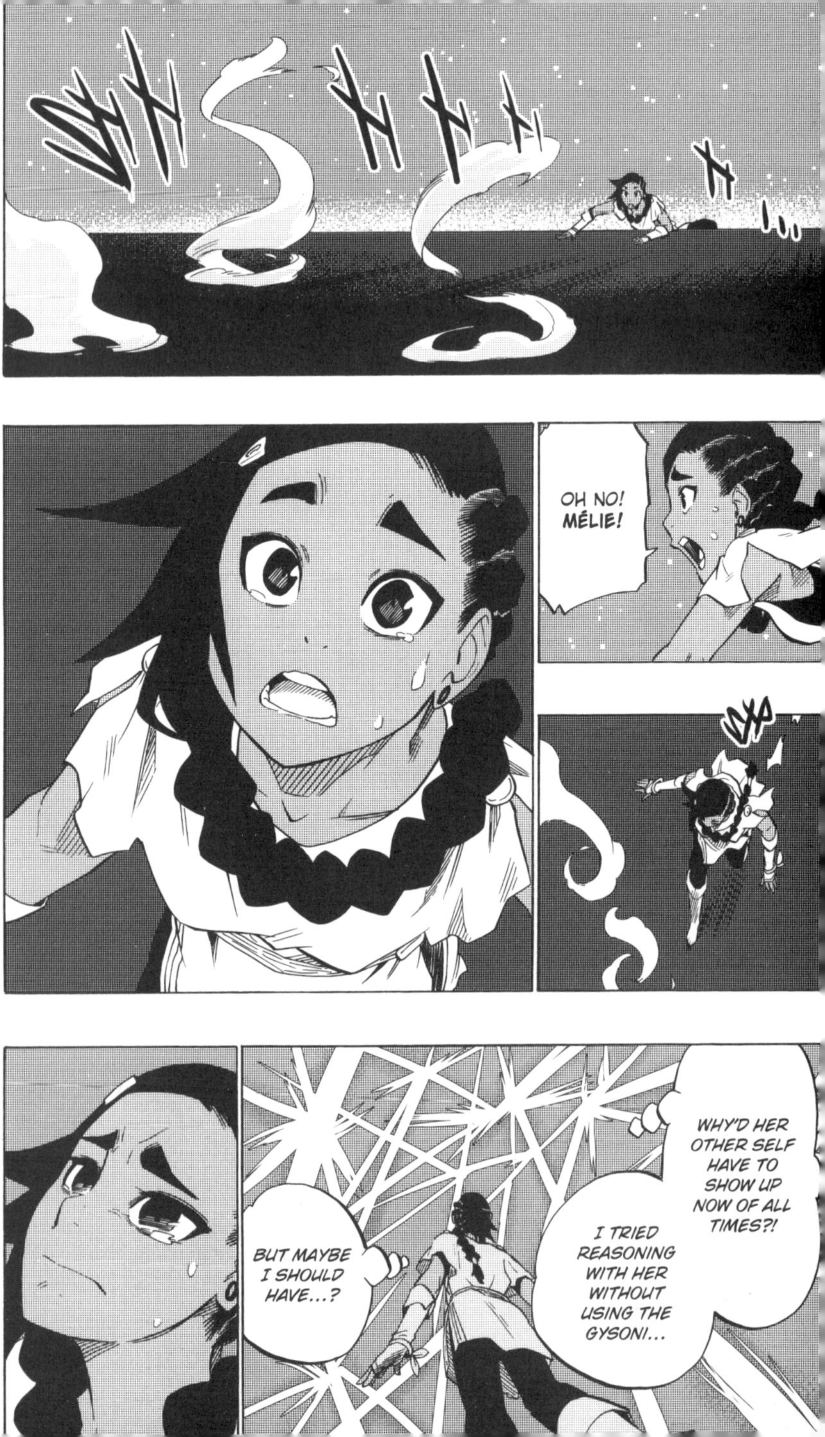
OH NO! MÉLIE!
WHY'D HER OTHER SELF HAVE TO SHOW UP NOW OF ALL TIMES?!
I TRIED REASONING WITH HER WITHOUT USING THE GYSONI...
BUT MAYBE I SHOULD HAVE...?

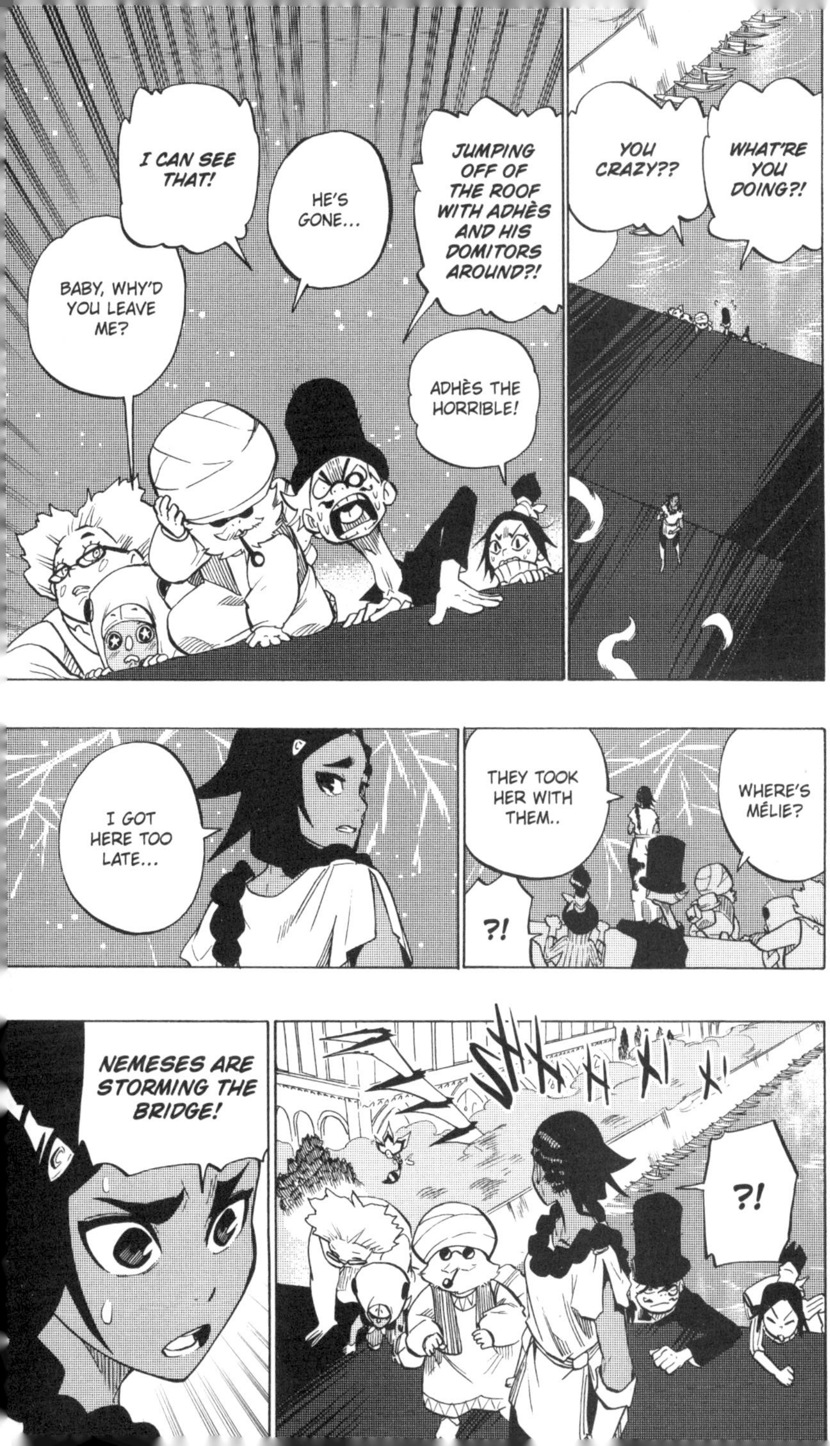
WHAT'RE YOU DOING?!
YOU CRAZY??
JUMPING OFF OF THE ROOF WITH ADHÈS AND HIS DOMITORS AROUND?!
ADHÈS THE HORRIBLE!
HE'S GONE...
I CAN SEE THAT!
BABY, WHY'D YOU LEAVE ME?
WHERE'S MÉLIE?
THEY TOOK HER WITH THEM..
?!
I GOT HERE TOO LATE...
?!
NEMESES ARE STORMING THE BRIDGE!

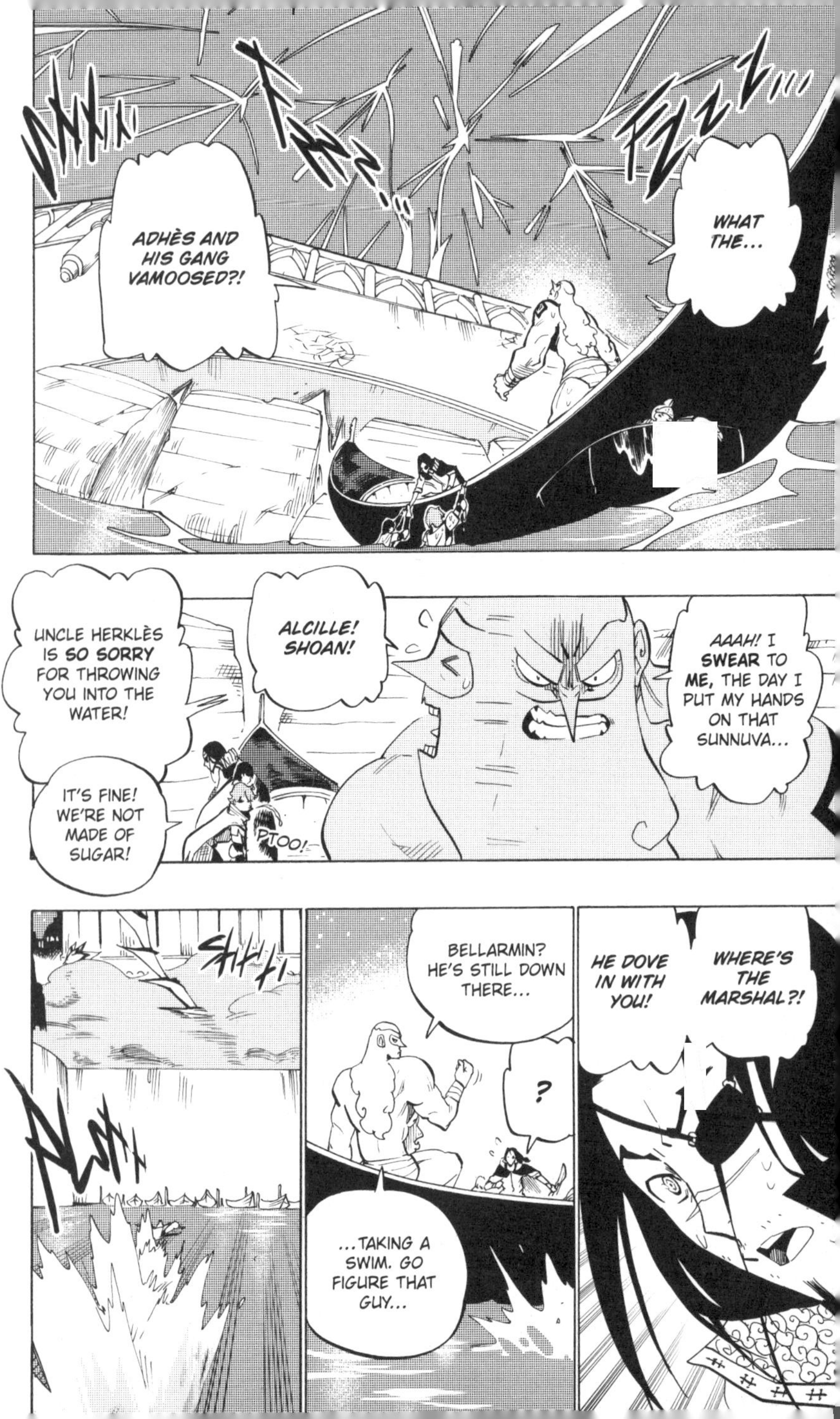
WHAT THE...
ADHÈS AND HIS GANG VAMOOSED?!
AAAH! I SWEAR TO ME, THE DAY I PUT MY HANDS ON THAT SUNNUVA...
ALCILLE! SHOAN!
UNCLE HERKLÈS IS SO SORRY FOR THROWING YOU INTO THE WATER!
IT'S FINE! WE'RE NOT MADE OF SUGAR!
PTOO!
WHERE'S THE MARSHAL?!
HE DOVE IN WITH YOU!
BELLARMIN? HE'S STILL DOWN THERE...
?
...TAKING A SWIM. GO FIGURE THAT GUY...

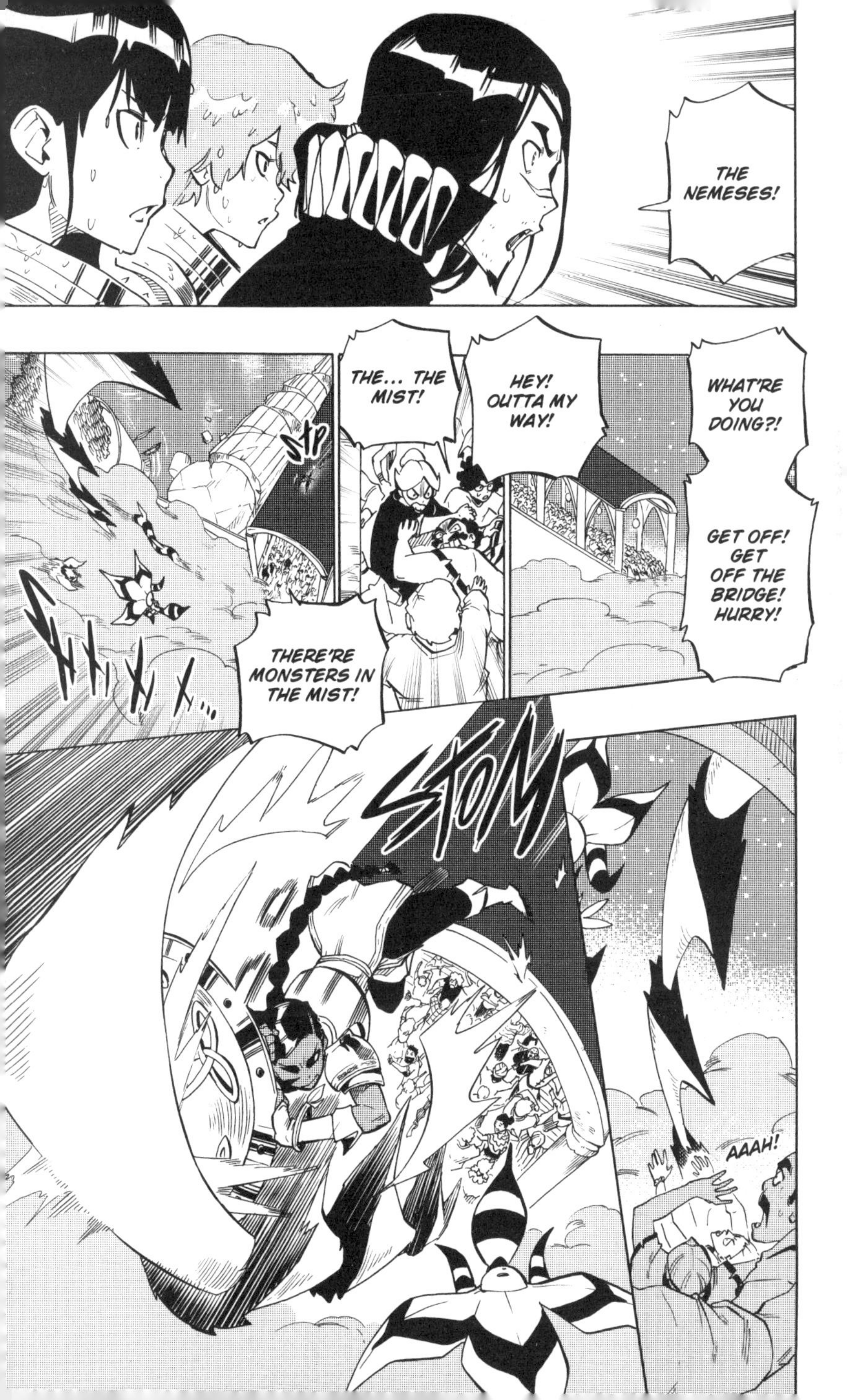
THE NEMESES!
WHAT'RE YOU DOING?!
GET OFF! GET OFF THE BRIDGE! HURRY!
HEY! OUTTA MY WAY!
THE... THE MIST!
THERE'RE MONSTERS IN THE MIST!
STP
STOM
AAAH!

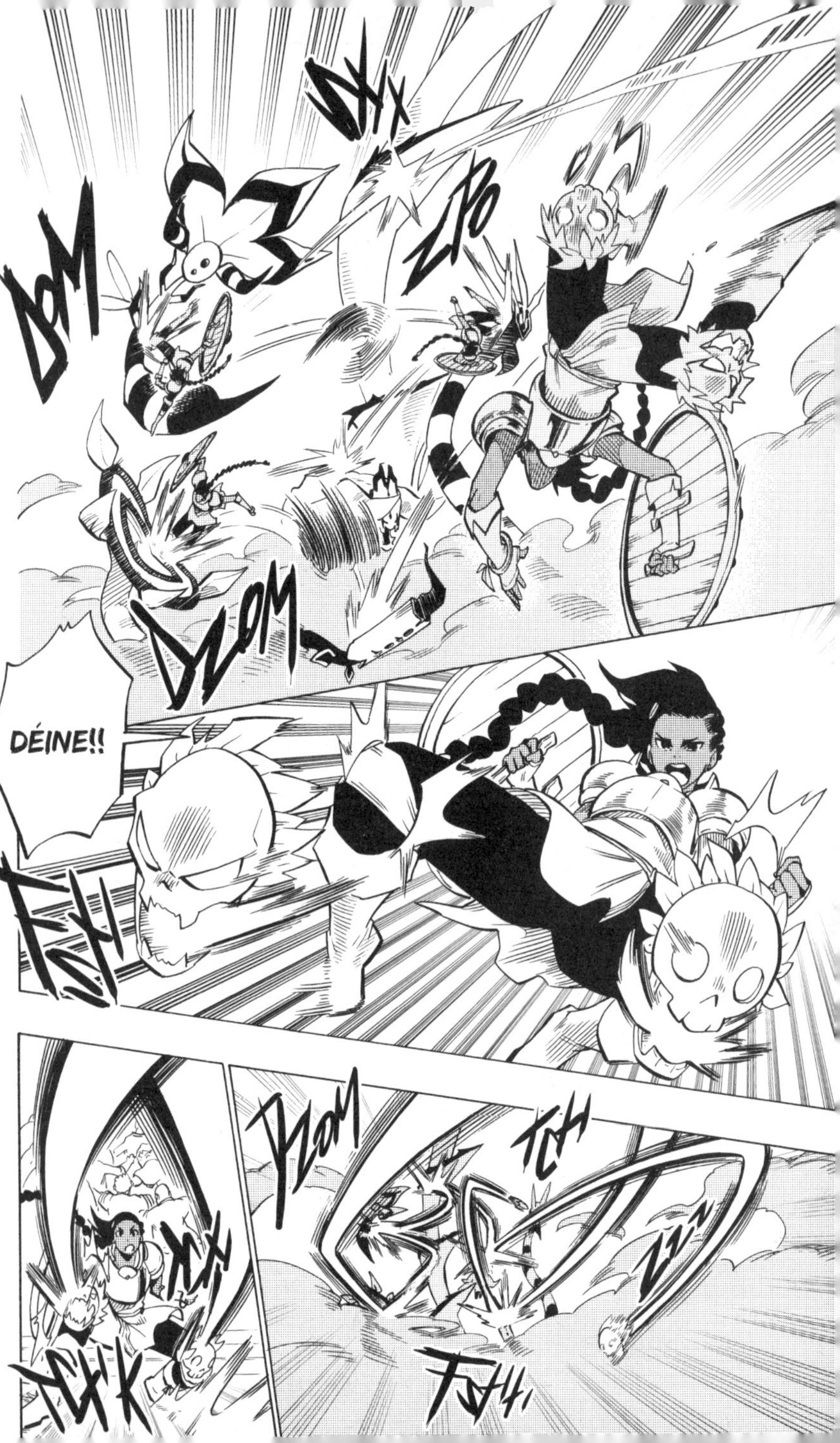
DOM
DZOM
DÉINE!!
DZOM
TCH

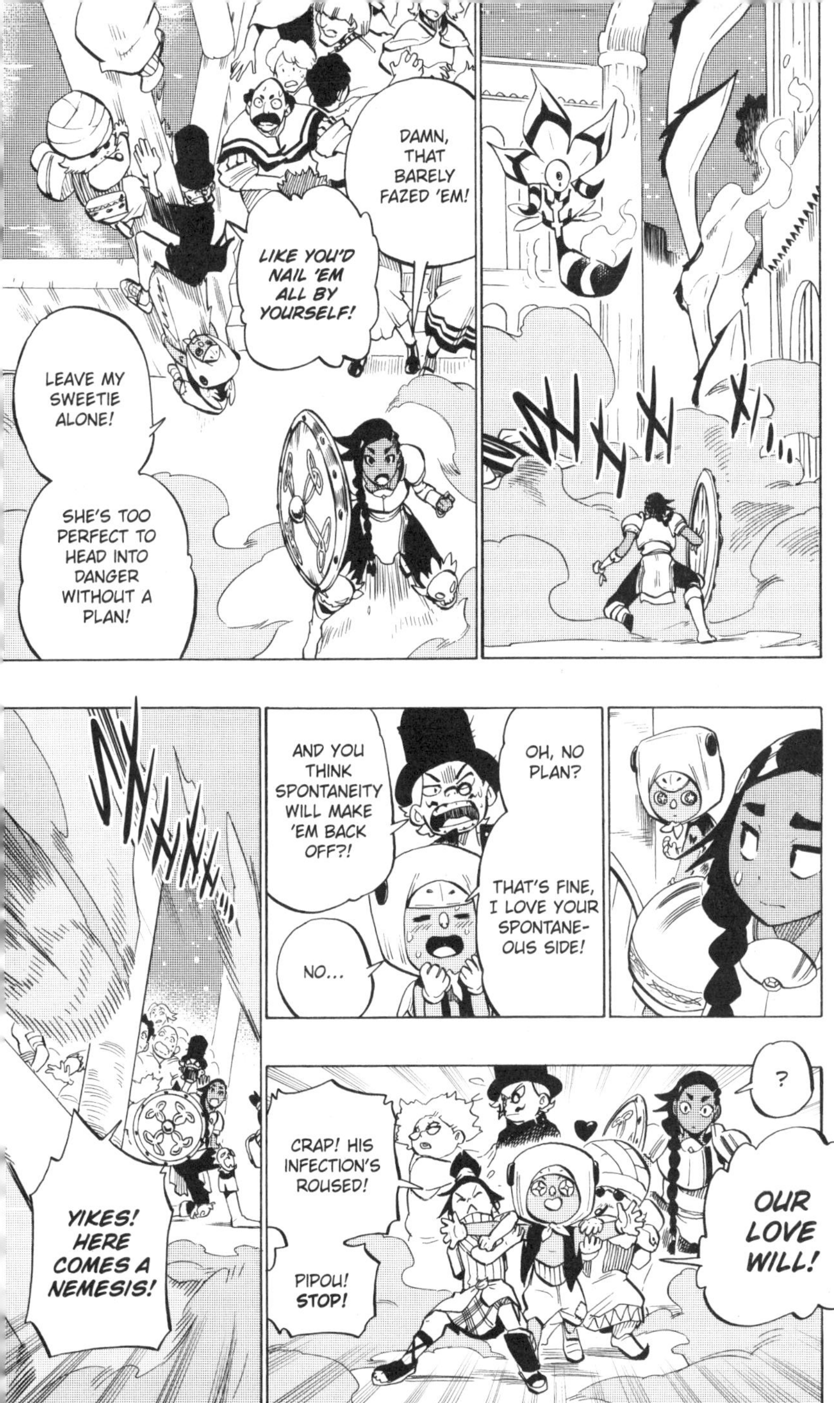
DAMN, THAT BARELY FAZED 'EM!
LIKE YOU'D NAIL 'EM ALL BY YOURSELF!
LEAVE MY SWEETIE ALONE!
SHE'S TOO PERFECT TO HEAD INTO DANGER WITHOUT A PLAN!
OH, NO PLAN?
AND YOU THINK SPONTANEITY WILL MAKE 'EM BACK OFF?!
THAT'S FINE, I LOVE YOUR SPONTANE-OUS SIDE!
NO...
?
OUR LOVE WILL!
CRAP! HIS INFECTION'S ROUSED!
PIPOU! STOP!
YIKES! HERE COMES A NEMESIS!

SETH'S
IMAGINATION...

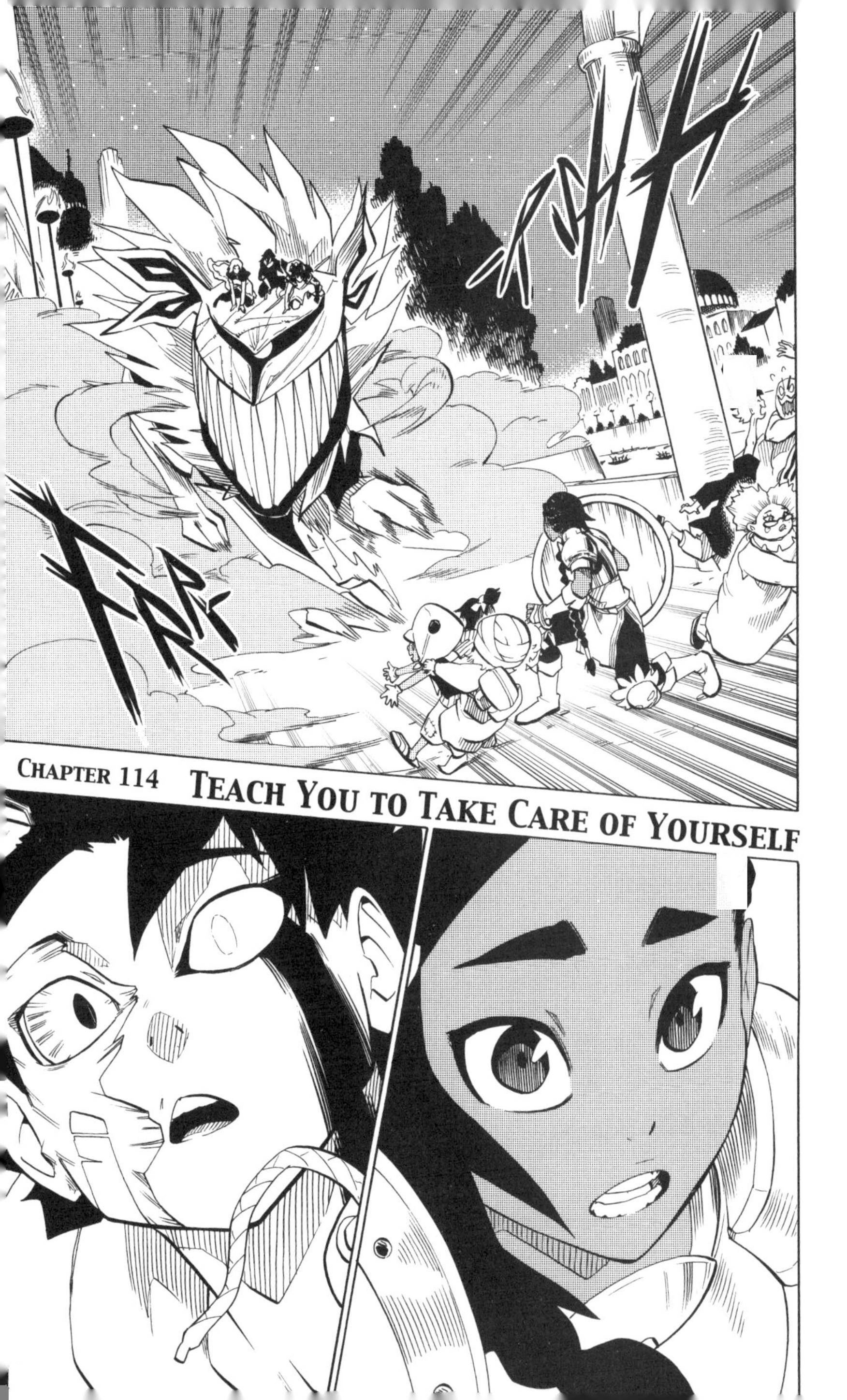
Chapter 114 Teach You to Take Care of Yourself

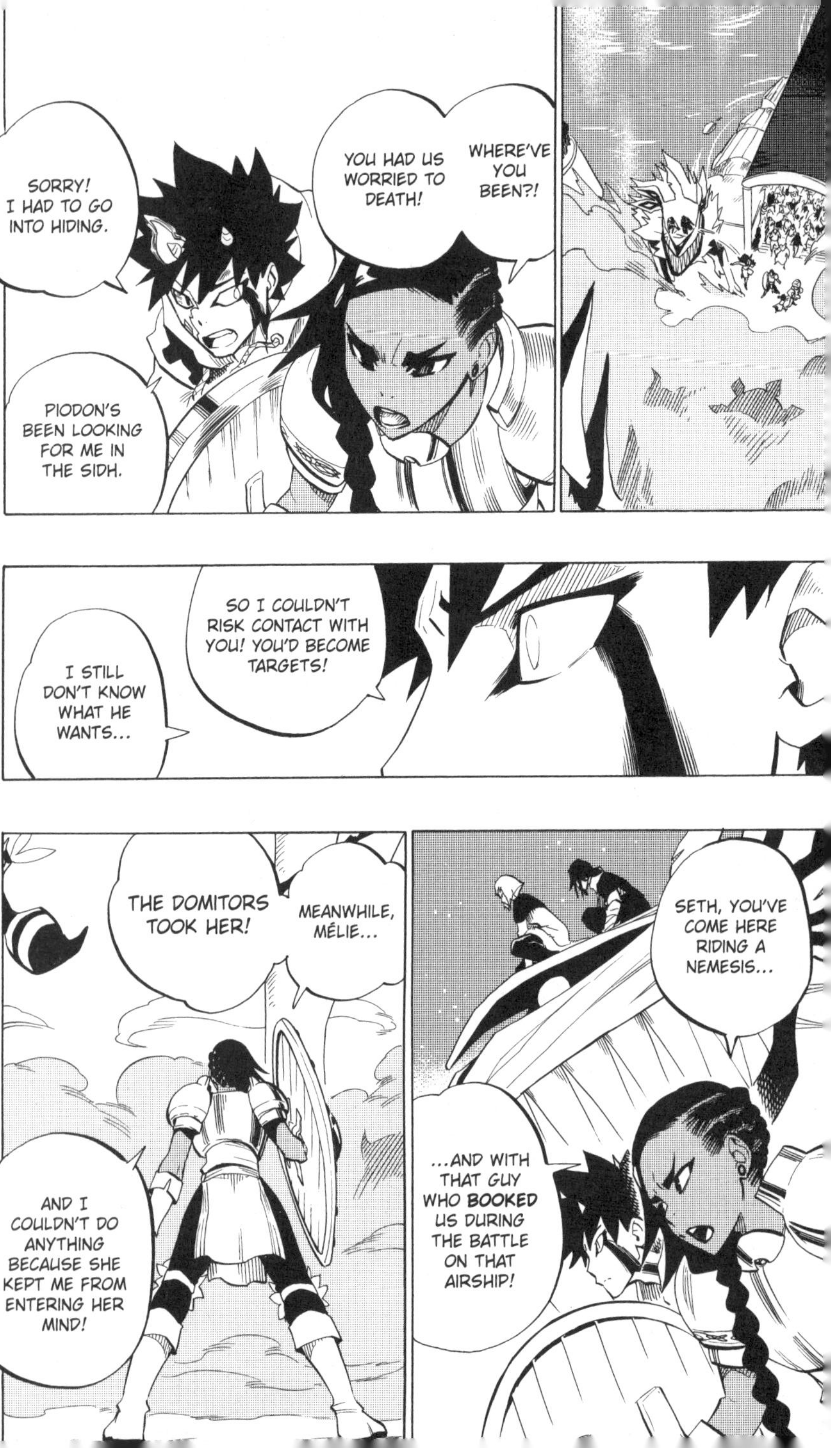
WHERE'VE YOU BEEN?!
YOU HAD US WORRIED TO DEATH!
SORRY! I HAD TO GO INTO HIDING.
PIODON'S BEEN LOOKING FOR ME IN THE SIDH.
SO I COULDN'T RISK CONTACT WITH YOU! YOU'D BECOME TARGETS!
I STILL DON'T KNOW WHAT HE WANTS...
SETH, YOU'VE COME HERE RIDING A NEMESIS...
...AND WITH THAT GUY WHO **BOOKED** US DURING THE BATTLE ON THAT AIRSHIP!
MEANWHILE, MÉLIE...
THE DOMITORS TOOK HER!
AND I COULDN'T DO ANYTHING BECAUSE SHE KEPT ME FROM ENTERING HER MIND!

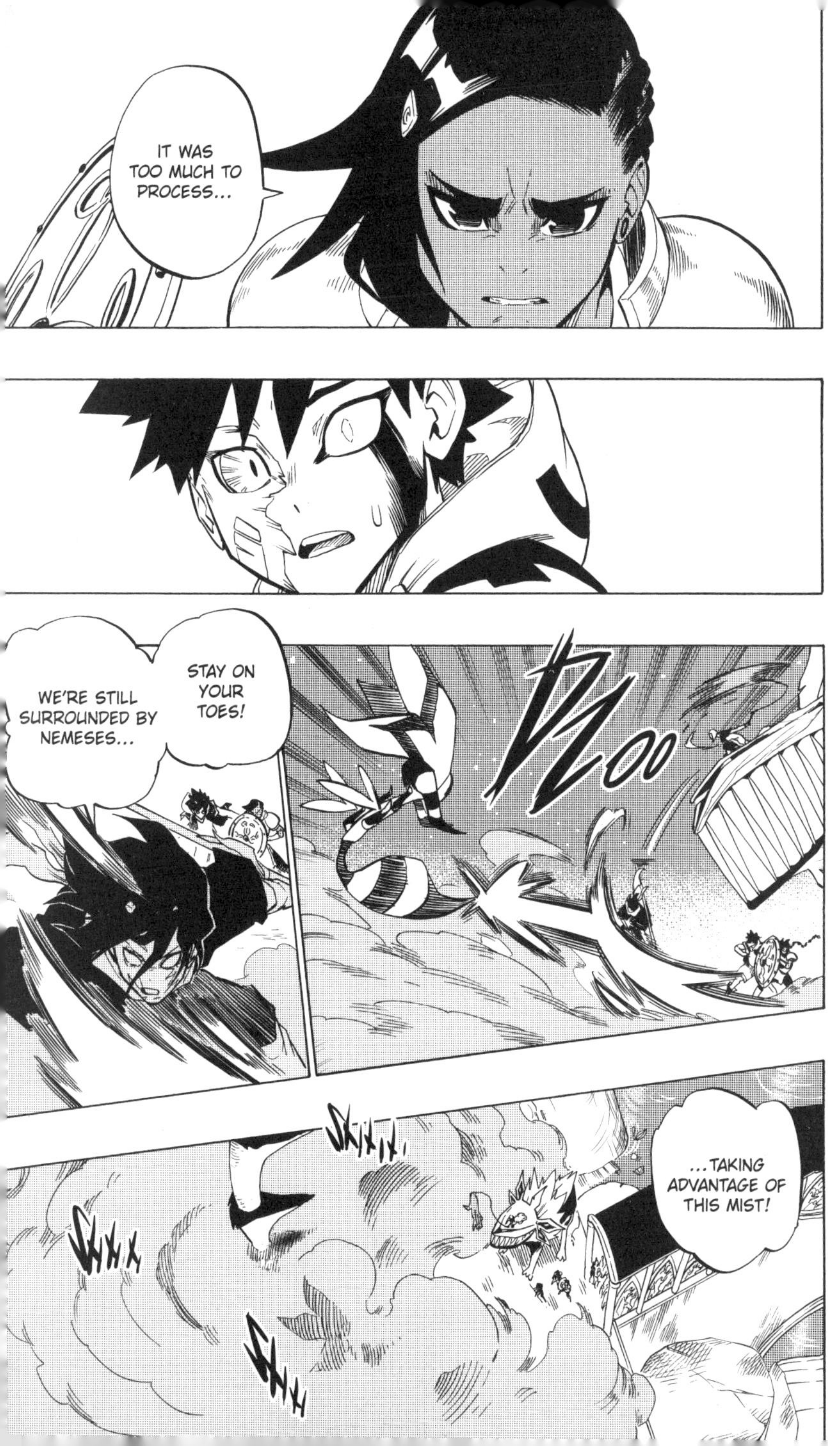
IT WAS TOO MUCH TO PROCESS...
STAY ON YOUR TOES!
WE'RE STILL SURROUNDED BY NEMESES...
...TAKING ADVANTAGE OF THIS MIST!

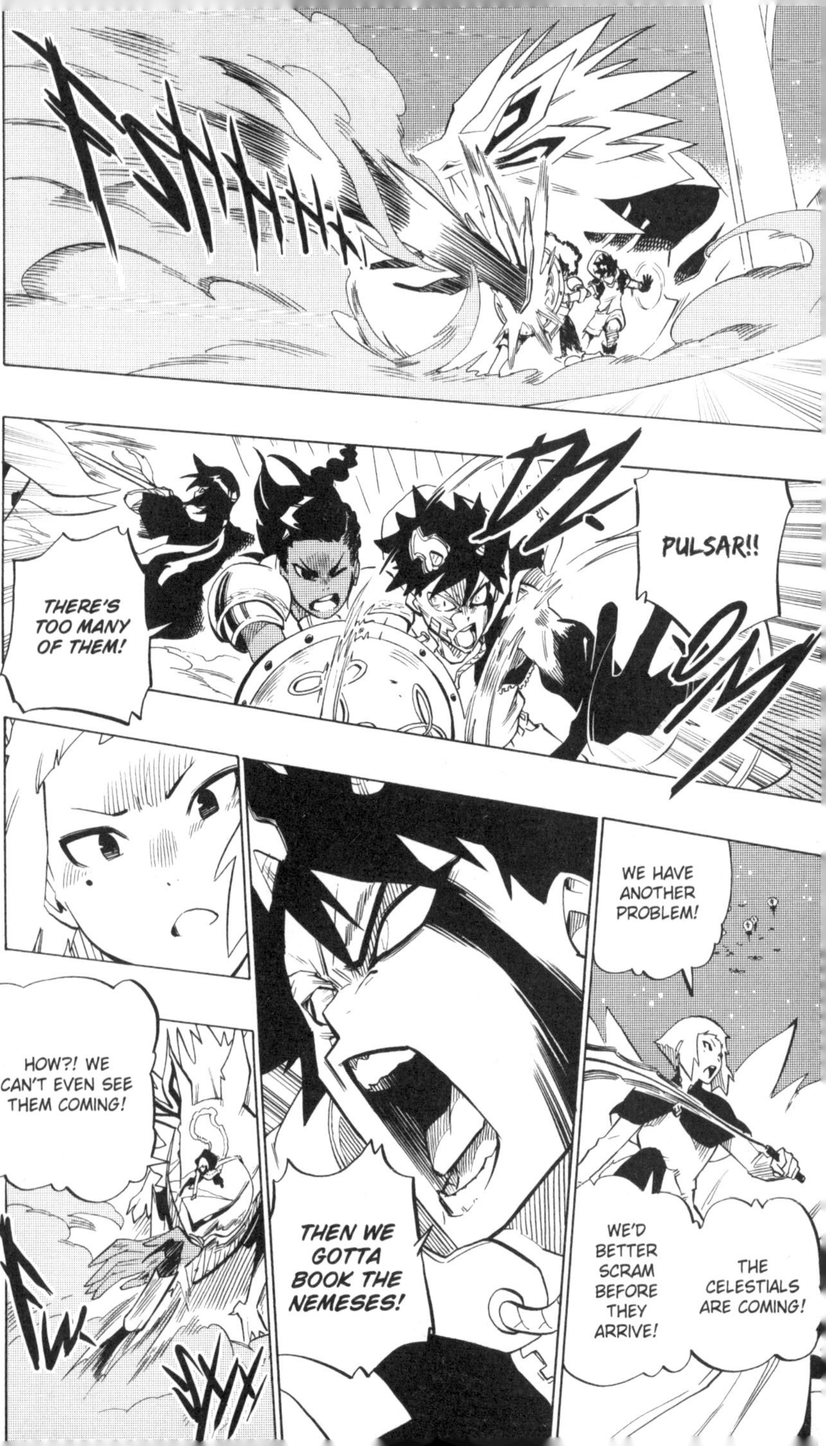
PULSAR!!
THERE'S TOO MANY OF THEM!
WE HAVE ANOTHER PROBLEM!
THE CELESTIALS ARE COMING!
WE'D BETTER SCRAM BEFORE THEY ARRIVE!
THEN WE GOTTA BOOK THE NEMESES!
HOW?! WE CAN'T EVEN SEE THEM COMING!

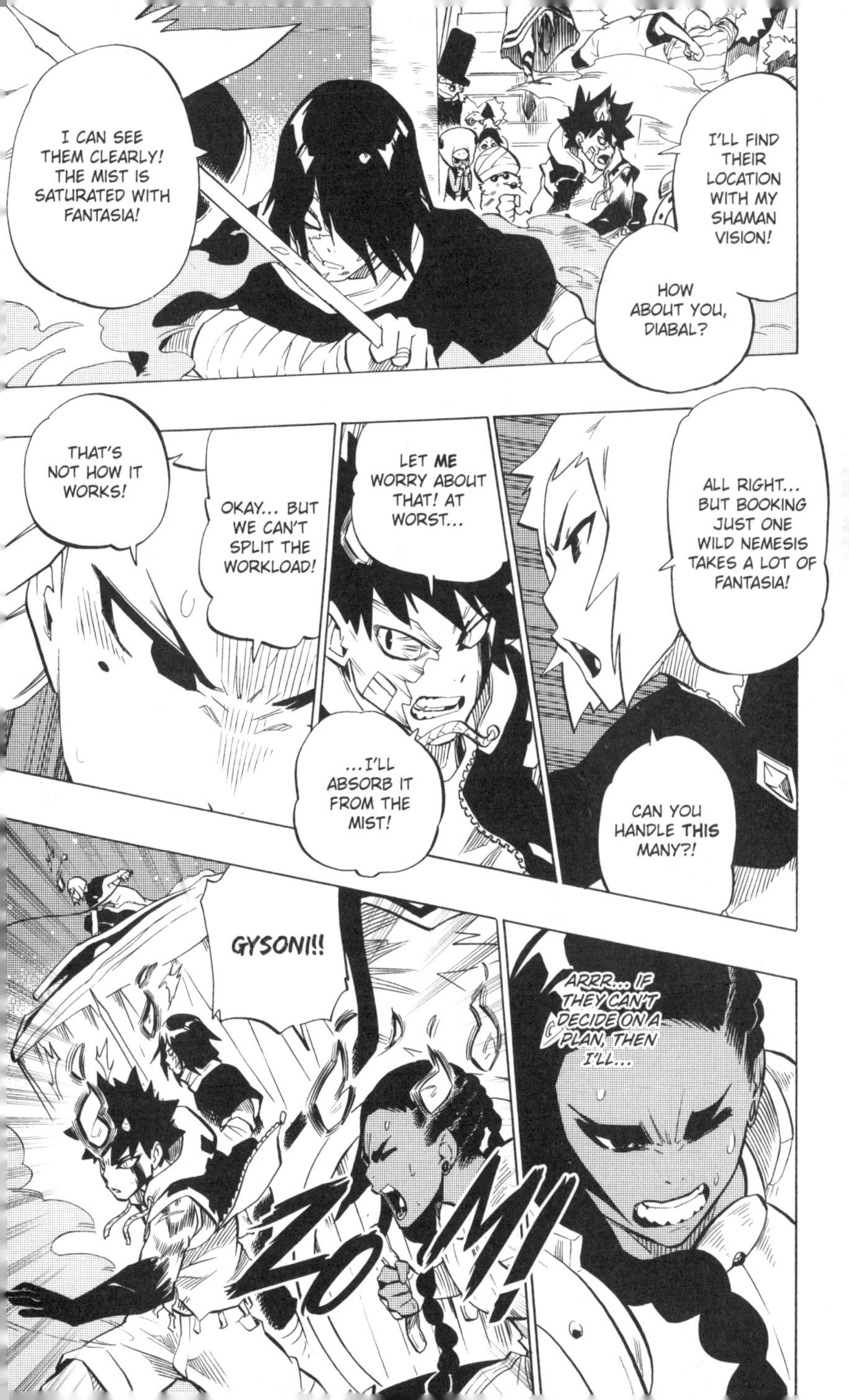
I'LL FIND THEIR LOCATION WITH MY SHAMAN VISION!
HOW ABOUT YOU, DIABAL?
I CAN SEE THEM CLEARLY! THE MIST IS SATURATED WITH FANTASIA!
ALL RIGHT... BUT BOOKING JUST ONE WILD NEMESIS TAKES A LOT OF FANTASIA!
CAN YOU HANDLE THIS MANY?!
LET ME WORRY ABOUT THAT! AT WORST...
...I'LL ABSORB IT FROM THE MIST!
OKAY... BUT WE CAN'T SPLIT THE WORKLOAD!
THAT'S NOT HOW IT WORKS!
ARRR... IF THEY CAN'T DECIDE ON A PLAN, THEN I'LL...
GYSONI!!
ZOOM!

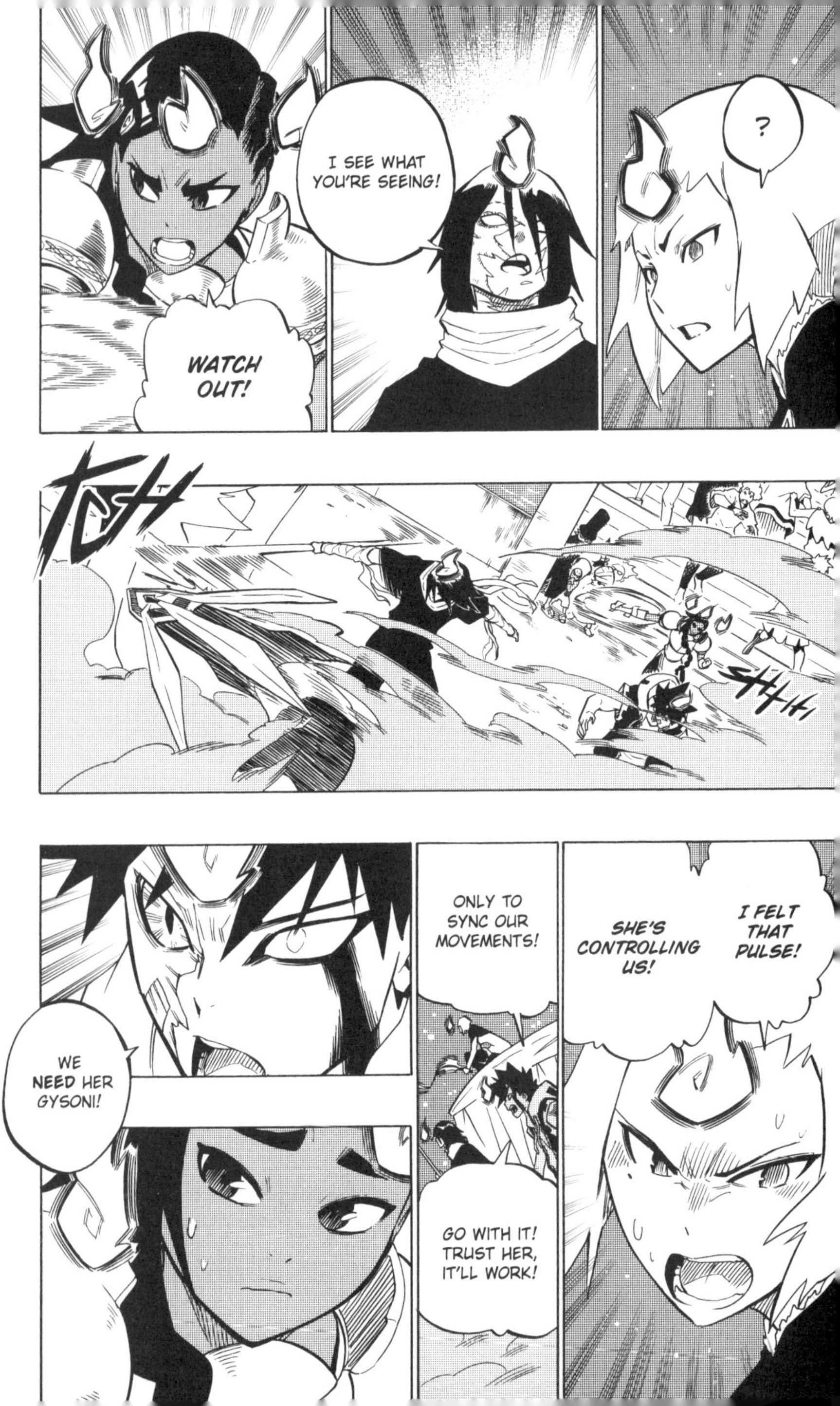
?
I SEE WHAT YOU'RE SEEING!
WATCH OUT!
I FELT THAT PULSE!
SHE'S CONTROLLING US!
ONLY TO SYNC OUR MOVEMENTS!
GO WITH IT! TRUST HER, IT'LL WORK!
WE NEED HER GYSONI!

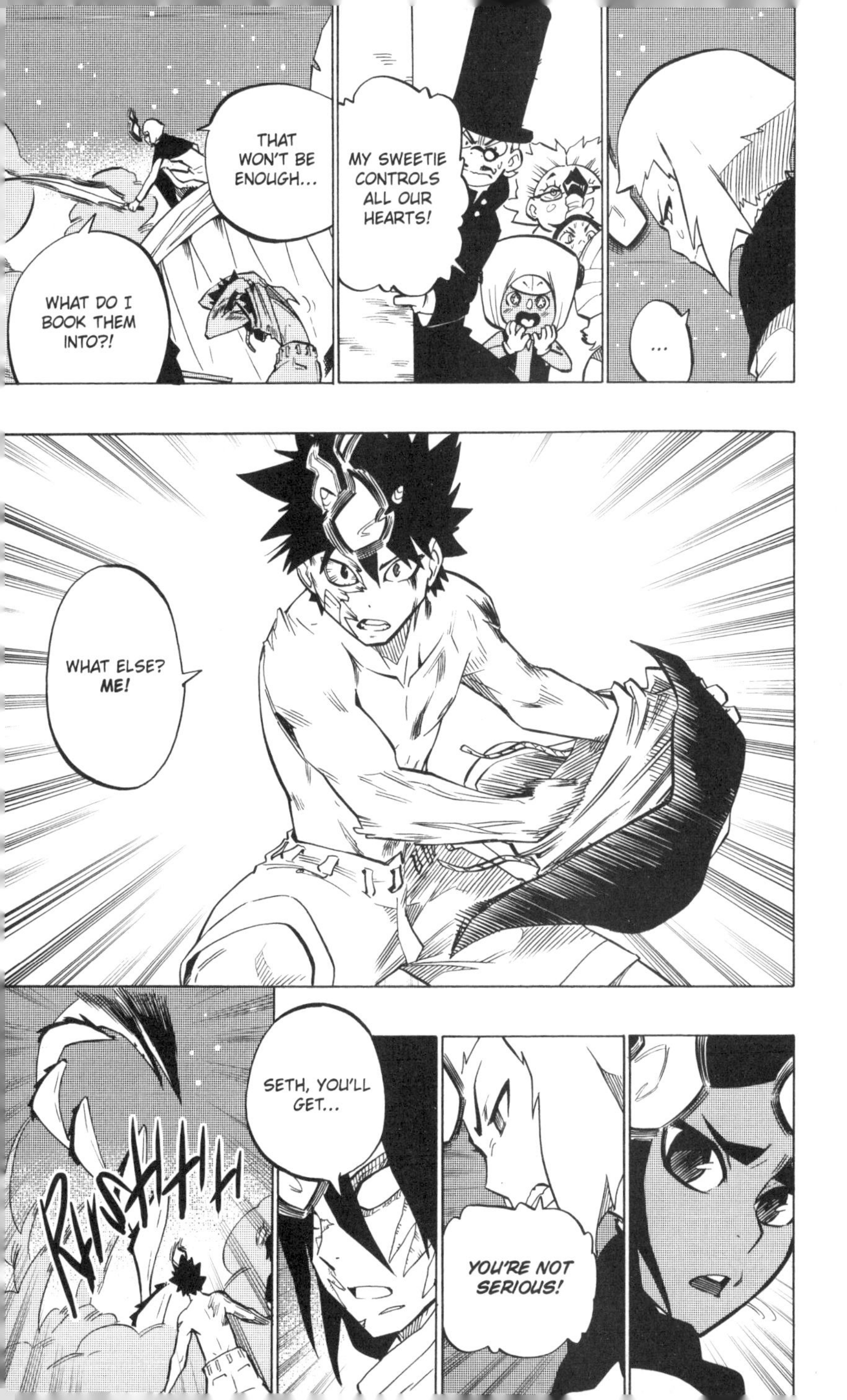
...
MY SWEETIE CONTROLS ALL OUR HEARTS!
THAT WON'T BE ENOUGH...
WHAT DO I BOOK THEM INTO?!
WHAT ELSE? **ME!**
YOU'RE NOT SERIOUS!
SETH, YOU'LL GET...

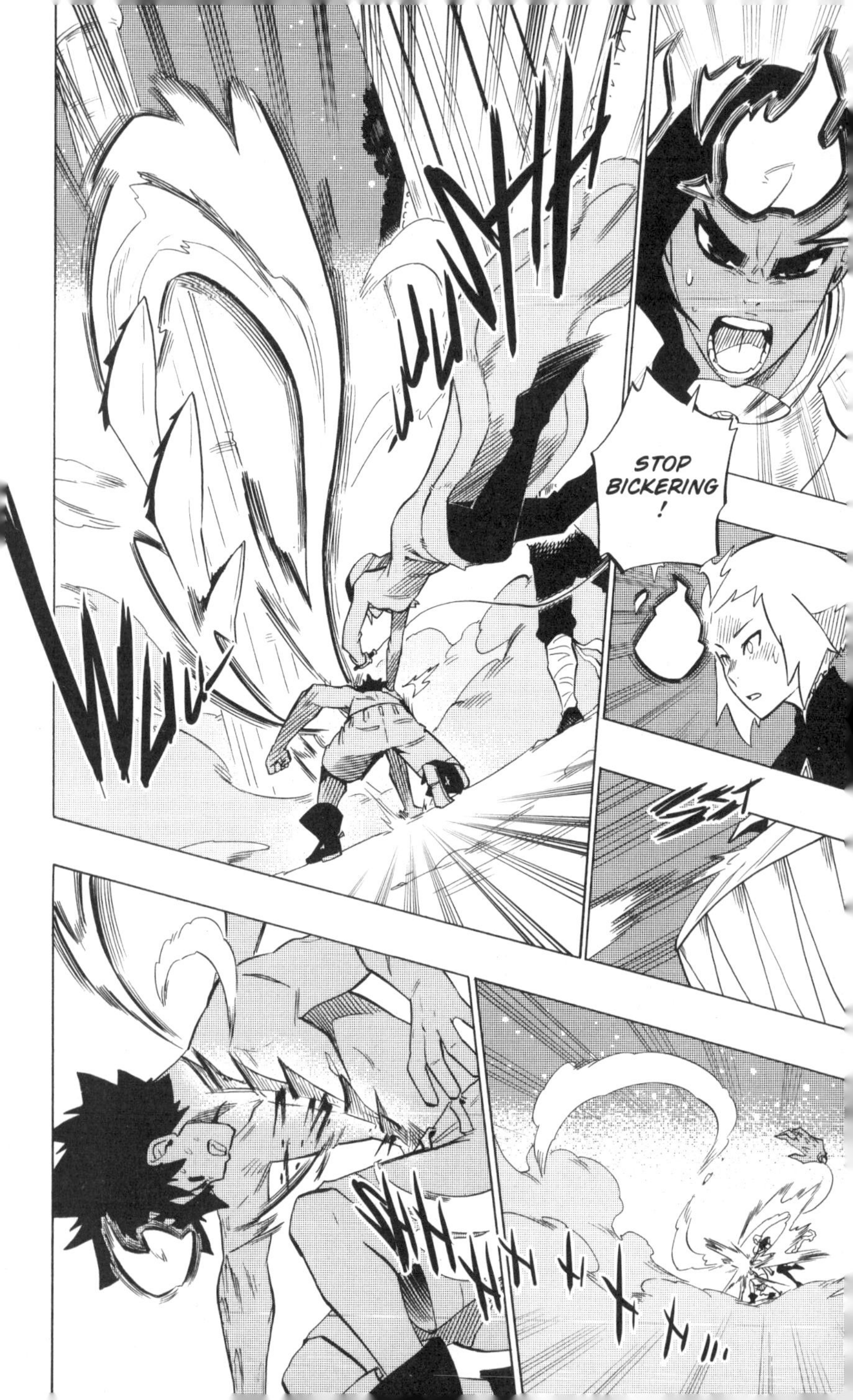
STOP BICKERING!

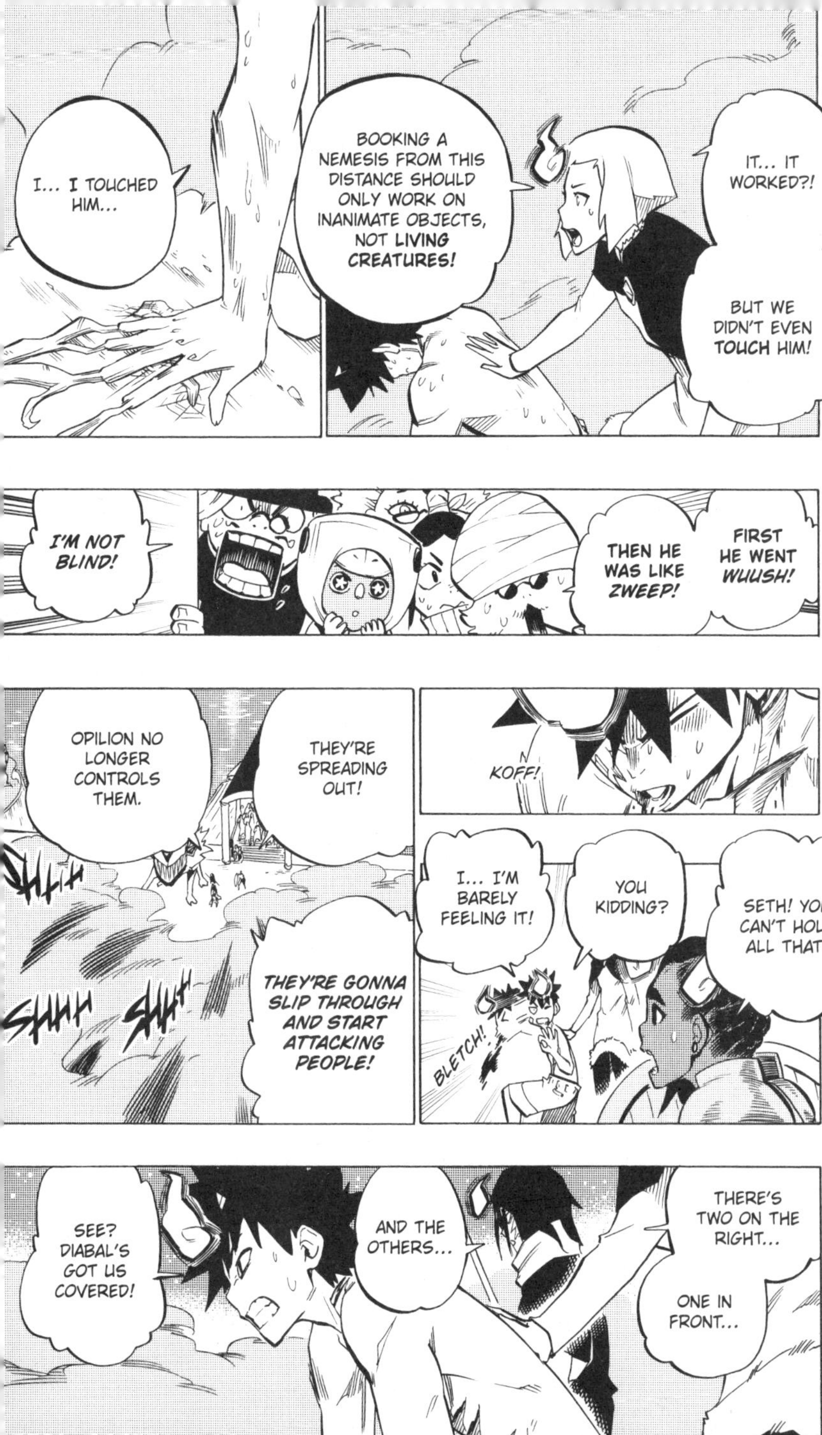
IT... IT WORKED?!
BUT WE DIDN'T EVEN TOUCH HIM!
BOOKING A NEMESIS FROM THIS DISTANCE SHOULD ONLY WORK ON INANIMATE OBJECTS, NOT LIVING CREATURES!
I... I TOUCHED HIM...
FIRST HE WENT WUUSH!
THEN HE WAS LIKE ZWEEP!
I'M NOT BLIND!
KOFF!
SETH! YOU CAN'T HOLD ALL THAT!
YOU KIDDING?
I... I'M BARELY FEELING IT!
BLETCH!
THEY'RE SPREADING OUT!
OPILION NO LONGER CONTROLS THEM.
SHHH
THEY'RE GONNA SLIP THROUGH AND START ATTACKING PEOPLE!
SHHH
SHHH
THERE'S TWO ON THE RIGHT...
ONE IN FRONT...
AND THE OTHERS...
SEE? DIABAL'S GOT US COVERED!

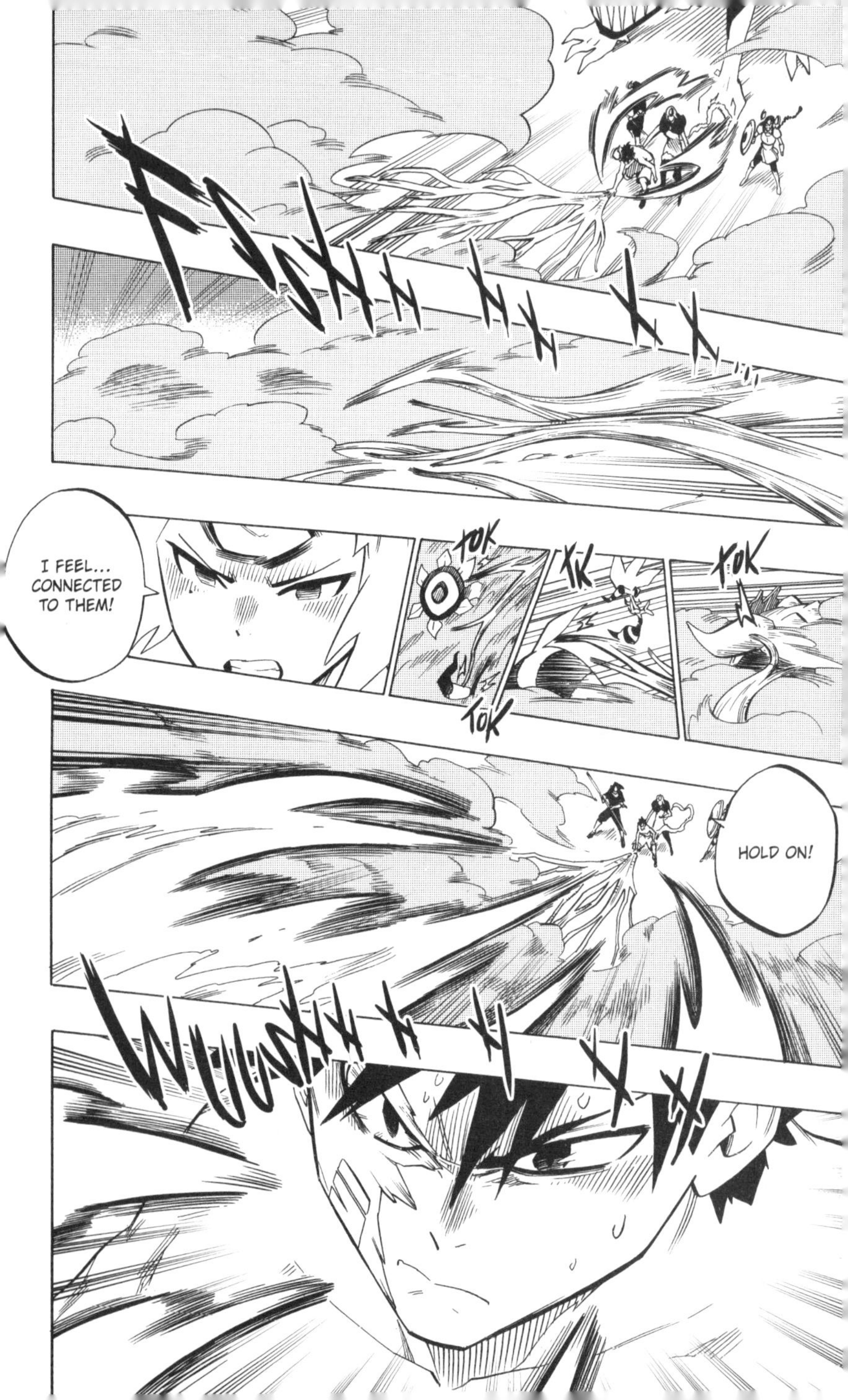
FSSHHHHHH...
YOK
TK
TOK
TOK
I FEEL... CONNECTED TO THEM!
HOLD ON!
WHUSHHHHHH

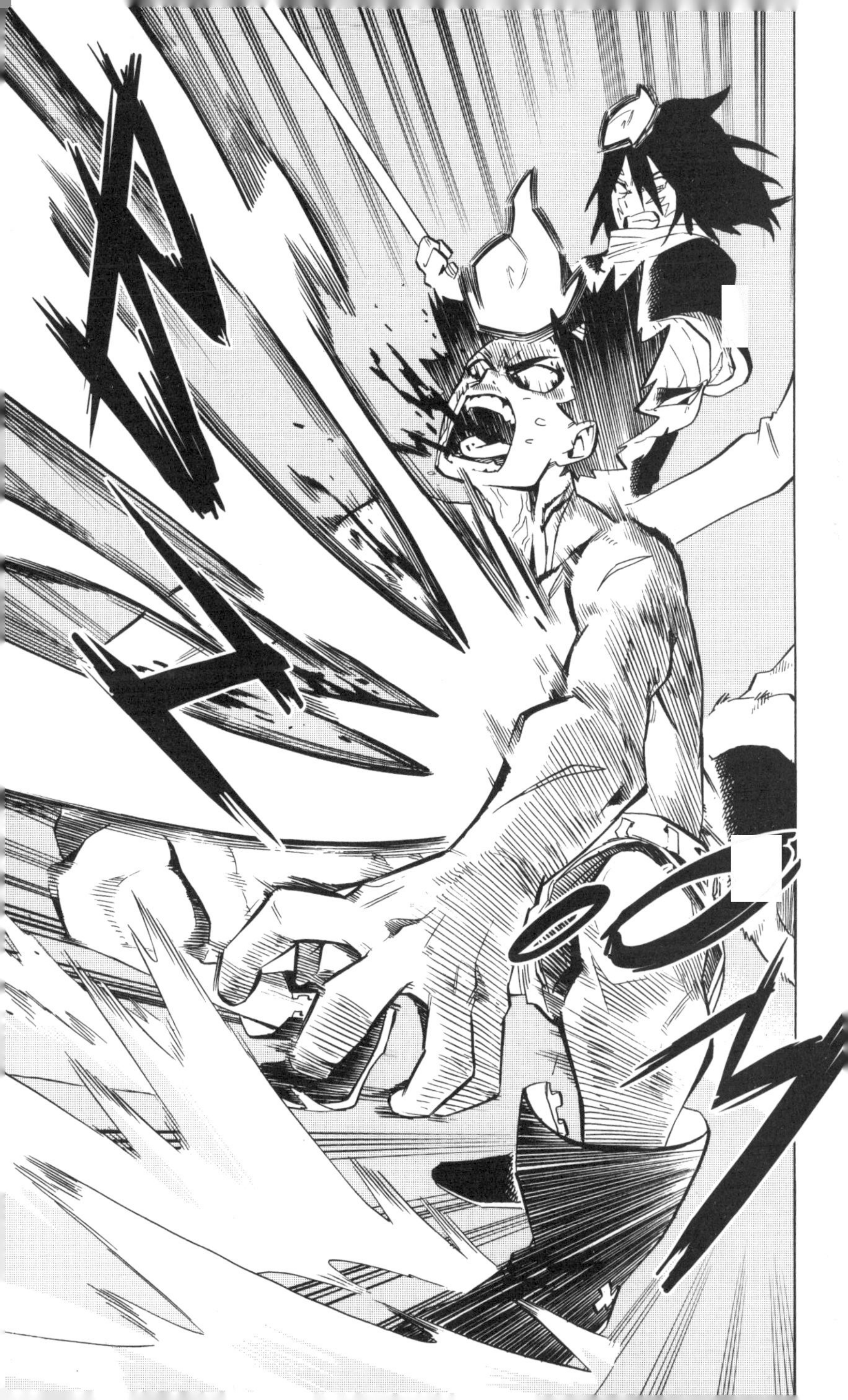

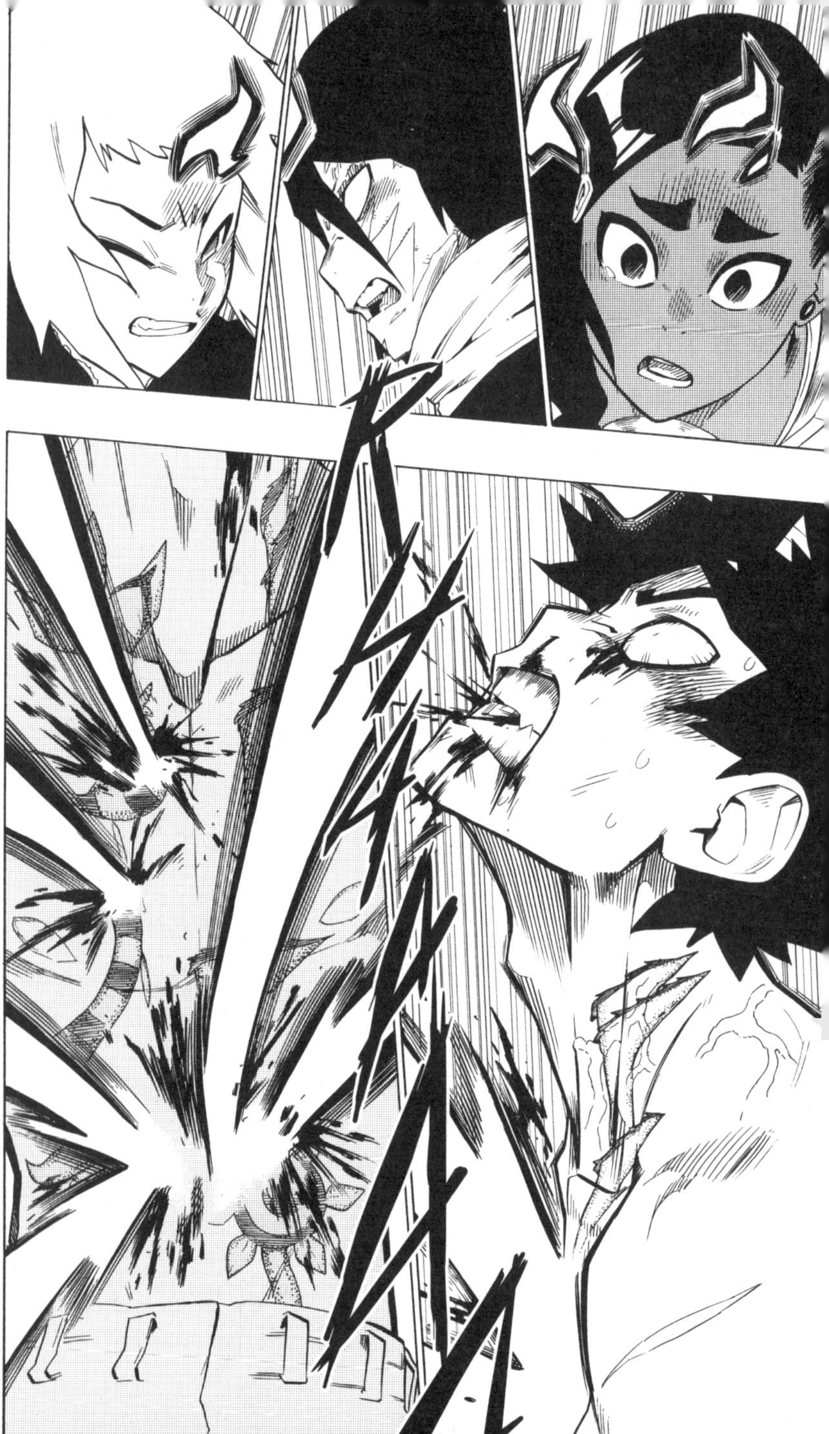

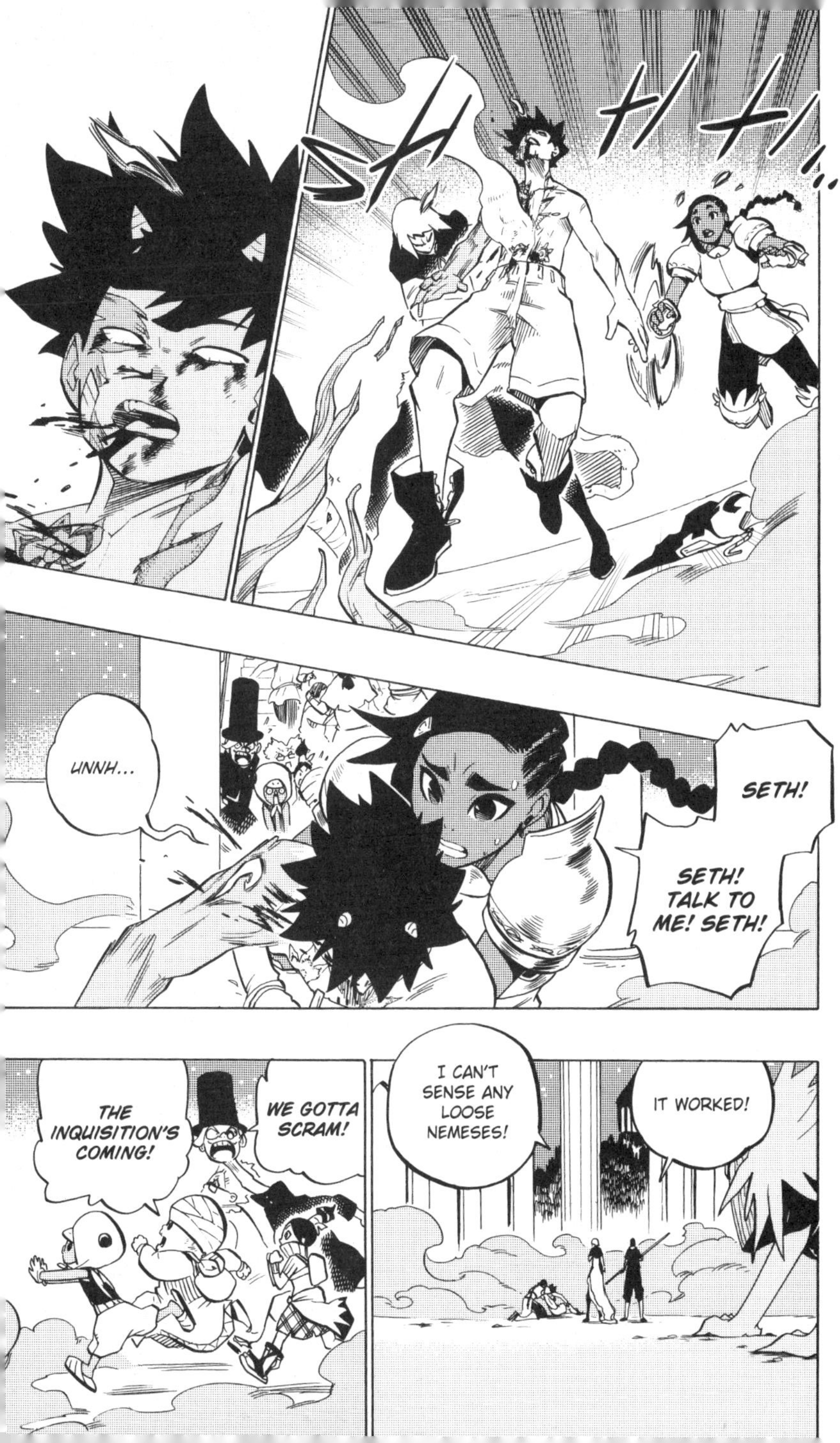
SH
HHH...
SETH!
SETH! TALK TO ME! SETH!
UNNH...
IT WORKED!
I CAN'T SENSE ANY LOOSE NEMESES!
WE GOTTA SCRAM!
THE INQUISITION'S COMING!

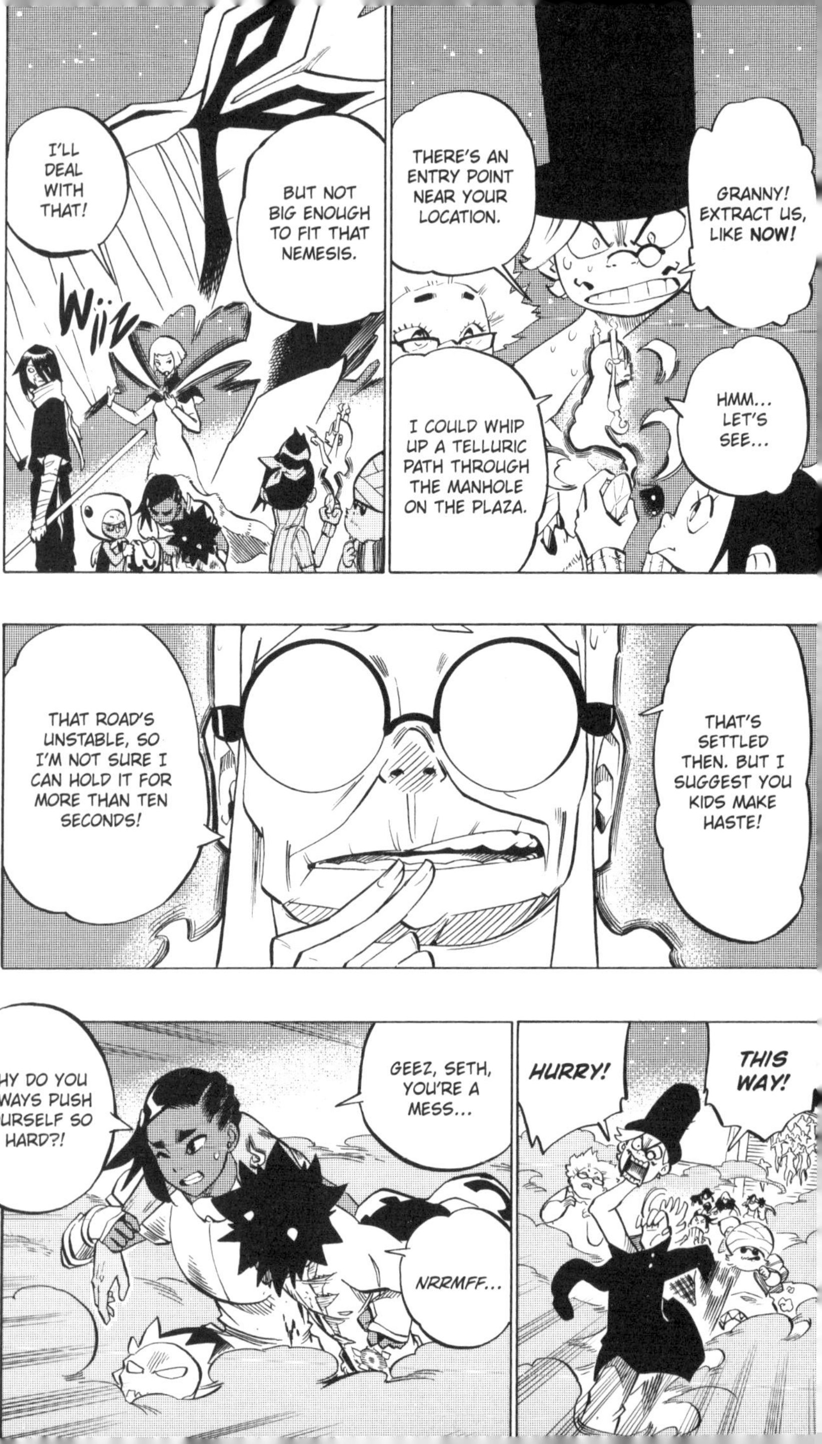
GRANNY! EXTRACT US, LIKE **NOW!**
THERE'S AN ENTRY POINT NEAR YOUR LOCATION.
HMM... LET'S SEE...
I COULD WHIP UP A TELLURIC PATH THROUGH THE MANHOLE ON THE PLAZA.
BUT NOT BIG ENOUGH TO FIT THAT NEMESIS.
I'LL DEAL WITH THAT!
WiiZ
THAT'S SETTLED THEN. BUT I SUGGEST YOU KIDS MAKE HASTE!
THAT ROAD'S UNSTABLE, SO I'M NOT SURE I CAN HOLD IT FOR MORE THAN TEN SECONDS!
THIS WAY!
HURRY!
GEEZ, SETH, YOU'RE A MESS...
WHY DO YOU ALWAYS PUSH YOURSELF SO HARD?!
NRRMFF...

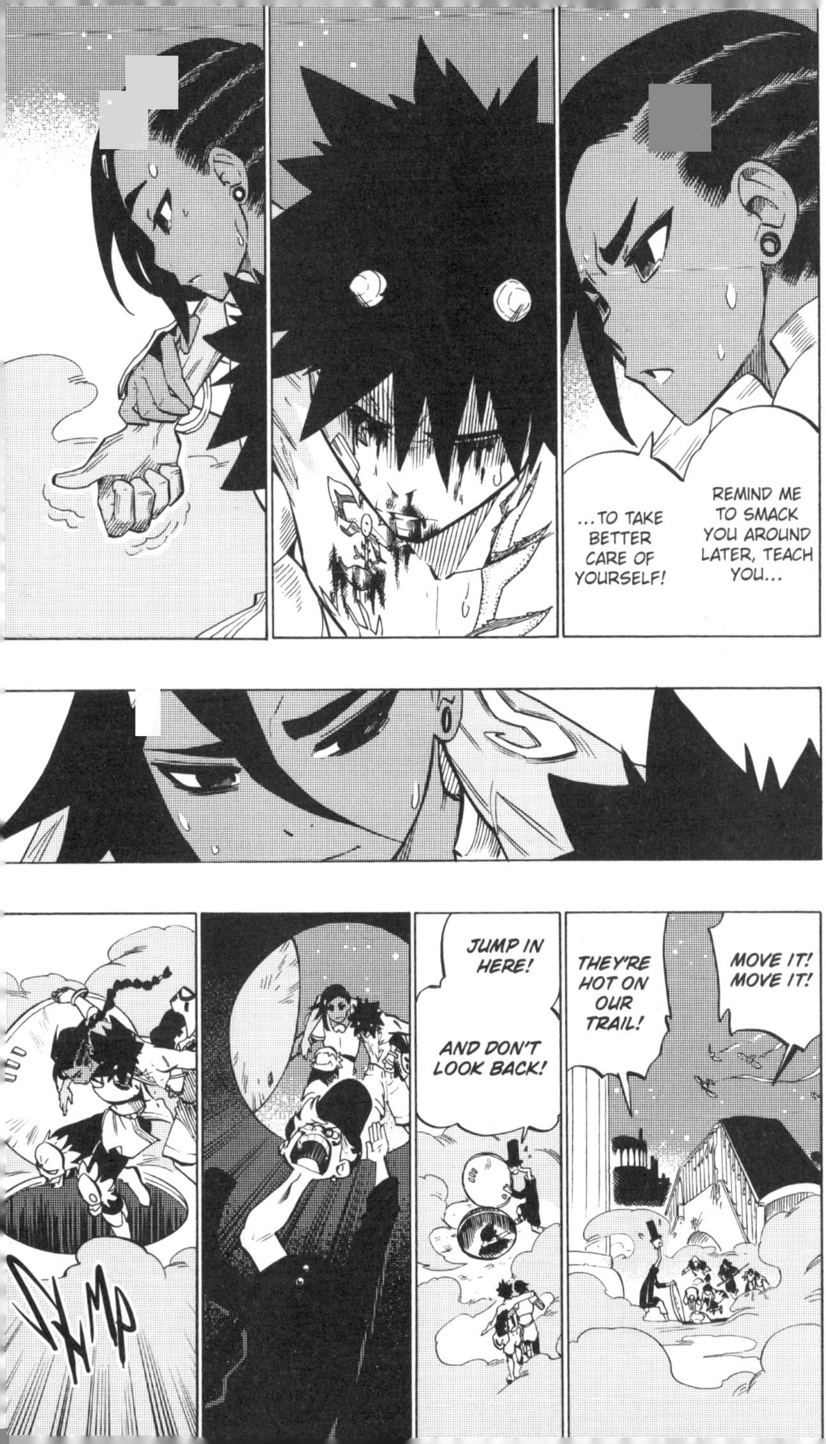
REMIND ME TO SMACK YOU AROUND LATER, TEACH YOU...
...TO TAKE BETTER CARE OF YOURSELF!
MOVE IT! MOVE IT!
THEY'RE HOT ON OUR TRAIL!
JUMP IN HERE!
AND DON'T LOOK BACK!

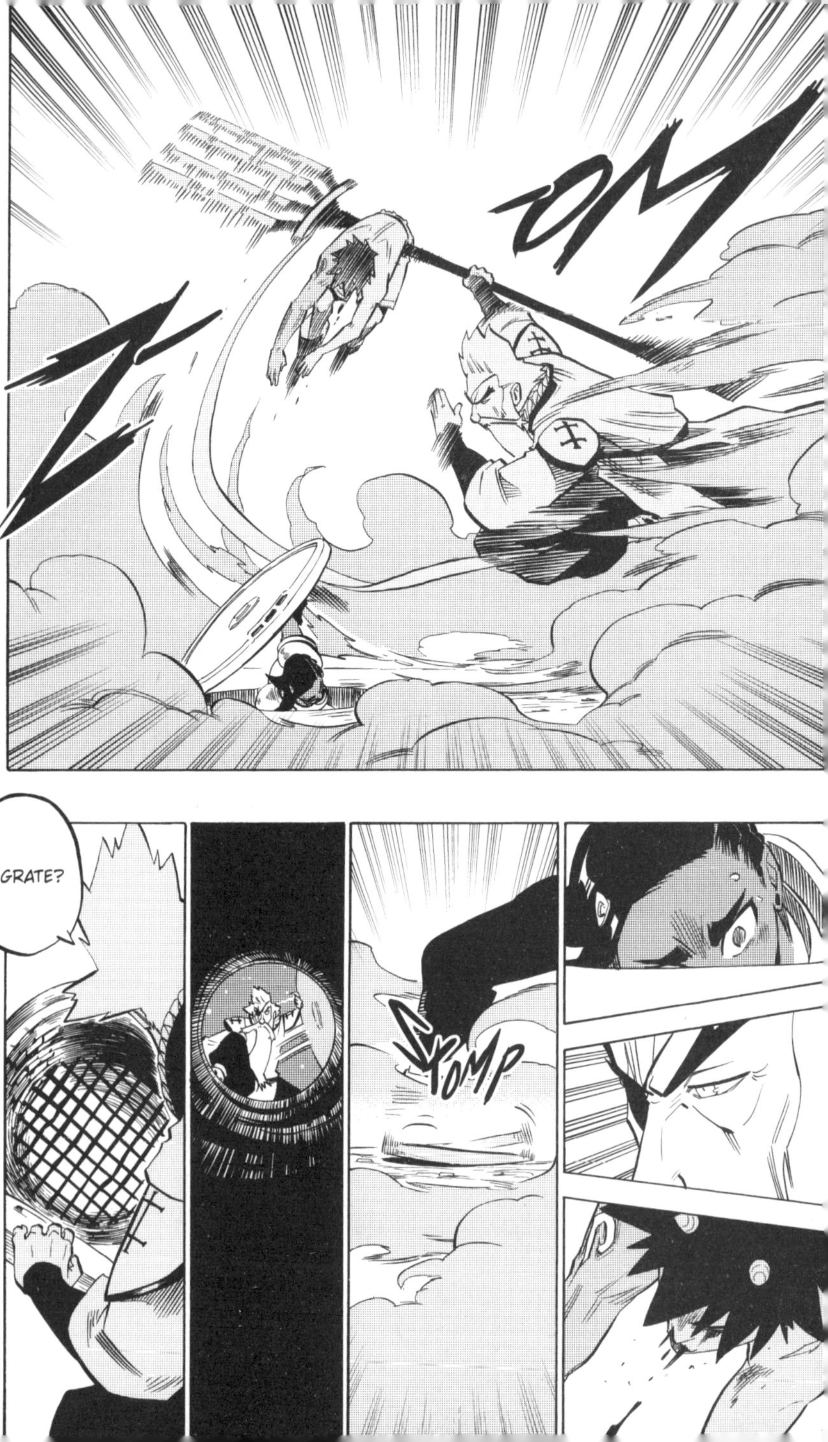
ZOM
STOMP
A GRATE?

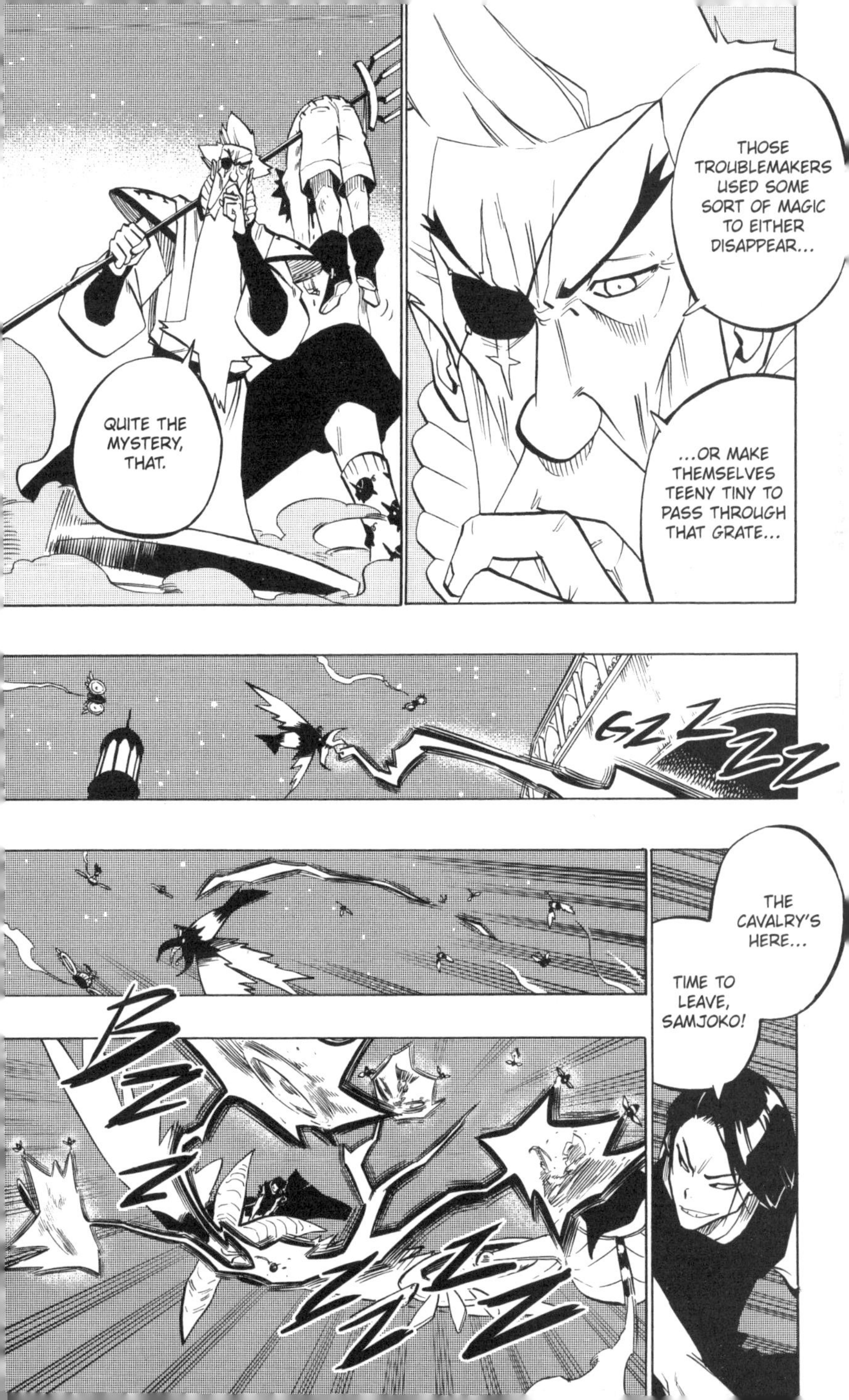
THOSE TROUBLEMAKERS USED SOME SORT OF MAGIC TO EITHER DISAPPEAR...
...OR MAKE THEMSELVES TEENY TINY TO PASS THROUGH THAT GRATE...
QUITE THE MYSTERY, THAT.
GZZZZZ
THE CAVALRY'S HERE...
TIME TO LEAVE, SAMJOKO!
BZZZZZZ

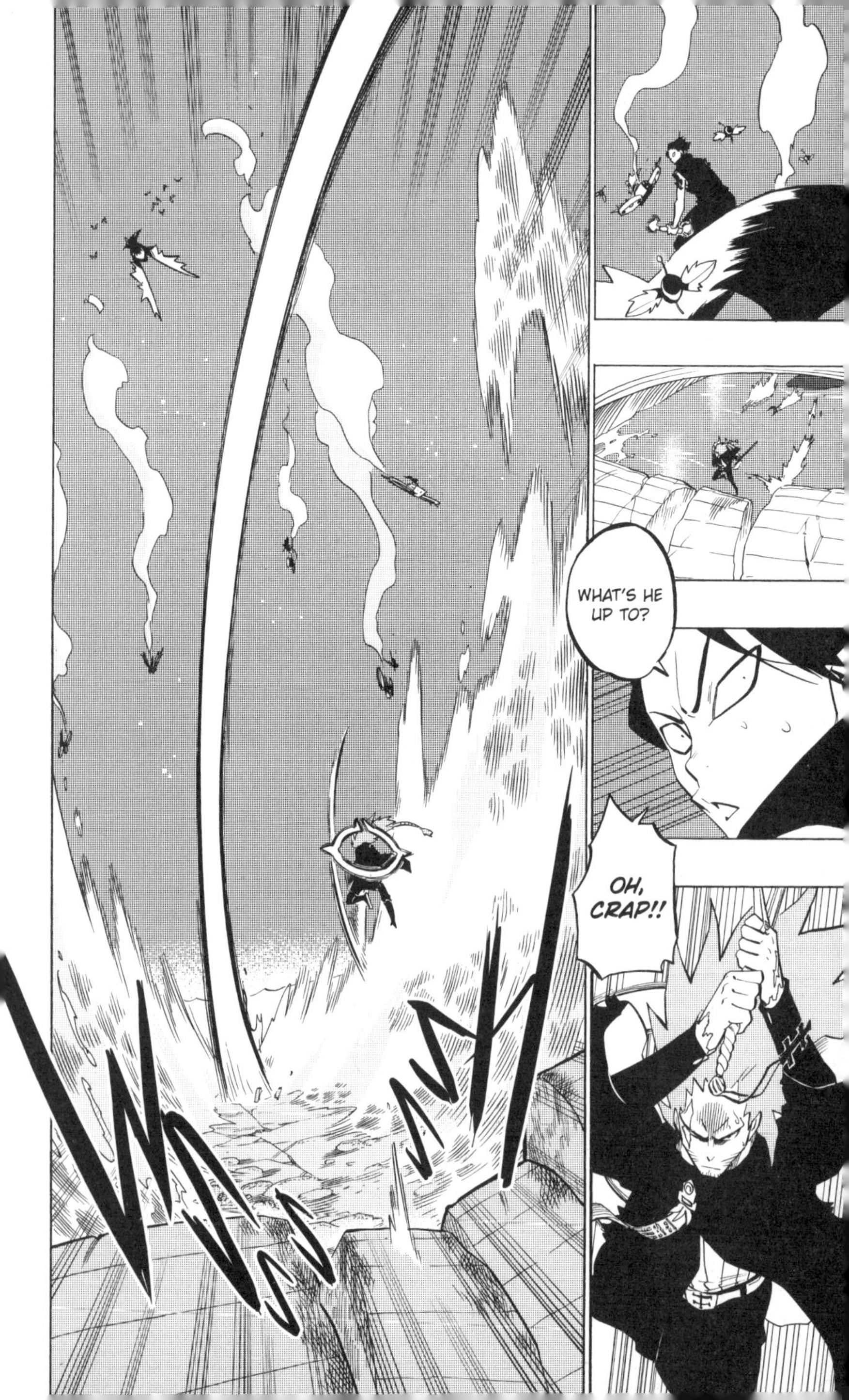
WHAT'S HE UP TO?
OH, CRAP!!

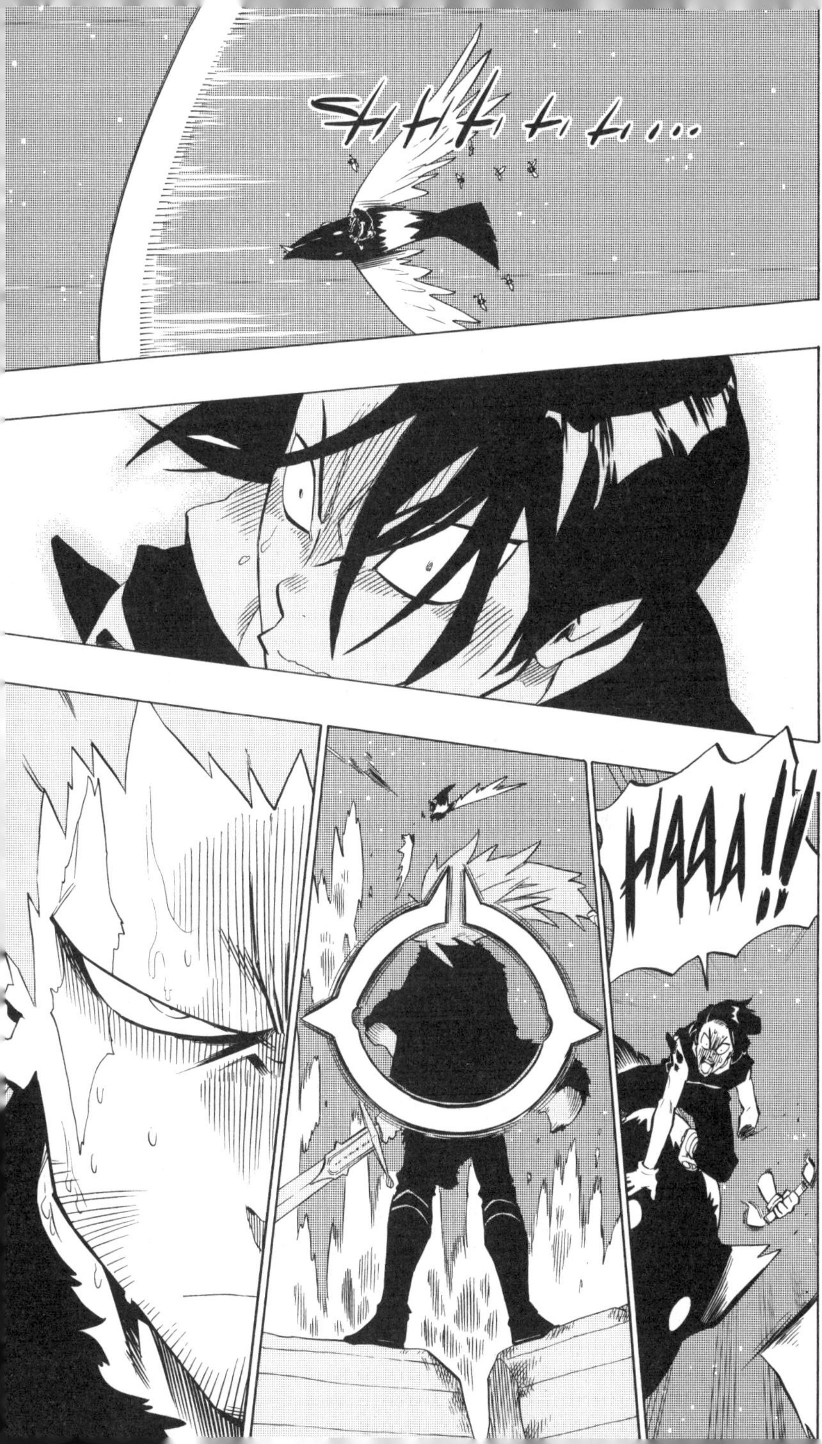
HAAA!!

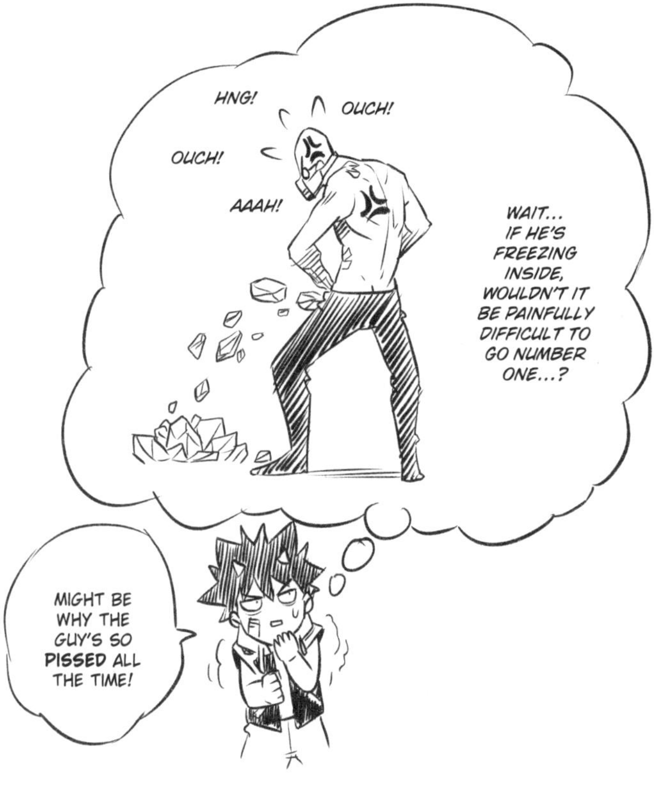
HNG!
OUCH!
OUCH!
AAAH!
WAIT... IF HE'S FREEZING INSIDE, WOULDN'T IT BE PAINFULLY DIFFICULT TO GO NUMBER ONE...?
MIGHT BE WHY THE GUY'S SO **PISSED** ALL THE TIME!

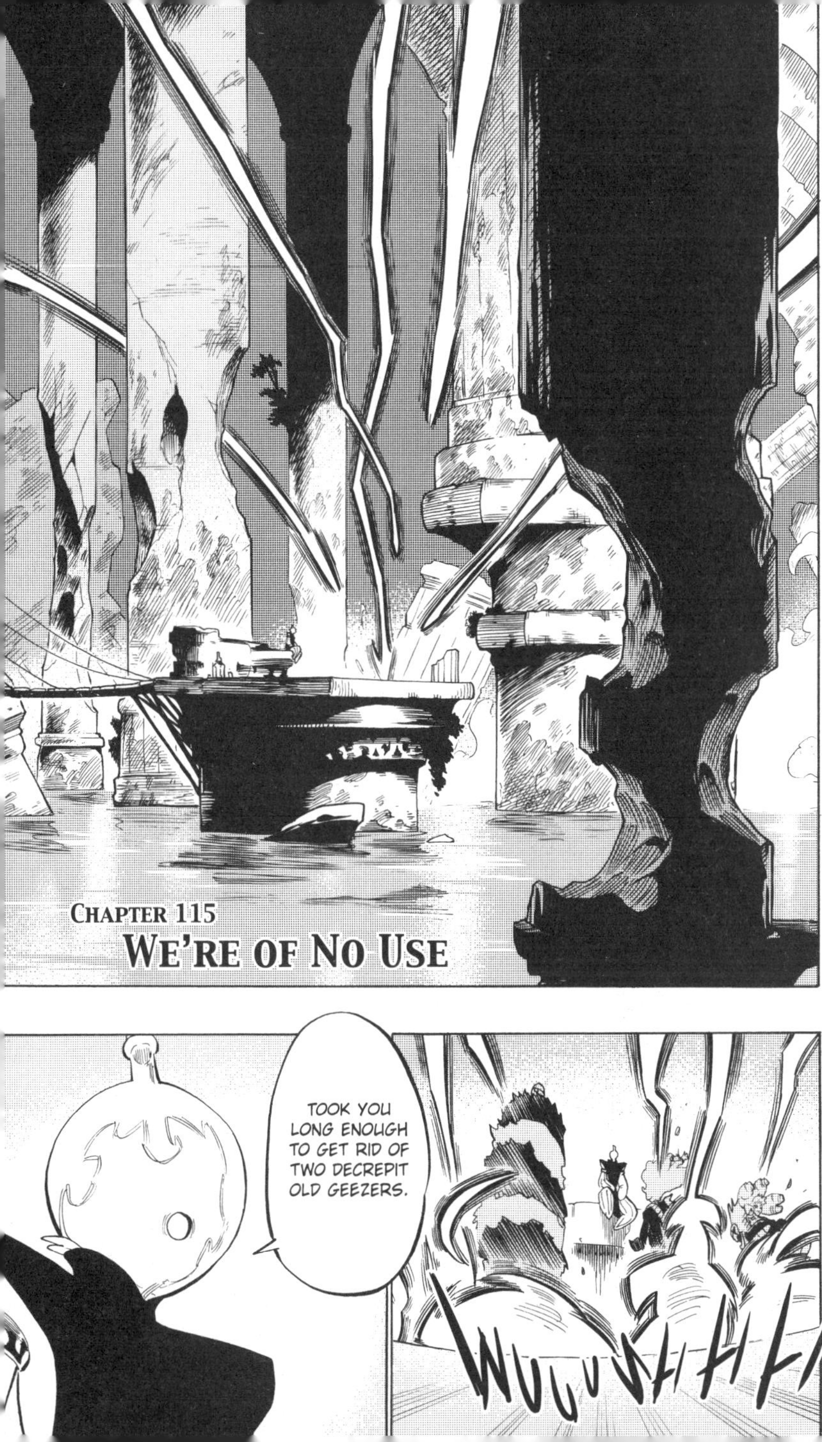
CHAPTER 115
WE'RE OF NO USE
TOOK YOU LONG ENOUGH TO GET RID OF TWO DECREPIT OLD GEEZERS.

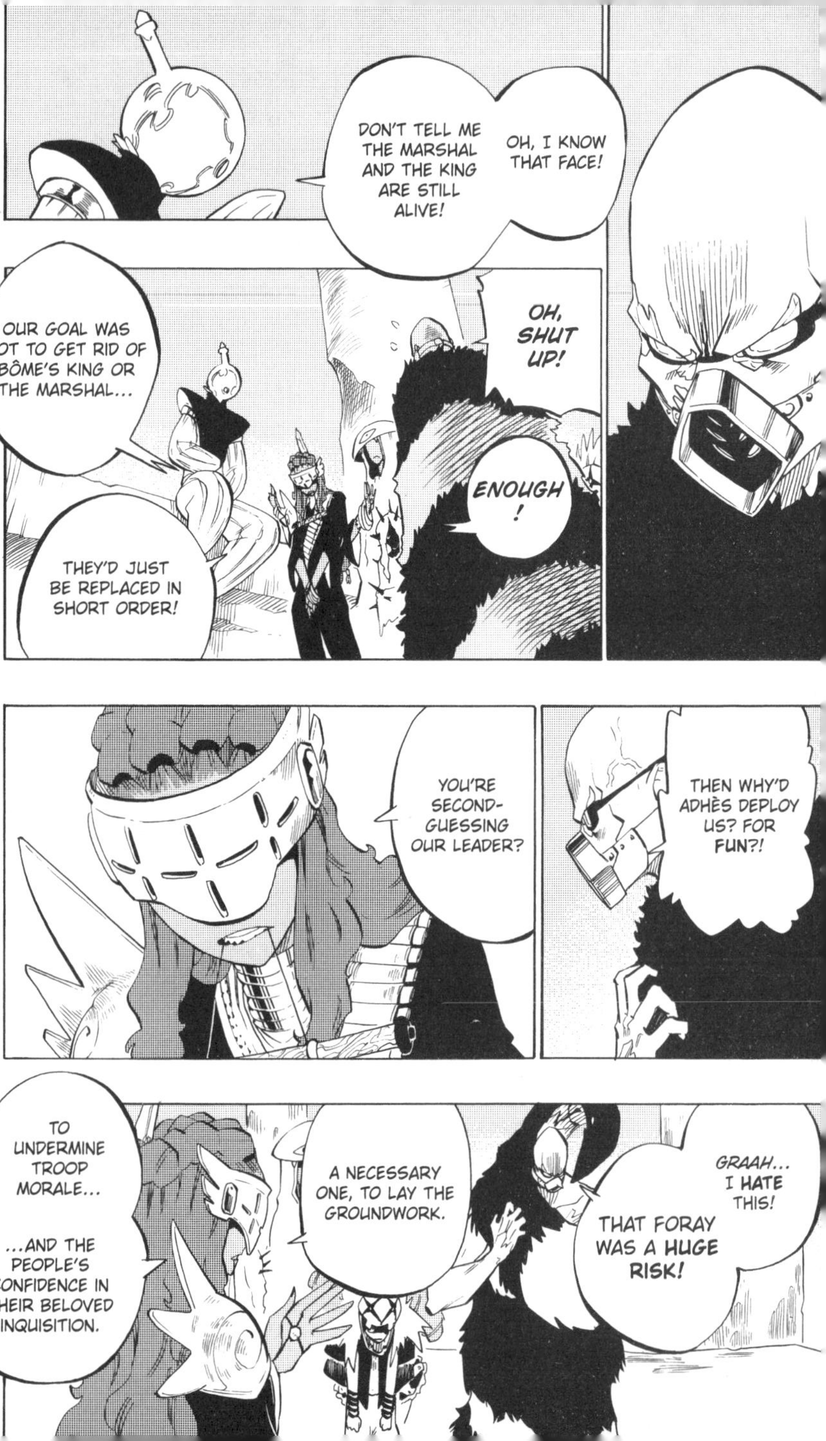
OH, I KNOW THAT FACE!
DON'T TELL ME THE MARSHAL AND THE KING ARE STILL ALIVE!
OH, SHUT UP!
ENOUGH!
OUR GOAL WAS NOT TO GET RID OF BÔME'S KING OR THE MARSHAL...
THEY'D JUST BE REPLACED IN SHORT ORDER!
THEN WHY'D ADHÈS DEPLOY US? FOR FUN?!
YOU'RE SECOND-GUESSING OUR LEADER?
GRAAH... I HATE THIS!
THAT FORAY WAS A HUGE RISK!
A NECESSARY ONE, TO LAY THE GROUNDWORK.
TO UNDERMINE TROOP MORALE...
...AND THE PEOPLE'S CONFIDENCE IN THEIR BELOVED INQUISITION.

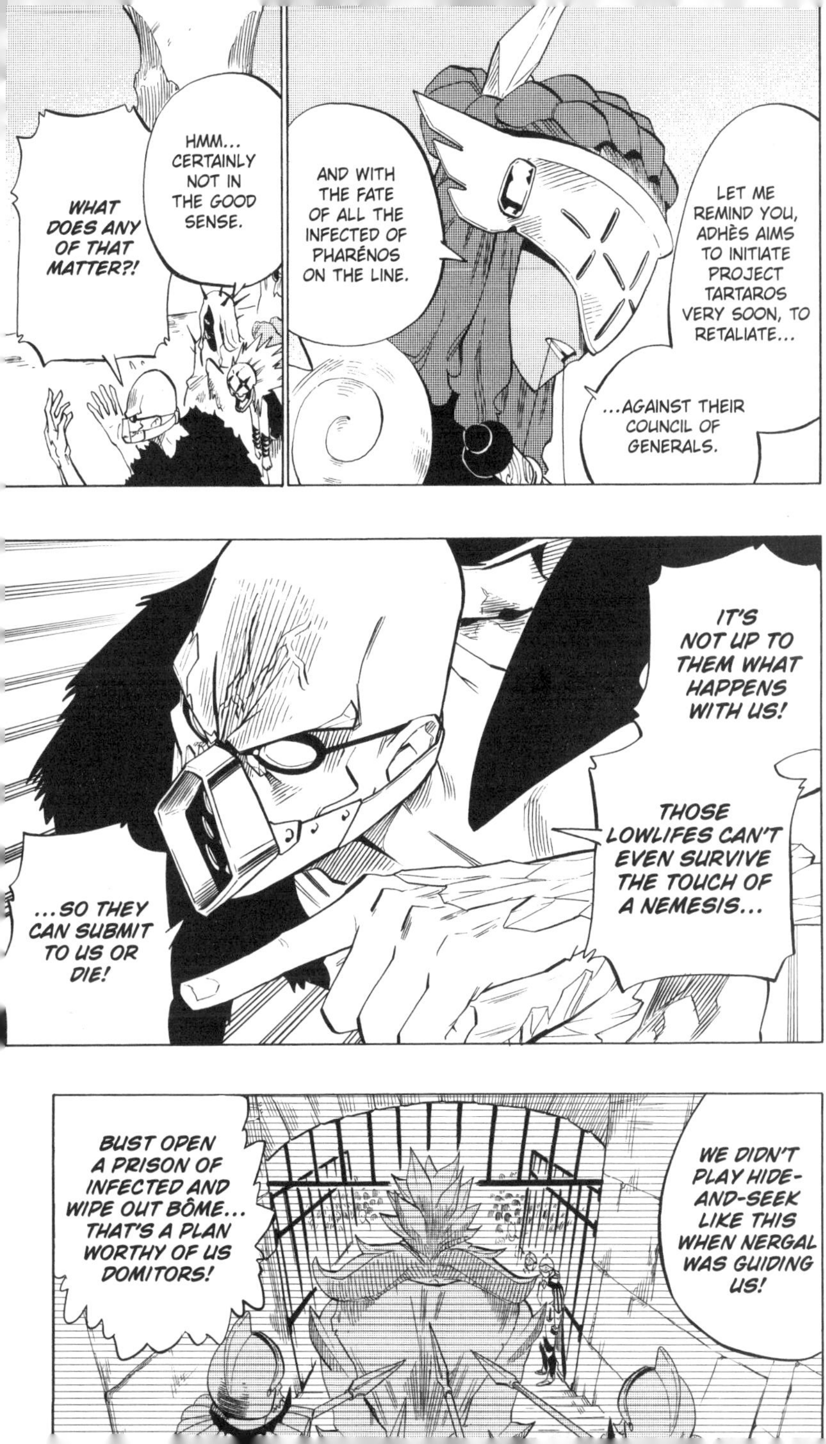
LET ME REMIND YOU, ADHÈS AIMS TO INITIATE PROJECT TARTAROS VERY SOON, TO RETALIATE...
...AGAINST THEIR COUNCIL OF GENERALS.
AND WITH THE FATE OF ALL THE INFECTED OF PHARÉNOS ON THE LINE.
HMM... CERTAINLY NOT IN THE GOOD SENSE.
WHAT DOES ANY OF THAT MATTER?!
IT'S NOT UP TO THEM WHAT HAPPENS WITH US!
THOSE LOWLIFES CAN'T EVEN SURVIVE THE TOUCH OF A NEMESIS...
...SO THEY CAN SUBMIT TO US OR DIE!
WE DIDN'T PLAY HIDE-AND-SEEK LIKE THIS WHEN NERGAL WAS GUIDING US!
BUST OPEN A PRISON OF INFECTED AND WIPE OUT BÔME... THAT'S A PLAN WORTHY OF US DOMITORS!

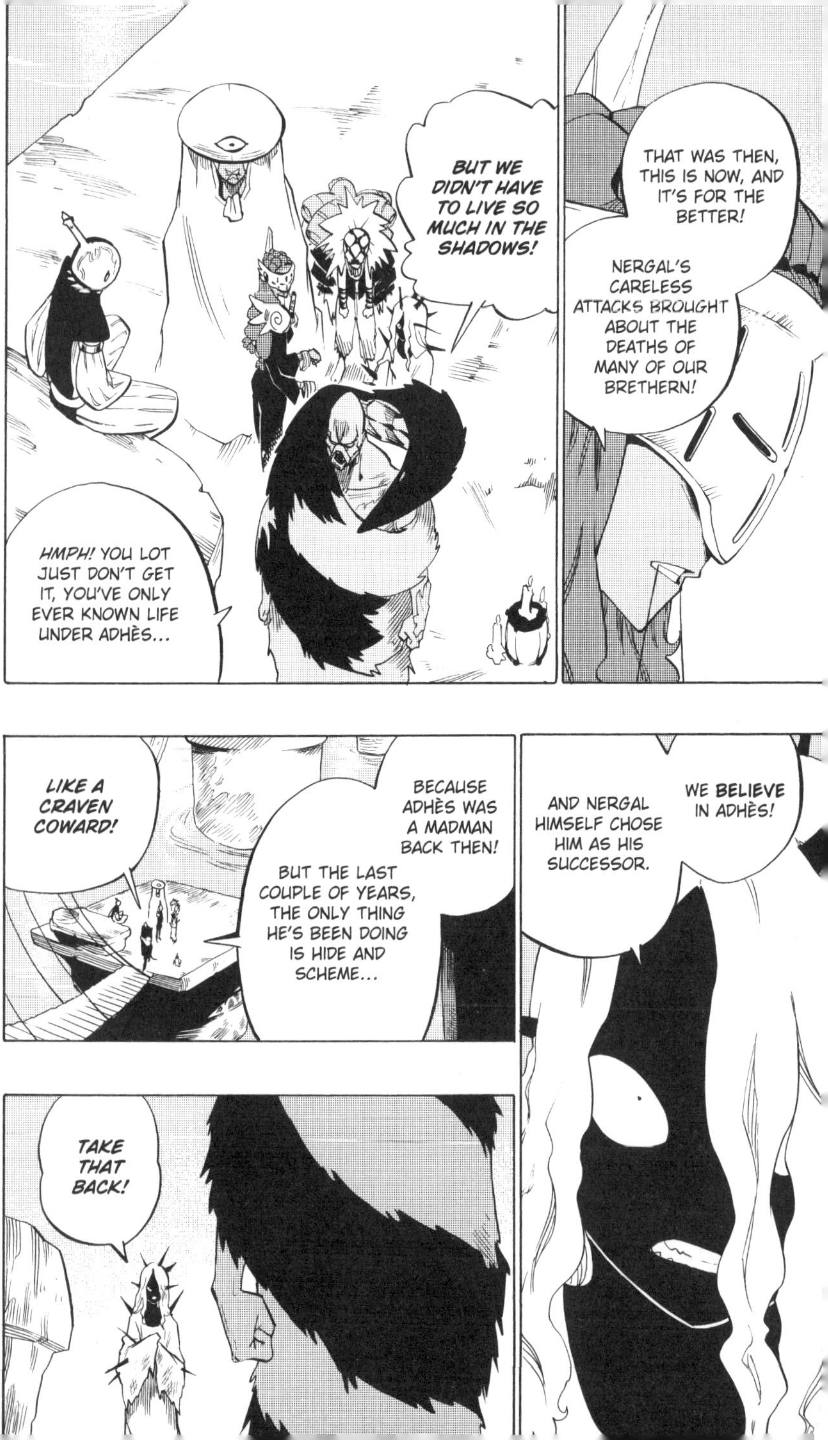
THAT WAS THEN, THIS IS NOW, AND IT'S FOR THE BETTER!
NERGAL'S CARELESS ATTACKS BROUGHT ABOUT THE DEATHS OF MANY OF OUR BRETHERN!
BUT WE DIDN'T HAVE TO LIVE SO MUCH IN THE SHADOWS!
HMPH! YOU LOT JUST DON'T GET IT, YOU'VE ONLY EVER KNOWN LIFE UNDER ADHÈS...
WE BELIEVE IN ADHÈS!
AND NERGAL HIMSELF CHOSE HIM AS HIS SUCCESSOR.
BECAUSE ADHÈS WAS A MADMAN BACK THEN!
BUT THE LAST COUPLE OF YEARS, THE ONLY THING HE'S BEEN DOING IS HIDE AND SCHEME...
LIKE A CRAVEN COWARD!
TAKE THAT BACK!

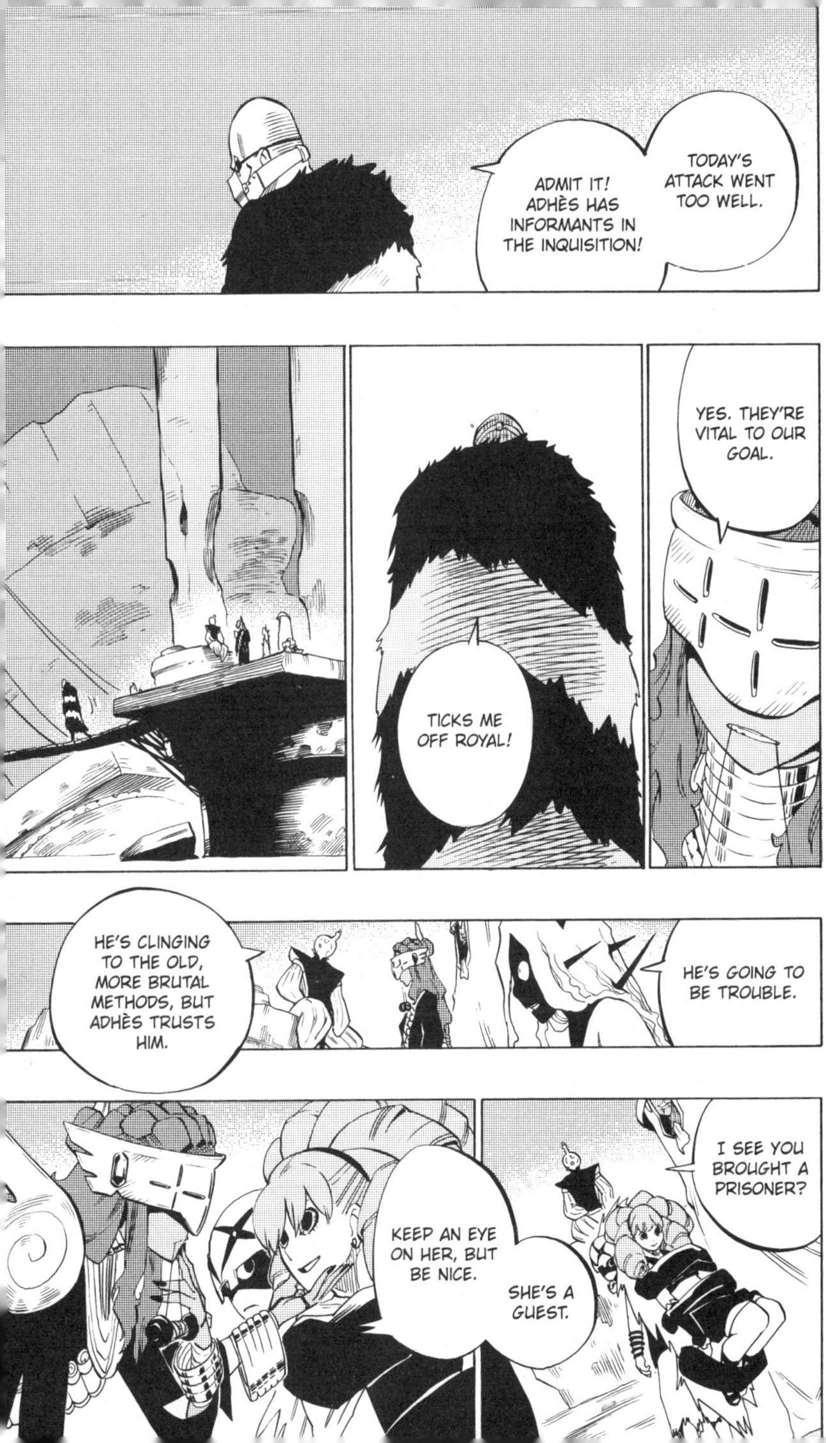
TODAY'S ATTACK WENT TOO WELL.
ADMIT IT! ADHÈS HAS INFORMANTS IN THE INQUISITION!
YES. THEY'RE VITAL TO OUR GOAL.
TICKS ME OFF ROYAL!
HE'S GOING TO BE TROUBLE.
HE'S CLINGING TO THE OLD, MORE BRUTAL METHODS, BUT ADHÈS TRUSTS HIM.
I SEE YOU BROUGHT A PRISONER?
KEEP AN EYE ON HER, BUT BE NICE.
SHE'S A GUEST.

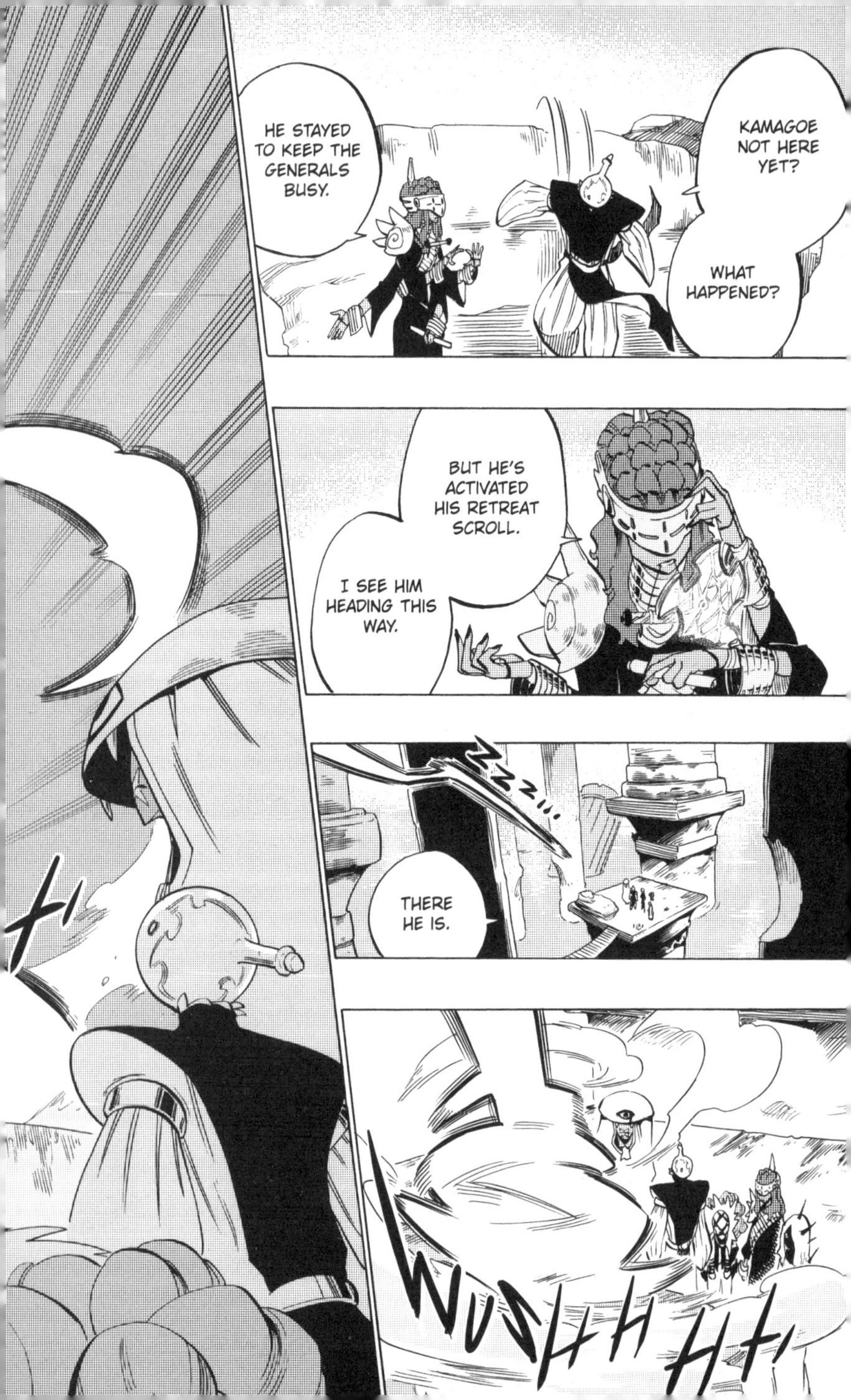
KAMAGOE NOT HERE YET?
WHAT HAPPENED?
HE STAYED TO KEEP THE GENERALS BUSY.
BUT HE'S ACTIVATED HIS RETREAT SCROLL.
I SEE HIM HEADING THIS WAY.
ZZZ!!!
THERE HE IS.
WUSHHHHT!

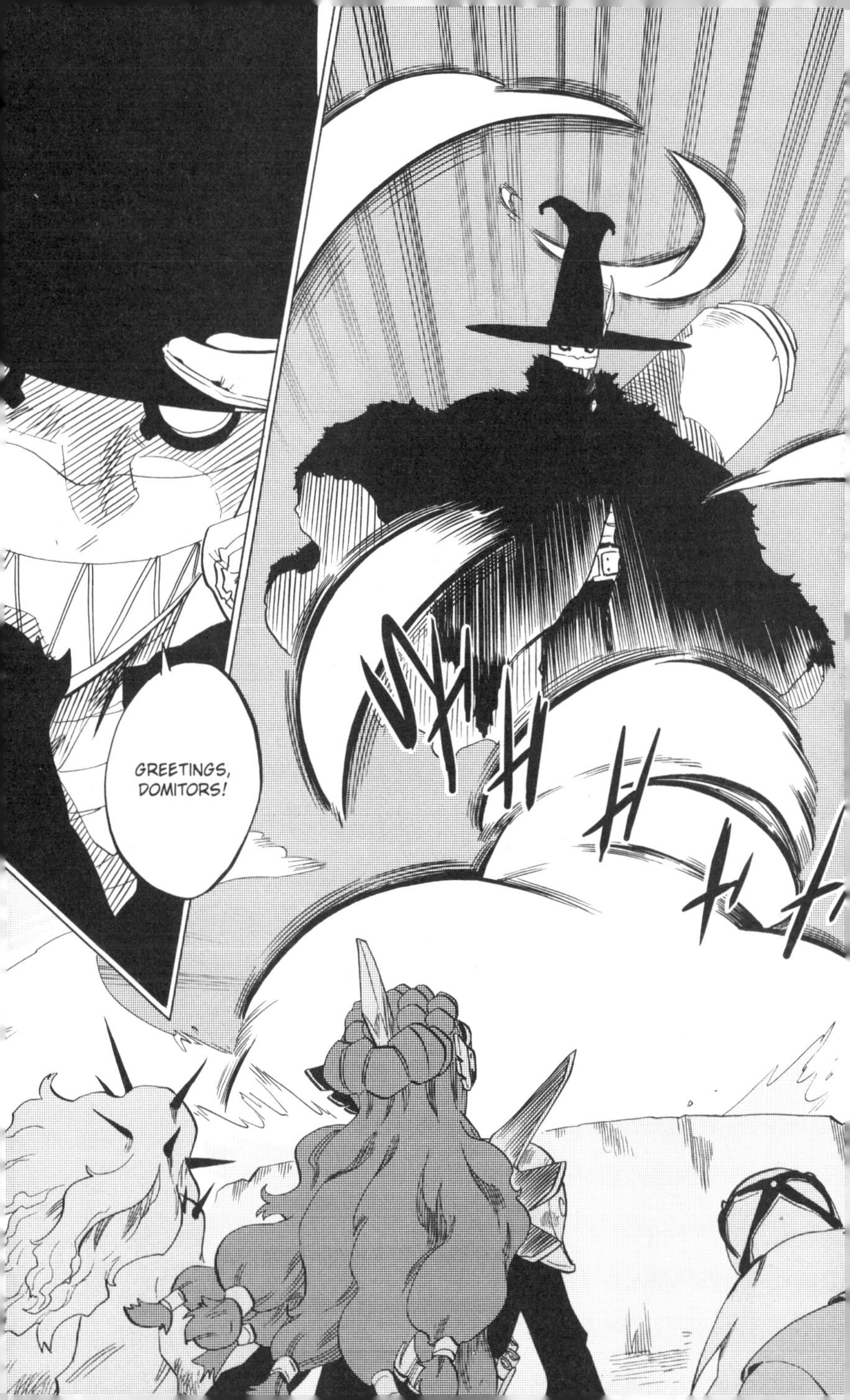
GREETINGS, DOMITORS!

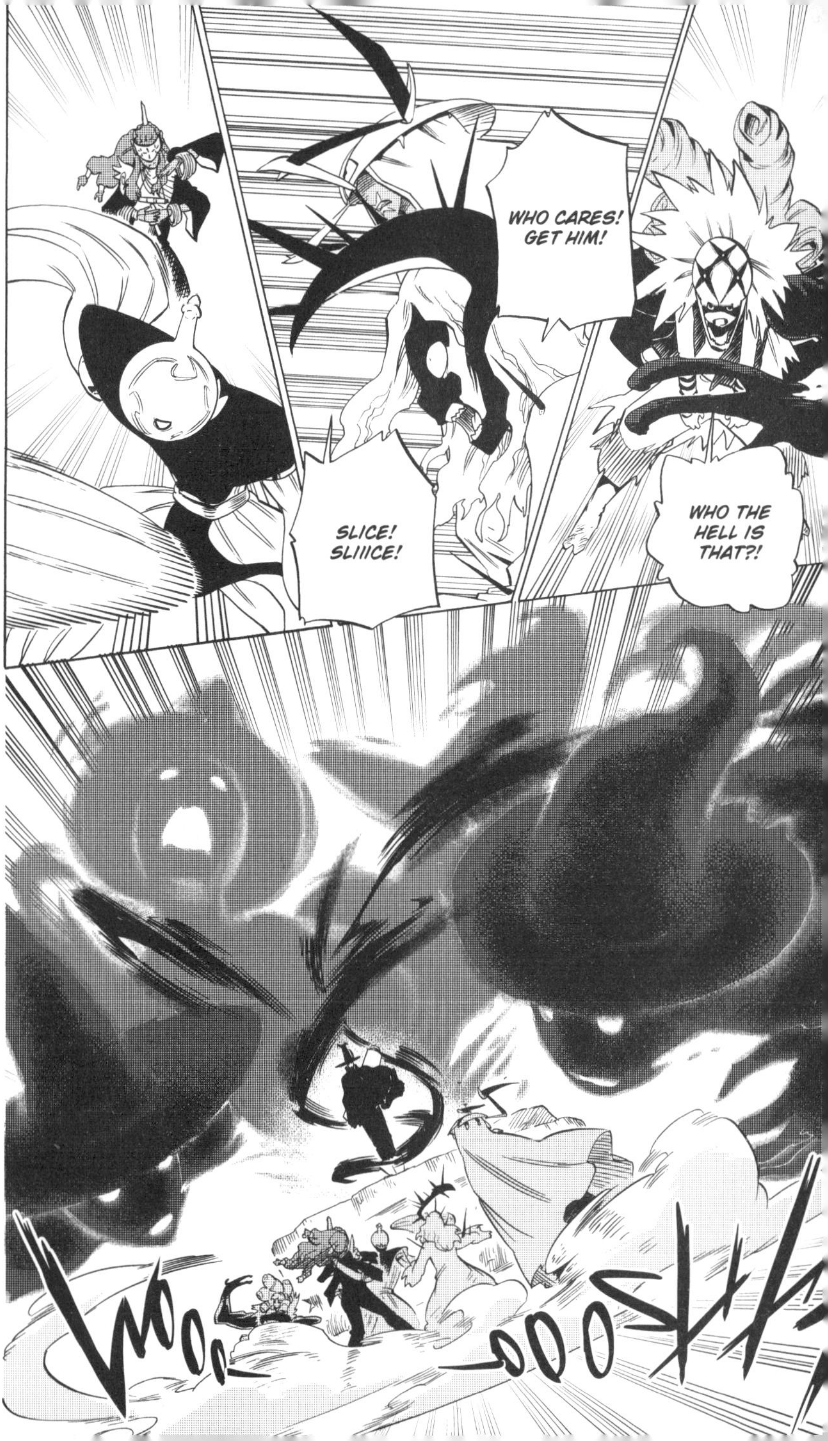
WHO THE HELL IS THAT?!
WHO CARES! GET HIM!
SLICE! SLIIICE!
WHOOOOOOOOSHH

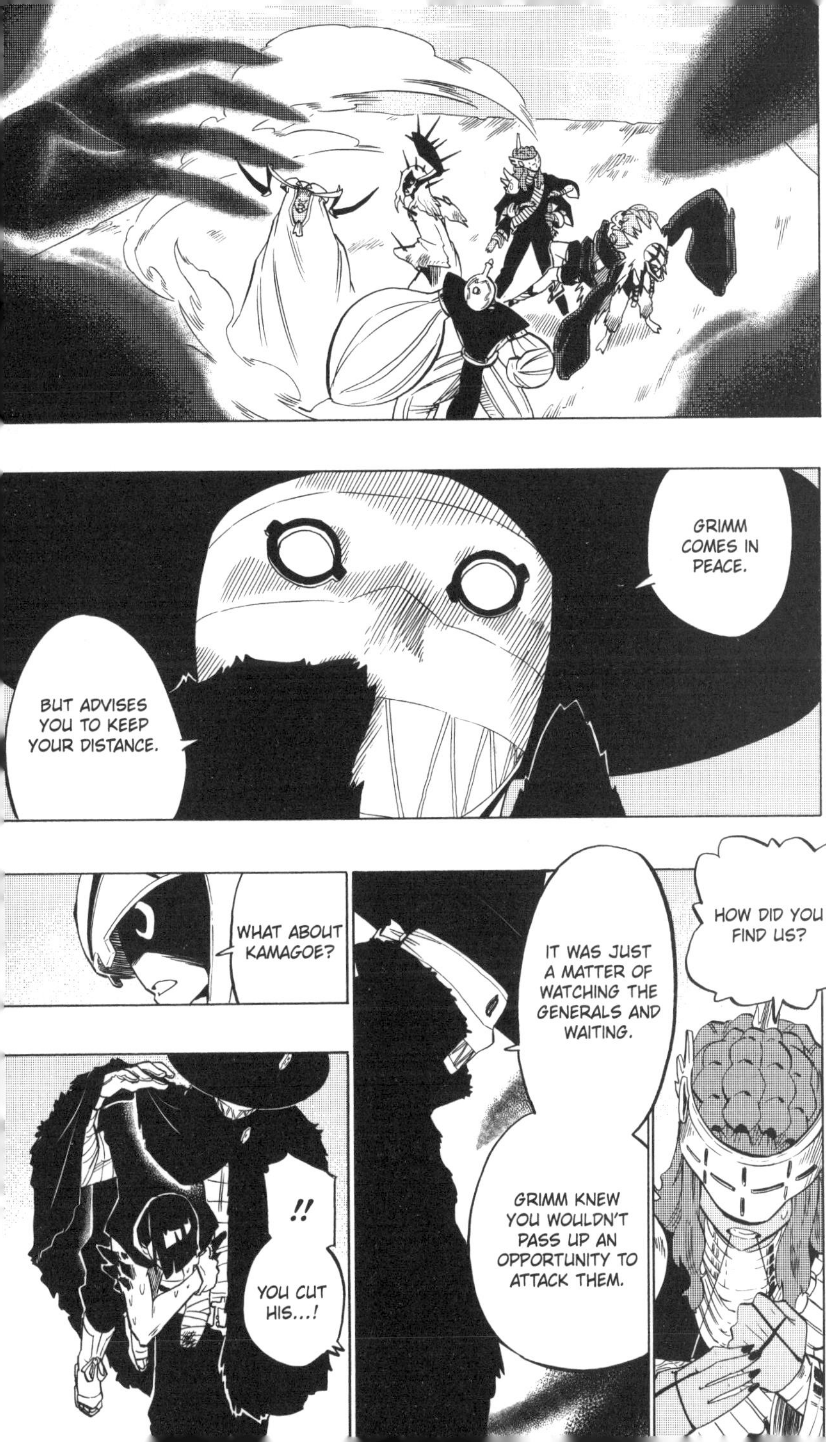
GRIMM COMES IN PEACE.
BUT ADVISES YOU TO KEEP YOUR DISTANCE.
HOW DID YOU FIND US?
IT WAS JUST A MATTER OF WATCHING THE GENERALS AND WAITING.
GRIMM KNEW YOU WOULDN'T PASS UP AN OPPORTUNITY TO ATTACK THEM.
WHAT ABOUT KAMAGOE?
!!
YOU CUT HIS...!

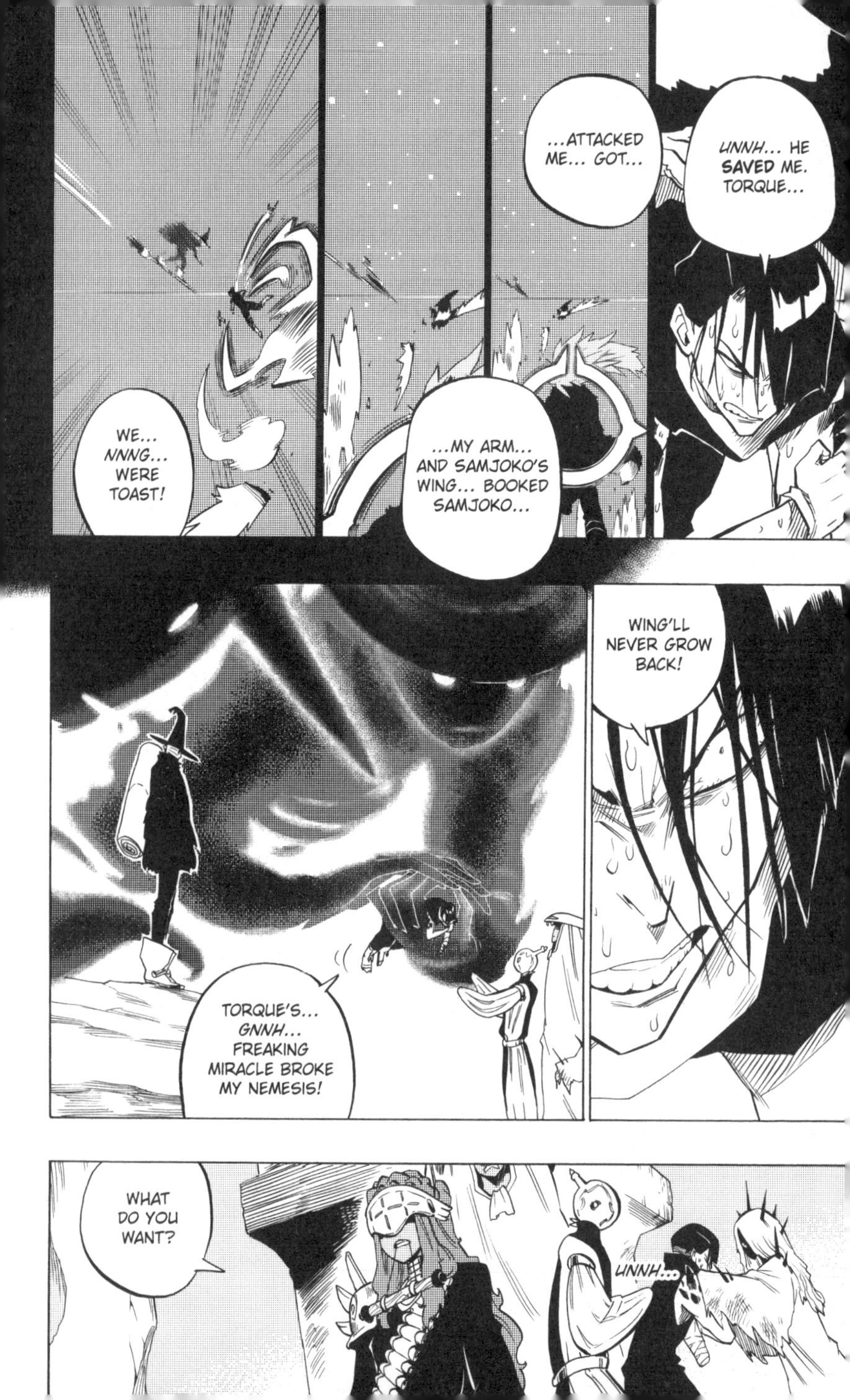
UNNH... HE SAVED ME. TORQUE...
...ATTACKED ME... GOT...
...MY ARM... AND SAMJOKO'S WING... BOOKED SAMJOKO...
WE... NNNG... WERE TOAST!
WING'LL NEVER GROW BACK!
TORQUE'S... GNNH... FREAKING MIRACLE BROKE MY NEMESIS!
UNNH...
WHAT DO YOU WANT?

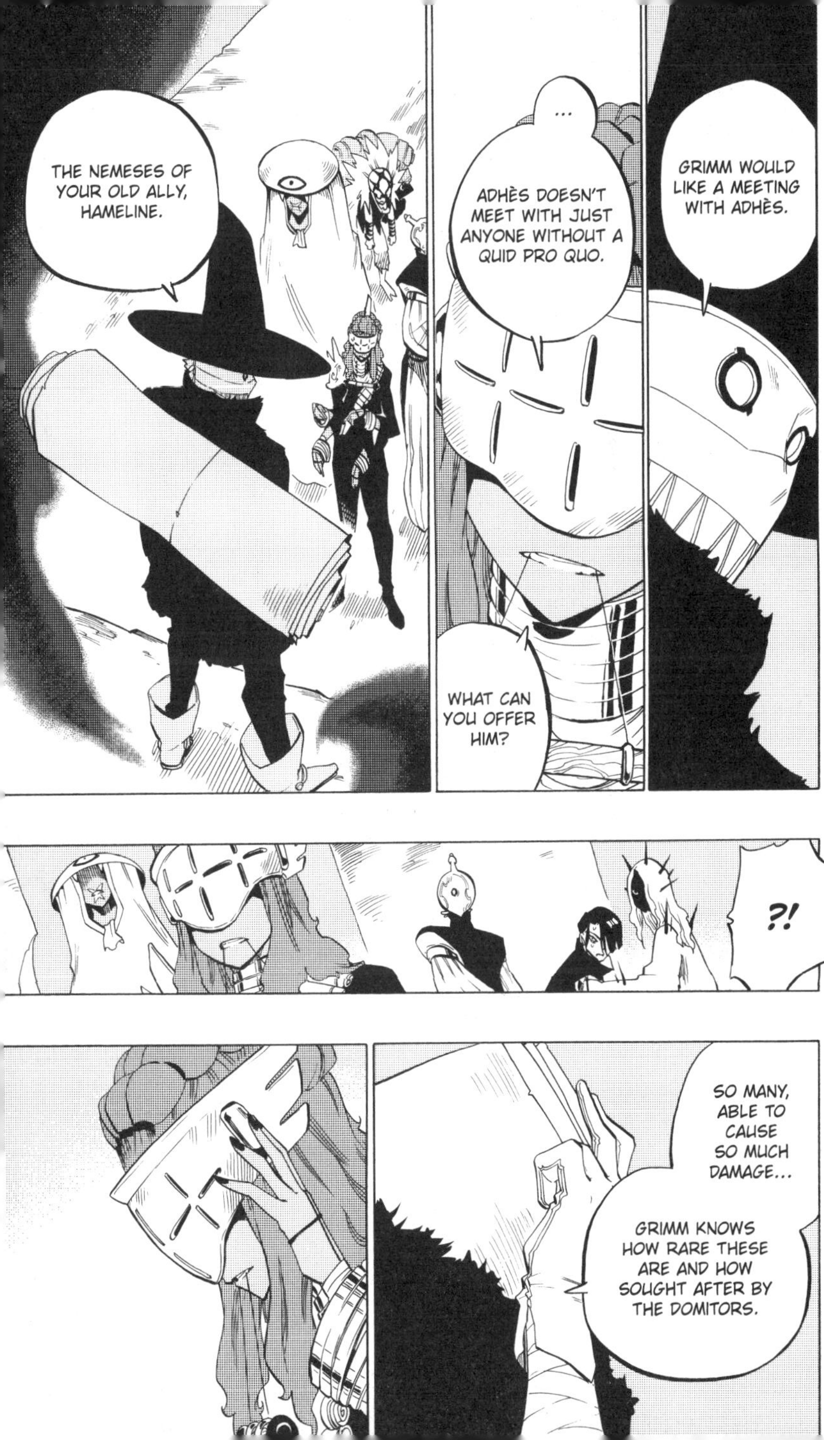
GRIMM WOULD LIKE A MEETING WITH ADHÈS.
...
ADHÈS DOESN'T MEET WITH JUST ANYONE WITHOUT A QUID PRO QUO.
WHAT CAN YOU OFFER HIM?
THE NEMESES OF YOUR OLD ALLY, HAMELINE.
?!
SO MANY, ABLE TO CAUSE SO MUCH DAMAGE...
GRIMM KNOWS HOW RARE THESE ARE AND HOW SOUGHT AFTER BY THE DOMITORS.

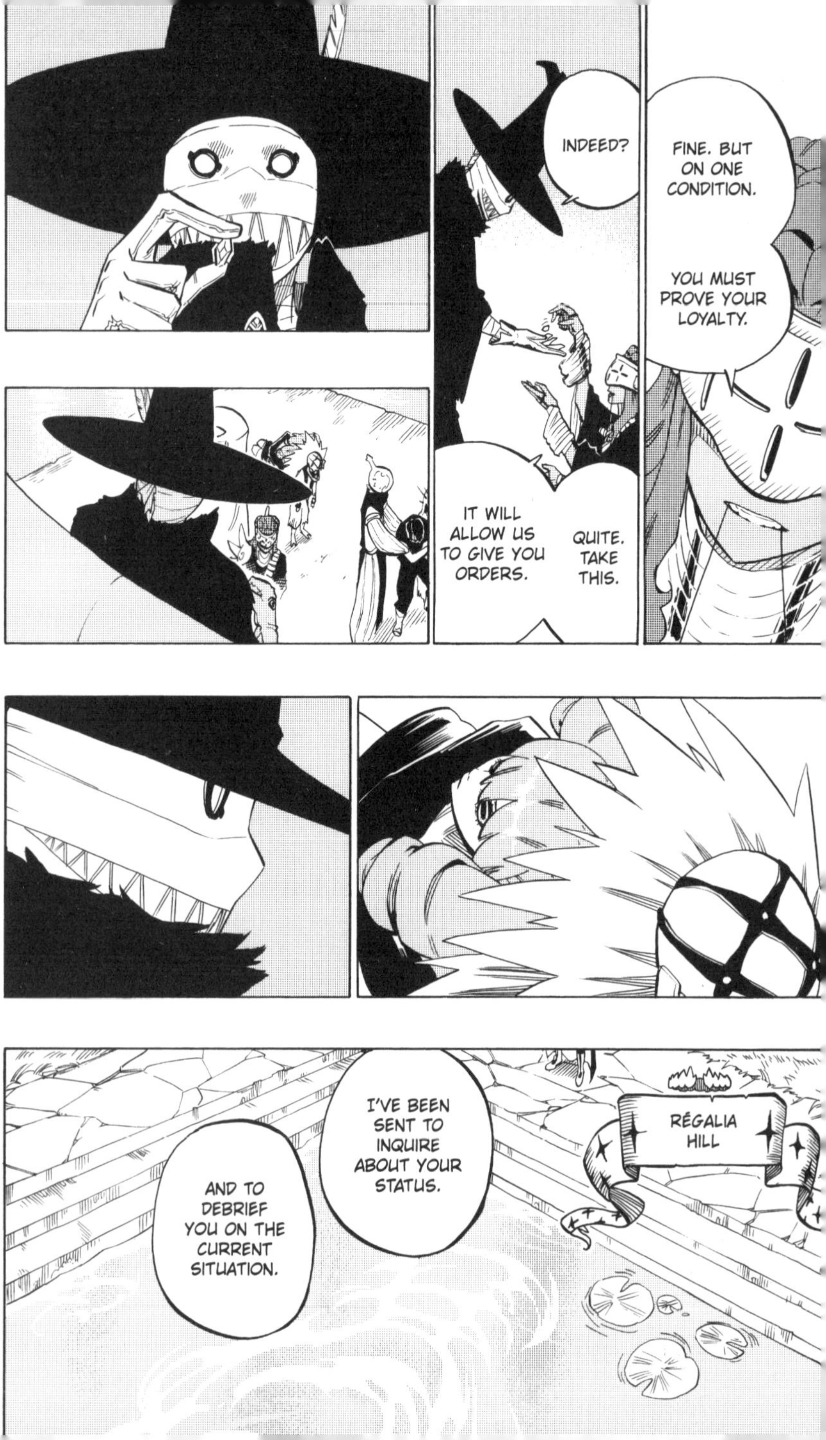
FINE. BUT ON ONE CONDITION.
YOU MUST PROVE YOUR LOYALTY.
INDEED?
QUITE. TAKE THIS.
IT WILL ALLOW US TO GIVE YOU ORDERS.
RÉGALIA HILL
I'VE BEEN SENT TO INQUIRE ABOUT YOUR STATUS.
AND TO DEBRIEF YOU ON THE CURRENT SITUATION.

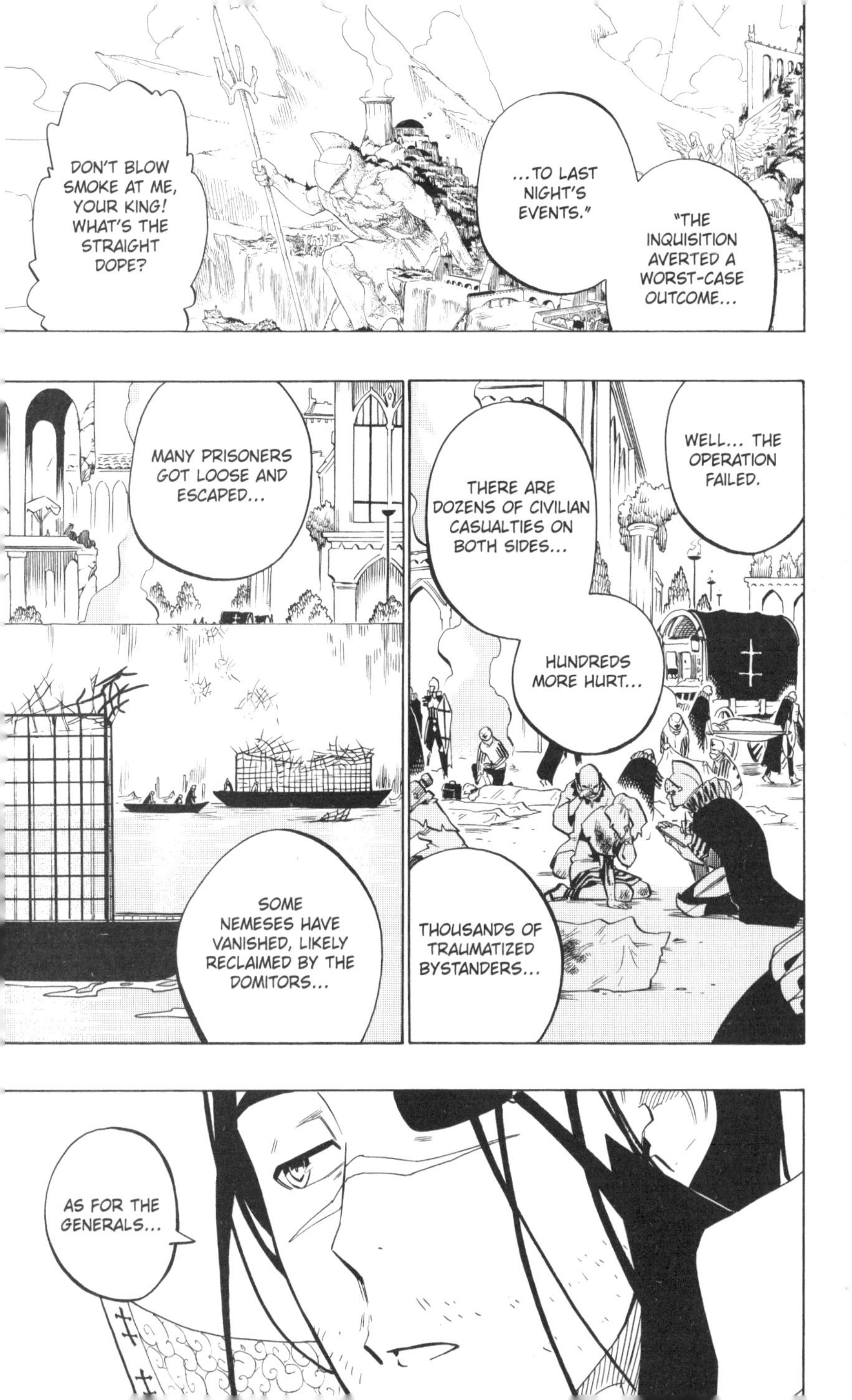
"THE INQUISITION AVERTED A WORST-CASE OUTCOME...
...TO LAST NIGHT'S EVENTS."
DON'T BLOW SMOKE AT ME, YOUR KING! WHAT'S THE STRAIGHT DOPE?
WELL... THE OPERATION FAILED.
THERE ARE DOZENS OF CIVILIAN CASUALTIES ON BOTH SIDES...
HUNDREDS MORE HURT...
THOUSANDS OF TRAUMATIZED BYSTANDERS...
MANY PRISONERS GOT LOOSE AND ESCAPED...
SOME NEMESES HAVE VANISHED, LIKELY RECLAIMED BY THE DOMITORS...
AS FOR THE GENERALS...

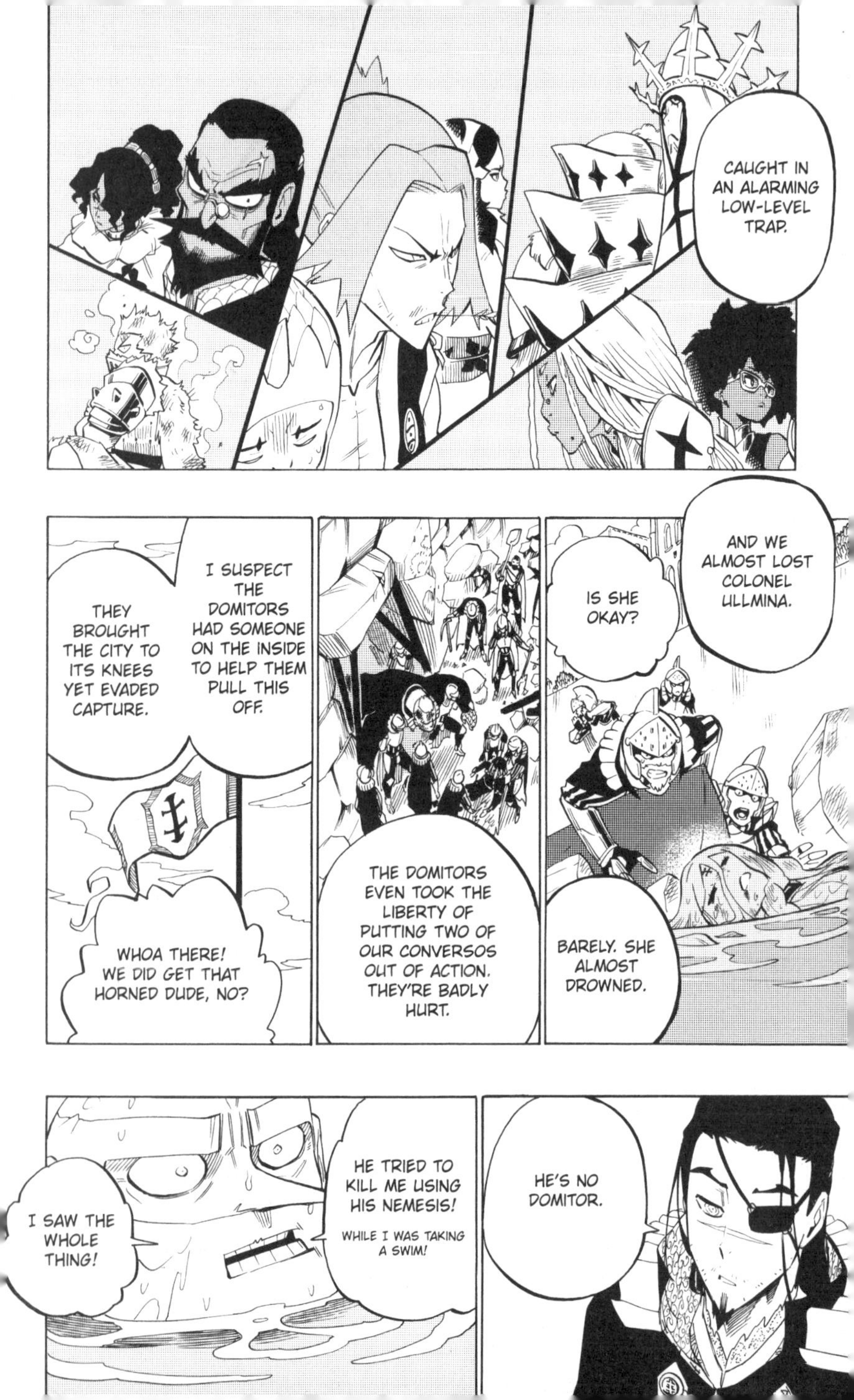
CAUGHT IN AN ALARMING LOW-LEVEL TRAP.
AND WE ALMOST LOST COLONEL ULLMINA.
IS SHE OKAY?
BARELY. SHE ALMOST DROWNED.
THE DOMITORS EVEN TOOK THE LIBERTY OF PUTTING TWO OF OUR CONVERSOS OUT OF ACTION. THEY'RE BADLY HURT.
I SUSPECT THE DOMITORS HAD SOMEONE ON THE INSIDE TO HELP THEM PULL THIS OFF.
THEY BROUGHT THE CITY TO ITS KNEES YET EVADED CAPTURE.
WHOA THERE! WE DID GET THAT HORNED DUDE, NO?
HE'S NO DOMITOR.
HE TRIED TO KILL ME USING HIS NEMESIS!
WHILE I WAS TAKING A SWIM!
I SAW THE WHOLE THING!

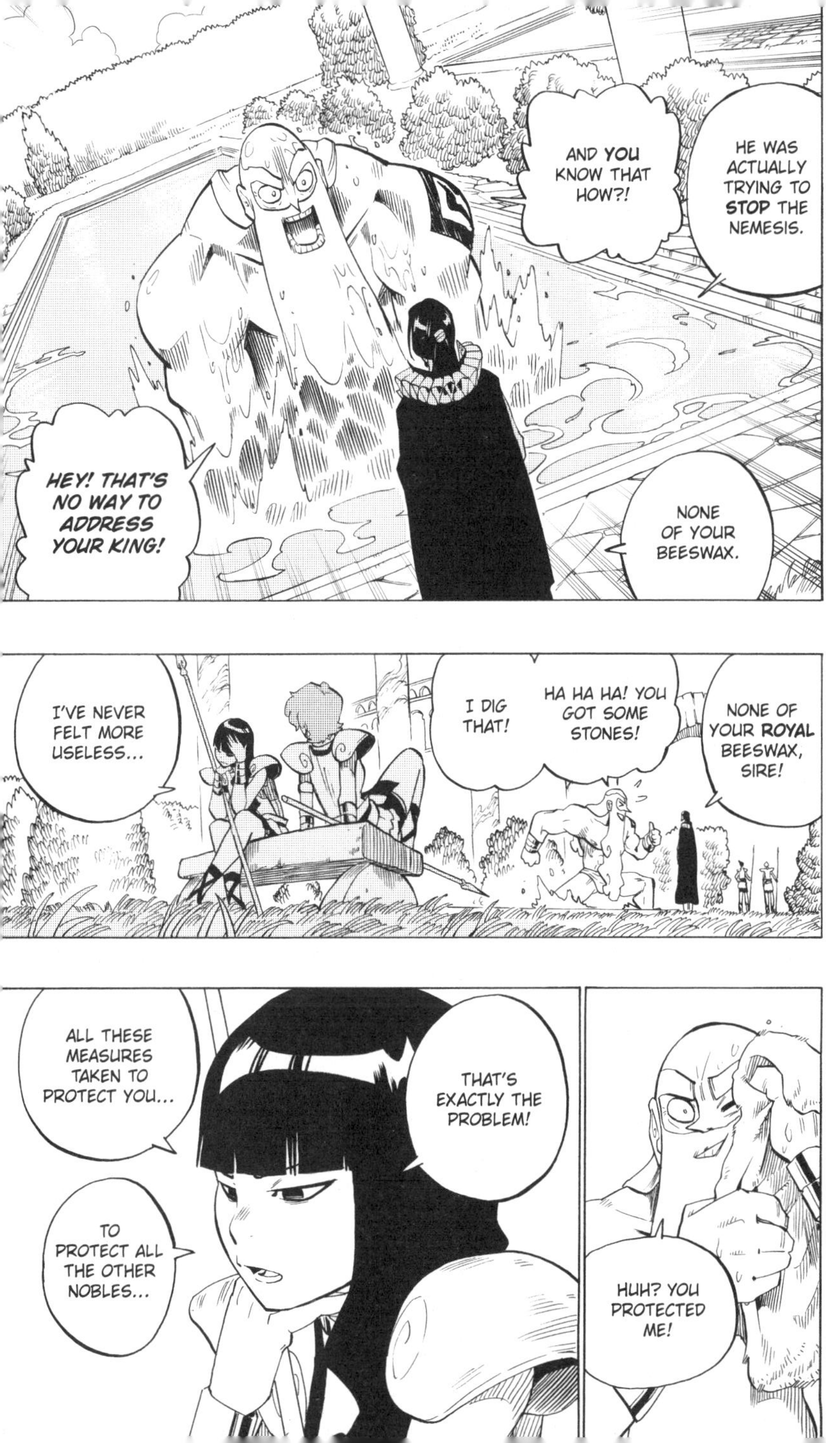
HE WAS ACTUALLY TRYING TO STOP THE NEMESIS.
AND YOU KNOW THAT HOW?!
NONE OF YOUR BEESWAX.
HEY! THAT'S NO WAY TO ADDRESS YOUR KING!
NONE OF YOUR ROYAL BEESWAX, SIRE!
HA HA HA! YOU GOT SOME STONES!
I DIG THAT!
I'VE NEVER FELT MORE USELESS...
HUH? YOU PROTECTED ME!
THAT'S EXACTLY THE PROBLEM!
ALL THESE MEASURES TAKEN TO PROTECT YOU...
TO PROTECT ALL THE OTHER NOBLES...

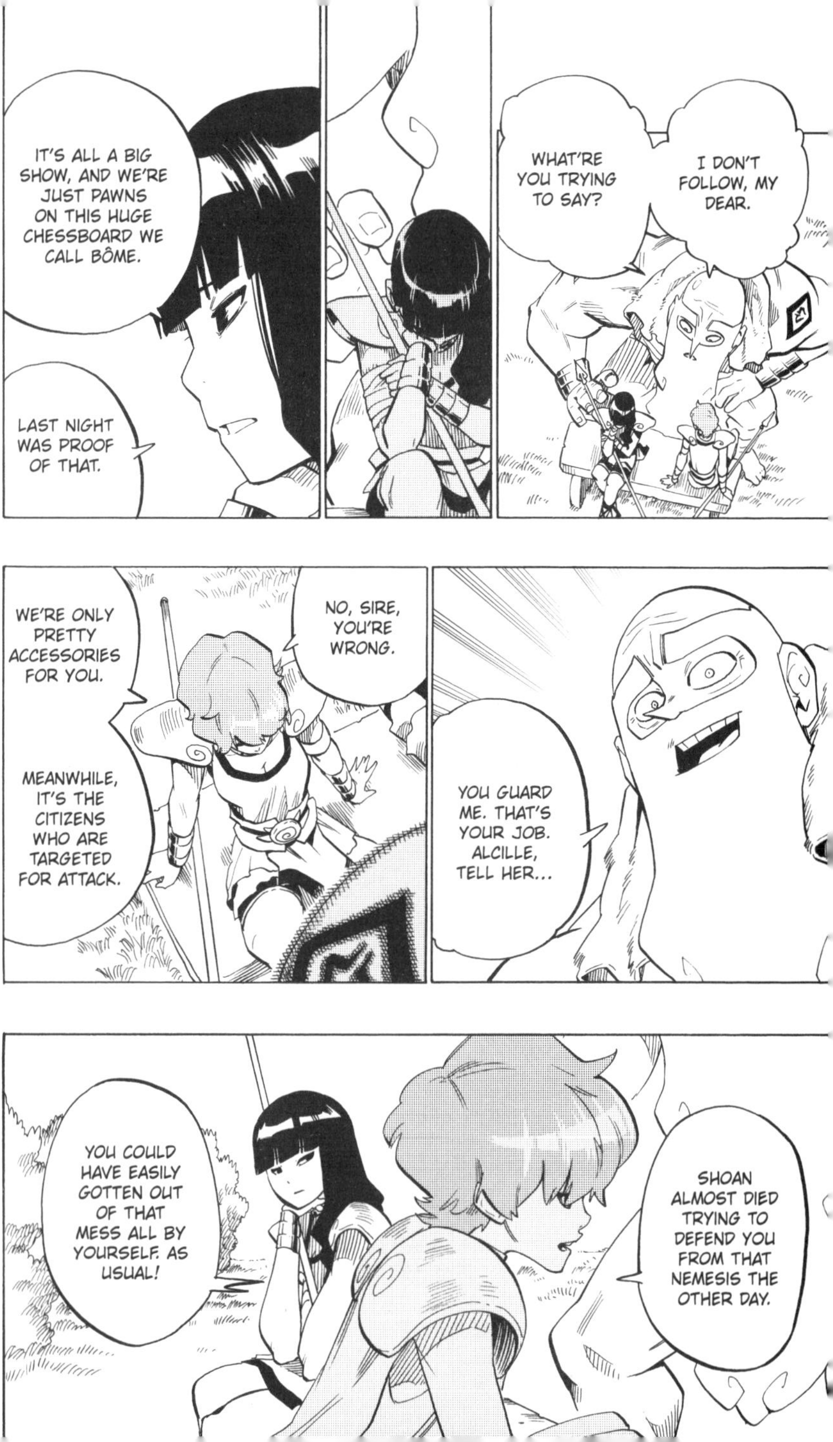
I DON'T FOLLOW, MY DEAR.
WHAT'RE YOU TRYING TO SAY?
IT'S ALL A BIG SHOW, AND WE'RE JUST PAWNS ON THIS HUGE CHESSBOARD WE CALL BÔME.
LAST NIGHT WAS PROOF OF THAT.
YOU GUARD ME. THAT'S YOUR JOB. ALCILLE, TELL HER...
NO, SIRE, YOU'RE WRONG.
WE'RE ONLY PRETTY ACCESSORIES FOR YOU.
MEANWHILE, IT'S THE CITIZENS WHO ARE TARGETED FOR ATTACK.
SHOAN ALMOST DIED TRYING TO DEFEND YOU FROM THAT NEMESIS THE OTHER DAY.
YOU COULD HAVE EASILY GOTTEN OUT OF THAT MESS ALL BY YOURSELF. AS USUAL!

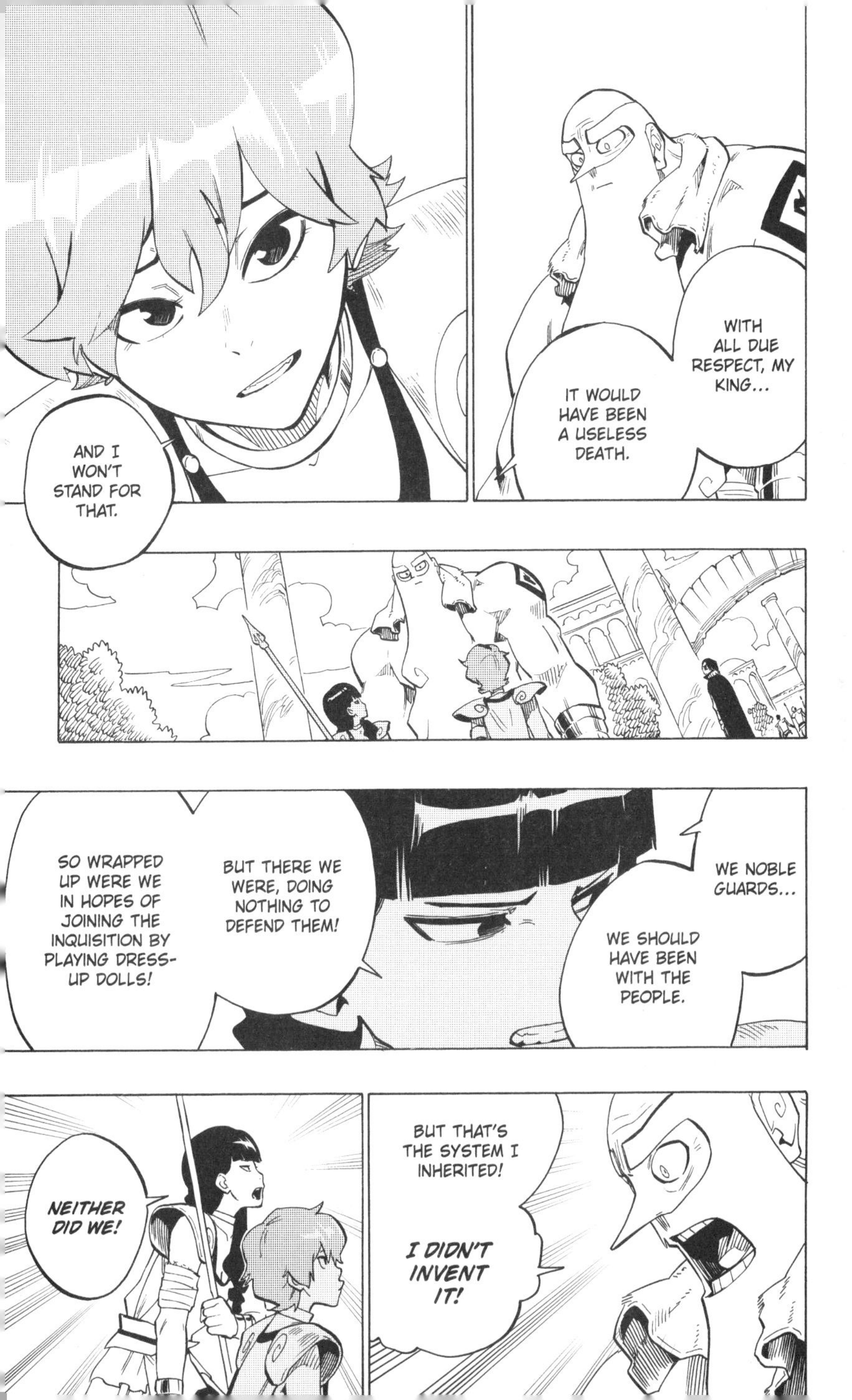
WITH ALL DUE RESPECT, MY KING…
IT WOULD HAVE BEEN A USELESS DEATH.
AND I WON'T STAND FOR THAT.
WE NOBLE GUARDS…
WE SHOULD HAVE BEEN WITH THE PEOPLE.
BUT THERE WE WERE, DOING NOTHING TO DEFEND THEM!
SO WRAPPED UP WERE WE IN HOPES OF JOINING THE INQUISITION BY PLAYING DRESS-UP DOLLS!
BUT THAT'S THE SYSTEM I INHERITED!
I DIDN'T INVENT IT!
NEITHER DID WE!

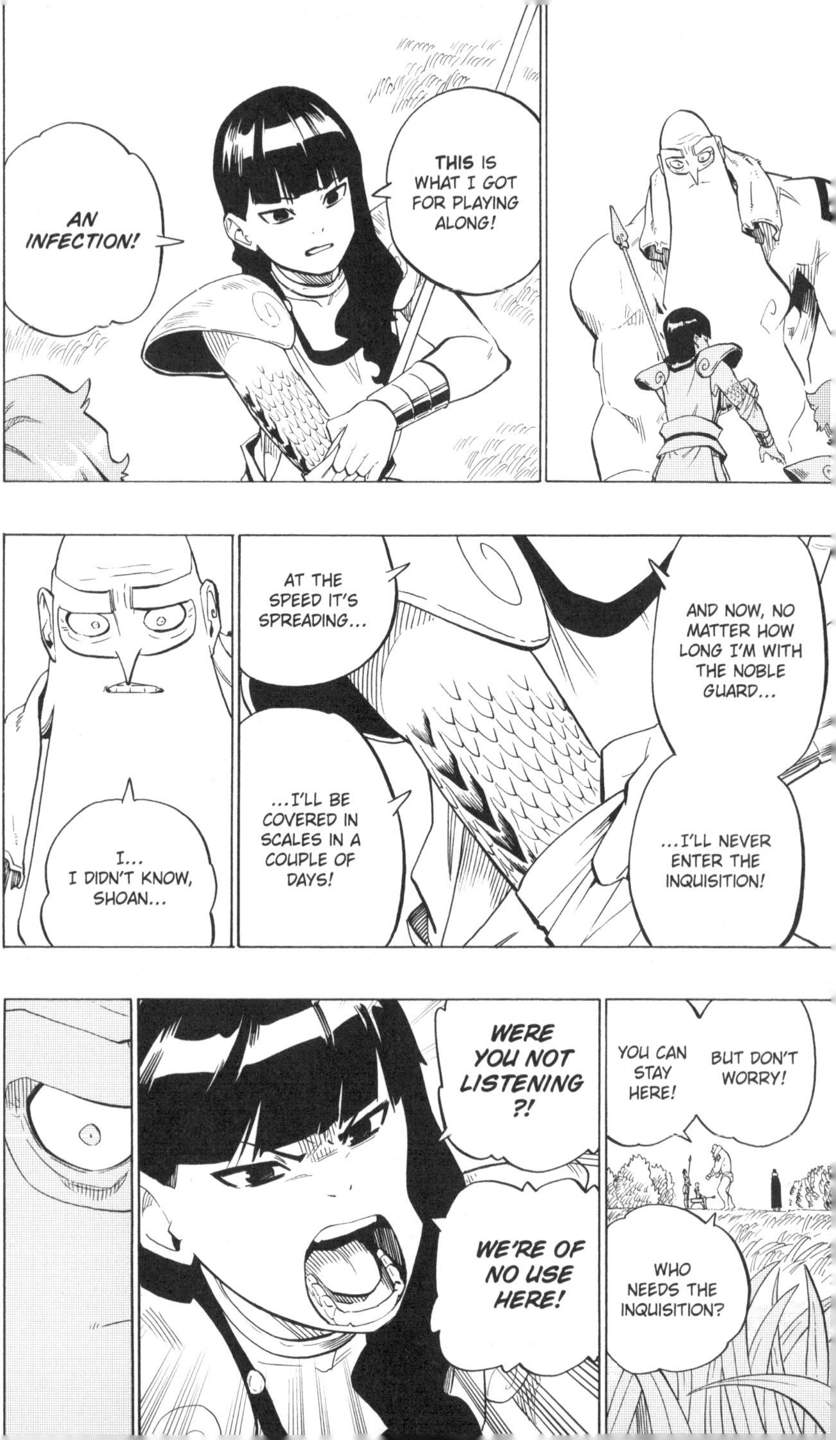
THIS IS WHAT I GOT FOR PLAYING ALONG!
AN INFECTION!
AND NOW, NO MATTER HOW LONG I'M WITH THE NOBLE GUARD...
...I'LL NEVER ENTER THE INQUISITION!
AT THE SPEED IT'S SPREADING...
...I'LL BE COVERED IN SCALES IN A COUPLE OF DAYS!
I... I DIDN'T KNOW, SHOAN...
BUT DON'T WORRY!
YOU CAN STAY HERE!
WHO NEEDS THE INQUISITION?
WERE YOU NOT LISTENING?!
WE'RE OF NO USE HERE!

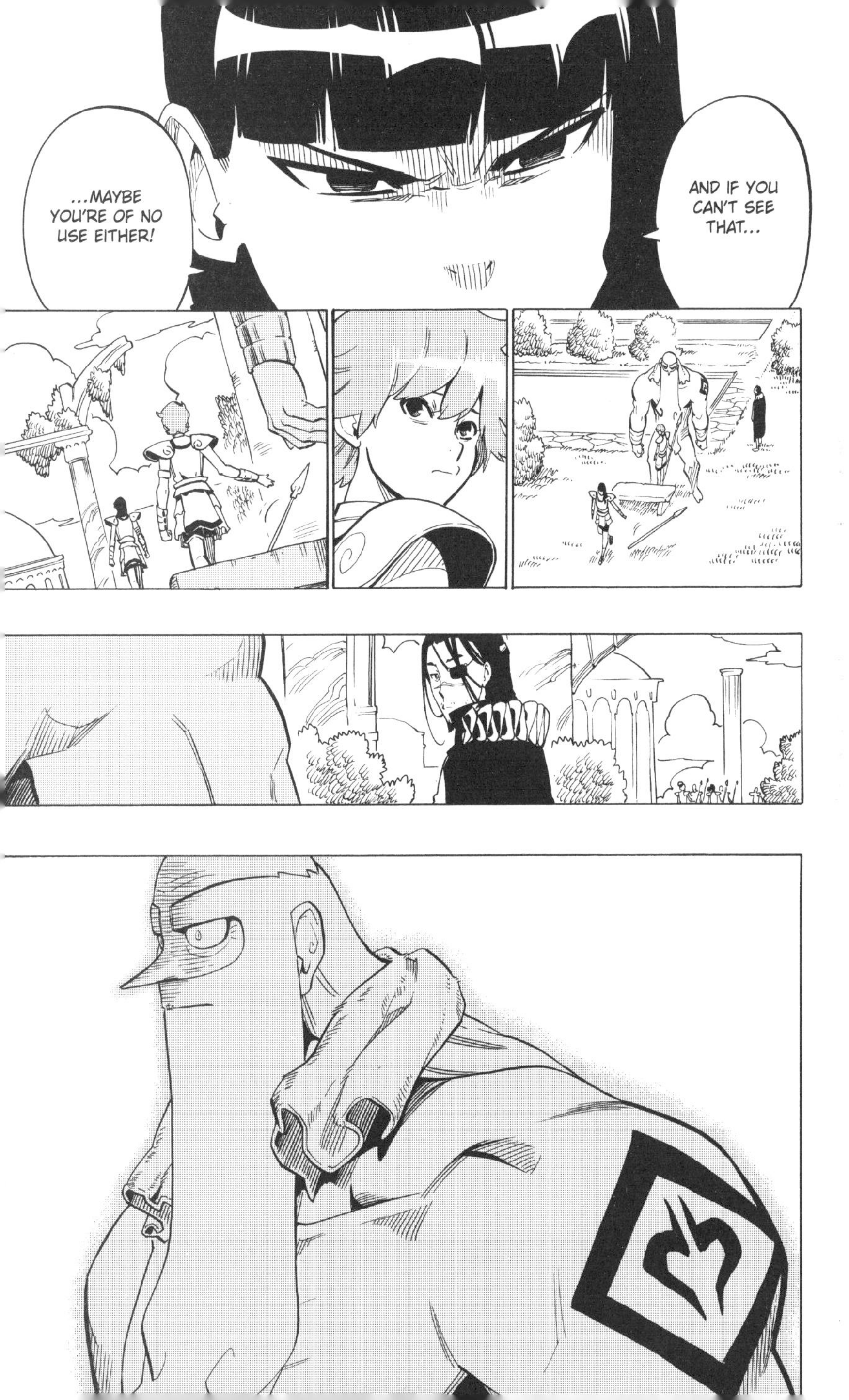
AND IF YOU CAN'T SEE THAT...
...MAYBE YOU'RE OF NO USE EITHER!

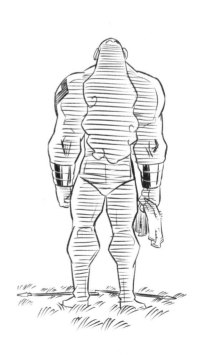

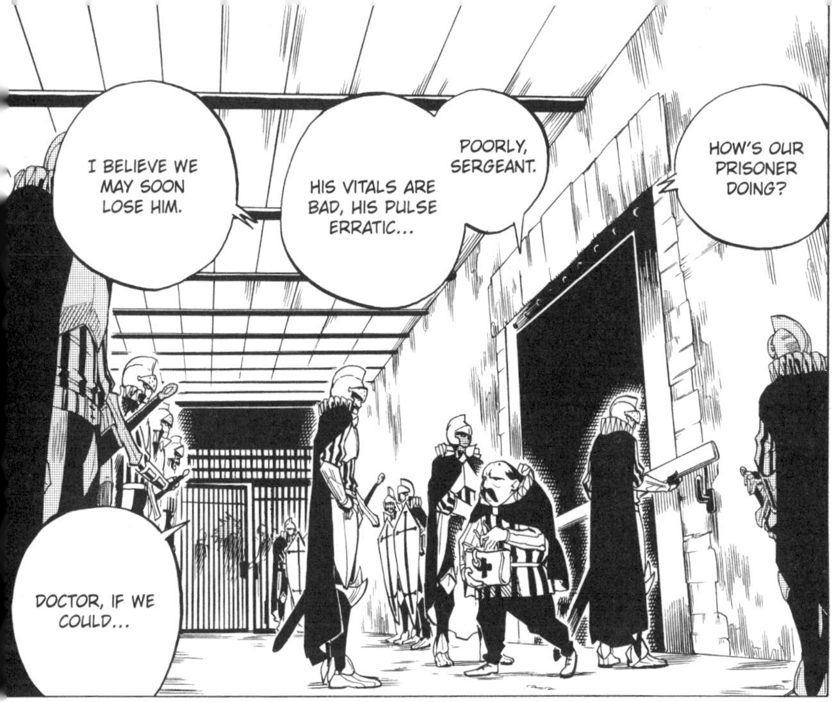
HOW'S OUR PRISONER DOING?
POORLY, SERGEANT.
HIS VITALS ARE BAD, HIS PULSE ERRATIC...
I BELIEVE WE MAY SOON LOSE HIM.
DOCTOR, IF WE COULD...

Chapter 116 Our Uniform

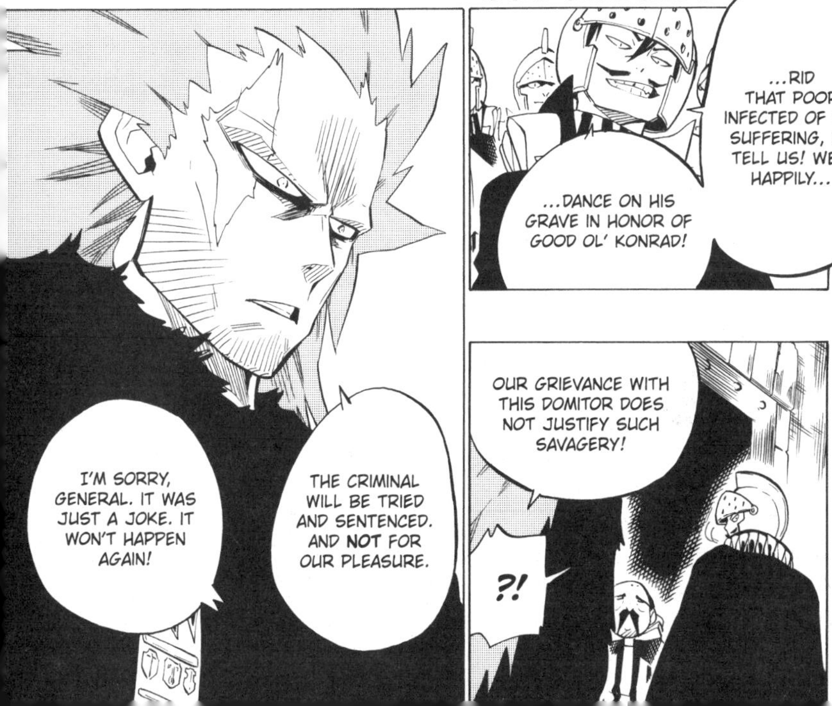
...RID THAT POOR INFECTED OF HIS SUFFERING, DO TELL US! WE'D HAPPILY...
...DANCE ON HIS GRAVE IN HONOR OF GOOD OL' KONRAD!
OUR GRIEVANCE WITH THIS DOMITOR DOES NOT JUSTIFY SUCH SAVAGERY!
?!
THE CRIMINAL WILL BE TRIED AND SENTENCED. AND NOT FOR OUR PLEASURE.
I'M SORRY, GENERAL. IT WAS JUST A JOKE. IT WON'T HAPPEN AGAIN!

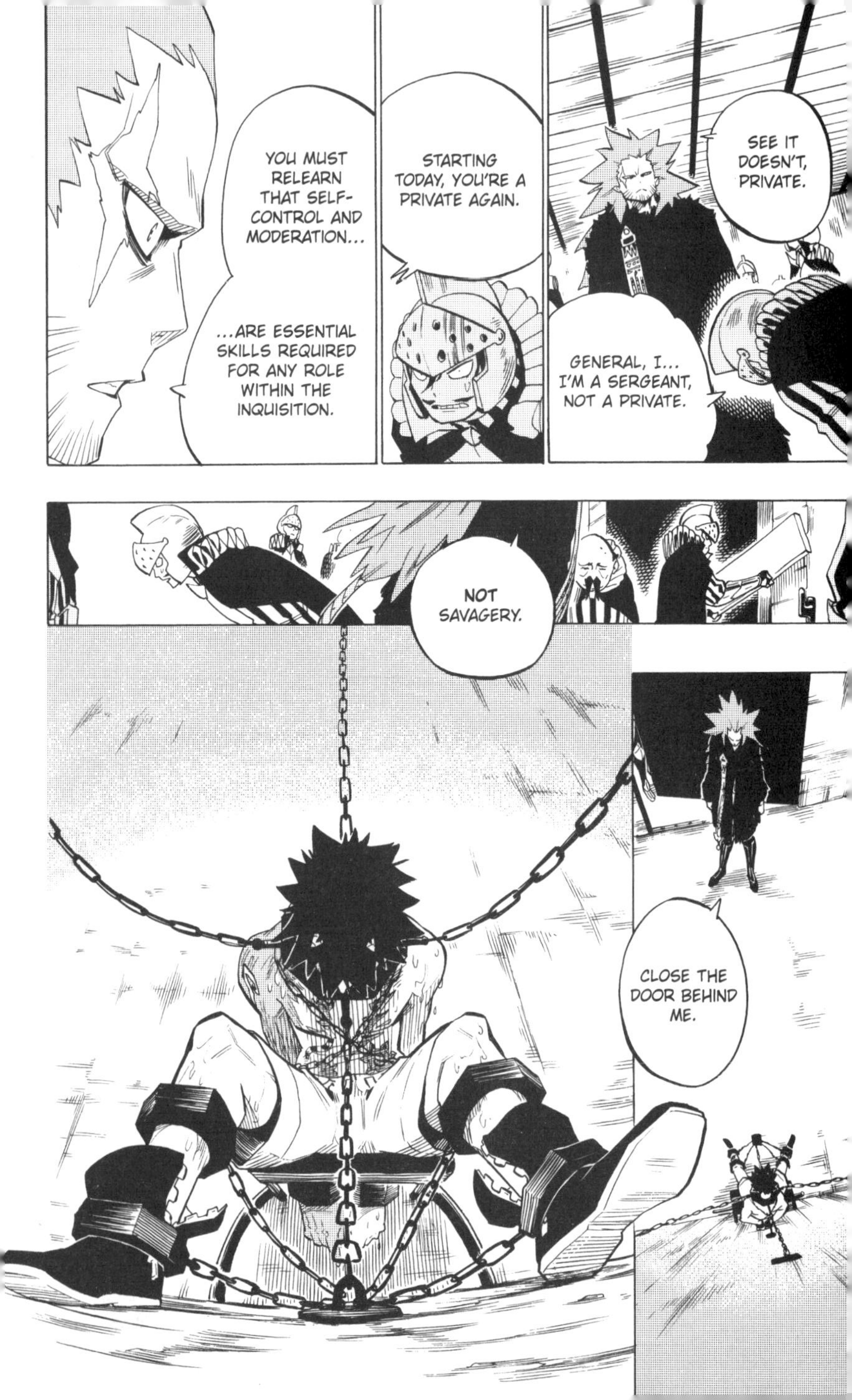
SEE IT DOESN'T, PRIVATE.
GENERAL, I... I'M A SERGEANT, NOT A PRIVATE.
STARTING TODAY, YOU'RE A PRIVATE AGAIN.
YOU MUST RELEARN THAT SELF-CONTROL AND MODERATION...
...ARE ESSENTIAL SKILLS REQUIRED FOR ANY ROLE WITHIN THE INQUISITION.
NOT SAVAGERY.
CLOSE THE DOOR BEHIND ME.

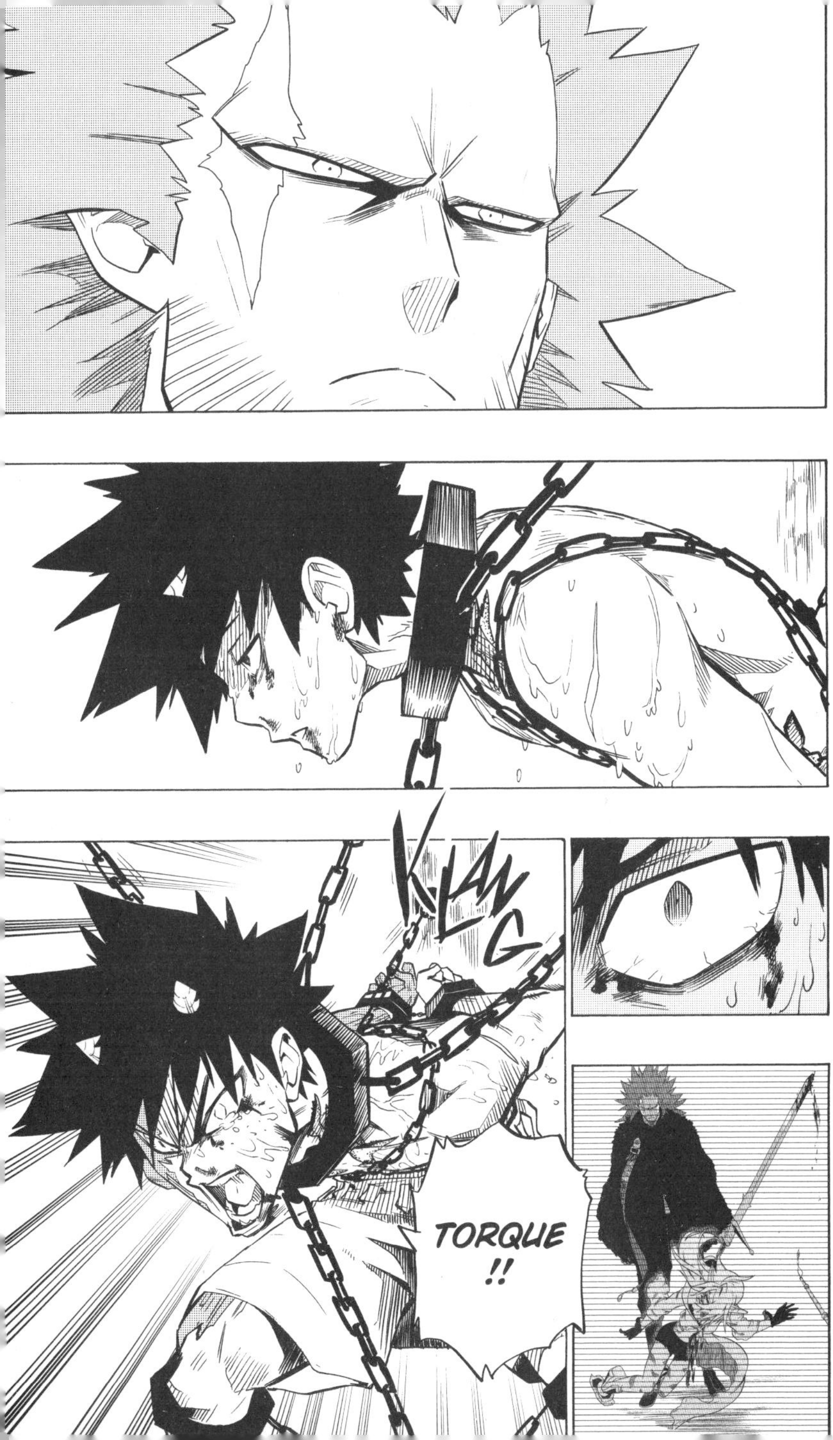
KLANG
TORQUE !!

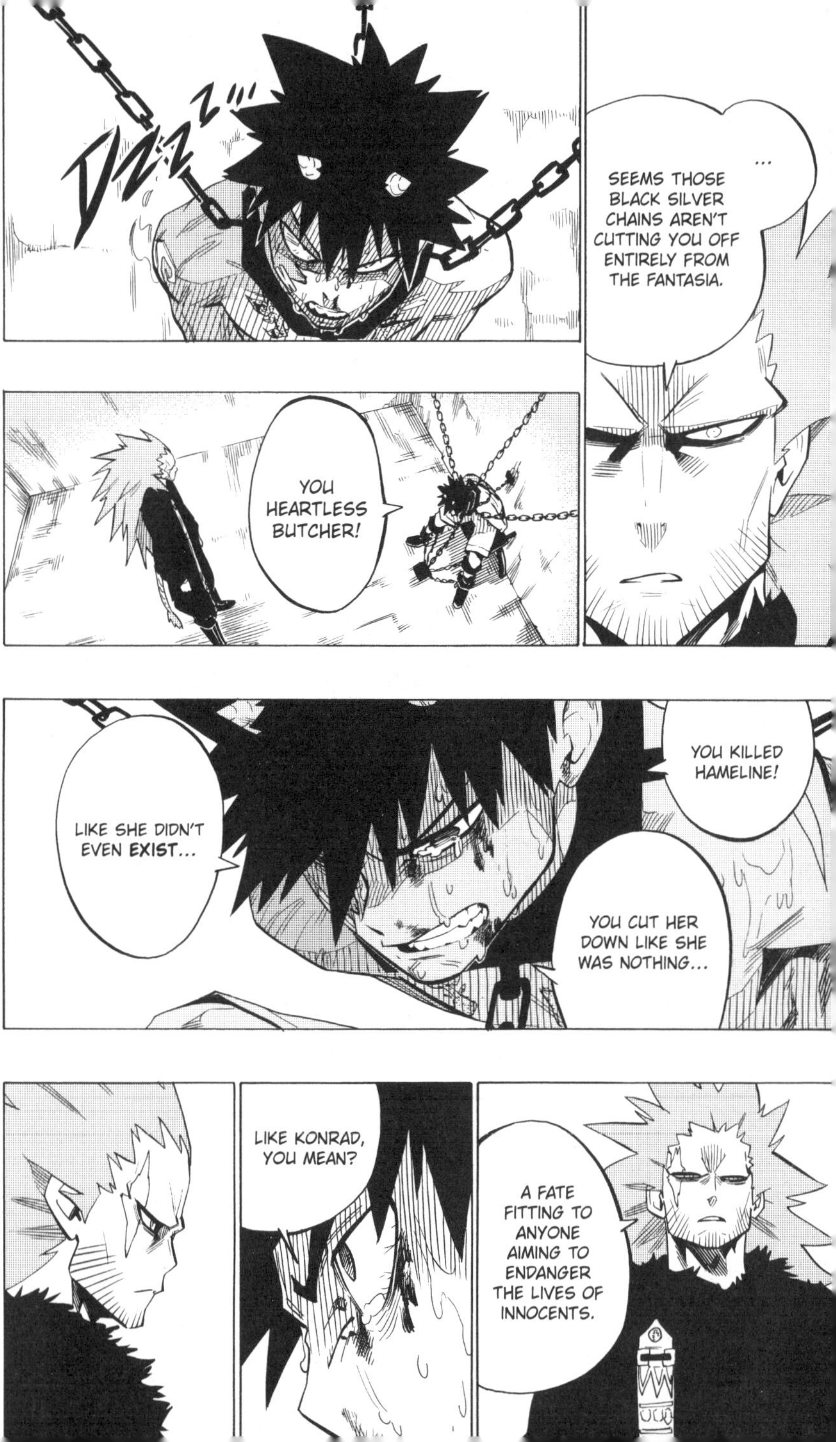
...
SEEMS THOSE BLACK SILVER CHAINS AREN'T CUTTING YOU OFF ENTIRELY FROM THE FANTASIA.
DZZZZ!!!
YOU HEARTLESS BUTCHER!
YOU KILLED HAMELINE!
YOU CUT HER DOWN LIKE SHE WAS NOTHING...
LIKE SHE DIDN'T EVEN **EXIST**...
A FATE FITTING TO ANYONE AIMING TO ENDANGER THE LIVES OF INNOCENTS.
LIKE KONRAD, YOU MEAN?

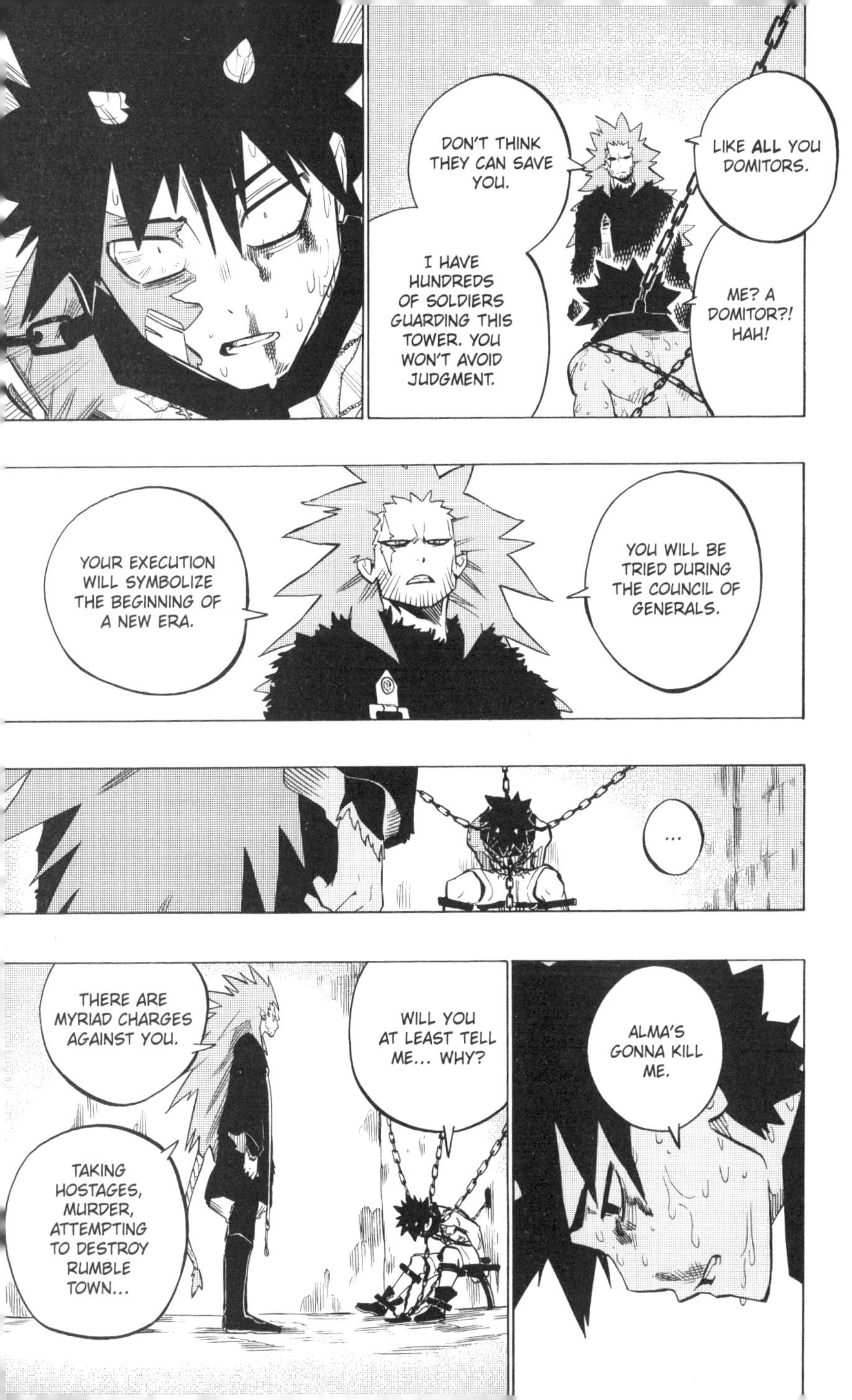
DON'T THINK THEY CAN SAVE YOU.
I HAVE HUNDREDS OF SOLDIERS GUARDING THIS TOWER. YOU WON'T AVOID JUDGMENT.
LIKE **ALL** YOU DOMITORS.
ME? A DOMITOR?! HAH!
YOU WILL BE TRIED DURING THE COUNCIL OF GENERALS.
YOUR EXECUTION WILL SYMBOLIZE THE BEGINNING OF A NEW ERA.
...
ALMA'S GONNA KILL ME.
WILL YOU AT LEAST TELL ME... WHY?
THERE ARE MYRIAD CHARGES AGAINST YOU.
TAKING HOSTAGES, MURDER, ATTEMPTING TO DESTROY RUMBLE TOWN...

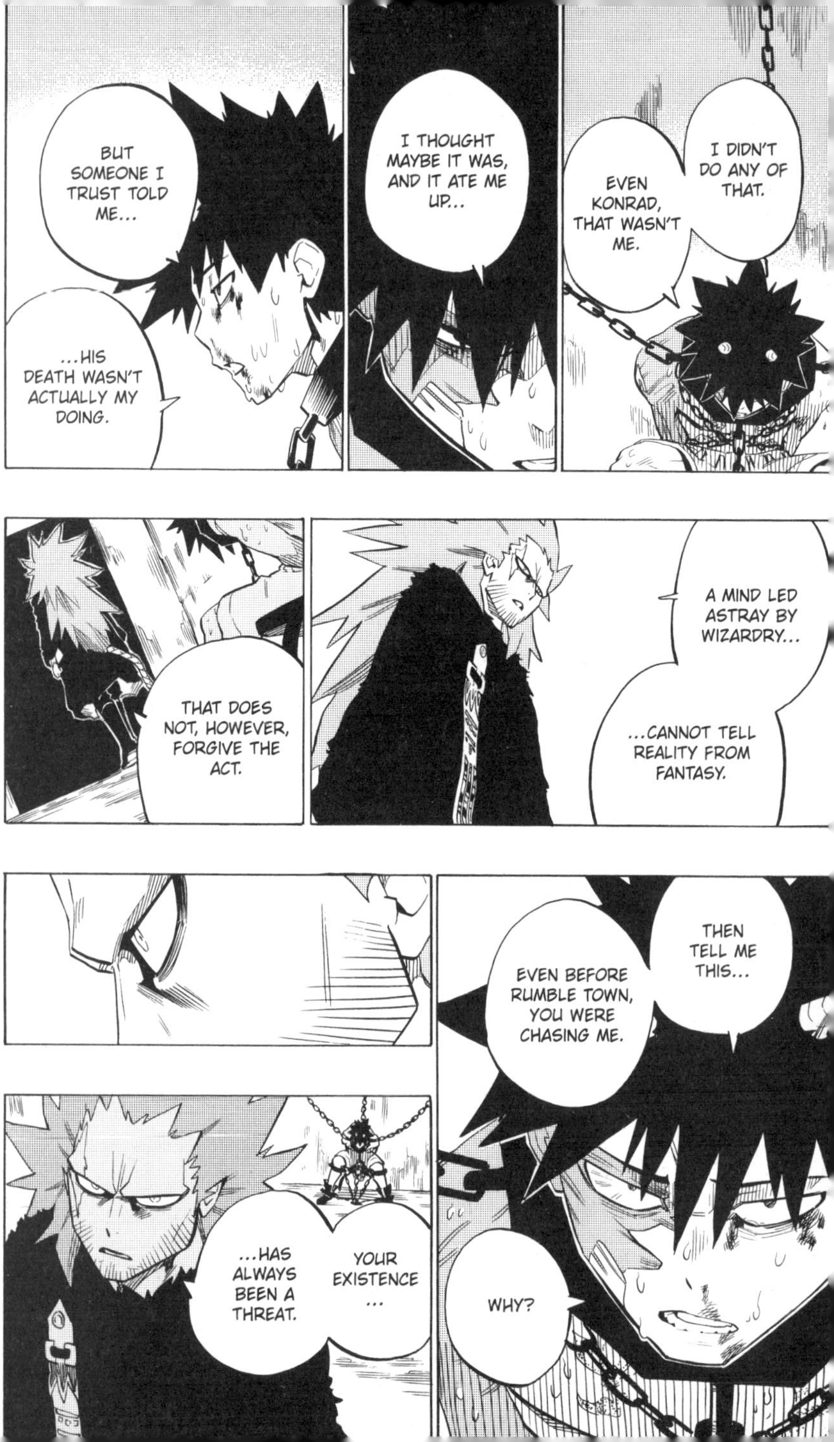
I DIDN'T DO ANY OF THAT.
EVEN KONRAD, THAT WASN'T ME.
I THOUGHT MAYBE IT WAS, AND IT ATE ME UP...
BUT SOMEONE I TRUST TOLD ME...
...HIS DEATH WASN'T ACTUALLY MY DOING.
A MIND LED ASTRAY BY WIZARDRY...
...CANNOT TELL REALITY FROM FANTASY.
THAT DOES NOT, HOWEVER, FORGIVE THE ACT.
THEN TELL ME THIS...
EVEN BEFORE RUMBLE TOWN, YOU WERE CHASING ME.
WHY?
YOUR EXISTENCE...
...HAS ALWAYS BEEN A THREAT.

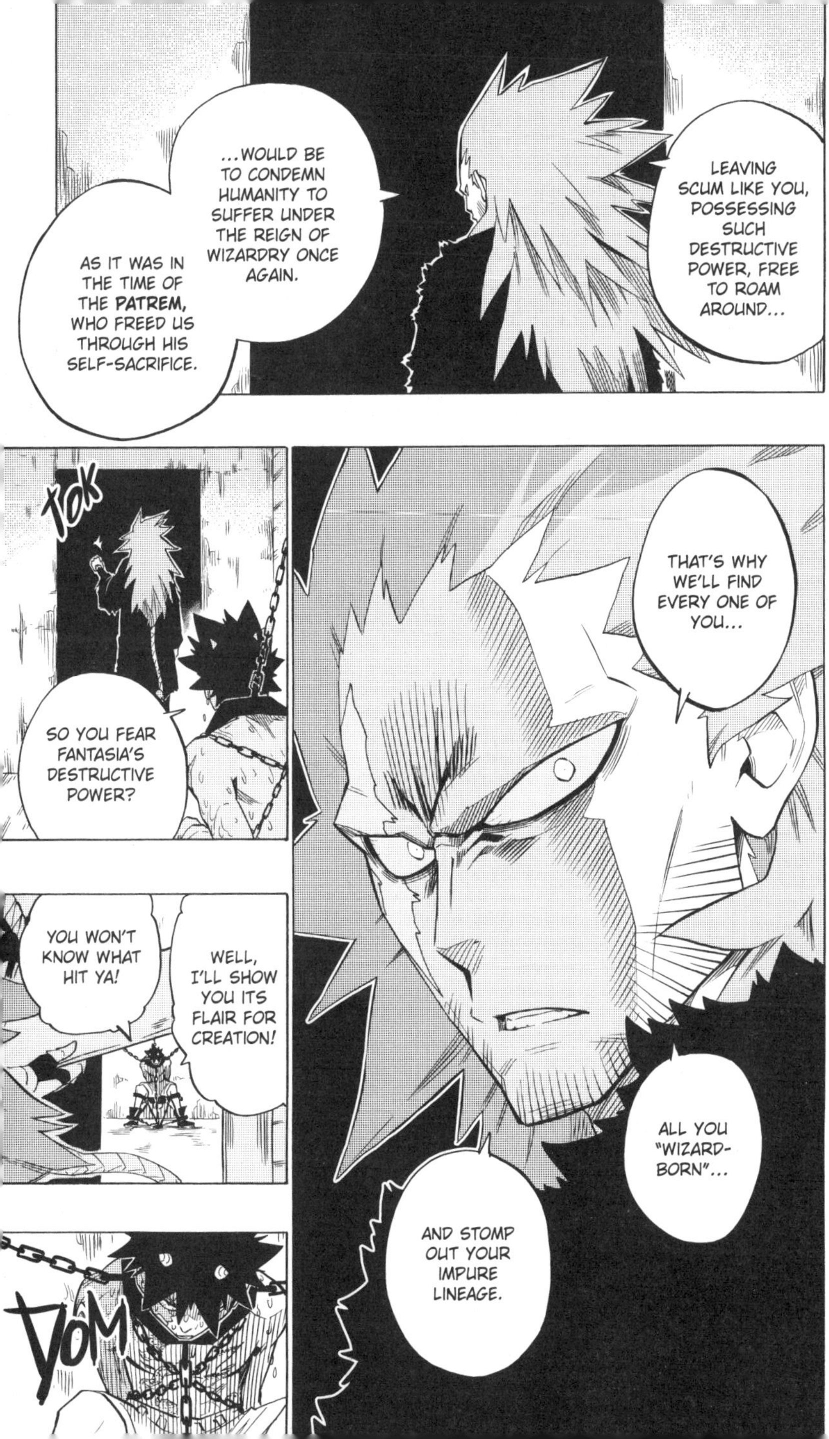
LEAVING SCUM LIKE YOU, POSSESSING SUCH DESTRUCTIVE POWER, FREE TO ROAM AROUND...
...WOULD BE TO CONDEMN HUMANITY TO SUFFER UNDER THE REIGN OF WIZARDRY ONCE AGAIN.
AS IT WAS IN THE TIME OF THE **PATREM,** WHO FREED US THROUGH HIS SELF-SACRIFICE.
THAT'S WHY WE'LL FIND EVERY ONE OF YOU...
ALL YOU "WIZARD-BORN"...
AND STOMP OUT YOUR IMPURE LINEAGE.
TOK
SO YOU FEAR FANTASIA'S DESTRUCTIVE POWER?
WELL, I'LL SHOW YOU ITS FLAIR FOR CREATION!
YOU WON'T KNOW WHAT HIT YA!
DOM

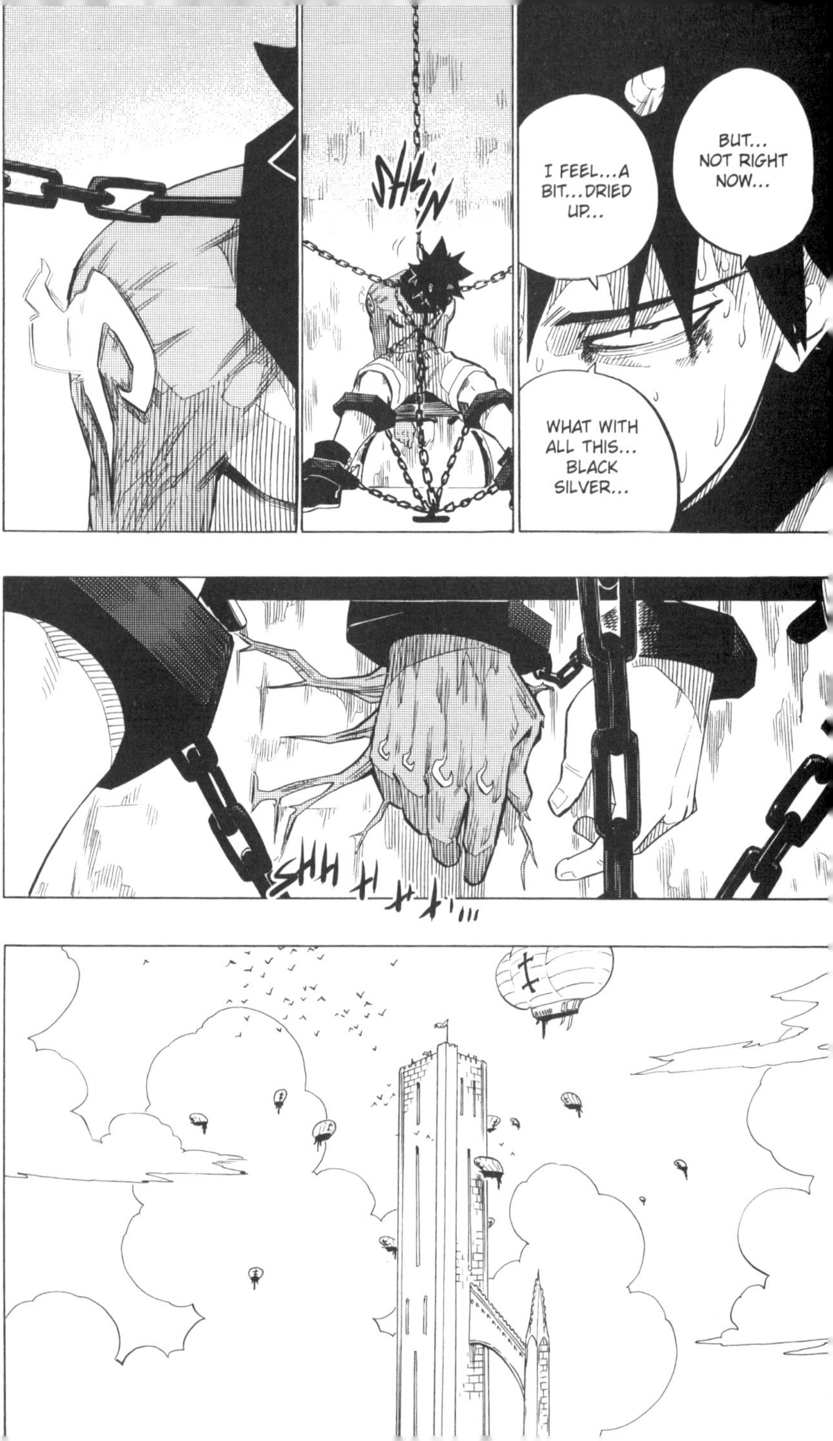
BUT... NOT RIGHT NOW...
I FEEL...A BIT...DRIED UP...
WHAT WITH ALL THIS... BLACK SILVER...
SHLIN
SHHH

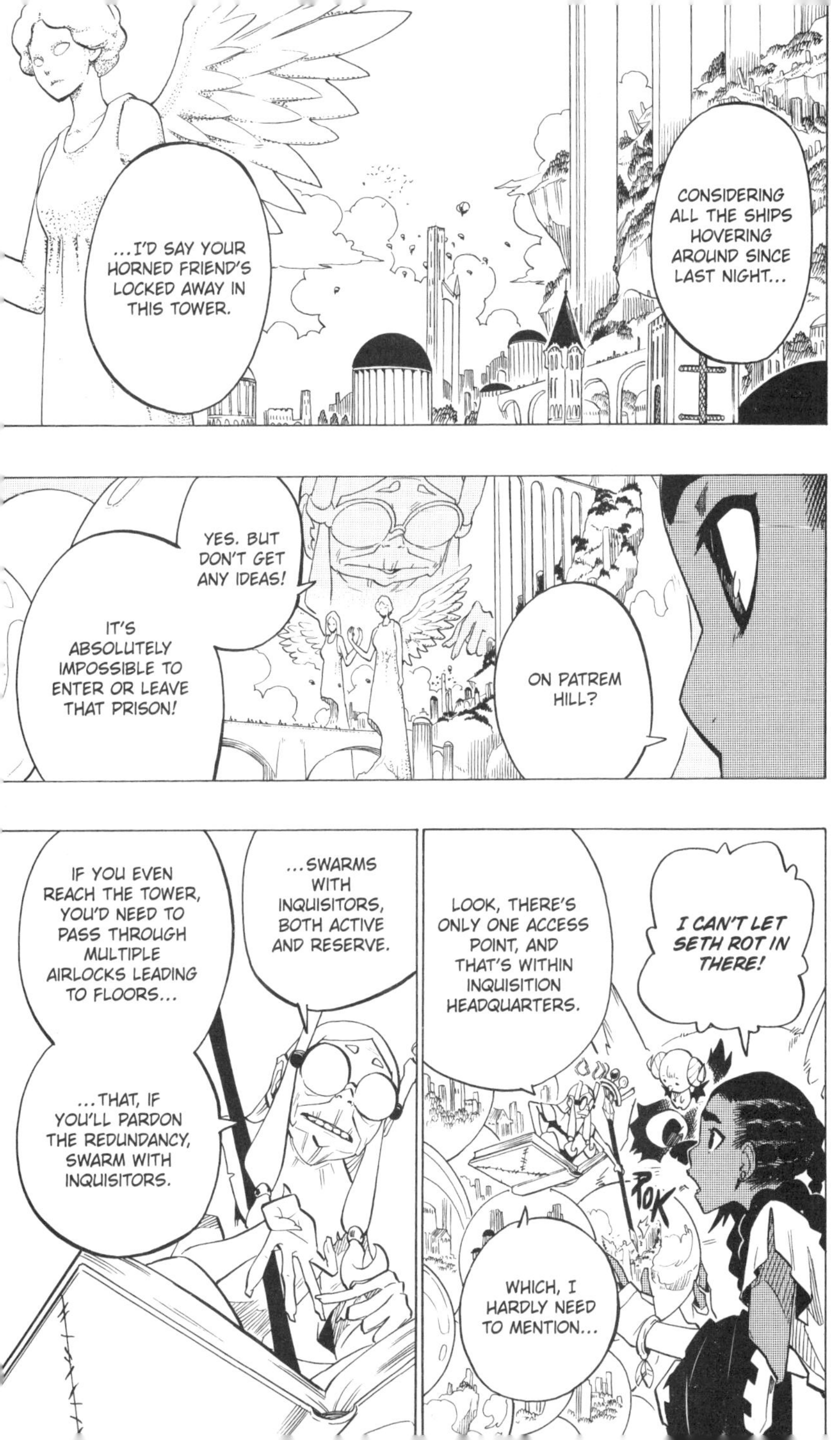
CONSIDERING ALL THE SHIPS HOVERING AROUND SINCE LAST NIGHT...
...I'D SAY YOUR HORNED FRIEND'S LOCKED AWAY IN THIS TOWER.
ON PATREM HILL?
YES. BUT DON'T GET ANY IDEAS!
IT'S ABSOLUTELY IMPOSSIBLE TO ENTER OR LEAVE THAT PRISON!
I CAN'T LET SETH ROT IN THERE!
POK
LOOK, THERE'S ONLY ONE ACCESS POINT, AND THAT'S WITHIN INQUISITION HEADQUARTERS.
WHICH, I HARDLY NEED TO MENTION...
...SWARMS WITH INQUISITORS, BOTH ACTIVE AND RESERVE.
IF YOU EVEN REACH THE TOWER, YOU'D NEED TO PASS THROUGH MULTIPLE AIRLOCKS LEADING TO FLOORS...
...THAT, IF YOU'LL PARDON THE REDUNDANCY, SWARM WITH INQUISITORS.

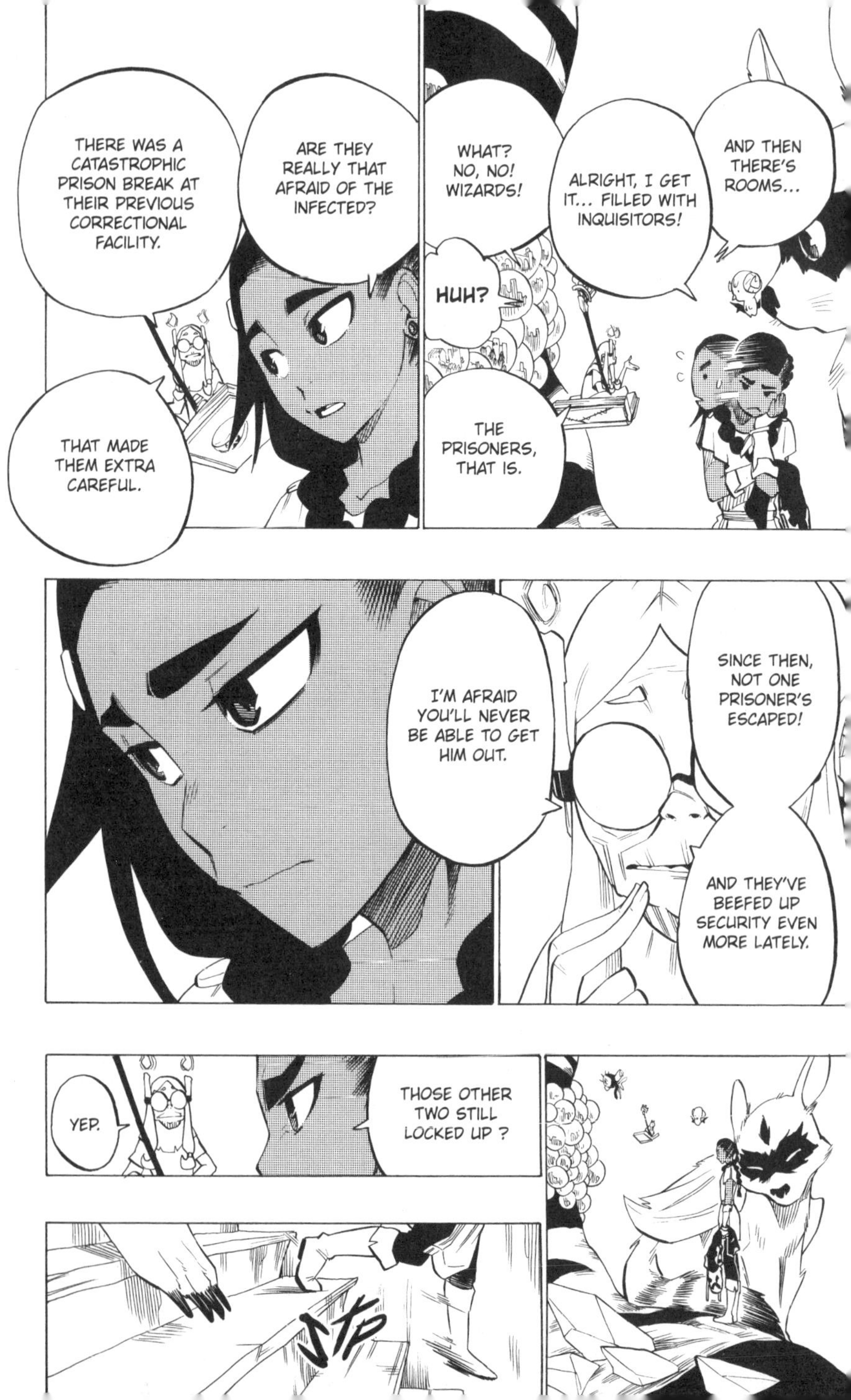
AND THEN THERE'S ROOMS...
ALRIGHT, I GET IT... FILLED WITH INQUISITORS!
WHAT? NO, NO! WIZARDS!
HUH?
THE PRISONERS, THAT IS.
ARE THEY REALLY THAT AFRAID OF THE INFECTED?
THERE WAS A CATASTROPHIC PRISON BREAK AT THEIR PREVIOUS CORRECTIONAL FACILITY.
THAT MADE THEM EXTRA CAREFUL.
SINCE THEN, NOT ONE PRISONER'S ESCAPED!
AND THEY'VE BEEFED UP SECURITY EVEN MORE LATELY.
I'M AFRAID YOU'LL NEVER BE ABLE TO GET HIM OUT.
THOSE OTHER TWO STILL LOCKED UP ?
YEP.
STP

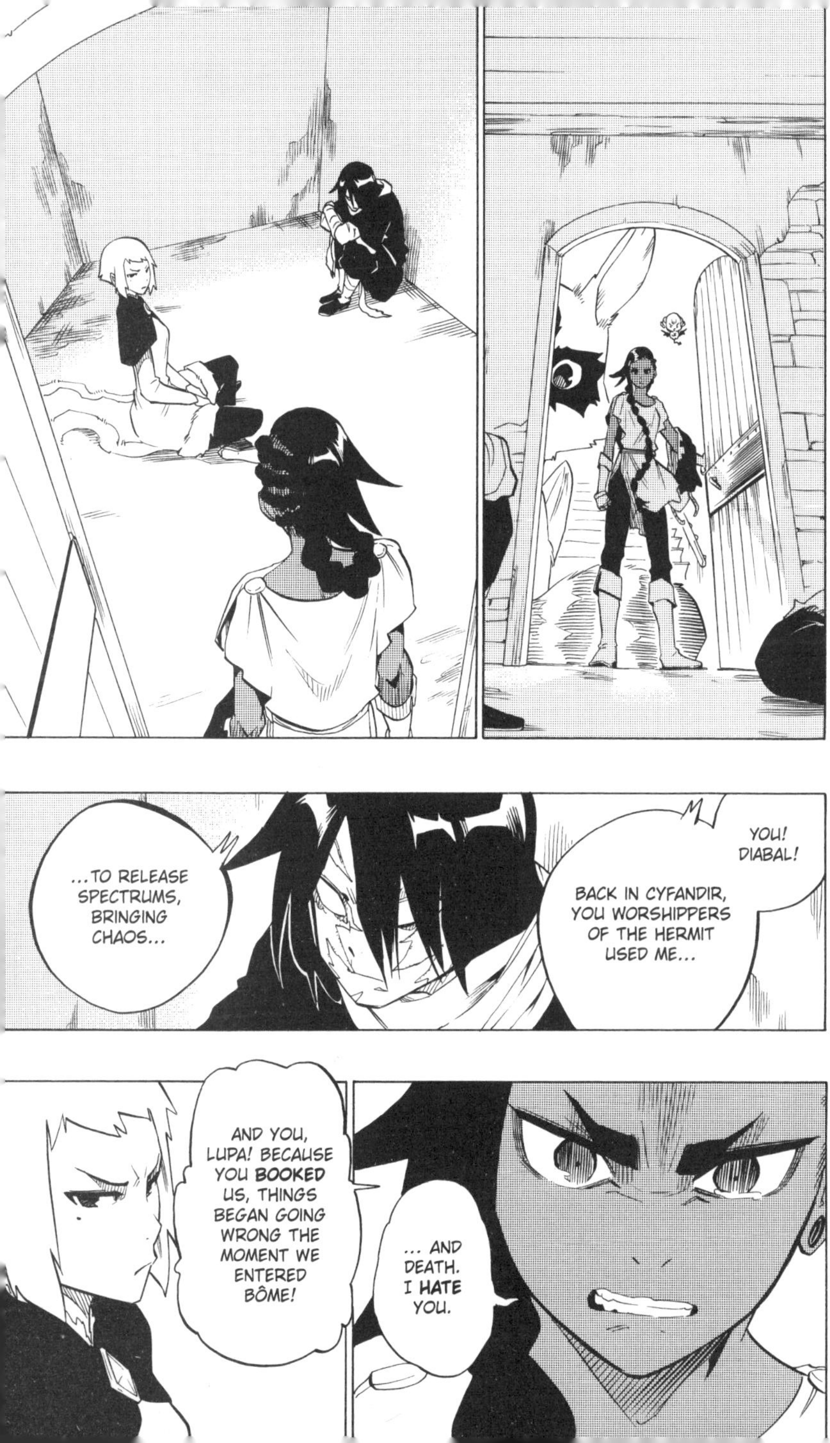
YOU! DIABAL!
BACK IN CYFANDIR, YOU WORSHIPPERS OF THE HERMIT USED ME...
...TO RELEASE SPECTRUMS, BRINGING CHAOS...
... AND DEATH. I HATE YOU.
AND YOU, LUPA! BECAUSE YOU BOOKED US, THINGS BEGAN GOING WRONG THE MOMENT WE ENTERED BÔME!

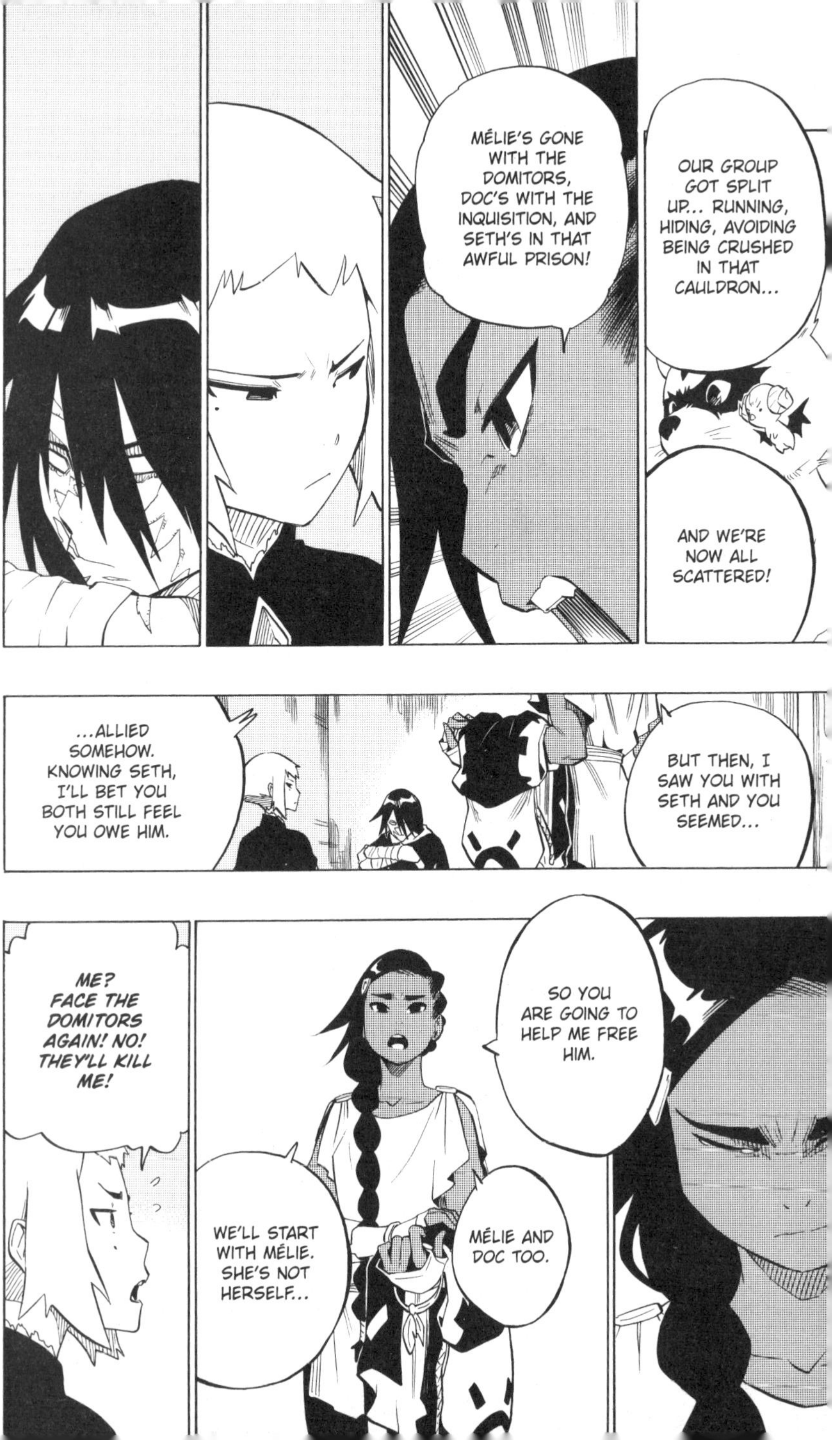
OUR GROUP GOT SPLIT UP... RUNNING, HIDING, AVOIDING BEING CRUSHED IN THAT CAULDRON...
AND WE'RE NOW ALL SCATTERED!
MÉLIE'S GONE WITH THE DOMITORS, DOC'S WITH THE INQUISITION, AND SETH'S IN THAT AWFUL PRISON!
BUT THEN, I SAW YOU WITH SETH AND YOU SEEMED...
...ALLIED SOMEHOW. KNOWING SETH, I'LL BET YOU BOTH STILL FEEL YOU OWE HIM.
SO YOU ARE GOING TO HELP ME FREE HIM.
MÉLIE AND DOC TOO.
WE'LL START WITH MÉLIE. SHE'S NOT HERSELF...
ME? FACE THE DOMITORS AGAIN! NO! THEY'LL KILL ME!

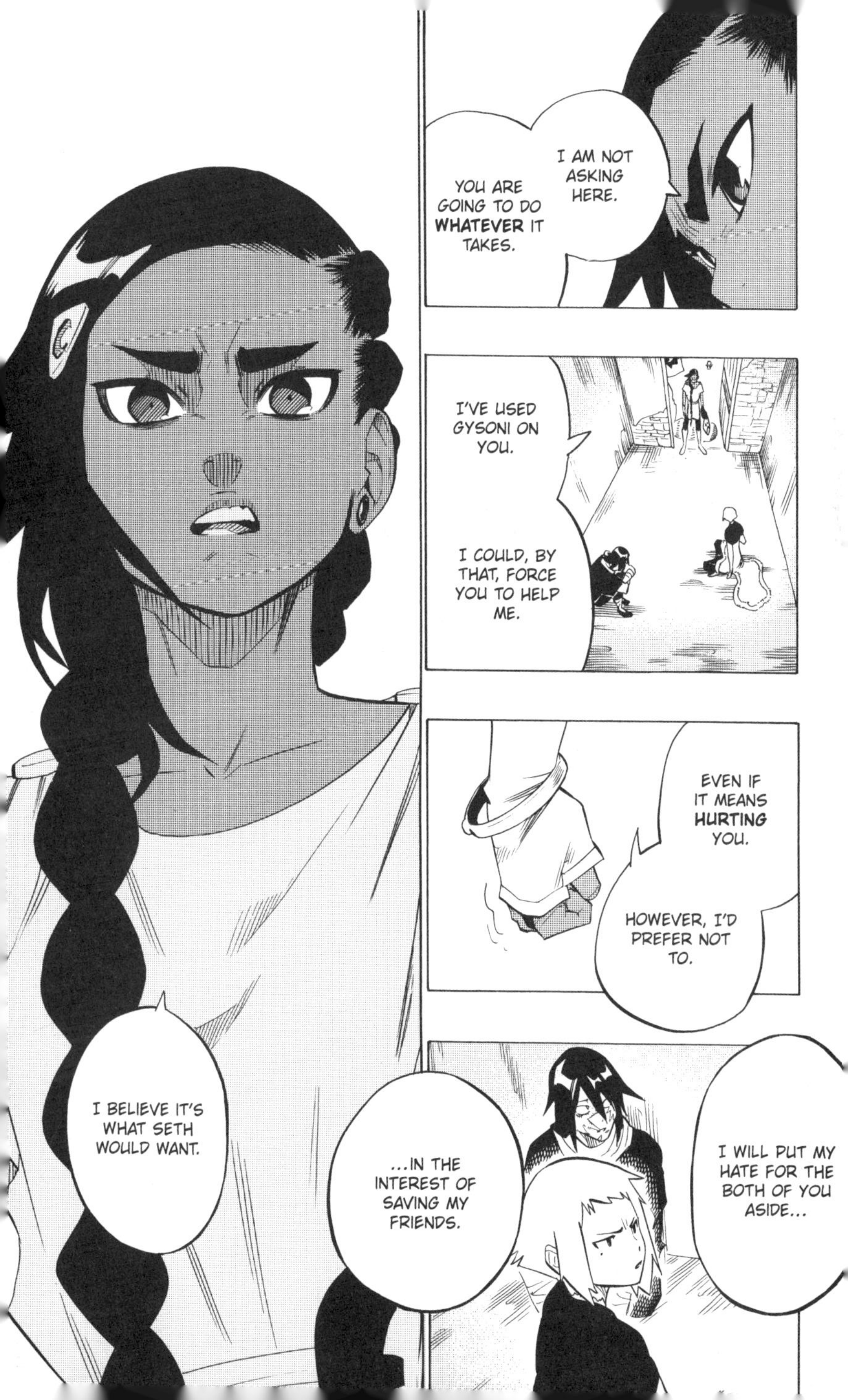
I AM NOT ASKING HERE.
YOU ARE GOING TO DO WHATEVER IT TAKES.
I'VE USED GYSONI ON YOU.
I COULD, BY THAT, FORCE YOU TO HELP ME.
EVEN IF IT MEANS HURTING YOU.
HOWEVER, I'D PREFER NOT TO.
I WILL PUT MY HATE FOR THE BOTH OF YOU ASIDE...
...IN THE INTEREST OF SAVING MY FRIENDS.
I BELIEVE IT'S WHAT SETH WOULD WANT.

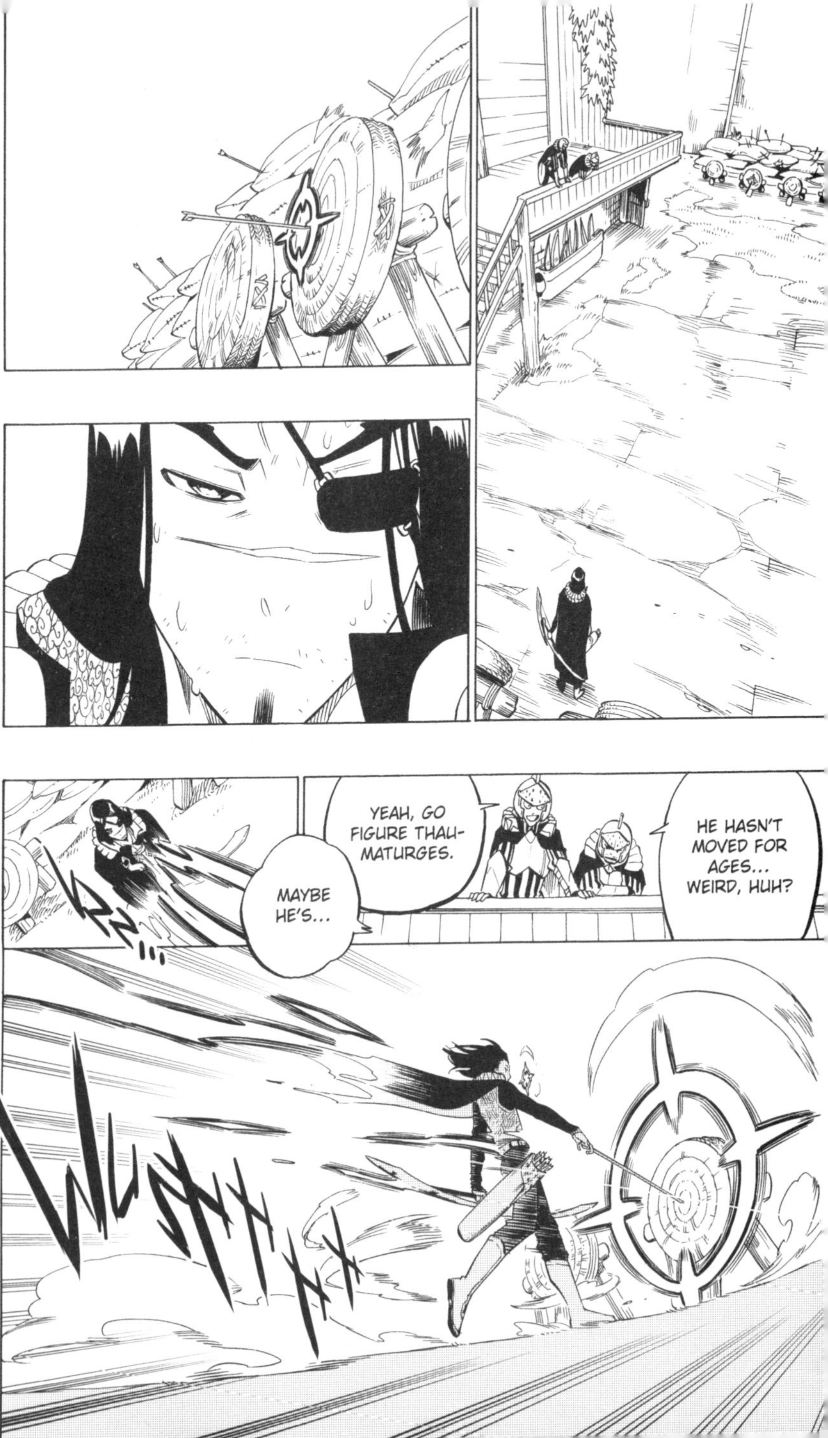
HE HASN'T MOVED FOR AGES... WEIRD, HUH?
YEAH, GO FIGURE THAUMATURGES.
MAYBE HE'S...

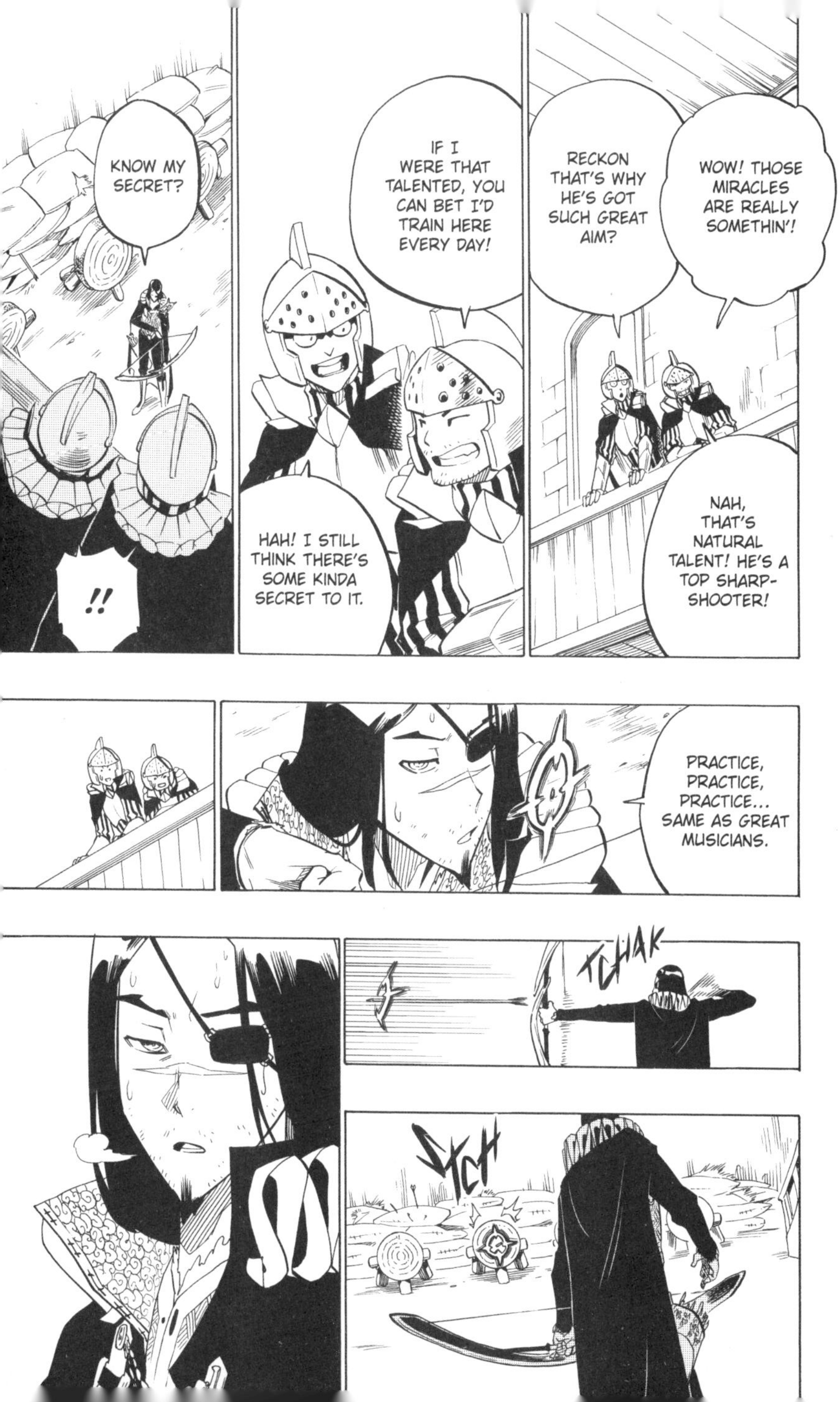
WOW! THOSE MIRACLES ARE REALLY SOMETHIN'!
RECKON THAT'S WHY HE'S GOT SUCH GREAT AIM?
NAH, THAT'S NATURAL TALENT! HE'S A TOP SHARP-SHOOTER!
IF I WERE THAT TALENTED, YOU CAN BET I'D TRAIN HERE EVERY DAY!
HAH! I STILL THINK THERE'S SOME KINDA SECRET TO IT.
KNOW MY SECRET?
!!
PRACTICE, PRACTICE, PRACTICE... SAME AS GREAT MUSICIANS.
TCHAK
STCH

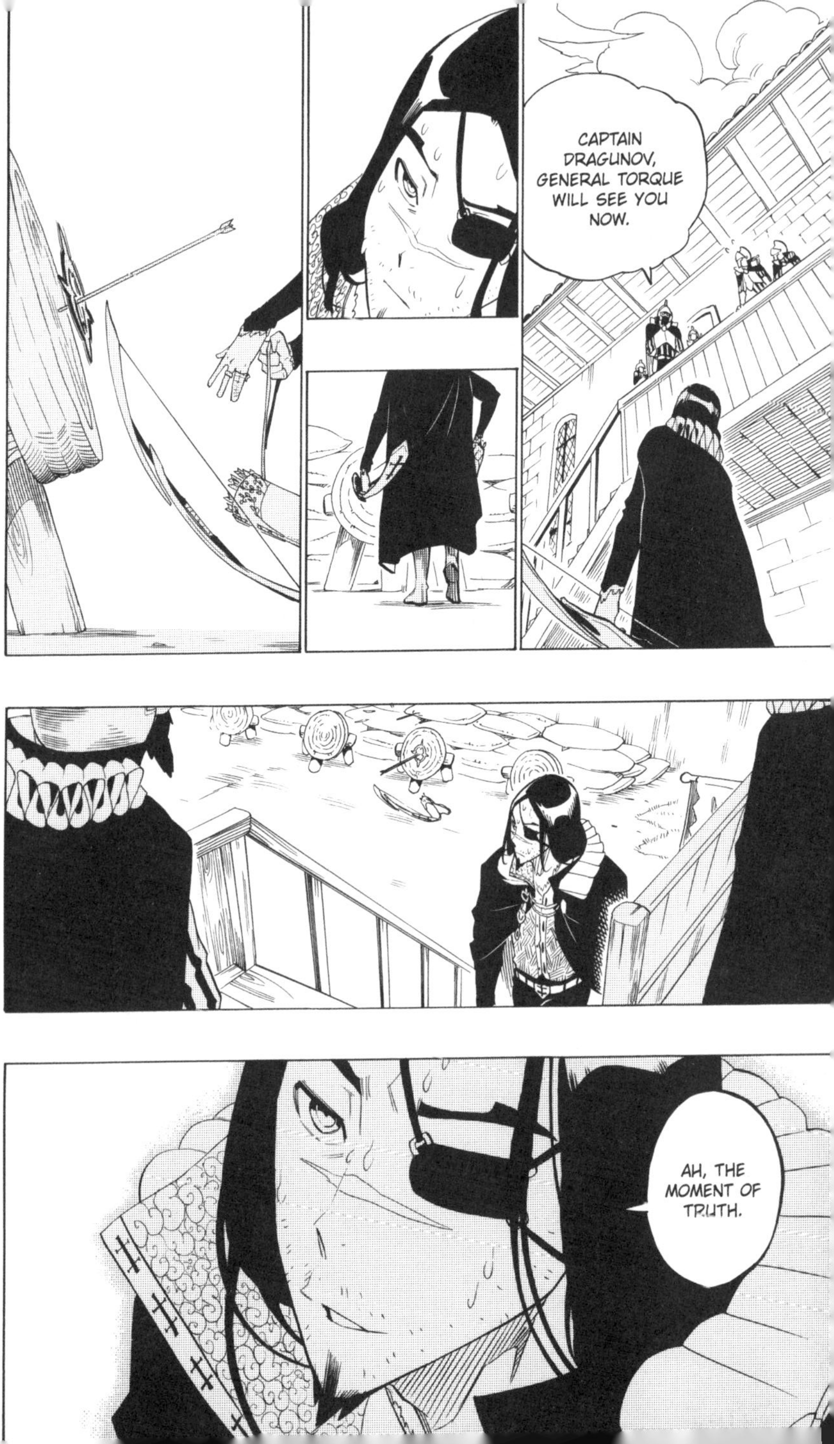
CAPTAIN DRAGUNOV, GENERAL TORQUE WILL SEE YOU NOW.
AH, THE MOMENT OF TRUTH.

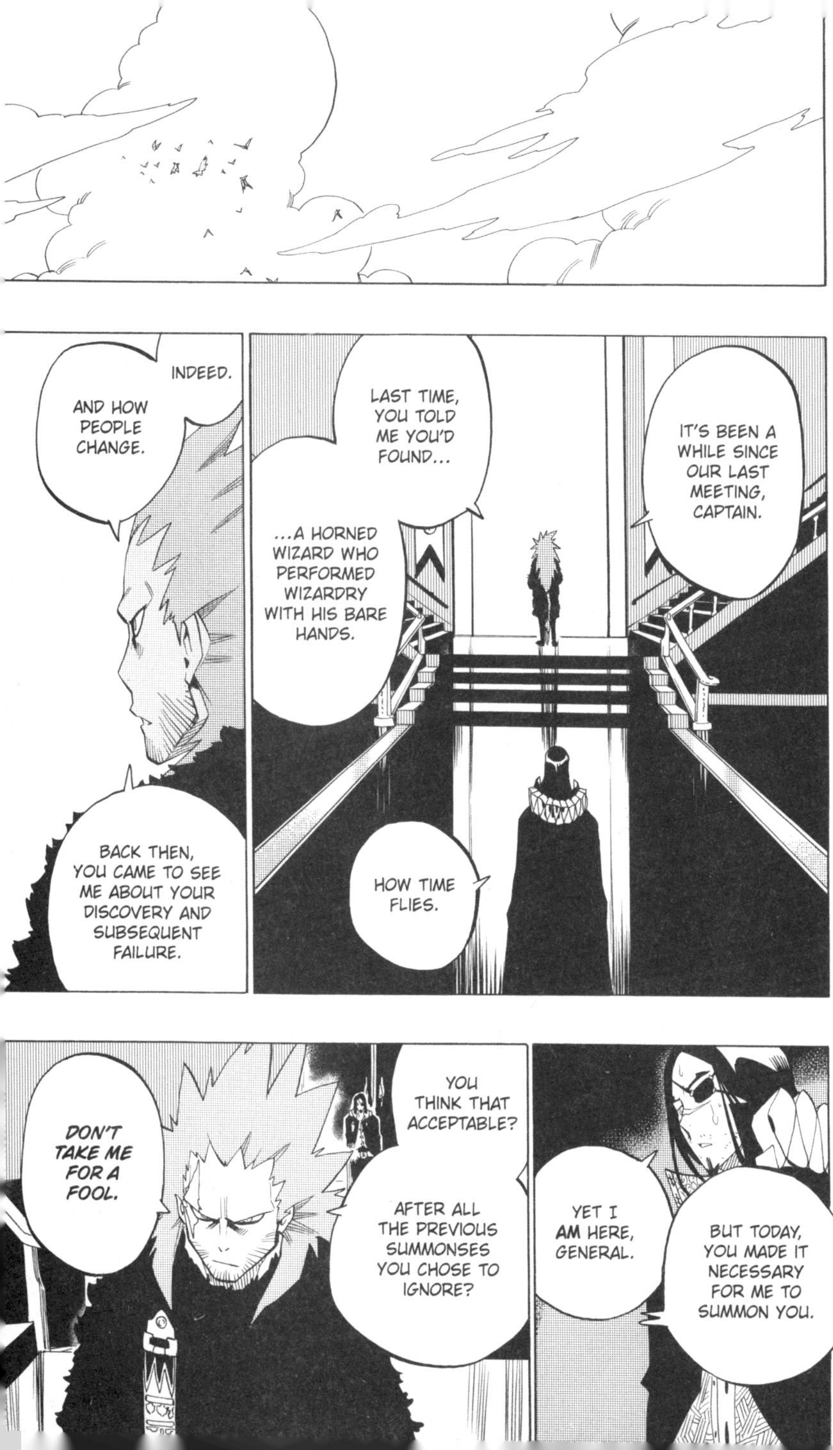
IT'S BEEN A WHILE SINCE OUR LAST MEETING, CAPTAIN.
LAST TIME, YOU TOLD ME YOU'D FOUND...
...A HORNED WIZARD WHO PERFORMED WIZARDRY WITH HIS BARE HANDS.
HOW TIME FLIES.
INDEED.
AND HOW PEOPLE CHANGE.
BACK THEN, YOU CAME TO SEE ME ABOUT YOUR DISCOVERY AND SUBSEQUENT FAILURE.
BUT TODAY, YOU MADE IT NECESSARY FOR ME TO SUMMON YOU.
YET I **AM** HERE, GENERAL.
YOU THINK THAT ACCEPTABLE?
AFTER ALL THE PREVIOUS SUMMONSES YOU CHOSE TO IGNORE?
DON'T TAKE ME FOR A FOOL.

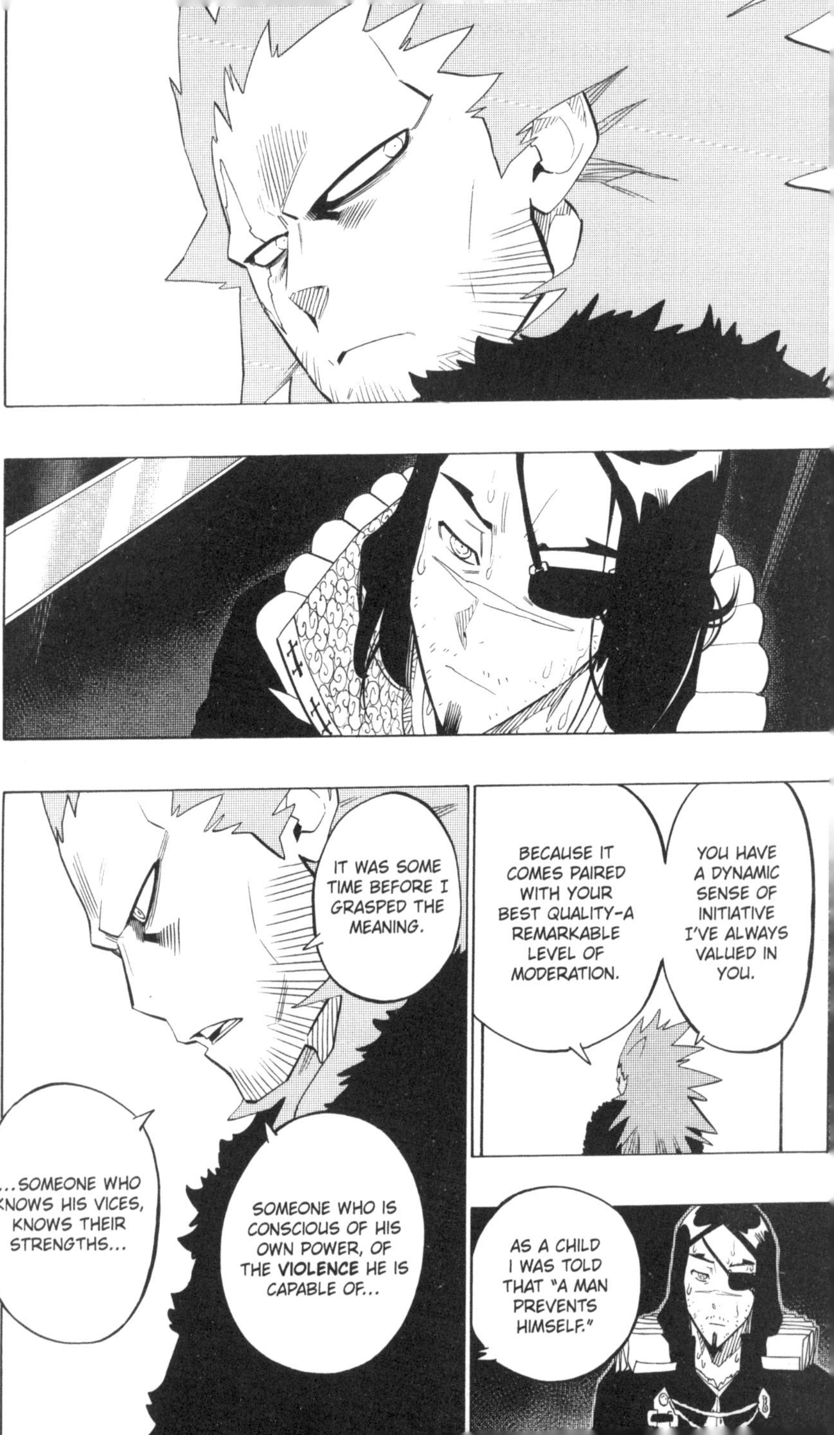
YOU HAVE A DYNAMIC SENSE OF INITIATIVE I'VE ALWAYS VALUED IN YOU.
BECAUSE IT COMES PAIRED WITH YOUR BEST QUALITY-A REMARKABLE LEVEL OF MODERATION.
AS A CHILD I WAS TOLD THAT "A MAN PREVENTS HIMSELF."
IT WAS SOME TIME BEFORE I GRASPED THE MEANING.
SOMEONE WHO IS CONSCIOUS OF HIS OWN POWER, OF THE **VIOLENCE** HE IS CAPABLE OF...
...SOMEONE WHO KNOWS HIS VICES, KNOWS THEIR STRENGTHS...

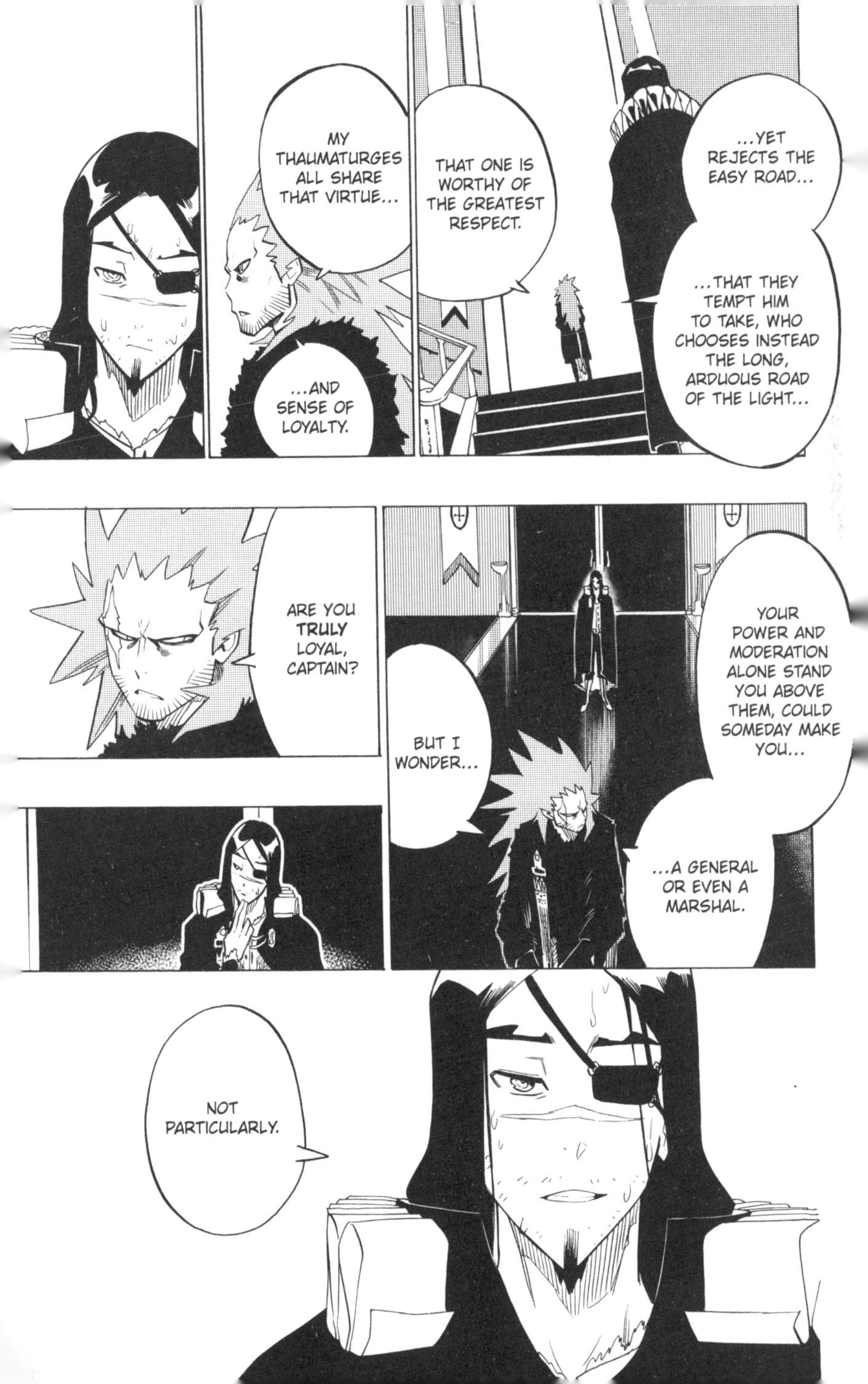
...YET REJECTS THE EASY ROAD...
...THAT THEY TEMPT HIM TO TAKE, WHO CHOOSES INSTEAD THE LONG, ARDUOUS ROAD OF THE LIGHT...
THAT ONE IS WORTHY OF THE GREATEST RESPECT.
MY THAUMATURGES ALL SHARE THAT VIRTUE...
...AND SENSE OF LOYALTY.
YOUR POWER AND MODERATION ALONE STAND YOU ABOVE THEM, COULD SOMEDAY MAKE YOU...
...A GENERAL OR EVEN A MARSHAL.
BUT I WONDER...
ARE YOU **TRULY** LOYAL, CAPTAIN?
NOT PARTICULARLY.

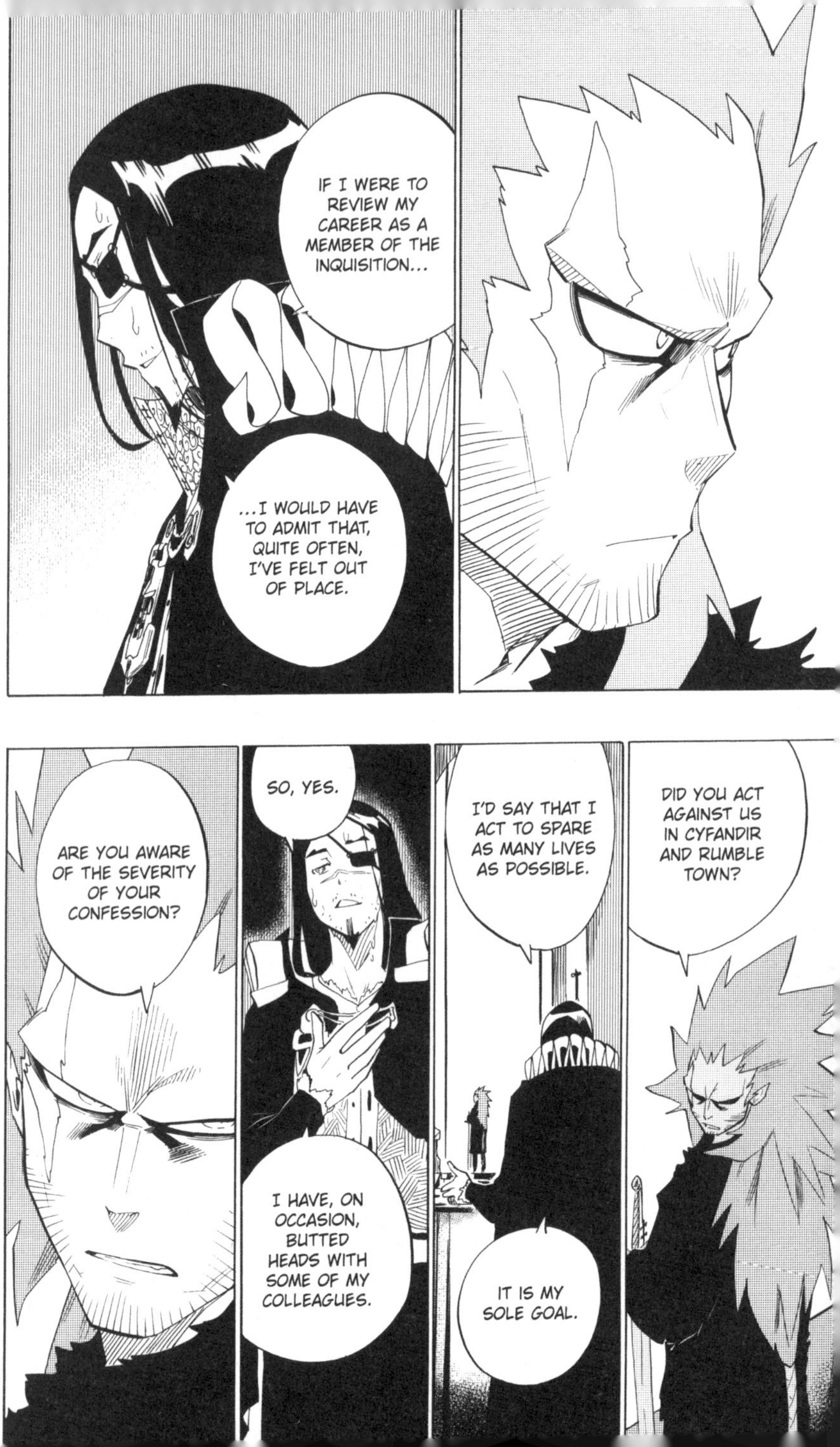
IF I WERE TO REVIEW MY CAREER AS A MEMBER OF THE INQUISITION...
...I WOULD HAVE TO ADMIT THAT, QUITE OFTEN, I'VE FELT OUT OF PLACE.
DID YOU ACT AGAINST US IN CYFANDIR AND RUMBLE TOWN?
I'D SAY THAT I ACT TO SPARE AS MANY LIVES AS POSSIBLE.
IT IS MY SOLE GOAL.
SO, YES.
I HAVE, ON OCCASION, BUTTED HEADS WITH SOME OF MY COLLEAGUES.
ARE YOU AWARE OF THE SEVERITY OF YOUR CONFESSION?

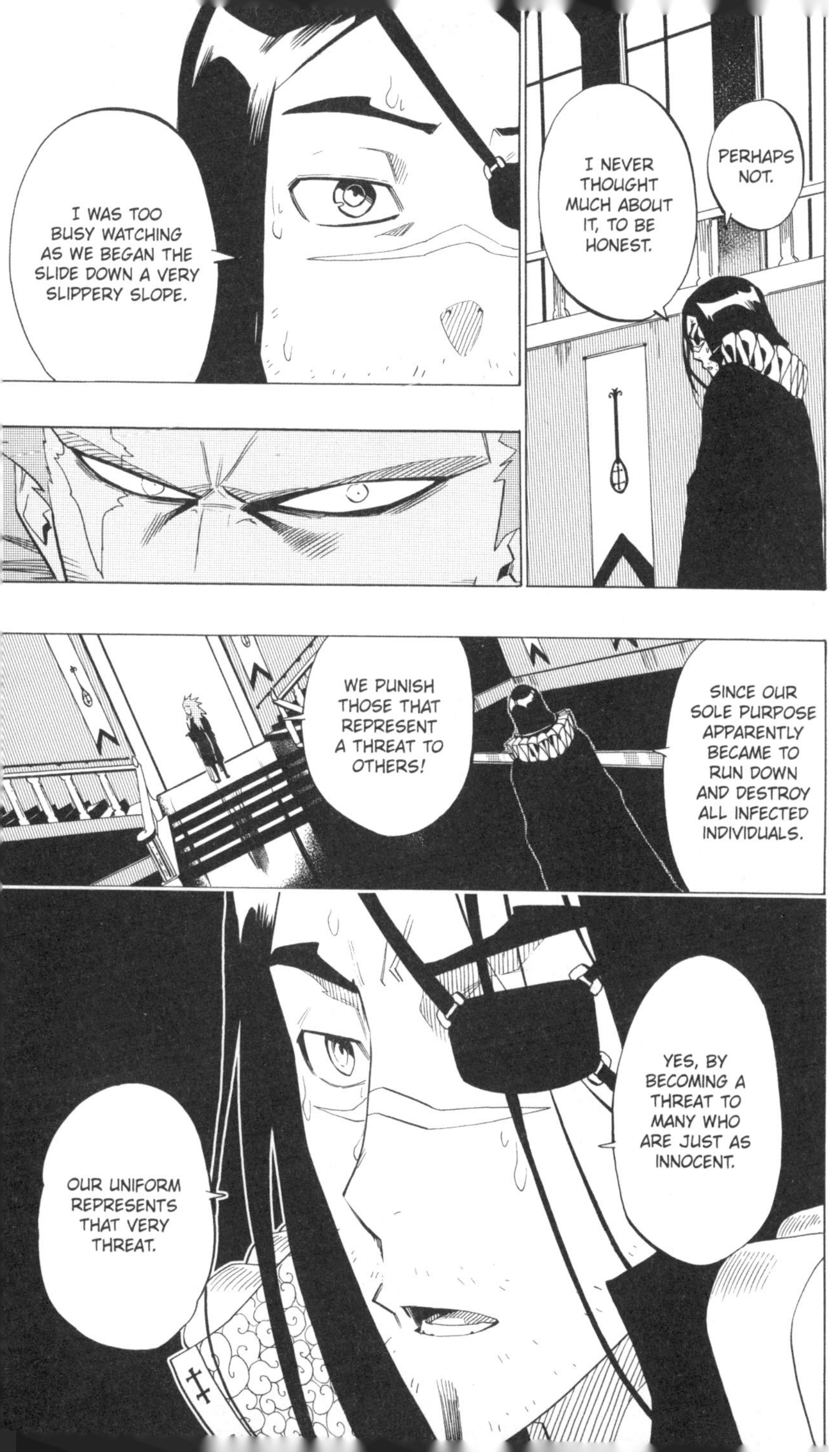
PERHAPS NOT.
I NEVER THOUGHT MUCH ABOUT IT, TO BE HONEST.
I WAS TOO BUSY WATCHING AS WE BEGAN THE SLIDE DOWN A VERY SLIPPERY SLOPE.
SINCE OUR SOLE PURPOSE APPARENTLY BECAME TO RUN DOWN AND DESTROY ALL INFECTED INDIVIDUALS.
WE PUNISH THOSE THAT REPRESENT A THREAT TO OTHERS!
YES, BY BECOMING A THREAT TO MANY WHO ARE JUST AS INNOCENT.
OUR UNIFORM REPRESENTS THAT VERY THREAT.

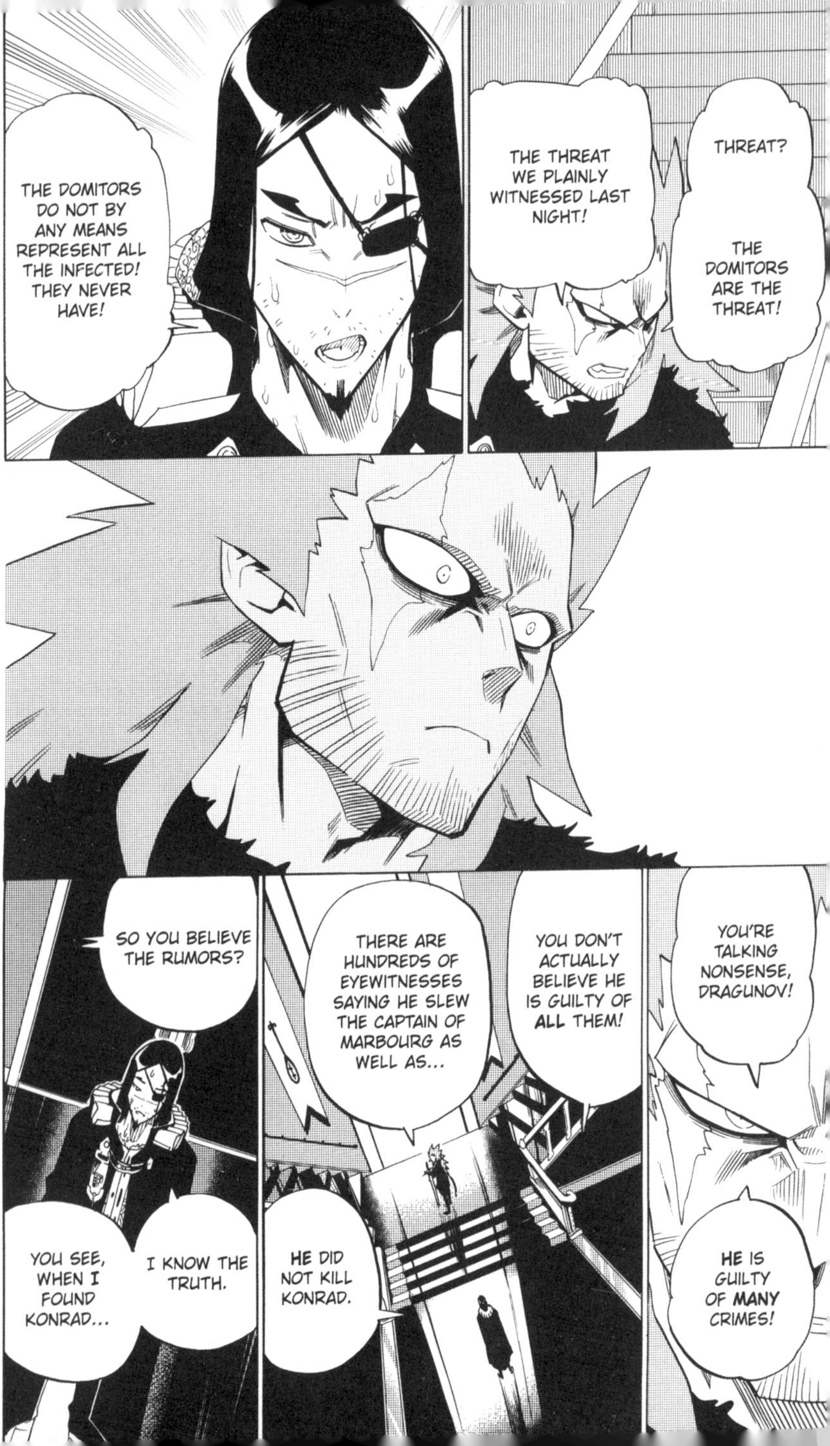
THREAT?
THE DOMITORS ARE THE THREAT!
THE THREAT WE PLAINLY WITNESSED LAST NIGHT!
THE DOMITORS DO NOT BY ANY MEANS REPRESENT ALL THE INFECTED! THEY NEVER HAVE!
YOU'RE TALKING NONSENSE, DRAGUNOV!
HE IS GUILTY OF MANY CRIMES!
YOU DON'T ACTUALLY BELIEVE HE IS GUILTY OF ALL THEM!
THERE ARE HUNDREDS OF EYEWITNESSES SAYING HE SLEW THE CAPTAIN OF MARBOURG AS WELL AS...
HE DID NOT KILL KONRAD.
SO YOU BELIEVE THE RUMORS?
I KNOW THE TRUTH.
YOU SEE, WHEN I FOUND KONRAD...

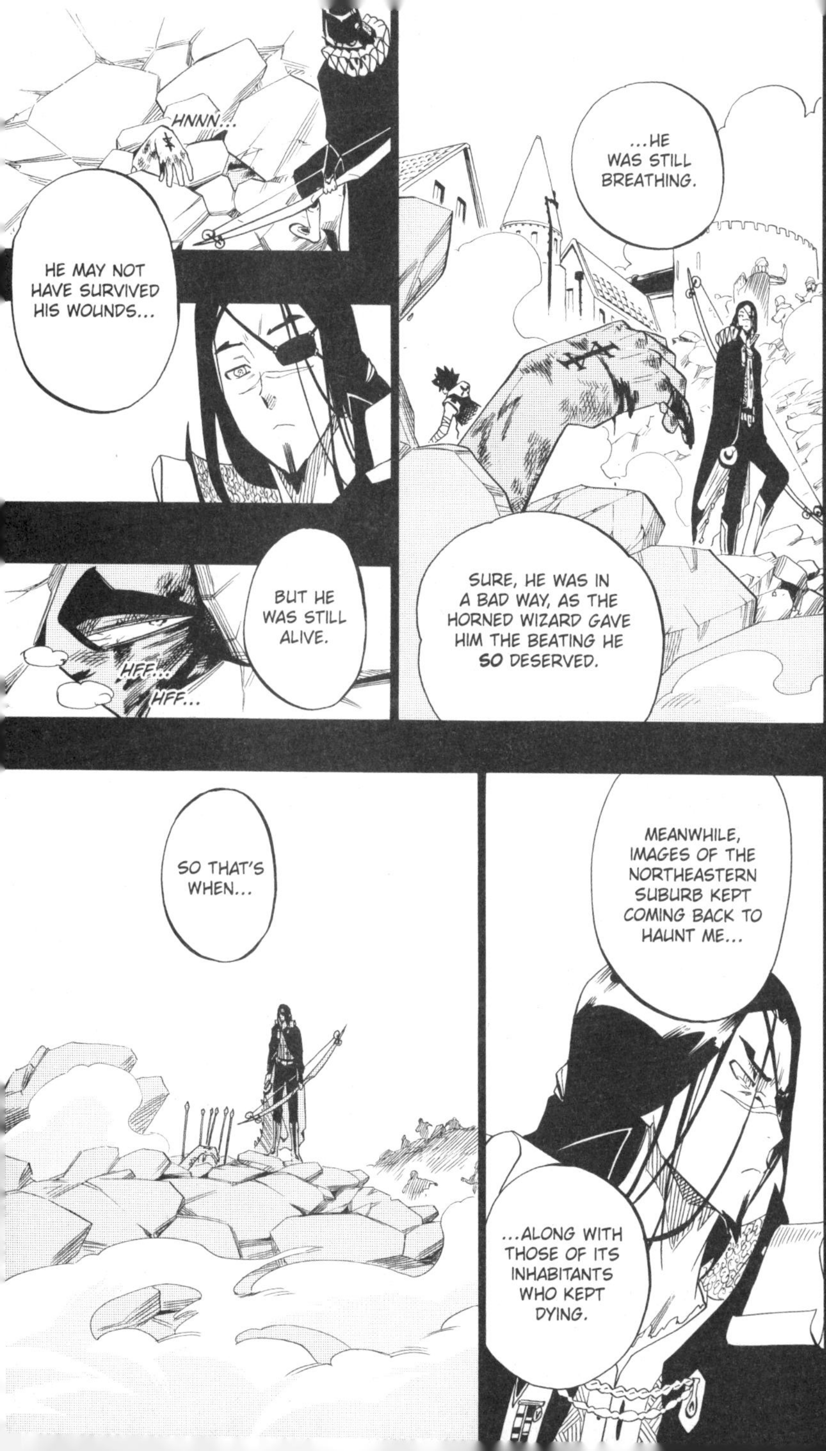
...HE WAS STILL BREATHING.
SURE, HE WAS IN A BAD WAY, AS THE HORNED WIZARD GAVE HIM THE BEATING HE SO DESERVED.
HNNN...
HE MAY NOT HAVE SURVIVED HIS WOUNDS...
BUT HE WAS STILL ALIVE.
HFF...
HFF...
MEANWHILE, IMAGES OF THE NORTHEASTERN SUBURB KEPT COMING BACK TO HAUNT ME...
...ALONG WITH THOSE OF ITS INHABITANTS WHO KEPT DYING.
SO THAT'S WHEN...

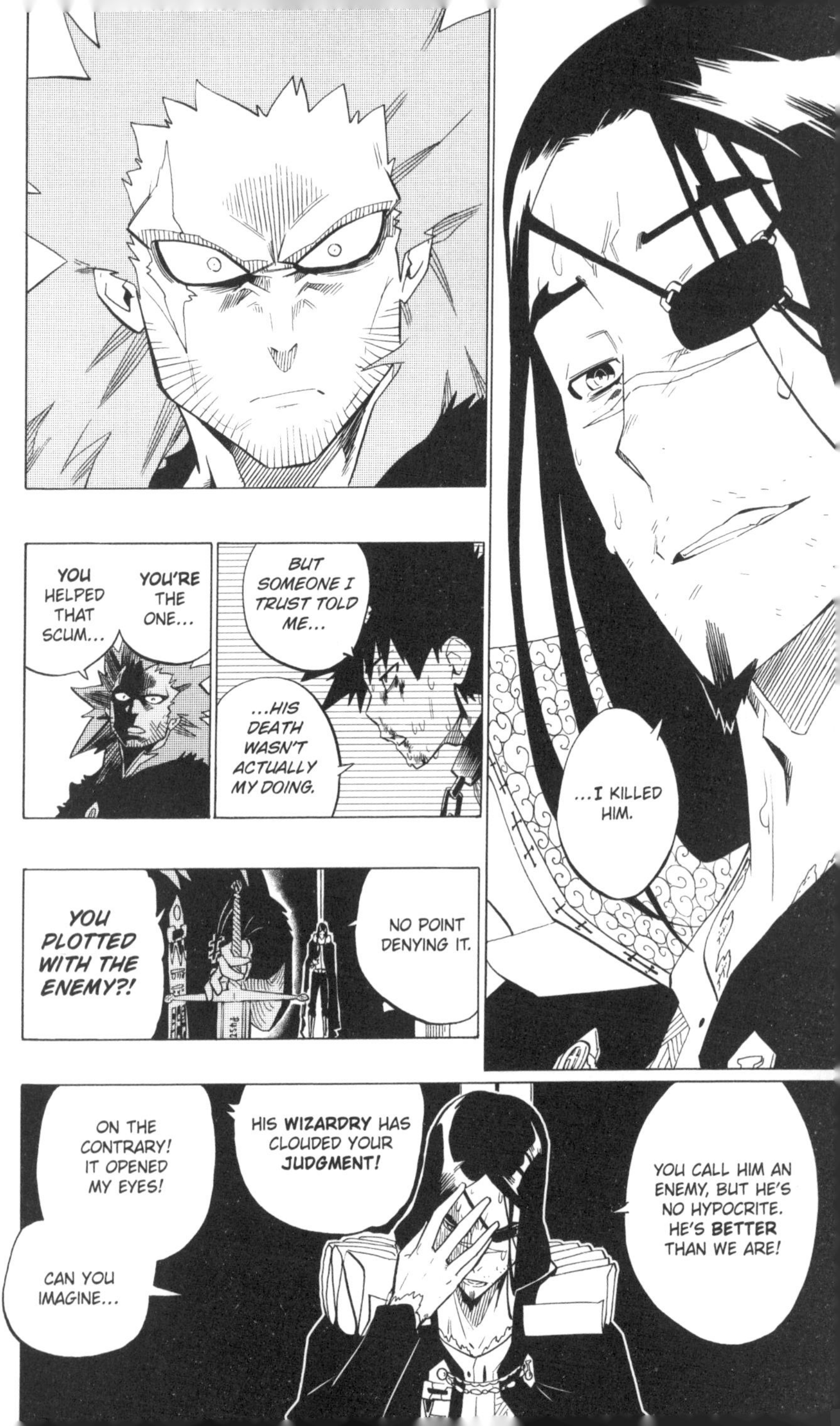
...I KILLED HIM.
BUT SOMEONE I TRUST TOLD ME...
...HIS DEATH WASN'T ACTUALLY MY DOING.
YOU'RE THE ONE...
YOU HELPED THAT SCUM...
NO POINT DENYING IT.
YOU PLOTTED WITH THE ENEMY?!
YOU CALL HIM AN ENEMY, BUT HE'S NO HYPOCRITE. HE'S BETTER THAN WE ARE!
HIS WIZARDRY HAS CLOUDED YOUR JUDGMENT!
ON THE CONTRARY! IT OPENED MY EYES!
CAN YOU IMAGINE...

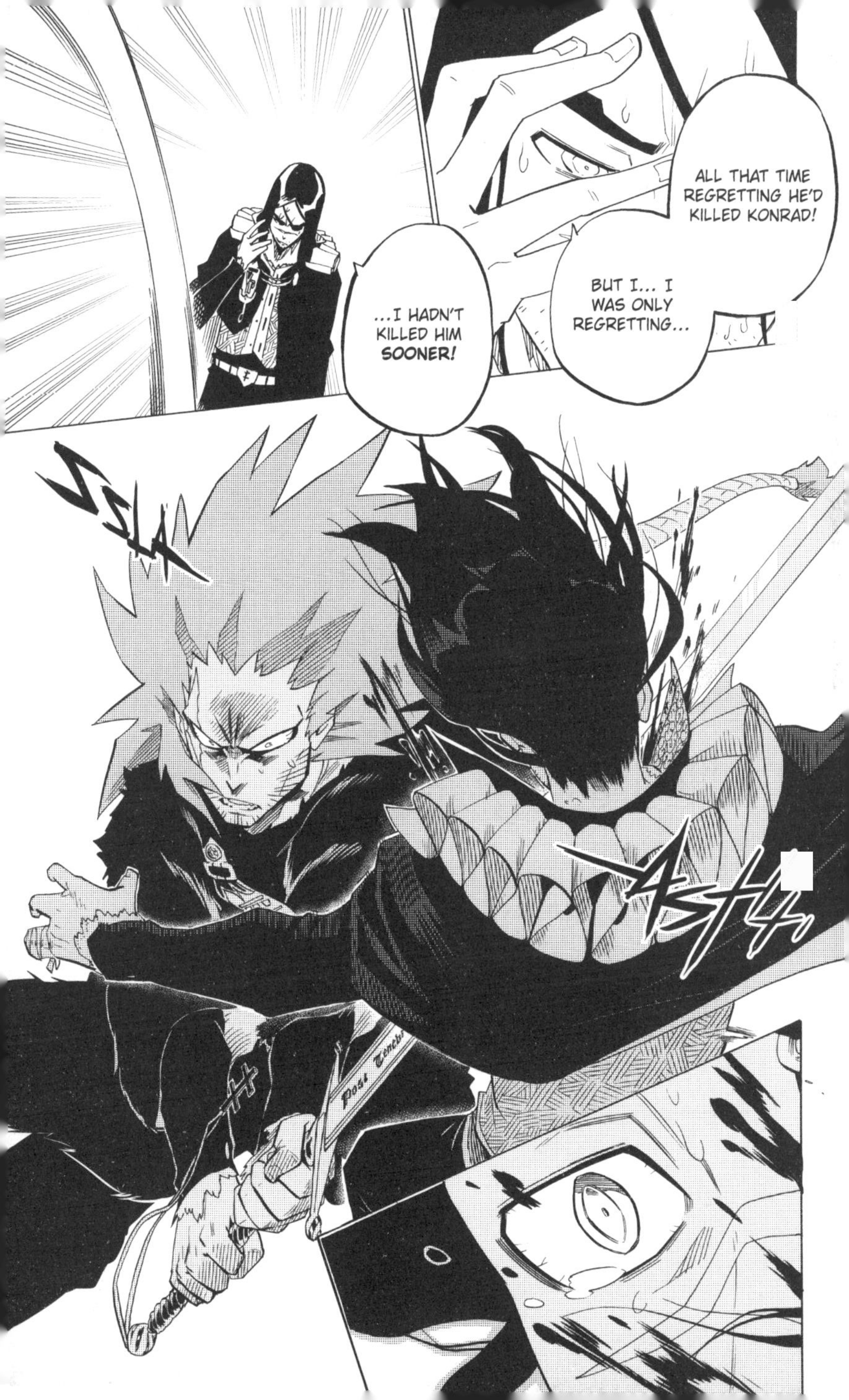
ALL THAT TIME REGRETTING HE'D KILLED KONRAD!
BUT I... I WAS ONLY REGRETTING...
...I HADN'T KILLED HIM SOONER!

TO BE CONTINUED...

Toum? STAK!!!

QUESTIONS...

ANSWERS!

Ponkuro (from Japan): Hello, Tony Sensei. I LOOOOOOVE *Radiant!* And I was wondering if I could ask you a couple of questions. The Inquisitor ships are super cool. Were you influenced in any particular way when creating those ships or did you start from scratch? Do you also happen to have an idea of their size?

Tony Valente: I wanted to make sure the airships had a pretty recognizable shape at first glance, so I had the idea of using the shape of a French police officer's cap rather than the shape of a balloon. And since the Inquisition is sort of like the police, I thought it'd fit in nicely on top of being original! As for the size, I have no idea…

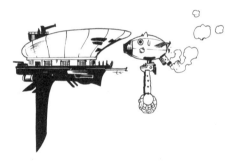

-How many brothers does Seth have in total?
Oh well, regarding his brothers, let me see… So there's Piodon, then Diabal, then of course Triton (mentioned in the flashbacks), then we have, eh… not taking into account, eh… minus, eh… and then you'll find out the final answer to that question in the upcoming story. XD

-Liselotte's outfit in Rumble Town had big pointy shoulder pads. Wouldn't those be a little too heavy and dangerous to wear?
Yes! But they reinforce her muscles and keep enemies at bay!

....

Stylo Bic: What would happen if the light emitted by Dragunov's arrow were to get split into two by some object at the moment it got sent off? For example: The Rumble Town Clock falls on Dragunov who sends out an arrow to escape, but the "teleportation" doesn't work with just the arrow reaching the other side.

Tony Valente: The ray of light that follows the arrow isn't actually Dragunov himself, it's just a sort of a representation of his teleportation skill, not *him* as such. When he disappears for those couple of seconds he's just simply…not there. So where is he? Dandandaaaaaan (suspenseful sound)… I'll tell you later in the story.

- I wanted to know if you had any good advice to give me on how to draw hands and feet.
You have to look at them, and try to draw them while understanding how they work! Just don't go around ogling people's feet randomly in public spaces without saying anything. First, greet them and then tell them what you want. Then run away from the police that've been alerted by people nearby who'll have reported you as being a deviant. And after you get out of custody, get your life back in order and never ask anyone else something like that out in public again. Just look at your own feet, that's much easier. As for the hands, rinse and repeat.

-I also just wanted to thank you for *Radiant*, because this manga isn't just great, it's *even better!* I wanted you to know that I love your art and that thanks to you, my own drawings have also become much better. I also wanted to tell you that I can HARDLY wait for all the new *Radiant* volumes. Oh, right! Would you by any chance come back to the International Comics Festival of 2020? Because I *just* missed you when you came over. Good luck on your future projects! From: your biggest fan.
Thank you for the kind words! As for the festivals and such, everything's been on hold since the beginning of the pandemic. I'll be back as soon as possible!

Paul O.: Hello hello! I discovered *Radiant* while at the annual Japan Expo event in Paris a couple years back and it quickly became in just a couple of volumes my favorite manga series! I'm planning on studying computer science in order to be able to make video games and my dream is to be able to make one using the world of *Radiant*, because I have like sooooo many ideas on how to adapt certain story elements into game mechanics! How about you, what type of game would you have *Radiant* adapted into? More a RPG adventure? Open world? Or a fighting game? (I'm leaning towards an RPG with a linear story, maybe even a multiplayer coop game).
Tony Valente: Heeeeey, but that would actually be super cool!! My heart would opt more for an open-world RPG game, but…. I think a linear RPG type game like *Ni no Kuni* or *Dragon Quest* would be totally compatible with the story I'm telling. Yeah, that'd be fun. So, when do we sign the deal? What do you mean, you're still in school? Come on, hurry up and get older so we can start working on this already!!!!!!

Emma T.: Hello hello! My name's Emma, and to start off with, I wanted to tell you that I LOOOOOOOOVE your manga SOOOOOOO MUCH (yup, really *that* much). No, but seriously, all the feels it brings, the art, the comedy, the story, it's really just a magnificent manga! Anyway, I wanted to know if Seth's parents are still alive? If so, will we ever get to see them?
Tony Valente: I LOOOOOOOOVE SOOOOOO MUCH that you seem to love *Radiant*! But no no no no no no! Despite this mutual admiration for each other, I will *not* spoil the story!

- Another thing I've been wondering about: the Queen, Boadicée, was she big at birth or did she just have some sort of gigantic growth spurt (no, seriously, because wouldn't it have been super hard for her to be born)?
Considering it's her Infection, she was not born that big!

- Oh, and I won't lie, but along with all the action, I'm also craving some romance, so will Seth be in any sort of romantic relationship anytime soon?
Maaaaaaybe….

- Does the word "Sidh" hold any particular meaning, or did you come up with it yourself?
Sidh is the Celtic name for their world of the dead. It's not like the "world beyond" like we know it in the monotheistic religions with the pure souls in one area and the sinners in another. The Sidh assembles all the dead, as well the cowards and the brave, the criminals as well as the heroes. I really liked that idea of a world after ours where there was no difference being made between one human to another. In certain Celtic stories, it's also said to be the world of the gods. I won't spoil too much here, but while these Celtic concepts *did* influence me, in *Radiant* they're neither one or the other. Where we are in the story you could see it more as a sort of "Internet" for the mind. That's actually also how I explained it to the animated series staff so they'd understand my idea!
- Do you also happen to have a how-to to help me get the same hairdo as Ocoho? Seriously,

because I literally spent an entire afternoon trying to re-create it (and failed miserably)...?
Whoa, you really spent a lot of energy on that then! Even if you did fail, I'm giving out a certificate of authenticity just for the effort! I'm sorry to say I won't be able to help you out with a how-to, though -_- Just as a little anecdote, Ocoho's haircut was inspired by one of the many haircuts of a certain singer called Janelle Monáe (in the music video for her song called *Yoga* to be more specific). Now, my version is a *little* different, but that's what gave me the final direction on how to do Ocoho's look!

- And finally: where do you get your inspiration to come up with all of this and to find such original (and magnificent, too) names?
A lot is inspired from historical events and myths, both the events in my story as well as the names. A lot of original creations as well though, by trying to make things sound as if they actually existed. I have difficulty with imaginary first names that sound like someone just randomly blurted out some vowels to make it sound like something out of a fantasy world, like "Yaeileal, Iluyohalé, Glaluilh," etc. I much rather prefer things like Ornicalom, Mérouvian, Ysarielle, Glandruf, Fouliriane, Clapion. Sure, I *may* have *just* come up with those first names and they *may* suck a bit… But you see what I mean, right? I like to find familiar-sounding names that might have had a role in producing actual existing names.

....

LINE G.: Hello, Tony Valente! First of all, I looooooove *Radiant* <3 (especially Ocoho!!!!). I noticed that in Rumble Town, when Santori uses his Miracle, Liselotte and Ullmina are both by his side and both had one eye closed (not the same one), and each with a hand on his shoulder (not the same one). But then in the Wizard-Knight Arc, when he's fighting against Seth, he doesn't need them to use it. Is he blind or does he only need help when he's projecting his voice? It's been bothering me!
<u>Tony Valente:</u> If you were to compare the size of his Miracle in Rumble Town to the one in Cyfandir, you'd see that there's a difference: he's much bigger in Rumble Town! Liselotte and Ullmina, as Miracle-holders themselves, were lending a bit of their strength to help Santori with his. As a result, the Miracle became much more imposing. He actually even mentions it in the battle against Diabal in volume 9 (chapter 67).

....

Baptiste M.: Hello Mr. Valente! Before I ask you a couple of questions I wanted to make sure you know (even though I'm sure people must be telling you this very, very, very often) that I LOOOOOOVE *Radiant*. It's a real manga masterpiece that very efficiently covers a lot of topics like prejudices, racism and ecology. Now, as for my questions: During his battle against Seth, Santori ends up without his hat and we can clearly make out his eyes. In that moment he looks almost like a crazy person, even though until then he'd always just looked like a joyful idiot. Is this on purpose?
<u>Tony Valente:</u> Yes, because under his playful grandpa exterior hides a maniac experienced in violent combat and wars. You can't forget that he came to Cyfandir with the intention to burn the city to the ground!

- When Seth was under the control of that dark force (you know, the black hole in the Sidh), some circles appeared on his hands. What were those? Disks? Vibrations in the air? Where did they come from?
It was the air dilating due to the sheer amount of Fantasia being concentrated in his hands.

- In a world where 80 percent of the population possesses some superpower, named a Quirk, All for One possesses the Quirk to steal others' quirks…
Whoa, you missed the exit and you arrived at a completely different series there! Go back! By the way: the voice of Torque in the Radiant anime is done by the great Kenta Miyake, who also voices All Might in *My Hero Academia* (and tons of other characters in other shows). What a voice!!

- Mordred, the aspiring Wizard-Knight with no emotions, has the same name as the nephew (or son, depending on the version) of King Arthur. Legend goes that Mordred killed King Arthur, thus destroying the era of peace Arthur brought. Is that why you gave him that name?
Yes, I took Mordred's legendary treachery and adapted it to fit my story!

- And finally, do you have any tips on how to write stories? I love coming up with scenarios, entire worlds, and am even planning on writing a book! The problem is that, when writing a story, I often can't seem to stretch it for very long. What should I do?

First, get to work by writing down your stories, even if they seem short! It's necessary to practice, meaning: you need to write down words, come up with dialogue, create transitions in between two scenes, structure your prose, etc. No matter how long or short a story, all of these skills will be put to the test. As you progress, I'm sure some of the stories will stick with you and you'll naturally want to work on them again later and expand further upon them!

. . . .

Pierre-Alexandre: Hi Tony. First of all, I wanted to tell you I love (times infinity) *Radiant*. My first question is: since when has Master Lord Majesty been scam-... I mean, when did he create the Artemis and how old is he?

Tony Valente: I can't answer that without risking spoiling some things. You'll get your answers later in the story!

- My second question is about Prince Vérone. Is he really the son of Colonel Ullmina (who btw should *really* go see a therapist) and the Marshal? Is he destined to become Marshal himself then?

Yes, he really is the son of Ullmina, but no, not of the Marshal. He was born out of the relationship between Ullmina and a Convictis lord. He might already imagine himself as being a Marshal, but he'll need to be named as such by his peers to become one. Nothing is handed out for free!

- My last question is more of a wish than a question: will we see a battle between General Torque and Captain Dart Dragunov (my favorite character)?

Ha ha ha ha! Seems like your question got submitted into just the right volume, huh!

. . . .

Sara D.: Hi Tony! Thank you for your manga. I didn't really have any question, but I just wanted to leave you this message. You know, I discovered *Radiant* during a time when I was wondering about a lot of things about myself and my identity and what you're doing really touches me.

I really like Doc! I feel like he's really underrated... He reminds me of myself, having been adopted by a Caucasian couple, realized she was black as a teen, and that everything was just starting! People really underestimate what it is being part of a community, my friends for example always argue on whether I'm "mixed" or "black". Because of that, I learned a lot on how they see me (I am BLACK), and I understood that it especially depends on the way they want to see me ("Or maybe an Oreo? Mixed sounds better... Then again, you're not really *that* black either."). Self-hate goes far down here, and I've paid the cost for it millions of times already.

I finished reading volume 14 and wow! Doc is in the land of neutrality and passes by the school level! Let's go learn who our ancestors are, those great explorers. Mine must not have been the one steering the ship, meanwhile everyone apologizes with their eyes and I just tuck in my head.

Doc is scared of the Infected, he just admitted it! How old is he now? He must be about middle school age, no? At that age I was totally rejecting any affiliation to black kids. Then again, there were barely three of us. Changing trains for me was a daily thing to do when I estimated there were too many black people in my train and so white people would feel more at ease. I was the product of a racist institution, and today I am revolted by what they made of me.

And that's where Ocoho comes in.

Tony, thank you. Thank you so, so so much!

I would cry so hard if I'd told you in real life, but I never had any black role models (and even less black *female* role models) when I was little. We didn't listen to rap, or hip-hop, sometimes a bit of jazz... But of the Glenn Miller kind. Fixed with the idea that I didn't exist, or cornered with light jokes with "African" undertones, to jeering and insults, to the media... I would have cried for hours in my bed had I seen her, just like when Yoruichi turned human in *Bleach* (what a SHOCK that was!). And no matter how great you are, you don't know just how much these things can resonate with kids. If I had to explain it, I'd compare it to taking off your sunglasses for the very first time.

Basically, thank you and sorry for taking up space in your Toum Stak!!! corner. I didn't have any question, just maybe this: Is Ocoho black or mixed?

Tony Valente: *_* Look, I'm a man, so of course I won't tell you that I let a tear drop while reading your message. But I actually did wipe away some tears while reading. Screw masculinity! I'll be honest: when I write my stories, I do it in quite the selfish way, by bringing in elements that scare me in people's mentalities… And sometimes, like with Doc (who flips out when he meets wizards), some things, while understandable, sadden me. The fact that female readers such as yourself (and others) find similarities with close-to-heart, personal experiences, is kind of crazy and unexpected. It's moments like these that remind me to take the role of storyteller seriously. We create a collective psyche that will infuse into the minds of the young and very young for a long time. Whether we like it or not, we have the power to slowly advance things, one story at a time. And I try to do the best I can in this role, but I know that there is still so much I need to work on… That's why these kinds of messages like yours really help a lot! I'll remember that punch line you wrote *"Let's go learn who our ancestors are, those great explorers. Mine must not have been the one steering the ship, meanwhile everyone apologizes with their eyes and I just tuck in my head."* That summarizes so many things! Thank you soooo much for your message, Sara!

And to answer your question: Ocoho is black.

<3

Please send your questions to: radiant@ankama.com

Torque is so great to draw! Yes, yes, even for me, who created him! I wanted his charisma to come not from a displayed power but from a contained and mastered violence. He must intimidate with a look! I have always pictured him as a lion hiding behind a human mask. A lion staring at you is intimidating, even lying down. It doesn't need to scream or brandish a nunchaku.

Torque must scare without doing anything...
He's so great to draw!!

—Tony Valente

Tony Valente began working as a comic artist with the series *The Four Princes of Ganahan*, written by Raphael Drommelschlager. He then launched a new three-volume project, *Hana Attori*, after which he produced *S.P.E.E.D. Angels*, a series written by Didier Tarquin and colored by Pop.

In preparation for *Radiant*, he relocated to Canada. Through confronting caribou and grizzlies, he gained the wherewithal to train in obscure manga techniques. Since then, his eating habits have changed, his lifestyle became completely different and even his singing voice has changed a bit!

RADIANT VOL. 15
VIZ MEDIA Edition

STORY AND ART BY **TONY VALENTE**
ASSISTANT ARTIST **SALOMON**

Translation/(´･∀･`)ｻｧ?
Touch-Up Art & Lettering/**Erika Terriquez**
Design/**Julian [JR] Robinson**
Editor/**Gary Leach**

Published by arrangement with MEDIATOON LICENSING/Ankama.
RADIANT T15
© ANKAMA EDITIONS 2021, by Tony Valente
All rights reserved

Printed in the U.S.A.

Published by VIZ Media, LLC
P.O. Box 77010
San Francisco, CA 94107

10 9 8 7 6 5 4 3 2 1
First printing, August 2022

PARENTAL ADVISORY
RADIANT is rated T for Teen and is recommended for ages 13 and up. This volume contains fantasy violence.

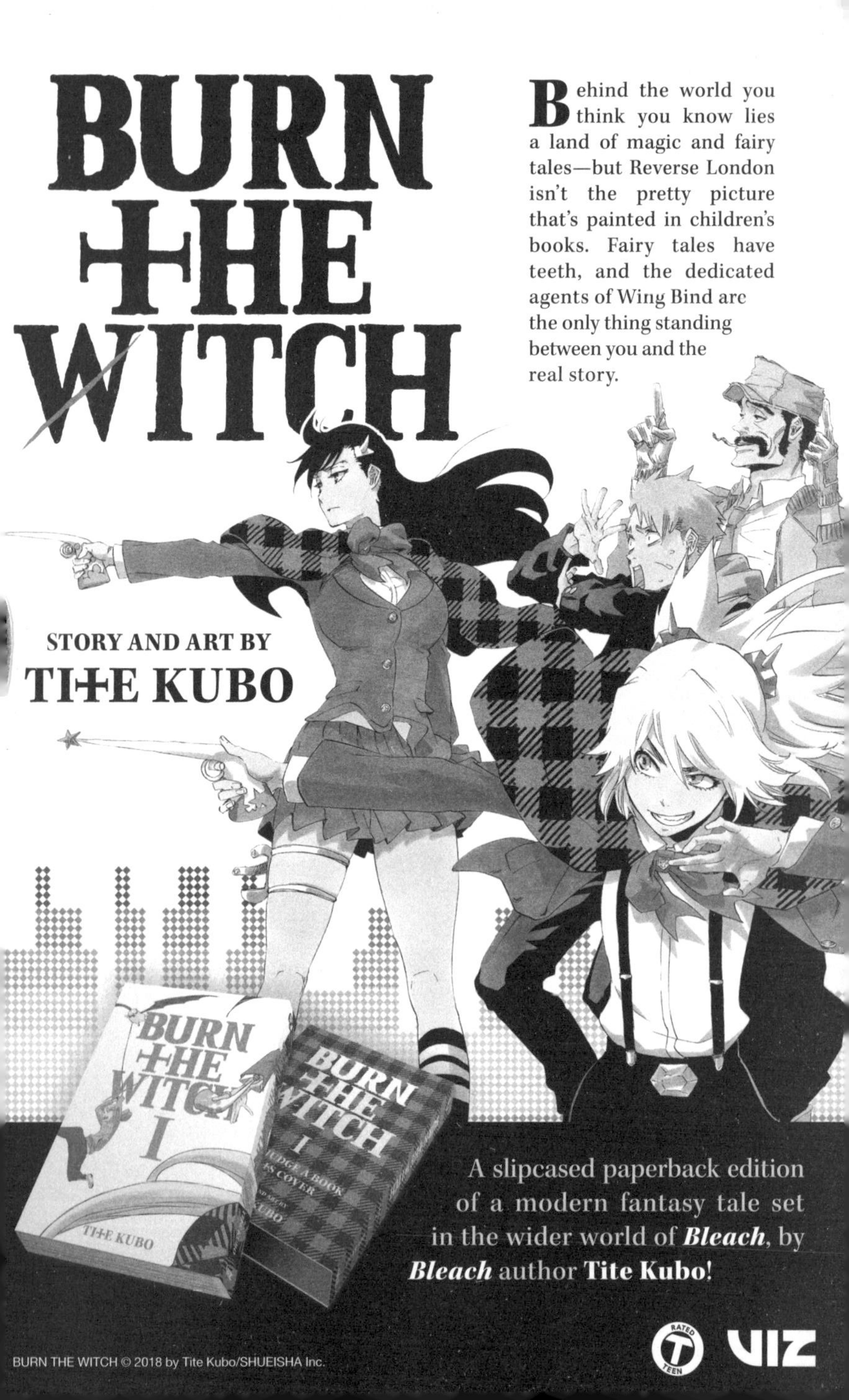
BURN THE WITCH
Behind the world you think you know lies a land of magic and fairy tales—but Reverse London isn't the pretty picture that's painted in children's books. Fairy tales have teeth, and the dedicated agents of Wing Bind are the only thing standing between you and the real story.
STORY AND ART BY
TITE KUBO
BURN THE WITCH
I
TITE KUBO
BURN THE WITCH
I
A slipcased paperback edition of a modern fantasy tale set in the wider world of Bleach, by Bleach author Tite Kubo!
RATED T TEEN
VIZ
BURN THE WITCH © 2018 by Tite Kubo/SHUEISHA Inc.

Kafka wants to clean up kaiju, but not literally! Will a sudden metamorphosis stand in the way of his dream?

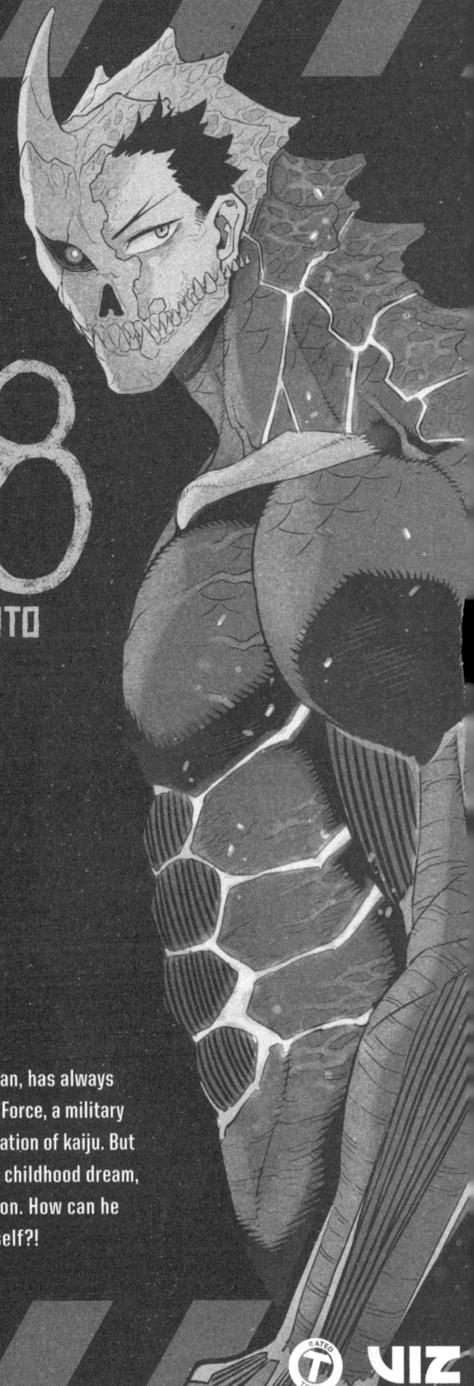

KAIJU NO.8

STORY AND ART BY **NAOYA MATSUMOTO**

Kafka Hibino, a kaiju-corpse cleanup man, has always dreamed of joining the Japan Defense Force, a military organization tasked with the neutralization of kaiju. But when he gets another shot at achieving his childhood dream, he undergoes an unexpected transformation. How can he fight kaiju now that he's become one himself?!

VIZ

EXPERIENCE THE INTRODUCTORY ARC OF THE INTERNATIONAL SMASH HIT SERIES *RWBY* IN A WHOLE NEW WAY—MANGA!

RWBY THE OFFICIAL MANGA

Story and Art by BUNTA KINAMI
Based on the Rooster Teeth series created by MONTY OUM

Monsters known as the Grimm are wreaking havoc on the world of Remnant. Ruby Rose seeks to become a Huntress, someone who eliminates the Grimm and protects the land. She enrolls at Beacon Academy and quickly makes friends she'll stand side-by-side with in the battles to come!

CAN MUSCLES CRUSH MAGIC?!

MASHLE

MAGIC AND MUSCLES

STORY AND ART BY
HAJIME KOMOTO

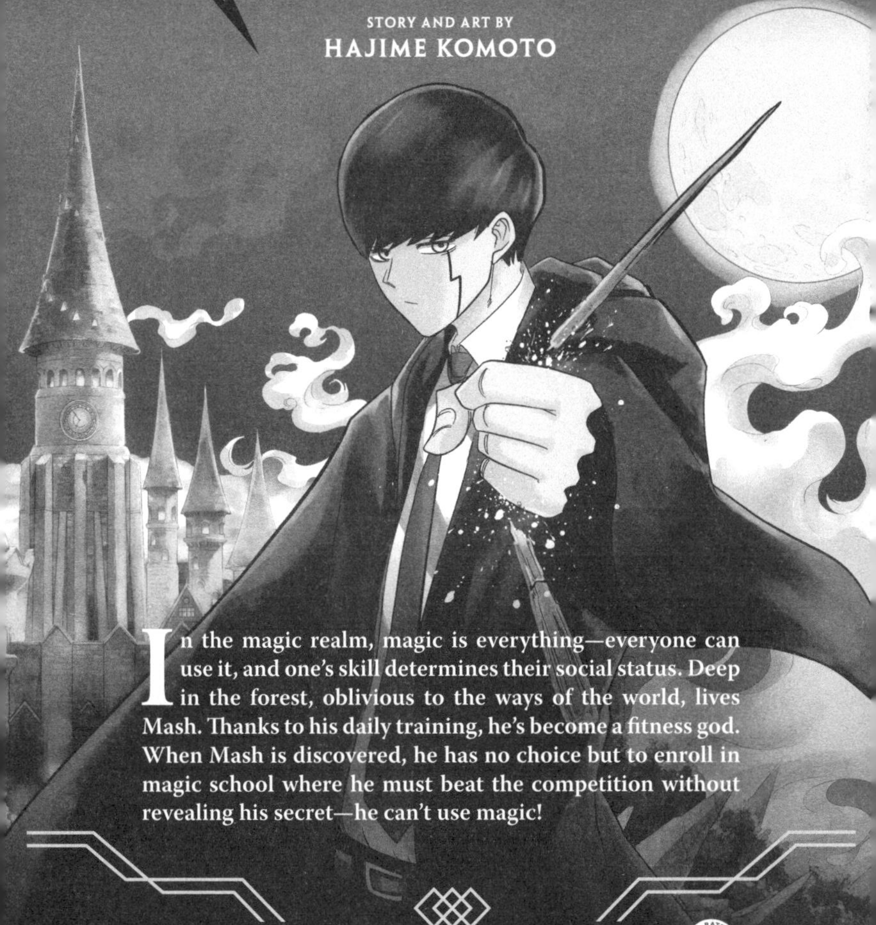

In the magic realm, magic is everything—everyone can use it, and one's skill determines their social status. Deep in the forest, oblivious to the ways of the world, lives Mash. Thanks to his daily training, he's become a fitness god. When Mash is discovered, he has no choice but to enroll in magic school where he must beat the competition without revealing his secret—he can't use magic!

YOU'RE READING THE WRONG WAY

RADIANT reads from right to left, starting in the upper-right corner, meaning that action, sound effects, and word-balloon order are completely reversed from English order.

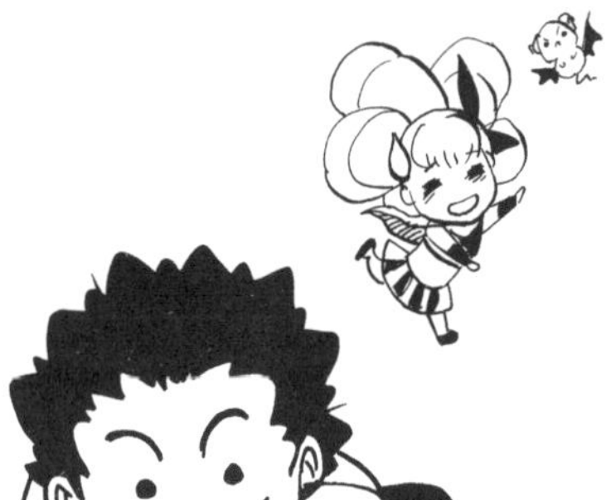

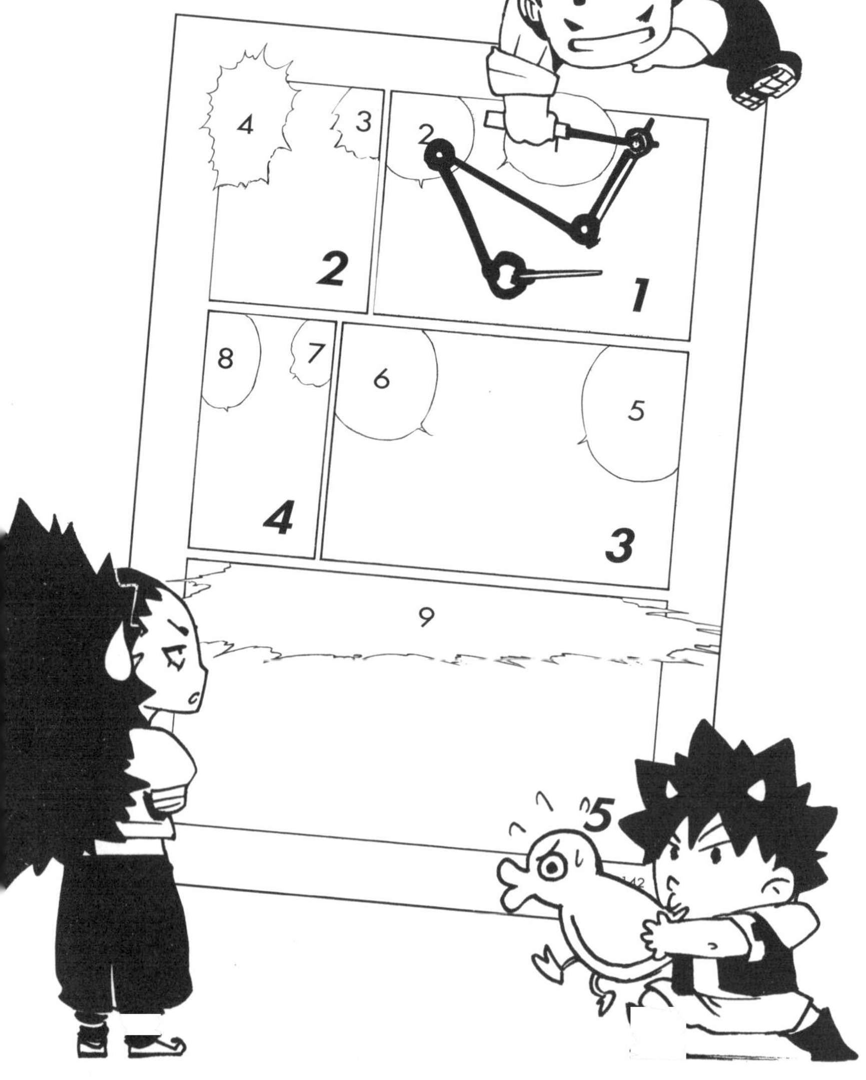
1
2
2
3
4
3
5
6
4
7
8
9
5